The Foreign Office and the Kremlin

British Documents on Anglo-Soviet Relations
1941–45

The Foreign Office and the Kremlin

British Documents on Anglo-Soviet Relations 1941–45

Edited with an Introduction by

GRAHAM ROSS

Lecturer in International Relations,
University of Leeds

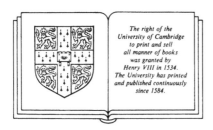

The right of the
University of Cambridge
to print and sell
all manner of books
was granted by
Henry VIII in 1534.
The University has printed
and published continuously
since 1584.

CAMBRIDGE UNIVERSITY PRESS

Cambridge
London   New York   New Rochelle
Melbourne   Sydney

CAMBRIDGE UNIVERSITY PRESS
Cambridge, New York, Melbourne, Madrid, Cape Town, Singapore,
São Paulo, Delhi, Dubai, Tokyo

Cambridge University Press
The Edinburgh Building, Cambridge CB2 8RU, UK

Published in the United States of America by Cambridge University Press, New York

www.cambridge.org
Information on this title: www.cambridge.org/9780521286572

First published 1984
Re-issued in this digitally printed version 2010

A catalogue record for this publication is available from the British Library

Library of Congress Catalogue Card Number: 83–18903

ISBN 978-0-521-24387-2 Hardback
ISBN 978-0-521-28657-2 Paperback

Contents

Acknowledgements

The Public Record Office documents which appear in this volume are Crown Copyright. The author wishes to thank the Controller of Her Majesty's Stationery Office for permission to reproduce them.

He also wishes to thank the British Academy for a grant which enabled much of the research for this book to be undertaken.

Mrs Maureen Hastie gave invaluable assistance in typing the manuscript.

Preface

There is now available in the Public Record Office an enormous, not to say overwhelming, amount of material concerning Anglo-Soviet relations during the Second World War. To make a selection of documents in one volume required the application of certain criteria. Firstly, the emphasis is very much on the viewpoint of the Foreign Office and the professional diplomats. How did the Secretary of State, his officials and ambassadors interpret Soviet policy? How did they react to the Soviet negotiating style? What degree of post-war co-operation did they think possible? Of course, to examine such problems from the viewpoint of one department leaves certain aspects of British policy only partially illuminated. Churchill's strong personality and close relationship with Eden meant that his incursions into foreign policy could not be ignored, however much the permanent officials may have resented them. The extent of Churchill's interest in policy towards Russia, and the degree to which his own views on the subject varied, appear in both the commentary and the documents. The service departments and the Treasury, however, are seen very much from the perspective of the Foreign Office. It has to be remembered that the dyspeptic view which the latter held of service attitudes to Russia, and especially of the Military Mission in Moscow, is only one side of the story.

Secondly, it seemed logical to reproduce documents which have not previously appeared in print or from which there has been little quotation. Equally, where there was already an extensive or recent secondary literature there appeared to be no point in going over well-trodden ground. Thus the Polish question, for example, is mentioned in the commentary only to remind the reader of the course of events. The last word has not been said about the conferences at Tehran, Yalta and Potsdam, but there is already an extensive literature on these meetings. It is true that there are voluminous British records for all three conferences which invite further research, yet to give only a few snippets from briefing and position papers would have added little that is new while necessitating the exclusion of other documents. Instead the aim has been to try and illustrate the evolution of Foreign Office attitudes during the war as a whole rather than to concentrate on the special occasions.

Some extracts have been included from conferences which have so far attracted less attention – such as the Moscow Foreign Ministers' meeting in 1943 and the first two post-war encounters in London and Moscow. This raises a third point: where should such a selection end? To stop with Potsdam would leave a number of problems in the air, whereas there is a case for continuing until the Moscow meeting of December 1945. By then the three allies are beginning to adjust to a new atmosphere in which wartime co-operation is being replaced by unease but not yet by despair. The United Nations is about to begin its life and control of atomic energy is one of the first questions to confront it. Moreover, the Moscow Conference produced agreement on a procedure for drafting peace treaties with the European allies of Germany. The road was now open to the first stage of what was still expected to be a general peace settlement. New faces are appearing on the scene; Bevin is beginning to settle into the role of Foreign Secretary and Clark Kerr is about to leave the Moscow Embassy. The end of the calendar year marks, therefore, the beginning of a new phase in Anglo-Soviet relations. It is, too, a phase in which Britain will become more and more aware of her economic weakness and dependence on the United States, but also one in which her doubts about American intentions will decrease. One theme that re-appears in the documents is uncertainty about Washington's post-war intentions and this in turn markedly affects the British view of Russia.

There is, however, little point in offering a selection of documents and then supplying a ready-made interpretation to go with it. It will be for individual readers to draw their own conclusions from the material included here. The commentary is intended as a linking narrative designed to put the documents in context and not to prejudge particular issues. Nor is this a book primarily about Soviet policy-making as such; here we have Stalin and Molotov as seen from the outside by British contemporaries whose knowledge and understanding of Soviet Russia were in varying degrees imperfect. Decision-makers always face the challenge of how to interpret incomplete information in the light of their own experience and assumptions. It is to be hoped that this book will give some indication of how well the Foreign Office met that challenge under the specific circumstances of global war and the first few months of peace. The weight of the documents selected lies in 1945 precisely because the pace of events in that year is so fast and bewildering. As far as possible one must try to avoid the advantage of hindsight in assessing the reactions of harassed and often overworked officials, without condoning what may be regarded as mistakes and errors of judgement in the light of the evidence then available.

Documents

INTRODUCTION

1 Prelude: Anglo-Soviet relations to the beginning of 1941

It is not possible to do more than mention some of the main developments – or lack of developments – in Anglo-Soviet relations between 1917 and 1941. Nevertheless, it is important to remember how bad those relations were before the German attack on Russia in June 1941 produced a new situation. The circumstances in which the Soviet Union was created ensured that relations between the two countries got off to the worst possible start. As one of the interventionist powers in the civil war, Britain was bound to be an object of Soviet suspicion. Given their virtual diplomatic isolation during the 1920s, it is scarcely surprising that Russian leaders continued to fear a renewed attack by the capitalist powers in general. Stalin used this fear to strengthen his own political position during the 'war-scare' of 1927. For their part, British governments saw Russia as a sponsor of subversion through the nominally independent Comintern. The alleged Zinoviev letter of 1924 was precisely the kind of communication which the British Right expected Comintern agents to produce. Attitudes to the Soviet Union, however, were not neatly divided on party lines. Within the Conservative party there was certainly a strong, not to say hysterical, suspicion of Russia, in contrast to the sympathy felt by some members of the Labour party. Moreover, it was the first Labour government which established diplomatic relations in February 1924 and the second which restored them in October 1929, following the break by the Baldwin government in May 1927. Yet in practice Labour policy towards the Soviet Union was scarcely less reserved and cautious than that of the Conservatives. Whatever their political complexion, British governments in the twenties viewed Russia as an irritant, if not quite an outright enemy. It was certainly difficult to see her as a potential ally.[1]

This attitude of doubt and suspicion changed only slowly as the international crisis of the thirties deepened. The Japanese take-over of Manchuria both threatened British interests in China and also implied a Japanese expansion at the expense of the Soviet Union. But the latter, still outside the

League of Nations, remained cautious and aloof during the Manchurian crisis. Although the National government in Britain was to become increasingly concerned about Japanese ambitions, it did not look to Russia as a counterweight. Nor had the Soviet Union much reason to help maintain Britain's imperial position in the Far East. Both countries conducted their policies towards Japan in separate compartments. The outbreak of the Sino-Japanese war in 1937 did not alter this situation. Both countries gave some aid to China; both continued to suspect each other's motives.

Hitler's rise to power in Germany produced a marked effect on Soviet policy in Europe. Relations with Germany never completely broke down, but Russia began to make signals that she was ready to join a combination to restrain Nazi revisionism. In 1934 she joined the League, obtaining a permanent seat on the Council; in May 1935 she signed treaties with France and Czechoslovakia; popular fronts against fascism were encouraged. The British reaction to these changes in Soviet policy was muted. Distaste for, and distrust of, Russia were combined with the hope that a comprehensive political settlement might meet German grievances. If Germany could be made a satisfied power there would be no need to look to Russia as a potential ally. Between 1934 and 1937 the Cabinet and the Foreign Office considered various means for reaching an agreement with Germany. That they came to nothing did not alter the basic fact that Britain was ignoring Russian signals. Indeed, co-operation with the Soviet Union might be positively dangerous. It is interesting to find Orme Sargent – then an Assistant Under-Secretary – arguing in January 1935 against the proposed Franco-Soviet alliance on the grounds that it would in effect re-create the Franco-Russian alliance of pre-1914 days and thus antagonise Germany. Vansittart, then Permanent Under-Secretary, shared some of Sargent's fears.[2]

Given such an attitude – which was not strongly challenged within the government or the Foreign Office – it is not surprising that the slight thaw which appeared in Anglo-Soviet relations in 1934 led to no positive agreement. Admittedly Eden (then Lord Privy Seal) visited Moscow in March 1935 and became the first minister from a Western power to gain an interview with Stalin, who stressed the need for collective action to restrain Germany. But the Cabinet did not attempt to follow up this contact, nor did Eden himself display any marked desire to improve relations with Russia after becoming Foreign Secretary in December 1935.[3] The outbreak of the Spanish Civil War in July 1936 made co-operation with Russia seem totally undesirable. The British government had no wish to be drawn into a general European conflict in which it might find itself aligned with Russia against Germany and Italy, nor to bring about a situation in which the Spanish struggle might be repeated in France. From the British point of view, non-intervention was the logical policy to follow. Soviet aid to the Spanish Republic and the development of the purges inside Russia combined to increase British suspicions of Russian intentions and to intensify doubts about her military capacity.[4]

The Munich crisis of 1938 demonstrated clearly the British reluctance to invoke Soviet assistance or to concede Russia a role as a major European power. The Russians declared their willingness to help Czechoslovakia but they were never put to the test. Their treaty commitment only came into force if the French moved first; Poland and Rumania would have had to agree to Soviet forces crossing their territory or using their airspace. From Moscow's point of view both Britain and France had demonstrated their lack of resolution. If they would not fight Hitler over the Sudetenland they were unlikely to resist further German expansion in eastern Europe. Worse still, they might positively encourage Hitler to turn against the Soviet Union in the hope that he would leave them unscathed. In the period after Munich an alliance between the Soviet Union and the Western powers seemed unlikely.[5]

But the German dismemberment of the rump of Czechoslovakia in March 1939 pushed Britain and France into giving guarantees to Poland and Rumania. Having thus abandoned her previous policy of avoiding commitments in eastern Europe, Britain now had to demonstrate both her resolution and her ability to make the guarantees effective. It was difficult to see how this could be done without some assistance from Russia. Confronted with this dilemma the Chamberlain Cabinet was to find itself pushed reluctantly towards a full-dress alliance with the Soviet Union. Much has been written about the Moscow negotiations of 1939, but largely in the context of the outbreak of the Second World War. Yet they were the first British attempt to negotiate a political and military agreement with the Soviet Union, and as such they were an important prelude to the talks and conferences that took place after June 1941. They also gave the British their first experience of the pleasures of negotiating with the dour, stubborn and rigid Molotov.[6]

Initially the British aim was something less than an outright alliance. On 14 April the British Ambassador, Sir William Seeds, conveyed to Litvinov a proposal that the Soviet Union should publicly declare her willingness to support her European neighbours against aggression. Litvinov produced eight counter-proposals on the 18 April. He wanted political and military agreements between Britain, France and Russia, combined with a promise to help those east European states between the Baltic Sea and the Black Sea who had common borders with the Soviet Union. The Russians clearly wanted to tie the Western powers down to specific commitments so that Moscow could not be left in the lurch. Equally, they wanted to broaden the proposed guarantees as a protection against threats to their security in the Baltic states and Finland.

The British Cabinet baulked at these wider commitments. It was still considering its next move when there came, early in May, the surprising news of Litvinov's replacement by Molotov. The latter lacked knowledge and experience of foreign affairs, and his negotiating style was far less flexible than that of the more cosmopolitan Litvinov. But the substance of Soviet policy had already been made clear in the proposals of 18 April. Molotov's personality added to, but did not create, the difficulties which the British and French negotiators faced between May and August. Seeds gave Molotov a revised version of the proposal for a public guarantee, only to have it rejected on 14 May. After much agonising and argument the Cabinet decided on 24 May to go ahead with negotiations for a political alliance. Chamberlain was still very reluctant but Halifax had come round to the view that it was worth making the attempt. He was anxious to avoid a breakdown in discussions yet did not wish to give too much scope for German propaganda that Britain was allying herself with the Comintern. His Permanent Under-Secretary, Cadogan, was also an unwilling convert; he saw an alliance as necessary to keep Russia away from Germany. The Cabinet and the Foreign Office were well aware of the danger that Russia might make a deal with Germany. Where they miscalculated was in assuming that she would not do so while still negotiating with the Western powers.[7]

The lack of conviction with which the British entered the negotiations facilitated Molotov's pushing them further and further along a path they did not wish to follow. By the end of June they had agreed to a list of named states which were to be guaranteed, including Estonia, Latvia and Finland (Lithuania was excluded because she did not then have a common border with Russia). Molotov did agree, however, that this list would be included in a secret protocol and not in the main treaty. By the end of July the British negotiators had also agreed to the start of military talks even though the political agreement had not been completed. The main difficulty was the definition of indirect aggression. The British did not want to give the Soviet Union too free a hand to intervene in her neighbours' affairs; Molotov continued to press for a broad definition and for a reference to indirect aggression in the treaty itself. No agreement had been reached on this issue by the time the political talks were adjourned.

Molotov had stuck rigidly to his own position and had taken one concession as a reason for pressing for another. Nor was his stubborn attitude relieved by any personal intervention from Stalin, as was to happen in later wartime negotiations. The dispatch of Strang to assist Seeds no doubt gave the impression that Britain did not take the talks seriously enough, but it is not certain that matters would have been much improved if Halifax himself had gone to Moscow. He had obviously no wish to do so since it might give the impression of being too anxious for an agreement. At a time of international crisis it would have been difficult for the Foreign Secretary to be away from London for lengthy periods. Moreover, Halifax's presence in Moscow would have made it necessary for the French to send Bonnet, which would have complicated the situation even further. As it was, Molotov was able to play upon the obviously greater willingness of the French to come to terms.

It was also unfortunate that the Anglo-French military mission was not particularly high-powered and that it took its time in reaching Moscow. Had it arrived earlier it would only have confronted sooner the question which Marshal Voroshilov posed on 14 August. Would Soviet troops be allowed to cross Polish and Rumanian territory? The British and French delegations could give no answer. The matter had not been raised previously with the Polish and Rumanian governments for fear that they would refuse. When their consent was still not forthcoming by 22 August, Voroshilov adjourned the talks. The announcement that same day of Ribbentrop's impending visit to Moscow signified the failure of the negotiations. The British and French governments had failed to foresee that Russia might conduct parallel negotiations with Germany. Nor were they aware of the eagerness with which Ribbentrop kept pressing for an invitation to Moscow from 14 August onwards. The British view that it was better to keep the negotiations going as a means of preventing a Russo-German agreement was thus demonstrated to be unsound. The lack of urgency shown by Britain and France roused Molotov's suspicions of their good faith. As early as 17 July he was complaining to his ambassadors in London and Paris how slow and untrustworthy the Western powers were. It is uncertain whether he was then already firmly in favour of an agreement with Germany.[8]

The Anglo-French guarantee to Poland could not save her from partition by Germany and Russia. A secret protocol to the Anglo-Polish treaty of 25 August made it clear that British help would only be given against German aggression. Britain was not obliged to go to war with Russia, nor did the government in fact contemplate doing so. Halifax also took the view that the guarantee to Rumania did not oblige Britain to intervene if the Soviet Union chose to regain the province of Bessarabia. The British reaction in September 1939 was confined to disapproval of Russia's forcible acquisition of Polish territory.[9] Behind this public attitude lay an ambiguity which was later to assume importance when the Polish question became a live issue. Britain did not recognise the partition of Poland but she was not automatically committed to the restoration of the Polish–Soviet frontier established by the Treaty of Riga in 1921. This had given Poland large Ukrainian and White Russian minorities which had not become reconciled to Polish rule. Successive British governments had shown some unease at the treatment of non-Polish minorities in the east.[10]

In the closing months of 1939 this was not an immediate problem for Britain. The next cause of friction with Russia was her attack on Finland at the end of November. The Russians had unsuccessfully pressed the Finns to make border changes and grant them bases, but it was not certain if their ambitions would remain limited to these objectives. They might seek to occupy the whole of Finland and perhaps even seize a port on Norway's Atlantic coast. Such speculations led Britain and France to give serious consideration to intervention on Finland's behalf. This might be combined with another operation – the occupation of the iron-ore mines in northern Sweden. This was expected to have a devastating effect on the German economy. Within the Foreign Office Sargent was to be found in December arguing the case for a dual-purpose expedition. But Chamberlain, Halifax and Cadogan all had reservations about provoking an outright conflict with Russia. On balance their main interest was seizing control of the mines, whereas the Daladier government was much more interested in aiding Finland. When the Supreme War Council met in Paris on 5 February 1940 the French proposed sending a force to occupy the port of Petsamo (already under Russian control) but were dissuaded by the British. Anglo-French disagreements, divisions within the British Cabinet, and the manifest unwillingness of Norway and Sweden to allow free passage to Allied forces all combined to prevent action before the collapse of Finnish resistance in March. An expedition was about to sail to occupy Narvik and seize control of the railway to the mines, but the project was abandoned on news of the Finnish surrender.[11]

A possible clash with the Soviet Union was thus avoided. Finland had to concede territory and bases but retained her independence. The obvious British sympathy for Finland had further increased Soviet suspicions. Moreover, Russia's expulsion from the League of Nations in December 1939 had been a public slight to her prestige, however limited its practical effects. The worsening of Anglo-Soviet relations was indicated by the recall of Sir William Seeds at the end of 1939; a new ambassador was not appointed. Since the Soviet Union had become a virtual ally of Germany there seemed to be little that Britain could usefully discuss with her – with the important exception of trade. A German–Soviet trade agreement was signed on 10 February 1940 after much hard bargaining in which Stalin personally intervened.[12] If Britain could get a similar agreement it might be possible to prevent Russia from falling completely under German influence and so limit her value as a loophole in the British blockade. But, at the end of April and again on 22 May, the Soviet Union made it clear that she would not accept any restrictions on her right to trade with Germany.

Despite the discouraging Soviet response the Cabinet decided to continue trade negotiations and to send Sir Stafford Cripps to Moscow for this purpose. At his own suggestion he had visited the Soviet Union in February and obtained an interview with Molotov which left him convinced that the Russians were genuinely interested in a trade agreement. At the time Halifax thought him over-optimistic. But this visit, and his expulsion from the Labour party in June 1939 for supporting the principle of popular fronts, seemed to make him a suitable candidate for a special mission. Molotov, however, would only accept him as successor to Seeds. So Cripps was formally appointed ambassador at the end of May and arrived in Moscow on 12 June. If he made little progress it would be difficult to recall him without admitting failure. Nor was it an opportune time to seek an improvement in Anglo-Soviet relations. Germany had occupied Denmark and Norway; France was on the verge of collapse; Italy had entered the war. Given Churchill's well-known antipathy towards communism, his replacement of Chamberlain as Prime Minister (on 8 May) did not suggest that British doubts about Russia would diminish. Cripps found that initial meetings with Molotov on 14 June and with Stalin on 1 July produced no follow-up. Discussions on trade with Mikoyan showed that the Russians wanted only a limited barter arrangement and confirmed their unwillingness to modify the existing agreement with Germany.[13]

Hitler's military successes pushed the Soviet Union into consolidating her own position. At the end of June she delivered an ultimatum to Rumania which forced the latter to cede Bessarabia and northern Bukovina. In the middle of June the three Baltic republics were forced to establish new governments more acceptable to the Russians. These governments held elections and the respective assemblies thus produced voted for incorporation into the Soviet Union in July. As in the case of the Russian acquisition of Polish territory, the British attitude was somewhat ambiguous. *De jure* recognition of the latest Soviet gains was out of the question in view of the damage it would do to Britain's reputation, especially in the United States. But *de facto* recognition might be considered if Britain could gain something in return. There was little that Britain could do to disturb the effective Russian possession of the Baltic states and Bessarabia.

But on what terms should Britain contemplate granting *de facto* recognition? Cripps saw it as a concession which could buy Russian goodwill and a tangible gesture which would help to break down Russian suspicions. Halifax and Cadogan were more cautious; they thought that the Russians would be influenced by a realistic calculation of what was in their own best interests. It would be pointless therefore to offer recognition without seeking something in return. This difference of opinion on how to deal with the Soviet Union foreshadowed similar arguments which were to reappear during the war years. Nevertheless, the possibility that Russia might come further under German influence led the Cabinet to accept Cripp's suggestion for attempting to reach a political agreement. On 22 October he gave the British proposals to Vyshinsky, the recently appointed Deputy Commissar for Foreign Affairs. Britain was prepared to concede *de facto* recognition of the Russian territorial gains of 1939 and 1940, would consult the Russians about the post-war settlement, and would avoid joining any anti-Soviet alliance. In return Britain would expect benevolent neutrality from Russia and was prepared to consider a non-aggression pact if circumstances were favourable. Cripps went beyond his instructions in referring to the territories of 'the former Polish state', a phrase which could have been construed as an acceptance of Soviet sovereignty and as a withdrawal of support from the Polish government in exile.

The problem did not arise, since Vyshinsky's initial expression of interest was not followed up by a formal reply. It was not until 1 February 1941 that Molotov confirmed the Soviet lack of interest. At that stage the value of *de facto* recognition was outweighed by the possibility of more tangible gains from Japan and Germany. In July 1940 the Japanese took the initiative in proposing a neutrality treaty. The Russian reply in August 1940 favoured a non-aggression pact and called for the ending of the Japanese oil and coal concessions in northern Sakhalin as a prerequisite for any political agreement. By continuing to insist on this for the rest of 1940 Molotov succeeded in blocking further progress. Moreover, he changed his position in November and now announced a preference for a neutrality treaty over a non-aggression pact. Either he was over-playing his hand or he deliberately wanted to avoid agreement.[14]

Similar tactics appeared in Molotov's dealings with Germany. The growth of the latter's influence in Rumania, amounting almost to a protectorate, and the signing of the Tripartite Pact on 27 September, were clear indications that Russia's freedom of action was likely to be severely limited unless she could strike a new bargain with Germany. Yet when Molotov visited Berlin in November, on Ribbentrop's invitation, he once again over-played his hand. He made it clear that Russia was unwilling to be diverted from the Balkans, the Black Sea and the Baltic Sea. She wanted bases in the Dardanelles and still harboured territorial ambitions against Finland and Rumania. Hitler showed his disapproval; he was only prepared to consider admitting Russia to the Tripartite Pact if she kept out of Europe and expanded towards the Persian Gulf and India. Molotov's visit did nothing to turn Hitler away from his plans for attacking the Soviet Union. Having returned to Moscow, Molotov gave the German ambassador on 26 November what amounted to the Soviet terms for joining the Tripartite Pact. German forces must leave Finland, Russia must be allowed to sign a treaty with Bulgaria, and the demand for an end to the Japanese economic concessions was repeated. Expansion towards the Persian Gulf was the only aspect of Hitler's proposals to attract Russian enthusiasm. These suggestions killed off any remaining German interest in further negotiations. It is not clear whether the ineptness of Soviet diplomacy during the second half of 1940 was the result of Stalin's placing particular reliance on Molotov's advice. The adoption of a rigid position and a high opening bid were very similar to the tactics used in the 1939 negotiations with Britain and France.[15]

Precisely because they over-estimated the strength of their bargaining position *vis-à-vis* Japan and Germany, Stalin and Molotov had little reason to accept the British offer of 22 October. There was in any case little point in antagonising Germany by an overt improvement in relations with Britain. Cripps found the lack of progress frustrating. This was his first encounter with the delays and difficulties which any ambassador can expect. The isolation of the diplomatic corps in Moscow, and Molotov's obvious unwillingness to see him, further increased Cripps's impatience. He began to favour a less conciliatory line, and was on the point of sending Mikoyan a critical letter complaining about Russian obstructiveness over a trade agreement, when on 23 December 1940 Eden returned to the Foreign Office and Halifax departed to become ambassador in Washington.[16]

2 Developments in 1941 to Eden's Moscow visit

Eden persuaded Cripps not to send the proposed letter to Mikoyan in case it was interpreted as signifying a change of policy by the incoming Secretary of State. Cripps in turn advised Eden against sending a personal message to Stalin on the grounds that it would be taken as a sign of weakness. Since the Soviet Union was essentially no more friendly to Britain than she was to Germany the best policy was to maintain a reserved attitude. During the summer of 1939 Eden had been a strong supporter of an alliance with Russia and had even volunteered to go to Moscow himself. At the beginning of 1941, however, he seemed to agree with Cripps and showed no inclination to take a new initiative. At a discussion on 6 January Cadogan found him well aware that little was to be expected from the Soviet Union. This attitude comes out clearly in a message sent to Cripps on 17 January (Document 1A).[1] In his letter on 26 January Cripps commented on the Russo-German agreements which had been signed on 10 January. These consisted of a Pact of Friendship signed in Berlin, a new economic agreement and a settlement of the Lithuanian frontiers with Germany and Poland. The two latter agreements were signed in Moscow.

In the light of what seemed to mark an improvement in relations between Germany and the Soviet Union, Cripps was apparently still in favour of a cautious policy (Document 1B). His attitude was soon to change. As the result of a complaint to Maisky, Molotov granted Cripps an interview on 1 February, the first meeting between the two men since October 1940. Molotov confirmed that Russia was not interested in the offer of 22 October and made various criticisms of British unfriendliness. This was not very promising, but the very fact of obtaining an interview stimulated Cripps into action. On the same day he presented Vyshinsky with a memorandum containing the warning that Soviet policies could affect Britain's attitude to any German peace proposals. This hint that Britain might leave Germany a free hand to deal with Russia was made entirely on Cripps's own initiative. He then proceeded on 2 February to urge upon Eden that the question of the

10

Baltic states should be reopened. Cadogan, Sargent and Collier, the Head of the Northern Department, all disagreed with this proposal, and Eden himself commented on Cripps's contradictory behaviour. He was instructed on 9 February not to reopen the question.[2]

In mid-February Eden set off on a trip to Egypt, Greece and Turkey. Cripps suggested that he visit Moscow as well, but Eden did not wish to appear too anxious to make contact with the Russians. Nor was Churchill in favour of the idea. So Cripps flew to Ankara at the end of the month to urge again the need for fresh discussions on the Baltic states. Once more he was unsuccessful, but Eden did agree that something should be done to improve Russo-Turkish relations. The Turks were particularly suspicious of Russian designs on the Black Sea Straits, for the Soviet Union had never been happy about the Montreux Convention of 1936. On his return to Moscow Cripps persuaded Russia and Turkey to exchange assurances on 9 March that if either became the object of aggression the other would show complete understanding and neutrality. This did something to reassure the Turks that in the event of a German attack Russia would not try to take advantage of the situation.[3]

This interlude did not divert Cripps from renewed appeals during March and April for a new approach over the Baltic states. If Britain appeared too hostile, he argued, the Soviet Union might be pushed closer to Germany. Sargent was not in principle opposed to conceding *de facto* recognition but thought that there was no possibility of an agreement with Russia until she abandoned her appeasement of Germany. Cadogan felt that the right moment for concessions had not arrived. Eden wanted to reduce Soviet suspicions but saw no point in making useless gestures. On 16 April he informed Cripps that he was prepared to concede *de facto* recognition of the take-over of the Baltic states but did not wish to commit himself to public *de jure* recognition. But there was no point in discussing the question until there were definite signs that Russia had decided to abandon co-operation with Germany. In other words, Eden felt that he ought to be making a diplomatic approach to Russia but did not see his way to achieving it.[4]

Meanwhile, Cripps's erratic behaviour was causing annoyance and alarm in the Foreign Office. On 3 April he was given a message from Churchill for transmission to Stalin concerning German troop concentrations in Poland. He showed considerable reluctance to pass this on and did not do so until 19 April. On the previous day he gave Vyshinsky a memorandum for Molotov in which he repeated the threat of 1 February that Britain's attitude to possible German peace offers could be influenced by Soviet policy. Once again he had no authorisation to make such a statement. To add insult to injury his reaction to Eden's message of 16 April was to repeat his arguments for re-opening the Baltic question. He had again to be told that Eden did not intend to take any action. The vagaries of Cripps's behaviour led Sargent to compile an indictment on 26 April (Document 2). Nevertheless, the suggestion of recalling Cripps was not taken up until the beginning of June.[5]

By then German military successes in Yugoslavia and Greece had further weakened Soviet influence in the Balkans. It was particularly unfortunate for the Russians that the signing of a non-aggression pact with Yugoslavia on 5 April came only one day before the German invasion of that country. Some evidence of Soviet concern was revealed by the conclusion of a five-year neutrality pact with Japan. When Matsuoka, the Japanese Foreign Minister, passed through Moscow in March on his way to Berlin and Rome, he had made no progress towards getting an agreement with Russia. On his return trip, however, Stalin intervened personally to obtain the signature of the pact on 13 April. The troublesome question of the economic concessions in northern Sakhalin was dealt with in a separate exchange of letters. The effusive send-off which Stalin gave to Matsuoka at the railway station indicated the importance of the treaty to Russia. The danger of a war on two fronts was reduced but not eliminated. The Soviet Union was not committed to any reduction in aid to China, and Maisky was careful to assure Eden that too much should not be read into the pact. The Foreign Secretary was not altogether reassured; he commented that it was difficult to know how well informed Maisky was about Russian policy.[6]

During the spring of 1941 the information being acquired by the various British intelligence agencies suggested more and more the possibility of a German attack on Russia, yet without being entirely conclusive. An appreciation drawn up by the Joint Intelligence Committee (JIC) on 5 April still thought a direct attack on the Soviet Union unlikely. The British had to count on the possibility that Germany was preparing for a thrust through Turkey into the Middle East. In any case it was a logical assumption that Germany would make demands on Russia first and would only resort to force if these were refused. So when Cripps was sent a summary of evidence on 20 April about German plans against Russia the Foreign Office was still as cautious in its predictions as the JIC. Publicly Soviet diplomats took the line that there was no danger of a German attack and that Russia would not let herself be drawn into the war. Oumansky, the Ambassador in Washington, spoke in these terms on 1 May to the Australian diplomat Casey. On 14 May Molotov assured the Japanese Ambassador that rumours of a German attack were merely propaganda. Vyshinsky said much the same to Steinhardt, the American Ambassador, on 25 May. Two days later Maisky told Eden that Russia did not wish to become involved in hostilities. Having discounted the possibility of a German attack he turned to the Baltic question and suggested that Britain make a definite statement of what she was prepared to offer and of what she wanted in return.[7]

Although Eden would have liked to make some approach to the Russians Britain still had little to offer. By the end of May, however, Foreign Office and military opinion was coming round more definitely to the possibility of a German attack. On 31 May Cadogan agreed with the Chiefs of Staff that Germany was prepared to move against Russia but thought that the latter would yield to German demands without a fight. Could Britain stiffen Russian resolve and how could she help if the Soviet Union was in fact attacked? There was some rather unproductive discussion within the Foreign Office. On 28 May there was a meeting between R. A. Butler (the Parliamentary Under-Secretary), Sargent, Horace Seymour, Bowker and Warner (recently appointed Head of the Northern Department in succession to Collier), which found little scope for improving relations with Russia. Nor did much come out of a discussion on 2 June between Eden, Cadogan, Butler and Warner as a preliminary to a meeting between Eden and Maisky later the same day. The latter continued to discount the possibility of a German attack. A memorandum by Coote of the Northern Department on 8 June argued that the British attitude might tip the scale if the Soviet Union was hesitating to submit to German demands. But he could see little that Britain could do in the way of economic assistance. Eden made another unsuccessful attempt to move Maisky on 13 June, offering to send a military mission to Moscow in the event of a German attack. Maisky remained sceptical and said that the conditions for such close collaboration did not exist. That same day the Soviet news agency Tass issued a denial that Germany had made demands on Russia and implied that Cripps was responsible for such rumours. On the eve of the German attack the Russians still seem to have suspected that Britain was trying to stir up trouble. On the British side the Foreign Office and the Service Departments were at least beginning to think about the implications of a Russo-German war.[8]

Germany's attack on Russia was quickly followed by Churchill's broadcast promising help to the Soviet Union. By itself this could not change attitudes and expectations overnight. There was considerable doubt about the Russian ability to withstand the German onslaught. In June the JIC was thinking in terms of German troops reaching Moscow in six weeks at most. At the end of June Cadogan found Dill pessimistic about Russian prospects. On 10 July Cavendish-Bentinck, Chairman of the JIC, said that the War Office did not expect the Russians to reach the Caucasus for another six weeks. Nevertheless, preparations for destroying the oilfields there should be put in hand within the next four weeks. Given such pessimism it was difficult to make long-term plans. On the other hand it was impossible for Britain to do nothing at all.[9]

Some persistent themes in Anglo-Soviet relations soon began to appear. Cripps returned to Moscow accompanied by the heads of economic and military missions, the latter led by Colonel Mason Macfarlane. The mission soon discovered that the Russians were unwilling to pass on information or reveal much about their own activities against the Germans. Annoyance on the part of the Military Mission was perhaps understandable; it is less clear why from an early stage the Foreign Office exhibited such hostility towards its activities. Warner minuted on 2 November that he was always nervous when Mason Macfarlane called for a firm line. Cadogan, Sargent and Strang all agreed with him in wanting to leave well alone and not press the Russians for military information. When Mason Macfarlane, on 22 November, complained about Russian obstructiveness and wanted to lodge a formal protest, Eden complained to Brooke, who had just taken over as Chief of the Imperial General Staff. On 30 November Eden minuted that Mason Macfarlane was a fusspot. Thus, fairly or not, a pattern was soon established of frustration on the part of the Military Mission and a feeling by the Foreign Office that its members were by and large clumsy and tactless.[10]

Aid to the Soviet Union fell into the two categories of civilian and military. An agreement on civilian aid was signed on 16 August, whereby Britain agreed to provide a credit of £10 million upon which the Soviet Union could draw for up to 60% of the goods she bought from Britain. For the time being this agreement produced no difficulties. The position over military aid was initially less clear, in part because of the attitude of the United States. Although Sumner Welles had issued a statement denouncing the German attack, President Roosevelt said on 1 August that the Soviet Union did not qualify for Lend–Lease. This reserved attitude disappeared as a result of Harry Hopkins's visit to Moscow at the end of July. He came away convinced that Russia would survive the German attack and that she deserved all the aid available. While in Moscow he had a conversation with Cripps on 31 July. The latter put to him the idea of a conference to discuss military aid to Russia. The upshot was the Beaverbrook–Harriman mission which visited Moscow at the end of September. It proved a success in so far as a protocol on supplies to Russia was signed. But this was achieved at the cost of a decision, not formally spelled out, to give Russia military aid unconditionally. Assistance to meet the Soviet Union's immediate needs was more important than any attempt to elicit detailed information, which seems to have been Cripps's original intention. Thus a pattern was set for later aid negotiations with Russia which was confirmed by the news on 6 November that Roosevelt had decided to extend a $1,000 million credit to the Soviet Union under the Lend–Lease Act. It was noticeable that Beaverbrook left Cripps out of the discussions during his mission. When the Allied Supplies Executive (ASE) was set up at the end of October with Beaverbrook as its first chairman, it was decided that all communications about supplies would be made through the Soviet Embassy in London. Cripps would only be kept informed. (Despite its imposing title, ASE was a purely British body.)[11]

There were two problems where Britain and Russia seemed to achieve some measure of co-operation. On 30 July the Soviet Union and the Polish government-in-exile re-established diplomatic relations. This did not prevent continuing mutual hostility and suspicion. Although the Russians agreed that their treaties of 1939 with Germany were now invalid, they did not abandon their territorial claims, while the Poles were still committed to regaining their 1939 frontiers. Britain reaffirmed that she did not recognise territorial changes which had taken place since the outbreak of war. The question of Polish frontiers was thus left unresolved, although temporarily concealed. The second instance of co-operation was the Anglo-Soviet occupation of Iran launched on 25 August. The Russians had argued that the German community in Persia was plotting a coup which would produce a pro-Axis government. The evidence for this allegation was dubious but it could be argued that as a preventive measure it was necessary for Britain and Russia to secure their position. Persia's value as an oil producer and as a potential route for supplies to the Soviet Union was obvious. The carrying capacity of the Persian railways was initially limited, but was to increase in later years. There was also perhaps another motive which influenced British policy: if Russian forces suffered a severe defeat in the south and German troops reached the Caucasus it would be well for British forces to be established in Iran. A treaty recognising the rights and position of the occupying powers was signed with the Persian government in January 1942. On the one hand British and Russian forces gained wide powers over communications, on the other they promised to withdraw not more than six months after the end of hostilities with the Axis powers. If the Iranians were not entirely happy, they had at least gained a promise in writing which they could hope to use to their advantage.[12]

In seeking a political agreement with Russia, Britain at an early stage found her hands tied by the United States. Winant, the American Ambassador, advised Eden against a formal treaty with Russia and on 21 July Hopkins and he repeated the warning, extending it to wartime commitments in general. Initially there seemed to be no problem. Cripps returned to Moscow on 27 June. When he saw Molotov the following day the latter raised the question of a political agreement. Cripps was cautious and as it turned out rightly so. When Cripps saw Stalin on 8 July he found that only a very general agreement was in question. The document which he and Stalin signed on 12 July merely said that the two countries would give each other aid and would not negotiate a separate armistice or peace. This suited the British Cabinet and Foreign Office and met American objections. The publication of the Atlantic Charter in August further committed Britain to following certain principles of international conduct.[13]

Cripps was genuinely anxious to promote both wartime and post-war co-operation with Russia. But he was not willing to remain ambassador indefinitely and was increasingly eager to return to British politics. These two themes appear in his messages from the end of July (Document 1C; Document 3A, C, E, F). Within the Foreign Office there were certainly doubts about Cripps's diplomatic ability. For Churchill there was also a political problem. If Cripps came back to London he was likely to want a place in the government or might set himself up in opposition. Given the uncertain military situation in Russia it would in any case be injudicious for Cripps to return home. This might be regarded as indicating a lack of faith in the Soviet Union. Eden therefore wrote to Cripps on 25 August that it would be a mistake for him to leave Russia, and added pointedly that Churchill regretted that there was no vacancy in the government at present. Cripps replied on 14 September that he did not intend to come home immediately and did not expect a place in the government. But, he added ominously, he was not prepared to put himself permanently out of British politics. Having at first praised the Beaverbrook–Harriman mission, he reacted angrily to Eden's account of its discussions.[14]

Russian resistance continued well beyond the six weeks originally expected but at the end of October the military situation was still precarious. The evacuation of the diplomatic corps to Kuibyshev in mid-October indicated how seriously the Russians regarded the threat to Moscow. Ismay was fairly optimistic on 26 October but the pessimistic Sargent thought three days later that Russia was already beaten. There was still considerable British concern about the Caucasian oilfields. On 21 November Britain and the United States promised to help Russia find alternative supplies during and after the war if the oilfields had to be destroyed. Early in December a British mission reached Mrasnodar but was shown little and was not allowed to stay long. Their improved military situation made the Russians less willing to consider destruction of the oilfields.[15]

The question of a more detailed political agreement was brought to a head by Stalin's message to Churchill of 8 November. Its tone as much as its content alarmed the Foreign Office. It was the first of several occasions on which Churchill was to find that corresponding with Stalin was a more uneasy and uncertain business than dealing with Roosevelt. Stalin was annoyed by, and suspicious of, the British unwillingness to declare war on Finland, Rumania and Hungary. He now wanted a more specific agreement than the joint declaration of 12 July. In a long minute Warner summed up the results of a talk with Sargent and Dew. They found it difficult to account for the tone of the letter. Stalin perhaps suspected that Britain wanted to see Russia crippled. The difficulty was that in trying to placate him Britain might find herself driven from one concession to another. Yet it was necessary to maintain Russian morale. The Soviet Union would probably want Finland, control of the Dardanelles, perhaps even an opening to the Atlantic by obtaining territory in north Norway, and heavy reparations from Germany. Perhaps remembering the experience of 1939, Warner argued that it would be better to keep political and military talks separate. He was also in favour of postponing any discussion of peace aims. Warner was saying in effect that Britain should avoid giving away too much to Russia.[16]

A further discussion, between Eden, Cadogan, Warner and Sargent on 14 November came to the conclusion that the Foreign Secretary would have to visit Moscow. Dew, on 15 November, and Warner, on 17 November, saw the need to allay Soviet suspicions. These speculations led up to the discussion held in Cadogan's room of which Dew produced a lengthy account on 21 November (Document 4). On the same day Churchill informed Stalin that Eden was willing to come to Moscow. Two days later Warner repeated his view that the talks should only be exploratory and added the interesting rider that Britain should avoid seeking detailed agreement in advance from the United States. The idea of Eden visiting Moscow was not entirely new. He had talked in early August of a possible visit in September; Churchill had thought that Eden might accompany the Beaverbrook–Harriman mission. In early September Beaverbrook himself suggested a visit by Eden, claiming that Cripps had lost his nerve. Just before the arrival of Stalin's letter, Eden was talking of a visit after Christmas. Thus the stage was set for the second British attempt to make a formal alliance with the Soviet Union.[17]

3 Eden's visit to Moscow and the Anglo-Soviet treaty

Britain's declaration of war on Finland, Rumania and Hungary on 6 December removed one cause for Soviet complaint. This was soon overshadowed, however, by the Japanese attack on Pearl Harbour and Germany's declaration of war on the United States. When Eden arrived in Moscow on 15 December he faced a new and disadvantageous situation for conducting delicate negotiations. American entry into the war offered the prospect of ultimate victory; in the short term Britain was confronted with the need to divert supplies and men to the Far East. These new military commitments would make it more difficult to maintain the flow of aid to Russia. In addition, Eden's hands had been tied by a warning from Hull on 6 December against making agreements on territorial changes and against secret treaties. The memory of Woodrow Wilson's problems at Versailles in 1919 haunted both Roosevelt and the State Department. It is true that Hull was merely repeating and emphasising the earlier warnings of Winant and Hopkins; but it was also significant that the United States was prepared to apply so much pressure even before she had become a belligerent. The British government, having publicly accepted the principles of the Atlantic Charter, would find it difficult to disown them too openly.[1]

In contrast, the Russian negotiating position had been strengthened. The Germans had been checked and pushed back before Moscow; for the winter at least the Soviet Union had gained a breathing space. Moreover, the Japanese move against British and American possessions removed any lingering fears that Tokyo might be tempted to break the Neutrality Pact. Stalin explained to Eden at their first meeting that he could not immediately join in the war against Japan. He did not add the obvious point that while she was embroiled in the Pacific and South-East Asia the Soviet Union was safe from a war on two fronts. For the next three years or so Russia was careful not to give Japan any cause to complain that the Neutrality Pact had been violated. On their side the Japanese found it useful to maintain the pact and were finally to abandon the Sakhalin concessions in 1942.[2]

18

Stalin had played the leading role in the negotiations with Harriman and Beaverbrook. He had used the tactics of a friendly opening approach followed by a stiffer attitude and then a later reversion to cordiality. Eden and his colleagues do not seem to have anticipated that they would face a similar approach. As in the 1939 negotiations Stalin proposed a political and military treaty but on this occasion was careful not to link them too closely together. He also used once again the idea of a secret protocol for various post-war territorial changes. He was, however, careful to appear flexible. The proposal of the Curzon line as the basis for the frontier with Poland could be made to look like a concession, since it would mean giving up some territory by comparison with the 1941 frontier. On the other hand Stalin hardened his position in the second and third meetings. If he did not get British agreement to Russia's 1941 frontiers he was not prepared to continue negotiations. Once again, therefore, the Russians were asking Britain for a clear-cut commitment. During the second meeting Stalin commented more than once that the negotiations with the Chamberlain government had broken down over the Baltic states and Finland. In 1939, of course, it had not been a question of frontiers, but of the degree of intervention which Britain was prepared to concede under the formula of indirect aggression. Nevertheless it is interesting that in the changed circumstances of 1941 Stalin still had in mind the British attitudes of two years earlier.

Eden had little freedom of action. The British statement of the previous July prevented him from making concessions on the Polish frontier; on other frontiers his hands were tied by the American warning. His two main assistants on the trip were dubious about making concessions; Cadogan thought Stalin was bluffing and Harvey, initially at least, felt that it would be wrong to write off the Baltic states even though Britain was hardly likely to dispute Soviet control in practice. Churchill, in Washington at the time, made clear in a message of 21 December that he was unwilling to approach Roosevelt, even informally, for American agreement to Stalin's proposals. He advised Eden not to be disappointed if it proved impossible to get a joint declaration in Moscow.[3]

The Foreign Secretary could therefore do no more than say that he recognised Russia as having *de facto* sovereignty over the Baltic states. Molotov indicated his displeasure to Cripps, in an interview on 19 December, at the failure to get an agreement on frontiers. Without this there could be no firm foundation upon which Anglo-Soviet relations might develop. This did not, however, represent Stalin's view. The latter could not allow a breakdown in negotiations which might well become public knowledge, nor was he in a strong enough military position to hope for successful overtures to Germany. So he agreed that Eden should return to London for consultations on the assumption that these would lead to agreement in two or three weeks

(Document 5). Eden felt that a good deal had been done to lessen Russian suspicions; Cripps was less optimistic. On 5 January 1942 he told the American Chargé d'Affaires, Thurston, that the visit had been unsatisfactory. He personally wanted Britain to accept the Soviet claims, although he did qualify this by saying that the United States should agree. Cripps's remarks to some extent represented a sense of failure. One result of Eden's visit was confirmation that Cripps would be recalled and replaced by a career diplomat. He left Moscow on 9 January with little show of regret from the Russians. His successor, Clark Kerr, then Ambassador in China, did not arrive in Moscow until March. A more lively, not to say idiosyncratic, personality than his predecessor, Clark Kerr was to prove as an individual more acceptable to the Russians, although he too encountered some of the difficulties which had so annoyed Cripps.[4]

During his first meeting with Eden, Stalin said that Russia had no objection to certain European countries establishing federations. Eden took up this point and specifically mentioned Poland, Czechoslovakia and the Balkans. Stalin made no response to this lead and the whole question disappeared from sight in the argument about frontier questions. But potential confederations in Eastern Europe were to remain a significant element in British policy until the Moscow Foreign Ministers' Conference of October 1943. On 15 January 1942 the Yugoslav and Greek governments-in-exile signed an agreement to create a Balkan Union; on 23 January the Polish and Czech governments also agreed to set up a confederation, following up a declaration of principle made in November 1940. There was from the start some ambiguity about these incipient combinations. Were they intended to be mainly barriers to a German revival or were they also meant to limit possible Soviet expansion after the war? Dixon, Howard and Sargent all tended towards the latter view; indeed Sargent wanted Britain to come out openly for a larger federation in the Balkans which would include Bulgaria and Rumania. Eden was more cautious. While approving of the Greek–Yugoslav union as a model for others to copy he did not wish to arouse Russian suspicions. Nor did he want to give Bulgaria and Rumania the impression that they could expect lenient treatment.[5]

Agreements between governments-in-exile were no more than paper plans, and in early 1942 the Soviet attitude was still unclear. The question of the proposed Anglo-Russian treaty was of much more immediate significance. It soon became clear that more time would be required than the two or three weeks of which Stalin had spoken. Even before his return from the United States in the middle of January, Churchill had revealed his continued opposition to accepting the 1941 frontiers. In resisting the opening of negotiations with Russia he thus, somewhat ironically, found himself in a similar position to Chamberlain in 1939. By the beginning of February divisions of opinion were clearly established. In the Cabinet Eden and Beaverbrook were in favour of recognising the 1941 frontiers while Attlee supported the Prime Minister; within the Foreign Office Sargent and Harvey followed Eden, but Cadogan was strongly against concessions. He saw dangers in alienating American opinion by too blatant an abandonment of the principles of the Atlantic Charter.[6]

It was decided, however, to approach Roosevelt and put the case for accepting Stalin's demands. The basic British argument was the need to give the Russians a sign of goodwill and support. Continued refusal to recognise the 1941 frontiers might, in the extreme case, tempt Stalin to try for a separate peace. Even if that danger were discounted, Russia might simply relax her military efforts once German troops had been forced off her territory. Such reasoning lay behind Sargent's memorandum of 5 February (Document 6). Of course it was possible to argue that if the Russians were hard-headed, self-centred and suspicious, then attempts to demonstrate goodwill would have little effect. Against that there was the possibility that a reasonable straightforward attitude might have a cumulative long-term effect. In any case there was the immediate problem of keeping the Soviet Union in the fight. A diplomatic gesture was the best that Britain could offer in the absence of a major military victory. These at times contradictory arguments can be followed in Document 7.

Roosevelt was to prove unreceptive to British attempts to win him over. He was well primed by a memorandum from Hull on 4 February which set out the case against an Anglo-Soviet treaty. It would establish the dangerous precedent that frontiers could be settled before the peace conference. To condone the methods by which Russia took over the Baltic states would weaken the Atlantic Charter and alarm the smaller European states. In any case, concessions to the Soviet government were likely to provoke further demands. During February and March, therefore, Roosevelt continued to withhold his support for a frontier agreement, notwithstanding the blandishments of Beaverbrook. Having resigned on 19 February, the latter went off to the United States, ostensibly for his health, in practice to win over the President. The American Chargé d'Affaires in London, Matthews, found himself subjected to a campaign of warnings that without a treaty the Soviet Union might make a separate peace.[7]

Roosevelt tried in March to deflect Stalin by appealing to him through Litvinov to postpone the frontier question until the end of the war. The United States would then be willing to help promote Russian security. At this stage of the war, however, the Soviet Union saw little need to worry about American susceptibilities. Roosevelt was rebuffed by a curt note which merely said that the Soviet government took note of his views. Meanwhile Churchill's resistance to concessions was weakening under the impact of British military reverses in the Far East. By 25 March he was prepared to consider opening negotiations with Russia, although it was not until 8 April that the Cabinet gave formal approval. Roosevelt indicated that despite his unhappiness he would try to avoid public criticism of any resulting treaty. He now made another attempt to distract Stalin by sending an invitation on 11 April for Molotov to visit Washington in order to discuss certain military operations. This cut across a British invitation, made through Maisky on 8 April, that Molotov should come to London to negotiate the proposed treaty. Whereas on 13 April Maisky pleaded pressure of work as a reason for Molotov's inability to visit London, Stalin replied to Roosevelt on 20 April that Molotov would certainly come to Washington and would visit London as well. He confirmed this to Churchill on 22 April. The prospect of a second front, at which Roosevelt was clearly hinting, combined with a British alliance, overcame whatever doubts Stalin may have had about allowing Molotov to conduct important negotiations abroad. His message to Churchill also suggests second thoughts about leaving the London talks in the hands of Maisky. This would have reversed the 1939 situation and gone against the general Soviet practice of leaving little leeway to ambassadors.[8]

As a sop to American opinion Eden included in the British draft treaty a provision designed to allow emigration from the Baltic states. He also took up a suggestion from Sargent on 17 April that the Russians be asked to make a declaration, outside the proposed treaty, which would preserve some degree of autonomy for the Baltic republics. The more window-dressing the better, as Sargent cynically put it. But Sir William Malkin, Legal Adviser to the Foreign Office, reported on 24 April that such a statement could do little more than refer to the relevant sections of the Soviet constitution. Dew and Sargent thought that this would only reassure the innocent and Cadogan made the same point in a different way when he commented that such a declaration would not reassure the opponents of recognition.

To Eden's disappointment at this news was added a report from Harvey Watt (Churchill's Parliamentary Private Secretary) of unrest in the House of Commons at the proposed treaty. Although Eden was inclined to discount the danger of a serious revolt, suspecting the Poles of stirring up trouble through Victor Cazalet, who was Political Liaison Officer to Sikorski in addition to being a Member of Parliament (MP), he could not afford to ignore the problem entirely. The Foreign Secretary's troubles were further increased when Maisky gave him the Soviet drafts on 1 May. The Soviet political treaty contained no reference to a right of emigration and no mention of encouragement for confederations. The question of the frontier with Poland was to be dealt with in a separate note which assumed direct negotiations between the Soviet Union and Poland and ignored previous British statements of interest in the matter. In addition, the Russians still wanted a secret protocol but now limited to allowing them to give guarantees to Finland and Rumania and to establish bases in those two countries. Hull had thus been proved a true prophet: granted one concession, the Russians now asked for another (Document 8).[9]

Faced with a possible deadlock in the negotiations, Eden responded by preparing two different positions. On 6 May he circulated to the Cabinet a new draft which dropped the provision for emigration from the Baltic states. This got a generally bad reception in a discussion held on 7 May, although it was not rejected outright. Only Cripps supported such a retreat and Churchill now seemed to think that the negotiations would fail. Eden also took up Cadogan's suggestion for an alternative treaty which would be essentially an alliance with no mention of frontiers. The Permanent Under-Secretary feared a repetition of the lengthy and fruitless discussions of 1939. The alternative treaty went through various revisions between 12 and 22 May; it was to be held in reserve for use if negotiations on the main treaty broke down. Signs of opposition continued to increase; as varied a group as Simon (Lord Chancellor), James Stuart (Chief Whip) and Cardinal Hinsley indicated their dislike of the proposed treaty.

The actual discussions proved difficult, even though Molotov did modify his position. He abandoned the attempt to exclude Britain completely from the question of the Polish frontiers but seemed unhappy at allowing a restatement of the British position to be inserted in the treaty itself. On the right of emigration he would concede only a limited formula, restricted to national minorities. As for Soviet guarantees to Finland and Rumania, he was prepared to drop the secret protocol but wanted a specific reference to Russian interests in certain parts of the Baltic Sea and the Black Sea included in the treaty. When the alternative treaty was first presented to him on 23 May he was initially cautious. A memorandum of 25 May shows that Eden had still not completely abandoned hope of getting agreement on the basis of the original treaty. He was prepared to drop the right of emigration, repeating Sargent's phrase that it was in any case only window-dressing. On Poland he could accept an exchange of letters. As for Rumania and Finland, Molotov could be invited to write a letter which could be acknowledged without giving open agreement. On the other hand further discussions might be put off until Molotov had visited Washington. Eden also considered the possibility of insisting that the alternative treaty was the only basis on which he would continue negotiations. In a paper for the Cabinet that same day he was much more cautious, concentrating mainly on a description of the outstanding points of disagreement.

Molotov solved the British dilemma by agreeing on 26 May to accept the alternative treaty. A talk with Winant had apparently convinced him of the importance of calming American susceptibilities before arriving in Washington.

Assurances of military aid were more important in the short run than securing all the Soviet political demands. A non-contentious treaty with Britain was better than none at all. Thus Eden was able to obtain a diplomatic triumph and avoid the twin dangers of parliamentary revolt and American disapproval. It is difficult to say how much trouble there would have been in the House of Commons; Eden himself admitted to surprise at the extent of opposition. His lack of concern for American dislike of the original treaty sprang in part from doubt about the post-war policies of the United States. In the summer of 1942 there was still no guarantee that she would play an active role in European affairs. Britain and Russia might find themselves left to control Germany (Document 9).[10]

The question of federations was scarcely touched upon during the talks. Maisky had indicated on 5 May that the Soviet Union had its doubts, but Molotov himself remained cautious and reserved. The suspicions of some officials in the Foreign Office about the extent of Soviet ambitions, as expressed in early May, implied that Russia was unlikely to welcome groupings that would limit her influence (Document 10). Sargent took account of this possibility in his memorandum of 1 June, but still found it worthwhile to speculate on the structure and purpose of the proposed federations. There appears to have been a significant shift in his attitude since January, for he now saw the confederations as an anti-German rather than an anti-Russian device. He may have thought that signature of a treaty without reference to frontiers indicated a Soviet willingness to be reasonable (Document 11).

Although the public Russian position on federations remained non-committal, in private they were beginning to move into opposition. On his return from Washington Molotov stopped in London. In a conversation with Benes on 9 June he extracted from the latter a promise not to proceed with the Polish–Czech federation against the wishes of the Russians. In return Benes obtained Soviet recognition of Czechoslovakia's pre-Munich boundaries. (It was not until 5 August that Eden announced in Parliament the British repudiation of the Munich agreement, but without making a commitment on specific frontiers.) Benes was soon called upon to fulfil his part of the bargain; on 16 July the Russians informed him in so many words of their dislike of the federation. The proposal was not formally abandoned but in practice negotiations between Poland and Czechoslovakia came to a halt. The Foreign Office, however, did not completely give up hope of further progress.[11]

Earlier on 9 June Molotov had had a conversation with Eden in which the latter raised the question of a proposed treaty between Russia and the Yugoslav government-in-exile. He wanted to avoid a situation in which Britain and Russia found themselves drawn into a network of treaties and commitments well before the peace settlement; he therefore proposed a 'self-denying ordinance' whereby Britain and Russia would avoid making treaties which had implications for the post-war period. After some queries Molotov said that he 'gathered Mr Eden would like an understanding between the Soviet and British governments that they would discuss and reach agreement between themselves before they concluded any treaty with any of the smaller allies'. Eden agreed, thinking that he had secured an informal agreement which would remove a possible source of friction. He failed to see that Molotov as usual was thinking in terms of a specific written agreement. This ambiguity, which was to cause some argument in the course of 1943, illustrated well the differences in diplomatic styles between the two Foreign Ministers and their respective governments. That an Anglo-Soviet treaty had been signed at all could be regarded as a considerable achievement.[12]

4 From the Anglo-Soviet treaty to the Russian break with Poland

The Anglo-Soviet treaty ended argument over the status of the Baltic republics and Bessarabia. The Russians were careful not to raise the question again. Eden was later to express the view that Britain had conceded her acceptance of the Soviet take-over in the discussions of May 1942 even though the original treaty was abandoned. He did not think anyone would be greatly concerned by Rumania's loss of territory.[1] But the disappearance of the frontier problem was only achieved at the cost of a dangerous and ambiguous commitment over the second front. While in Washington Molotov induced Roosevelt to agree to a communiqué containing the fatal phrase that 'full understanding was reached with regard to the urgent tasks of creating a second front in Europe in 1942'. In London there was annoyance at the lack of consultation or warning, but it was impossible to show public dissent. The British communiqué, released on 11 July simultaneously with the American communiqué, therefore contained identical wording.[2]

Churchill tried to repair the damage by giving Molotov an *aide-mémoire* on 10 June setting out British reservations about the possibility of a cross-Channel operation in 1942. But Molotov made clear to Benes in their conversation on 9 June that he intended to take the communiqué as a firm promise of action and this was indeed the line he followed on his return to Moscow. Clark Kerr reported on 28 June that Molotov had spoken to him as if a definite promise had been made. As a result Clark Kerr was instructed to see him and make clear the difficulties facing such an operation. This he did on 4 July and found Molotov privately willing to admit that he understood the British reservations. Publicly, however, the Soviet government continued to maintain that an early second front could be expected. It would of course have been difficult to change course without lowering Russian morale.[3]

It could be argued that Roosevelt misled Molotov by failing to make clear that only a limited cross-Channel operation ('Sledgehammer') was being contemplated for 1942. General Marshall certainly thought the wording of the communiqué was too strong. At least 'Sledgehammer' was intended to help the Russians if their position seriously worsened and was meant to be the prelude to a major invasion in 1943; it could therefore be regarded as a second front in miniature. Roosevelt's ambiguity on this question, however, was soon overtaken by Churchill's opposition to 'Sledgehammer' and growing preference for the invasion of French North Africa. Marshall, King and Hopkins came to London on 18 July to argue the matter out, but by the end of the month President Roosevelt had agreed to abandon 'Sledgehammer' in favour of 'Torch', as the invasion of French North Africa was now named. Marshall was annoyed, not only at the British change of front but also by the delay this would mean for a major operation in western Europe. The British Chiefs of Staff themselves recognised that it would be impossible to carry out 'Torch' and a cross-Channel invasion within twelve months of each other, although both Churchill and Roosevelt, in their anxiety to get 'Torch' under way, overlooked the implications of their decision.[4]

The immediate problem was how best to break the news to Stalin at a time when the German offensive in southern Russia was still making good progress. Here Churchill, urged on by Clark Kerr, was right in thinking that this could best be done at a face-to-face meeting. To leave the information to correspondence alone, and to tell Stalin very little of Anglo-American plans, as Roosevelt suggested, could have had serious consequences, to judge by Stalin's reaction to similar news in the more favourable circumstances of June 1943. As it was, Churchill's first encounter with Stalin in August almost ended in disaster; it looked at one stage as if Churchill would leave Moscow without signing an agreed communiqué, which would have been tantamount to an admission of open disagreement. Like Eden before him, Churchill seems to have been surprised by Stalin's change of attitude from friendliness to hostility between their first and second meetings. Nevertheless, Churchill persuaded Stalin to accept 'Torch' as a worthwhile operation, although the British Prime Minister made some dangerously loose references to a major cross-Channel operation in 1943 which were to lead to further accusations of bad faith.[5]

During his visit Churchill proposed an exchange of information on weapons and equipment, which in practice had little effect. There was an exchange of notes on 29 September but in practice the Russians rarely invoked the agreement when asking for information and remained consistently unwilling to disclose much to the British. Although the agreement was almost a dead letter from the start the Foreign Office and the Service Departments continued to agonise during 1943 and 1944 about how much information to give, especially when the equipment concerned was, in part at least, of American origin. In the end, the United States released some 246 items to the Russians in October 1944, whereas the British Military Mission continued with a policy of limited disclosure. Given the small amount of information released by the Russians it is perhaps surprising that the Foreign Office spent a disproportionate amount of time on this matter; in part it was the result of a continuing fear that hard bargaining by the Service Departments would alienate the Russians and make them even more difficult to handle. In fact it is doubtful whether different tactics would have altered the Soviet policy of asking for as much information as possible and giving the minimum in return.[6]

Another suggestion of Churchill's also failed to bear fruit – the proposal to establish an Anglo-American force of bombers in the Caucasus, codenamed 'Velvet'. Although Roosevelt had shown earlier some enthusiasm for the idea it was not until October that he confirmed his willingness to join in, and Stalin did not agree to preliminary talks until 8 November. Air Marshal Drummond arrived in Moscow on 19 November only to encounter a signal lack of enthusiasm on the part of the Russians. They soon made clear that they wanted the planes, but did not want Anglo-American personnel stationed on their soil. This would have destroyed the whole aim of the proposal, which was to give a practical demonstration of Allied co-operation. Drummond left Moscow on 26 December with nothing accomplished. This was not quite the end of attempts to establish a base for British planes on Soviet soil. In February 1943 the Russians objected to a proposal that Royal Air Force (RAF) units be established in the north to help protect the Arctic convoys (operation 'Grenadine'). The appeals for British forces to fight in Russia which Stalin made in the early months of the German invasion proved to be only a temporary phase. During 1942 the Russians reverted to a policy of limiting British service personnel to what they regarded as the minimum necessary. It was perhaps also significant that in April and June the Russians agreed to the evacuation of Polish units which had been raised in the Soviet Union so that they could fight under British command in the Middle East. Apart from the ostensible difficulties of feeding the Polish units the Russians may have been unwilling to retain a force which might play a role similar to that of the Czech Legion during the civil war and intervene. A conversation which Patrick Hurley, Roosevelt's special envoy, had with a Soviet general in December revealed that the Russians were particularly suspicious of Allied designs on the Baku oilfields. This was an added reason for keeping foreign units out of the Caucasus.[7]

Thus attempts to display a spirit of co-operation either met with little response or proved counter-productive by apparently stirring up Soviet suspicions of an ulterior motive. Meanwhile, the continued advance of German troops in the summer and early autumn of 1942 raised once again the two questions which had worried the British government a year earlier. Would Russia be able to hold out or would she be tempted by a separate peace as a means of gaining a breathing space? On the whole, British miliary assessments were more optimistic than might have been expected. Mason Macfarlane, who had by now been recalled from the Military Mission in Moscow, thought in mid-June that the Russians would hold out. Appreciations by the JIC tended to the view that the Russians would suffer some reverses but would not collapse completely even if they failed to hold Stalingrad and the northern Caucasus. Nevertheless the Foreign Office could not ignore entirely rumours of a separate peace or the hints of their difficulties put out by Soviet spokesmen (Document 12). It was of course difficult to be sure whether peace rumours were being planted by the Germans to sow dissent or by the Russians to reinforce their propaganda for a second front. The gloomy views expressed by Maisky, Bogomolov and Vyshinsky might well be exaggerated for the sake of effect. Similarly Oumansky (in charge of Tass) told an American visitor in September that Stalin had raised the question whether Russia should cut herself off from her allies and 'stand alone' since he had doubts whether she would be treated fairly after the war. A further worry was how the Soviet Union would react if there was in fact no second front in 1943. Sargent and Bruce Lockhart both feared she might make a separate peace; Clark Kerr arrived home on leave at the end of November with similar doubts. Some of these emerged in a talk he gave to the Dominion High Commissioners on 3 December when he spoke of the deep-seated Soviet mistrust of Britain. His dispatch of 25 November, however, concentrated on Russian post-war aims without mentioning the possibility of a separate peace. He developed the theme, which was to become widely accepted in Britain and America, that the Soviet Union would find herself so immersed in reconstruction after the war that she would be unable to pursue an energetic foreign policy (Document 14).[8]

Apart from these private fears and speculations, Anglo-Soviet relations in the last four months of 1942 did not appear especially harmonious. There continued to be Soviet complaints over slow deliveries of supplies. Stalin sent only a curt acknowledgement of Churchill's message of 8 October that convoys would have to be suspended because escort craft were needed for 'Torch'. Soviet press agitation for a second front continued with some slight lulls; in October *Pravda* raised the question of trying Hess as a war criminal. The Russians perhaps feared that he might be used as a contact for German peace offers to Britain. It was possible that in his speech to celebrate the twenty-fifth anniversary of the October Revolution Stalin might make open criticisms of his allies and create a public rift. At Churchill's instigation Beaverbrook sent Stalin a telegram explaining why Britain was failing to keep up deliveries, and this appears to have been reasonably well received. Clark Kerr saw Stalin and Molotov on 5 November and had some success in reassuring the former at least that Britain did not intend to return Hess to Germany. Stalin's speech of 6 November was fairly mild in its criticisms of the Allies and was interpreted by both Cadogan and Henderson (the American

Chargé d'Affaires in Moscow) to indicate a willingness on Stalin's part to try out co-operation with the Western powers. From one point of view, therefore, the occasion passed off better than might have been expected. But the distinction which Stalin drew between Hitler and the German armed forces could be construed as a hint to the latter that if they overthrew the Nazi regime they could hope for a settlement with Russia. It is uncertain how seriously the Russians took the possibility of a separate peace. There is an unconfirmed account of a Soviet approach in Stockholm in December. On the other hand, Hitler told the Japanese Ambassador in May 1943 that he had made an approach at the end of 1942 which the Russians had rejected.[9]

The Allied landings in French North Africa on 8 November might have been expected to reinforce the fairly friendly attitude detected in Stalin's speech. In fact, however, the arrangement with Darlan to end the fighting with Vichy forces tended to rouse Soviet suspicions that the Allies were prepared to back Fascists. Maisky asked officially about Allied intentions towards Darlan on 20 November and it appears that some Soviet officers were critical of the ceasefire, although Stalin himself reacted calmly. Russian disquiet was directed more against the Americans than the British, but the affair contributed to the uneasy mood in which Anglo-Soviet relations ended the year, despite military successes in French North Africa and around Stalingrad, where the German forces had been surrounded by the end of November. Commenting on the interview between Hurley and a Soviet general Baggallay wrote bitterly: 'Nothing we can do is likely to have any substantial effect on this suspicion except at the peace settlement to give them everything they want on a platter.'[10]

It might not seem the most suitable moment to approach the Russians and ask them about their post-war aims. But Eden had already launched a general examination of British intentions for the peace settlement. This seems to have been motivated as much by a desire to forestall any grandiose plans which Roosevelt might produce as by a specific concern with Soviet aims. Yet the two themes were closely related and of particular importance for Britain if she were to play a significant role as middleman or interpreter between the other two. Warner had argued in July against simply confronting Russia with Anglo-American plans. Britain should be able to consult Russia directly since both would have to agree if effective European policies were to be attained. There is here the unspoken assumption that the United States would have only a limited role in post-war Europe.[11] There was also the problem of how to advance the British interest in federations in eastern Europe in the face of obvious Soviet resistance which as yet stopped short of open opposition in principle. At the end of September Wilson seemed inclined to retreat in the light of public Russian pronouncements but his colleagues were not at that stage prepared to abandon the idea entirely (Document 13).

Foreign Office research into the problems of post-war collaboration led to the production of a paper by Gladwyn Jebb which became known as the 'Four-Power Plan'. Eden gave Churchill a summary of the paper on 5 October and the full version as it then stood on either Friday 16 or Saturday 17 October. Future American policy was still regarded as uncertain; the United States was obviously going to play a major role but it was not yet clear how far she would seek to co-operate with Britain and Russia or follow an independent line. The main Soviet concern was security, which she might seek in various ways, for example by setting up a communist state in Germany or by playing off the smaller European states against Britain and America. For the time being Stalin seemed willing to try out a policy of collaboration but he would judge his allies by results. In particular he would want to be assured that Britain and America would join in effective control over Germany. (That the way to win Soviet friendship was to pursue a firm line towards Germany was to become an article of faith in the Foreign Office.) If on the other hand Russia proved uncooperative and simply pursued her own interests in Europe and the Middle East, Britain would be pushed into seeking American support, and that remained a doubtful quantity. Britain, however, had a good bargaining position, since neither America nor Russia would like to see her definitely lined up with one against the other. It would be necessary to make some concessions to Russia in eastern Europe and perhaps in the Middle East but if she showed herself too grasping Britain could always use the threat of an Anglo-American alliance to restrain her.

Churchill found this speculation premature. It was too early to say what kind of Russia would emerge from the war and what demands she would make. Nevertheless he agreed that Eden could circulate the paper to the Cabinet, which he did in a revised form on 8 November. This spurred Cripps into producing his own ideas on 19 November. The upshot was an inconclusive Cabinet discussion on 27 November; no attempt was made to launch exploratory talks with either the Americans or the Russians. In January 1943 Eden submitted to the Cabinet yet another version of the paper now called the 'United Nations Plan' but did not succeed in obtaining any discussion of it.[12] Churchill's obvious lack of enthusiasm made it likely that Eden would have to act on his own initiative if he was to obtain clarification of Allied war aims. Within the Foreign Office there was a general feeling that British policy in eastern Europe needed to be more sharply defined. On 22 October 1942 the Dutch Foreign Minister van Kleffens asked Eden if he could be told something of British views on the future of eastern Europe and the Balkans. This request produced a rash of minutes. There was general agreement that nothing should be said to van Kleffens, if only because British ideas were still so vague.[13]

It was Rendel's dispatch of 19 December which spurred the Foreign Office into action. Rendel himself was concerned mainly with the problem of Bulgaria and the possible role of the Turks. Discussion on his dispatch led to the decision to make a formal approach to the Russians when Clark Kerr returned to Moscow (Document 15). The idea of giving up completely any British interest in eastern and south-east Europe was explicitly rejected. Sargent had previously criticised the policy advocated by E. H. Carr in *The Times* in January 1942. On that occasion Barrington Ward had sent Eden a memorandum by Carr which proposed leaving the Soviet Union a free hand in eastern Europe. But, argued Sargent, Britain could only establish good relations with Russia by careful bargaining and not through a self-defeating series of abdications. Twelve months later he still assumed that Britain would be able to influence events in the Balkans.[14]

Clark Kerr's instructions mentioned the question of confederations in eastern Europe but ranged far beyond that particular point. Here was an ambitious attempt to promote Anglo-Soviet discussions on post-war Europe as a whole and to do so before approaching the United States (Document 16). Eden had not consulted Churchill; perhaps the latter's rather contemptuous attitude to the 'Four-Power Plan' still rankled. If Eden could obtain some fairly specific statements of objectives from the Russians he could present Churchill with a *fait accompli*. If they only made a vague reply little was lost; at least the British had shown themselves willing to talk. But Clark Kerr pressed too hard on the question of the interpretation of Stalin's speech of 6 November. Molotov may have been genuinely unprepared to commit himself without instructions or he may have suspected Clark Kerr of probing for some ulterior motive behind Stalin's references to Germany. Stalin's response was to propose a formal meeting that would reach a formal agreement on the treatment of Germany. The Foreign Office was in no position to make such an agreement so that even if an attempt had been made to continue with discussions it would have run into difficulties. Churchill's anger was sufficient, however, to force Eden into retreat. Once again he had been foiled in an attempt to consider post-war aims, and he had not succeeded in extracting from Stalin and Molotov any inkling of their views. What they made of the British failure to follow up the initial approach is not known. Nevertheless in early April Clark Kerr found Stalin in a better mood than he had ever known him and reported on a general growth of friendliness towards Britain.[15]

This was to prove a false dawn. On 13 April the Germans announced the discovery of a mass grave of Polish officers at Katyn. When the Polish government-in-exile supported the German suggestion of an investigation by the International Red Cross the Soviet government formally broke off relations on 25 April. It would have been difficult for the Russians to ignore the implication that they had been responsible for the massacre. Russia could now build up an alternative Polish government if she wished; a new complication had been added to Anglo-Soviet relations, and prospects for a Polish–Czech federation now seemed even gloomier. It was ironic, therefore, that at the end of April, O'Malley, Ambassador to the London Poles, should write a dispatch challenging the whole policy of encouraging federations and expressing fears about Soviet intentions. Yet his colleagues in the main discounted his arguments (Document 17). Initially both the Moscow Embassy and the Foreign Office somewhat underestimated the seriousness of the Soviet break with Poland, seeing it as an attempt by Stalin to extract frontier concessions.[16]

5 From Katyn to Tehran

Even before the Russo-Polish rupture, Stalin's attitude to his allies was wary and uncertain. In December 1942 he had declined an invitation to meet Roosevelt and Churchill in North Africa, pleading military exigencies as his reason, and for the rest of the war he was to demonstrate a continued unwillingness to attend meetings outside Soviet-controlled territory. This made it difficult for the Russians to influence Anglo-American discussions, yet they complained of their isolation and of not being treated as equals. The latter was a favourite theme of Maisky. This created a problem for Britain and the United States; in so far as they did want better co-ordination and closer consultation with the Soviet Union they needed to deal with Stalin directly. Molotov might again travel abroad as he had done in 1942 to speak for Russian political interests, but his powers of initiative were obviously limited, and there was no comparable figure who could represent Stalin in military matters.

Thus Roosevelt and Churchill met at Casablanca in January 1943 on their own. The decision to continue operations in the Mediterranean once the Germans had been cleared from Tunisia was logical enough. It would avoid a hiatus in which manpower and shipping were left unused. At the same time, however, it made a cross-Channel invasion in 1943 virtually impossible. In their messages to Stalin from the end of January to the middle of March, Roosevelt and Churchill did not openly admit this, although the latter did point out the difficulties involved in a major attack on France. Stalin for his part kept probing for more definite information and on 15 March sent Churchill a cryptic warning of the dangers of any further delay. Nor was his temper improved by Churchill's message of 30 March that the next convoy scheduled for North Russia had been cancelled and that after May there could be no more convoys until the autumn because escort ships would be needed for the projected invasion of Sicily.[1]

Stalin's reply on 2 April was curt but might perhaps have been worse, and in an interview with Clark Kerr on 12 April he was in an extremely genial mood. Indeed, the Ambassador was able to report a few days later on a growing mood of friendliness towards Britain. Yet during April rumours of Soviet–German peace negotiations again began to circulate, this time emanating from Turkey. At the end of the month it was announced that Litvinov was being recalled to Moscow. This was an uncertain omen, since at that stage there was little reason for Russia to indicate displeasure with the United States. Moreover, the Soviet Embassy was careful to indicate that the breach with Poland was not the reason for Litvinov's departure. He himself said before leaving for Moscow that he did not expect to return.[2]

On the other hand the announcement on 22 May of the dissolution of the Comintern could be taken as an indication that the Soviet Union wished to encourage co-operation with her allies and cast off her revolutionary image. Maisky took this line in a conversation with R. A. Butler on 2 June. The Soviet Ambassador on this occasion produced a curious mixture of blandishments and threats. On the one hand he spoke of the need for Anglo-Russian co-operation to restrain the United States and mentioned the prospect of increased post-war trade if Britain offered sufficient credits. On the other hand he raised the dormant issue of the 1941 frontiers, saying that Britain would be wise to make concessions on this issue now, since the Soviet Union intended to secure them in any case. Eden was impressed by this frank speaking; although it is not clear how far Maisky was acting on his own initiative.[3]

On the same day that Maisky was thus opening his mind to Butler, Roosevelt informed Stalin that the cross-Channel invasion would not now take place until the spring of 1944. Not surprisingly this news provoked recriminations and accusations of bad faith from Stalin, culminating on 24 June in a detailed but selective recital of extracts from earlier correspondence. Although the Prime Minister sent a restrained reply on 27 June, both he and Eden sought Clark Kerr's advice about future relations with Stalin. As late as 21 June the Ambassador had written to Warner that relations with the Kremlin had improved steadily since Stalin's speech of 6 November 1942 because the Russians now thought the British were treating them fairly; his optimism was shaken by the latest developments. Without seeking to defend the Russian attitude completely Clark Kerr tried to explain why Stalin should react so brusquely to yet another postponement of the seond front. He argued that, despite the unpleasant nature of the Soviet regime, it would be necessary to maintain co-operation both during the war and after it. As a result, he was opposed to ending the Churchill–Stalin correspondence. Clark Kerr seems to have thought that this advice might bring about his dismissal. Churchill took it in good part but decided to let the correspondence lapse for the time being. Propaganda in the Soviet press on the subject of the second front revived at the end of June and reached a peak in August. That month brought rumours of fresh German–Soviet contacts in Stockholm. At the very least the Russians were publicly indicating displeasure; at worst they might be contemplating a change of policy. Against this gloomy background the decision to replace Maisky by the inexperienced Gusev (conveyed to Clark Kerr by Molotov on 26 July) created considerable alarm in the Foreign Office. Clark Kerr was reassuring but then in August there came the announcement of Litvinov's replacement by Gromyko, previously Chargé d'Affaires at the Washington Embassy (Document 18).[4]

Yet by the end of July the case for an arrangement with Germany, if Stalin seriously contemplated one, had been weakened by the Russian victory at Kursk and by the fall of Mussolini on 25 July. The military balance on the eastern front was now moving in Russia's favour and the Anglo-American invasion of Sicily which began on 10 July was already paying political dividends. On 8 August Stalin wrote to Roosevelt and on 9 August to Churchill. While declining a proposal by Roosevelt for a meeting *à deux* (this suggestion had been made in May) he now showed interest in a tripartite meeting even if he could not attend personally. The upshot of the messages and further exchanges between the three heads of government was agreement on a Foreign Ministers' conference in Moscow to be followed by a meeting of the 'Big Three' themselves in Tehran. Even before Stalin's show of interest Eden had been much concerned about the need for better and more frequent consultation with the Russians. In July he presented Churchill with a paper drafted by Cadogan which argued the case for regular meetings in London between Eden himself, Winant and Maisky. This idea was to bear fruit later with the creation of the European Advisory Commission (EAC). In the short-term the proposal lost some of its attractions because of Maisky's recall and in any case it did not meet the immediate problem of how to ease the strain in Anglo-Soviet relations (Document 19).

At the end of July Eden suggested that he go on to Moscow from the Quadrant Conference due to be held in Quebec in August. Churchill did not object to this but he turned down an alternative suggestion by the Foreign Secretary that Molotov be invited to Quebec. (This was in part inspired by a telegram from Clark Kerr urging the importance of Russian representation at the next tripartite meeting.) Churchill's ostensible objection was the fact that it would embarrass the Russians to be present at a conference where the war against Japan would be discussed. It is more likely that he did not want to give Stalin the opportunity to raise the second front issue directly at an Anglo-American gathering where Churchill could still hope to gain support for a full-scale rather than a limited invasion of Italy. Eden now took up the idea of inviting Molotov to London for talks. He may have been influenced by a paper which Bruce Lockhart presented to Sargent on 9 August entitled 'Russia and the Allied governments'. It argued the need for an early and businesslike approach to the Russians and put forward two propositions which were becoming standard elements in Foreign Office thinking – that it was important to treat the Russians as equals and that there was no guarantee of American co-operation after the war. Eden certainly took this paper with him to Quebec. At almost the same time Geoffrey Wilson was expressing to Clark Kerr strong criticism of Churchill's attitude to the Russians (Document 20).[5]

Stalin soon made an advance on his proposal for a tripartite conference. On 24 August Clark Kerr informed the Foreign Office of Stalin's intention to propose a three-power commission to examine the surrender of Italy and other European allies of Germany. Clark Kerr interpreted this as a response to the Russian absence from Quebec. Eden saw wider implications: here was a specific Russian proposal which could be amended to produce the kind of clearing house which he had already suggested to Churchill. Moreover, as Harvey noted in his diary, if the Soviet Union were not given some role in Italian affairs she might exclude her allies from influencing events in the Balkans and eastern Europe. The message in which Stalin actually made the proposal to Churchill was rather surly in tone but at least it gave an opening for negotiation. There were further signs of the in-and-out nature of Soviet attitudes. In September Sobelev, the Russian Chargé d'Affaires in London, passed to the Foreign Office an *aide-mémoire* giving details of a Japanese proposal to send a high-ranking personage to Moscow who would then go on to visit western Europe. Molotov rejected what looked like an attempt at mediation; it was perhaps too reminiscent of Matsuoka's 1941 trip. Yet on 13 October, with the Foreign Ministers' conference only a few days away, Stalin sent Churchill a rude message about convoys and the treatment of British personnel in North Russia. This was the famous document which Churchill returned to Gusev as *nul et non avenu*. When Warner wrote to Clark Kerr at the end of September he had no foreknowledge of this particular episode. Nevertheless he summed up the doubts in the Foreign Office about Russia's ultimate intentions even on the part of those inclined to be well-disposed towards her (Document 21).[6]

Two other issues which developed during 1943 illustrated the difficulties of dealing with the Russians. The first of these was the Tizard mission. In December 1942 the Allied Supplies Executive (ASE) agreed that a scientific mission should be sent to Moscow under Sir Henry Tizard. Some of its members would remain in Moscow and become attached to the Military Mission. The aim was to improve the exchange of scientific information and breathe some life into the September agreement. It was not until the end of April that Clark Kerr was instructed to approach the Soviet government about the proposed mission. He got no response until 16 June when Molotov said that the Russians wanted the mission to come but were not ready to receive it. As a result the mission was disbanded. Thus an attempt to elicit and exchange information on a large scale had encountered the same kind of passive resistance which so frustrated the Military Mission. The latter did not prosper in 1943. Eden had lost confidence in its first head, Mason Macfarlane, but his successor, General Martel, who arrived in April 1943, was to prove no more satisfactory. Moreover, a violent personality clash developed when Air Marshal Babington arrived to head the RAF section of the mission in June. Clark Kerr found himself in the unedifying position of having to hold the ring in a bitter inter-service squabble.[7]

The second problem arose from the self-denying ordinance upon which Eden and Molotov had apparently agreed in June 1942. Benes saw the Soviet–Polish break as an indication that he ought to improve relations with Moscow. On 16 June he told Eden of his intention to visit Russia and sign a treaty, whereupon Eden told him of the ordinance. As a result the Russians advised Benes to postpone his visit in view of British misgivings, but they also presented an *aide-mémoire* to the Foreign Office on 26 July in which they claimed that they had expected Eden to follow up his general proposal with more specific suggestions. At the end of September Eden gave Sobelev a draft ordinance and also circulated a paper to the War Cabinet explaining the tactics he intended to follow in Moscow. He would oppose the early conclusion of a Soviet–Czech treaty since it would be aimed against Poland. He would also seek Soviet agreement to a self-denying ordinance and if the atmosphere was favourable he would suggest a Soviet–Czech–Polish agreement. Given the state of Russian–Polish relations this last proposal was somewhat optimistic. At least, however, Eden seemed to have a firm plan.[8]

The Foreign Ministers' Conference, which met in Moscow from 19 to 30 October, was not only well organised but also remarkably lacking in friction between the participants. Once reassured that the cross-Channel invasion would go ahead in the spring or early summer of 1944, Molotov seemed anxious to make the conference go smoothly. His usual stubbornness and argumentativeness were much reduced. Cordell Hull had come to Moscow to secure agreement on a four-power declaration that the three allies and China would work together after the war and would establish a new international organisation. Having attained his objective he was careful not to commit the United States on other issues. The conference succeeded because contentious issues were largely avoided; very little was said about Poland but that was enough to demonstrate the continuing Russian hostility towards the Polish government-in-exile. Other questions such as reparations, the dismemberment of Germany or a Russian share in the Italian fleet were either discussed in general terms or left over for further discussion. The restoration of Austrian independence was one of the few specific points agreed upon at the conference.[9]

As far as British interests were concerned the results were mixed. Eden secured the establishment of the European Advisory Commission (EAC) in

London as a body quite distinct from the Advisory Commission on Italy. It now remained to be seen whether he could in fact make it into an effective clearing house. A private talk with Molotov on 22 October settled the irritating question of the treatment of British personnel in North Russia; the return of Stalin's letter seems to have had some effect. Here, however, Eden perhaps gave away more than he gained. He agreed not to increase the existing establishment in North Russia by more than 10% without Soviet permission but agreed in turn that there should be no restriction on the number of Russian personnel entering Britain. Over confederations and the self-denying ordinance he had to accept defeat. The Soviet insistence that the time was not suitable for confederations meant in practice that the whole idea was now dead. Circumstances were unlikely to become more favourable as the Red Army moved westwards (Document 22). The decision to drop the self-denying ordinance seems to have been taken for a number of reasons. The Russians made clear their annoyance at the postponement of Benes's visit but were prepared to allow for later Polish accession to the Soviet–Czech treaty; the American delegation was bored and uninterested in the question; the treaty itself seemed innocuous, and as Cadogan pointed out, once Eden had agreed to let it be signed he would merely tie his own hands by insisting on an agreement. On 29 October Eden wrote a letter to Molotov which formally abandoned the proposal for a self-denying ordinance but re-peated the view that Britain and Russia should consult each other before making treaties or agreements with the lesser European allies. In his reply of 2 November Molotov reasserted the right of the Soviet Union to make agree-ments with neighbouring allies without having to consult Britain. Since the Russians also rejected a British proposal for a declaration that the allies would not try to establish separate areas of responsibility in Europe, it was clear that Molotov had succeeded in considerably reducing British claims to influence events in eastern Europe while retaining freedom of action for the Soviet Union. At the end of November Sargent drew the conclusion that the Russians were contemplating an exclusive sphere of influence in eastern Europe. Eden did not think this was 'quite fair'. In any case it was still possible for the Post-Hostilities Planning Staff (PHPS) to assume in February 1944 that Britain ought to play a significant role in the military occupation of south-east Europe (Document 23).[10]

Tehran was the first meeting of the Big Three and that in itself gave it significance. Apart from that, Churchill found himself isolated in his rear-guard action to prevent a fixed date for the cross-Channel invasion leading to a withdrawal of resources from Italy. Roosevelt and Stalin insisted on giving priority to the invasion of France and the latter took up with enthusiasm the proposal for a simultaneous invasion of the south of France. (In the event this operation took place after the Normandy landings.) There was, therefore, clear evidence of a decline in British influence on strategic matters, in part the result of Roosevelt's determination to avoid the appearance of an Anglo-American front against the Russians. On political matters the conference went over a good deal of ground already covered at Moscow, but at Tehran the discussion was more hurried and haphazard. Once again there seemed to be general agreement that Germany should be dismembered but details were left unsettled. On Polish frontiers there appeared to be a consensus but here too no formal agreement was made and there was no progress towards restoring Russian–Polish relations. When Stalin put in a bid for the port of Königsberg (now Kaliningrad) neither Roosevelt nor Churchill showed alarm or doubt.

The affair of the Italian fleet showed how promises casually made could later generate ill will. Churchill agreed at a lunch on 1 December that the Russians ought to get some Italian warships. Roosevelt and he spoke of handing them over by the following February. Then difficulties began to arise. The Combined Chiefs of Staff began to have doubts about losing Italian goodwill. Italy after all had been a co-belligerent since October 1943. It also seemed unwise to move ships from the Mediterranean especially when they were unsuitable for Arctic conditions. Moreover, Churchill discovered that Roosevelt was under the impression that the Russians had been promised one-third of the Italian fleet. The Russians became restless and suspicious at the delay. In March Stalin agreed to accept an American cruiser and some British destroyers on loan as a substitute for the Italian ships. Even then there was further friction. The Russians complained at having to send crews to Britain to collect the destroyers. When they arrived the Soviet contingent insisted on a thorough refit of what were admittedly old ships. The problem dragged on until July 1944.[11]

The cordiality of the Moscow and Tehran Conferences was deceptive partly because a number of issues were left blurred or unresolved. Moreover the meetings took place at a time when strategic issues were receding into the background but problems of the post-war settlement had not yet become acute. There was thus a breathing space in October and November 1943 when Anglo-Soviet relations seemed to lose much of their acrimony. In one sense there had been a considerable improvement compared with the atmosphere of Churchill's visit in 1942, and the negotiations of 1939 now seemed to belong to a different world. It had yet to be shown, however, that the new mood of goodwill could survive exposure to specific clashes of interest.

6 From Tehran to Yalta

The more relaxed negotiating style displayed by the Russians at Moscow and Tehran produced a mood of euphoria in the British camp. The Foreign Ministers' Conference convinced Eden and Clark Kerr that the important thing was to treat the Russians as equals. In January 1944 Churchill is to be found writing to Eden of his new-found confidence in Stalin and withdrawing his reservations about the Soviet take-over of the Baltic states, although he did not wish to make any public statement. He also professed to detect great changes in the character of the Russian state. This optimism was reinforced by the comments of Benes after his visit to Moscow. Having signed a treaty with the Soviet Union in December he returned to London convinced that she would co-operate with her allies after the war in holding Germany down. According to the Czech President, Stalin had spoken enthusiastically of the decisions taken at Tehran. Over Poland, however, he struck a warning note. Stalin regarded the question of Polish frontiers as settled, and was not prepared to renew relations with the London Poles unless their government was reconstructed.[1]

In any case the mood of goodwill could not be expected to last, and irritating incidents began to recur. The argument over the Italian ships has already been mentioned. On 17 January an article in *Pravda* claimed that two prominent British figures had made contact with Ribbentrop in Spain in an attempt to get a separate peace. In the face of British protests the Soviet government was careful to deny that it attached any importance to the report, and the allegation was not repeated. Thus the incident was passed over, but it showed how quickly Soviet suspicions could reappear.[2]

More serious was the Polish question. It was becoming increasingly clear to British observers that the London Poles would find it difficult, if not impossible, to re-establish themselves in Warsaw. Stalin continued to insist on a major reorganisation of the London government as a *sine qua non* for reopening relations. Moreover the London Poles were unwilling to swallow the frontier settlement sketched out at Tehran. To accept the Curzon line would mean giving up territory to Russia and they were dubious about taking over large amounts of German territory. As a result, a British attempt to mediate, which was launched at the beginning of February, made little progress. It produced abrasive letters from Stalin on 3 and 23 March, and by the beginning of April Churchill had decided to give up. As in the summer of 1943, he expressed doubts and disillusion about the value of his correspondence with Stalin. This could not alter the fact that by the spring of 1944 the Red Army had regained most of the territory lost to Germany and in some places had crossed the June 1941 frontiers. Stalin would be in a strong position to establish what might be regarded as friendly governments in Poland and in Rumania.[3]

The argument over Poland revived the suspicions of Churchill and Eden about Soviet intentions, although the two men found cause for concern in rather different areas. On 13 March, without consulting her allies, the Soviet Union announced the reopening of diplomatic relations with the government of Marshal Badoglio. Eden read into this a Russian plan to communise Italy and perhaps even to seek domination of the Mediterranean. Churchill was more concerned about Poland and Rumania; he also reacted strongly to the news that Japan had agreed to abandon the Sakhalin concessions. He suspected the Russians of wanting to settle outstanding disputes with Japan so that they could drive a hard bargain as a price for entering the Pacific war. (At Moscow and Tehran Stalin had indicated his intention of joining in after the defeat of Germany but had not specified what rewards he would expect.) Eden took the line that little could be deduced from the Sakhalin agreement. The Russians would realise the necessity of joining in the war against Japan if they were to play a major part in the Far Eastern peace settlement.[4]

By the beginning of May, however, Churchill had lost interest in Japan and was again concentrating on the Balkans. Since Harriman had left Moscow for a visit to the United States, Churchill wondered if Clark Kerr should be recalled as a sign of British displeasure at Russian intrigues. Was the Soviet Union to be allowed to communise the Balkans and perhaps Italy? Now it was Eden's turn to be reassuring. There was no good reason to make such a serious move as recalling Clark Kerr. First of all it would be necessary to find out how far British and Soviet interests in south-east Europe did in fact clash. So far the Russians had not shown their hand in Rumania and Bulgaria. Whatever their long-term aims, it would be difficult to prove that they had set out to communise the Balkans and Italy. Eden did agree, however, that it would be necessary to examine the long-term implications of British support for Tito in Yugoslavia and for the communist-led resistance in Greece. Churchill did not rise to this bait, but simply minuted on 21 May: 'You are right'. Despite his reassuring tone Eden was in fact afraid that British propaganda in the Balkans was giving too favourable a picture of Soviet policy.[5]

The respective fears of the two men make a curious contrast with the relative optimism of Dana Wilgress, the Canadian Ambassador in Moscow and of the Foreign Office paper on post-war Soviet policy (Documents 24 and 25). Both assumed that Russia's energies would be largely taken up with problems of post-war reconstruction and that she could be induced to co-operate in a post-war international security system. Her goodwill would largely depend on the continued subjection of Germany. Things might go wrong, but the Foreign Office paper assumed that for five years or so after the defeat of Germany Russia would not present a threat to British strategic interests. The gloomier paper of W. H. Young on Soviet policy in Persia was prepared at the suggestion of Ivor Pink of the Economic and Industrial Planning Staff (EIPS). This body wanted some guidance in connection with draft directives on economic and industrial problems that would have to be dealt with in the British draft of an armistice with Germany. Young's pessimistic conclusions seem to have made little impact on the Foreign Office or on the EIPS (Document 26).[6]

At the beginning of May the main point of argument with the Soviet Union was Rumania. A group of British agents had been parachuted into Rumania in December 1943 but had soon been captured. The Antonescu government had used the group as a means of putting out peace feelers to Britain. The Russians were informed of the mission and its capture in January, but their reaction was muted until at the end of April Molotov accused Churchill of acting in bad faith by trying to reach an agreement with Rumania behind Russia's back. This naturally provoked a sharp reaction from Churchill and led to some un-profitable exchanges with Molotov. In an effort to smooth things down Eden saw Gusev on 5 May and suggested that if the Russians would not interfere in Greece the British would keep out of Rumania. This was a variation on the idea of a self-denying ordinance which Eden had unsuccessfully tried on Molotov in 1942. Now, two years on, the Foreign Secretary was once again probably thinking of an informal understanding. A few days later he minuted that there was not enough contact with the Russians on Balkan questions.[7]

On 18 May Gusev informed him that the Soviet Union would like an agreement over Rumania and Greece but first wanted to know if the proposal had been cleared with the United States. The Russians were again running true to form in asking for a specific arrangement. Eden said he would approach the Americans and rather light-heartedly assumed that they would not make difficulties. This is surprising in view of Hull's dislike of anything that smacked of spheres of influence. Halifax was instructed to take the matter up with Hull and Eden suggested that Churchill give support by writing directly to Roosevelt. This proved to be a maladroit suggestion. When Halifax saw Hull on 30 May he somewhat disingenuously failed to reveal that Eden had already approached Gusev. Churchill's letter to Roosevelt of 31 May gave the game away. Moreover, a message from Churchill to Halifax on 8 June further alarmed Hull by bringing in Bulgaria and Yugoslavia. Roosevelt was induced by his Secretary of State to send a refusal on 10 June. He could not approve an arrangement, said the President, which might lead to the creation of spheres of influence, notwithstanding Churchill's argument that it would only apply to the wartime period. In a long and angry reply on 11 June Churchill asked that the agreement be given a three-month trial. Without consulting Hull, Roosevelt gave his consent on 12 June; on the same day the State Department sent the British Embassy a memorandum rejecting the proposal! Hull induced the President to send Churchill a rebuke on 22 June over the British concealment of their initial approach to Gusev. Churchill's tart rejoinder the following day pushed Roosevelt into partial retreat. Meanwhile on 19 June Eden had asked Gusev if the Soviet Union was still interested despite American reservations. Gusev did not reply until 8 July when he said that the Soviet government must give the matter further consideration and would seek the views of the Americans. Eden took this to mean that the arrangement had broken down. In fact the Soviet Embassy in Washington had already approached the State Department on 1 July; the latter replied on 15 July with a memorandum which gave heavily qualified support to the three-month trial. When this document came to Churchill's attention at the beginning of August he was puzzled by its ambiguity. Eden interpreted it to mean that the Americans had given in reluctantly but hoped nothing would come of the agreement. In the face of obvious American doubt the Soviet Union simply left the proposal hanging in the air.[8]

While time had thus been taken up in fruitless discussion the military, and therefore the political, situation in eastern Europe moved further in Russia's favour. At the end of June the Soviet Union broke off the contacts it had made with the London Poles. The latter again showed themselves unwilling to accept the Curzon line or to carry out major changes in their government. It was now logical for the Soviet Union to set up a potential provisional government of its own. On 25 July it recognised the Committee of National Liberation based in Lublin as temporary administrator of Polish territory liberated from the Germans. Stalin hinted to Churchill that it might become the basis for a provisional government. The committee had only been created four days earlier; Stalin could now use it as a bargaining counter when the time seemed ripe. The failure of the Warsaw rising, which began at the end of July, further strengthened the Russian position. The destruction of the non-communist resistance removed the main element which could have challenged the Committee of National Liberation on the ground. Nor did the Russians do much to help the rising in Slovakia which began at the end of August and was finally crushed in October, although the Slovaks were much less overtly anti-Russian than the Polish resistance.[9]

At the end of August a Bulgarian representative arrived in Cairo to negotiate an armistice with Britain and America. The Soviet Union short-circuited this move by herself declaring war on Bulgaria on 5 September. The Red Army's rapid occupation of the country killed off any British hopes of establishing effective influence there. On 12 September Rumania signed an armistice in Moscow which gave the Soviet High Command a dominating position on the Control Commission; Russian influence was less obvious in the armistice signed with Finland a week later. Although the Finns had broken off earlier talks in April, Russian terms in September were not much more severe; indeed the amount of reparations demanded now was half that asked in April. Britain faced a dilemma in trying to limit the spread of Russian influence. A paper circulated by Eden to the Cabinet on 7 June pointed out that it would be difficult to change course suddenly and, for example, abandon support for Tito in Yugoslavia. Nor was it feasible to give all-out support to communist resistance groups in the Balkans in the hope of weaning them away from Russia. The best that Eden could suggest was that Britain should try to consolidate her position and avoid an open clash with Russia. There was perhaps some hope to be derived from the fact that the Soviet Union did not appear to be seeking outright communisation of the Balkans. Yet later in the month Sargent was to express pessimism about the kind of government which Stalin would tolerate: 'What he requires is a strong autocratic government administering a system of state socialism and pro-Russian policy irrespective of the whims and prejudices of the population.' On 9 August Eden circulated a second paper to the Cabinet which in practice dealt with Soviet policy in Europe excluding the Balkans. Here it was again assumed that Russia would tolerate friendly but not exclusively communist governments, this time in Czechoslovakia, Hungary and Poland. Much stress was laid on the need to convince the Soviet Union that her allies would help to keep Germany weak and would not build up an anti-Russian combination.[10]

In the light of these views it is interesting to read Clark Kerr's assessment of Soviet policy at the end of August. In this delayed reaction to the Foreign Office paper of 29 April, the Ambassador pointed out the possible dangers that could arise from the combination of Soviet pride and sensitivity, especially since Russia retained complete freedom of action. He assumed that communist parties abroad would simply be used to foster Russian interests. His dispatch of 19 November laid considerable stress on the importance of reassuring Russia by keeping strict control over Germany (Documents 29 and 31). Russia was a growing problem for the Foreign Office, but not necessarily an insuperable one. There were also signs of hope; Eden found the Soviet memorandum on the proposed international organisation encouraging when he circulated it to the Armistice and Post-War Committee early in September.

Clark Kerr reported Molotov as anxious to maintain four-power co-operation within the new body.[11]

Lack of American support and the weakening of British influence in eastern Europe led Churchill to pay his second visit to Moscow, in another attempt to strike a bargain with Stalin. This time he was much more cautious in what he told Roosevelt. At the end of September he informed the President that the two main objects of his Moscow trip were to confirm the arrangements for Soviet entry into the war against Japan and to reach a settlement of the Polish question. Greece and Yugoslavia were mentioned only as incidentals. On Hopkins's advice Roosevelt decided against allowing Churchill to speak for American interests; Harriman was accordingly instructed to participate in the discussions as an observer only. This was in fact consistent with Roosevelt's previous policy of avoiding commitments over Poland and the Balkans especially in an election year. Up to a point this weakened Churchill's bargaining position; on the other hand if Harriman had been present at all the discussions as a formal representative of the United States it is doubtful whether he could have approved of the percentages agreement which Churchill put to Stalin on 9 October. Harriman did not get the full story until 12 October; he then advised Churchill not to send Stalin a letter dated 11 October which expounded Churchill's understanding of the percentages agreement. Harriman argued that Roosevelt would be forced to repudiate the letter. It is not clear on what Harriman based his objection; perhaps it was Churchill's statement that the agreement would have to remain secret for the time being. Here was a piece of secret diplomacy which made no reference to the Atlantic Charter. The President could hardly be expected to approve of it. Harriman's reports to the President and the State Department were general and guarded; he did not refer to the percentages in so many words. The State Department, however, had a shrewd idea of the kind of agreement that Churchill and Stalin had made. Perhaps mindful of the Prime Minister's wrath in June, Roosevelt was careful not to reproach Churchill directly.[12]

The percentages symbolised the degree of influence Britain hoped to have in each country. Given that a secret treaty delimiting spheres of influence was out of the question, the figures were a useful shorthand. Churchill himself argued that the percentages were only a guide, intended to provide an interim arrangement for the wartime period and subject to review at the peace conference. Eden was therefore able to reassure Sargent in London that the figures did not represent specific numbers of personnel to be placed on Control Commissions. Yet it was precisely this kind of interpretation which the ever practical Molotov had tried to impose in some hard bargaining with Eden. The latter held out for a 50/50 division in Yugoslavia but conceded 80/20 to the Russians in Hungary. This was a considerable retreat from the equal division which Churchill had originally proposed, given that Hungary was making peace overtures at the time (an armistice was not signed until January 1945). The concession to the Russians of 80/20 against the opening bid of 75/25 in Bulgaria might be seen as academic. More surprising was Eden's agreement that the Russians should predominate on the Bulgarian Control Commission until the end of hostilities with Germany; it was unlikely that British and American representatives could later regain lost ground. Nevertheless Sargent thought Eden had done well to maintain equal influence in Yugoslavia and to secure the withdrawal of Bulgarian troops from Greek territory. This lessened fears that the Russians would encourage Bulgarian irredentism (Document 30).[13]

What was the balance sheet? Britain was able to maintain her position in Greece, but it is not clear whether Stalin had decided to avoid active involvement on behalf of the Greek Communist party even before his meeting with Churchill. The latter was prepared to agree in principle to some modification of the Montreux Convention but was careful to leave it to Stalin to make specific proposals. Thus little had been given away over Turkey. Rumania, Bulgaria and Hungary were left effectively under Soviet predominance. The agreement on Yugoslavia would in practice depend on Tito's behaviour. At the end of October he struck a bargain with Dr Subasich, Prime Minister in the royal government-in-exile. King Peter would appoint three regents to represent him pending a final decision on Yugoslavia's form of government. Since this left Tito in effective control inside Yugoslavia the prospects for the return of the monarchy were not enhanced. Much discussion over Poland produced only failure. The Polish Prime Minister, Mikolajczyk, was unable to persuade his London colleagues to accept the Curzon line and to leave the city of Lvov to the Russians. His resignation on 24 November further weakened the already poor bargaining position of the London Poles. There were some talks about the war against Japan in which the Americans took the lead. Churchill and Eden left Moscow delighted by the general atmosphere of goodwill. A summing-up by Dixon, which the Secretary of State approved, concluded that the good relationship achieved would make it easier to handle unresolved difficulties. Because of their anxiety to maintain good relations, the Russians would be more cautious in handling problems in which Britain had an interest. Once again a short period of personal contact with Stalin had produced a mood of somewhat frenetic over-optimism.[14]

Between the Moscow meeting and the end of the year it was American rather than Soviet policy which worried Churchill. On 18 November Roosevelt informed him that after the defeat of Germany it would be necessary to bring American troops home as quickly as possible. An early withdrawal from Europe was not an entirely new strand in United States thinking. In March John Ward had minuted that the American Chiefs of Staff had stated their intention to withdraw troops as soon as possible. 'We have grave doubts how long they will be prepared to occupy their zone in Germany', he commented. In July General Spaatz of the United States Air Force warned Bruce Lockhart that Britain could not rely on American interest in Europe for more than two years after the war. But it was Roosevelt's message which brought home to Churchill the possibility that Britain would be left to control the western half of Germany virtually unaided. In putting these fears to Roosevelt on 19 November he did not openly express the corollary that Russia would be left in a dominant position on the Continent. The President's reply on 26 November was not comforting. A French occupation force could no doubt be equipped from captured German equipment, but he had no authority to equip foreign armies after the war and it was doubtful if Congress would let him so do. In other words, once the need for Lend–Lease disappeared Congress was unlikely to be generous. Nor was it certain what level of American post-war defence spending would be politically acceptable.[15]

December 1944 was a gloomy month for Anglo-American relations. Eden's statement in the House of Commons on 1 December that Britain would not welcome the appointment of Count Sforza as Italian Foreign Minister produced a critical communiqué from the State Department on 5 December. By implication this also attacked British policy in Greece. When Churchill complained Roosevelt pointed out that Eden's speech had been made without prior consultation with Washington. The atmosphere was made worse on 9 December when the columnist Drew Pearson quoted from orders which Churchill had sent to the British commander in Greece, authorising the use of force against the communists. Roosevelt warned Churchill that however much he might sympathise with British difficulties in Greece he could not publicly support the Prime Minister's policy. By the end of the year British forces had pushed the communists out of Athens and Anglo-American hostility had simmered down. Nevertheless Churchill had been reminded that he could count only intermittently on United States support against the Soviet Union. Yet such support was likely to be needed more and more. On 31 December the Committee of National Liberation constituted itself the provisional government of Poland and on 3 January Stalin informed Churchill of the Soviet intention to recognise it. Could Britain still hope to have any influence on developments in Poland?[16]

During 1944, therefore, Churchill's influence on both Stalin and Roosevelt had been eroded. At a lower level the EAC had not proved to be the influential clearing house for which Eden had hoped. As early as November 1943 he had foreseen that there would be some American suspicion and that Gusev was unlikely to make a large contribution. In practice, Roosevelt's doubts and the rivalries between the State Department and the American service departments meant that Winant was often left without instructions. The same was true of Gusev who for most of the year slowed down the pace of business by insisting that the EAC should only deal with one topic at a time. Some of his inflexibility was no doubt the result of instructions: he blocked discussion on armistice terms for Bulgaria until after the Soviet declaration of war. During the October visit to Moscow Eden complained to Molotov about the slowness of the EAC's progress, seemingly with some effect, for Gusev became much more co-operative from the end of November. Major differences had to be settled outside the EAC; American unwillingness to accept an occupation zone in south-west Germany and the equally strong British resistance to giving up a zone in the north-west had to be resolved between Roosevelt and Churchill at the second Quebec Conference in September.[17]

In the course of the year Churchill and Eden had little time to concern themselves with problems of post-war trade. But awareness of the difficulties that Britain would face in rebuilding exports sharpened the interest of Foreign Office and Treasury officials in securing a trade agreement with the Soviet Union. Given the widespread assumption that she would need much help in reconstruction, this was a logical aim; unfortunately Britain could not afford large and extended credits. Developments got under way in May when the Soviet Foreign Ministry informed Clark Kerr of its interest in expanding post-war trade. At the same time it complained that the terms of the 1941 agreement for financing non-military supplies to Russia were too onerous and should be renegotiated. This produced a mixed reaction in the Foreign Office: Wilson and Warner saw the opportunities for increasing trade with Russia whereas Coulson and Ronald felt Britain could not afford large credits. During June discussions on a possible offer continued between the Foreign Office and the Treasury. On 27 June the Russians revealed their hand when Gifford, Commercial Secretary at the British Embassy, was told that they wanted credit for about 25 years at 2% interest. The British proposal, which was not handed over until 11 September, was much more modest – a credit of £30 million over five years at $2\frac{1}{4}$%. In addition Britain was prepared to reduce the interest rate under the 1941 agreement from 3% to $2\frac{1}{4}$%. The Russians did not send a formal rejection in writing, but made clear that the proposals were unacceptable. By the end of the year the British offer was still in a state of suspended animation, and in January 1945 the Russians cancelled virtually all non-military orders from Britain under the fourth Lend–Lease protocol. They took an equally hard line in bargaining with the United States when the latter suggested a credit for post-war trade under article 3(c) of the Lend–Lease Act. Discussions in Washington from May to September ended in deadlock.[18] The Russians appear to have over-estimated American and British anxiety to secure post-war markets. The rigid Soviet bargaining position helps to explain British fears about Soviet attitudes to the United Nations Relief and Rehabilitation Administration (UNRRA). Although set up in November 1943 it was only coming into effective operation by the end of 1944 as the number of liberated areas increased. Russian unwillingness to allow UNRRA observers into Soviet-controlled territory and the danger that relief would be siphoned off for Russia's benefit combined to illustrate the difficulties of practical day to day co-operation (Document 32).

The Foreign Office view of the Military Mission in Moscow became if possible more jaundiced in the course of 1944. Babington departed in the summer of 1943 and Martel came home in February 1944. His successor, General Burrows, arrived in Moscow at the beginning of April. Initially the Foreign Office had hopes that Burrows would avoid his predecessors' mistakes and not insist on a rigid policy of bargaining for information. Unlike Martel, Burrows got on well with Clark Kerr. By the beginning of May, however, Burrows was complaining about Soviet obstructiveness over letting him visit the front. He did not conceal his frustration and Vyshinsky complained to Clark Kerr in June that the Russians found Burrows difficult and unsympathetic. The Ambassador smoothed things over, and by having a word with Molotov obtained a visit to the front for Burrows at the end of June. But when the latter visited London in August he talked of applying more forcible methods to extract information from the Russians. Sargent, Warner and Bruce Lockhart doubted whether these methods would work and they were proved right. On 24 September Stalin made clear to Clark Kerr that Burrows was *persona non grata*, and he was recalled in November. No doubt the Foreign Office would have been even more irritated if it had known that the Russians had effectively bugged the Military Mission's offices and so could hear Burrows's views at first hand.[19]

Exasperation with the Military Mission helps to explain the angry Foreign Office reaction to the activities of the PHPS. This body began life as the Post-Hostilities Planning Sub-committee of the Chiefs of Staff in August 1943, although it did not become truly active until after the Moscow Foreign Ministers' Conference. It changed its name as the result of a reorganisation in May 1944 and thereafter produced a series of papers on the strategic problems likely to face Britain over the next ten years. There had already been signs of divergence between the services and the Foreign Office in February, when the Chiefs of Staff expressed their doubts about the 'Four-Power Plan'. Under the guidance of Jebb this paper had continued to evolve from the version which Eden had circulated to the Cabinet in January 1943. The Chiefs of Staff were sceptical about the practicality of organising international security in collaboration with the Soviet Union under the auspices of the proposed new world organisation. They assumed that Russia would develop her own sphere of influence and therefore thought that the best course for Britain and America would be the continuation of the Combined Chiefs of Staff. This episode did not in itself provoke any great reaction in the Foreign Office; the turning point was the PHPS paper explaining its basic assumptions for the forthcoming examination of strategic problems. Leaving aside the possibility of a German or Japanese revival, only the United States or the Soviet Union could pose a serious threat to Britain. Relations with Russia were more likely to deteriorate than those with the United States, but the attitude of the latter to post-war problems was uncertain. Although it was reasonable to hope for continued three-power co-operation, Russia's long-term intentions were very much a matter of guesswork and there were areas in which her interests might clash with those of Britain. The PHPS therefore decided to assume on the one hand that the three powers would continue to co-operate. On the other hand, however, it also assumed that Britain would dispose of sufficient forces and bases to enable her, in co-operation with the United States, to deter the Soviet Union from trying to promote her own interests to the detriment of the other two powers.[20]

It was this second assumption which sparked off the angry and bitter comments in the Foreign Office which began in early June and continued until October. Sargent was horrified by the suggestion that British policy might be based on the assumption of a need to fight Russia, whereas Cadogan concentrated on the danger of fixed assumptions. Although the PHPS dropped the basic assumptions, the Foreign Office was not mollified. It remained unhappy about the anti-Russian tone of PHPS papers; it was worried by indiscreet talk by army officers; it especially disliked any suggestion of using Germany as an ally against the Soviet Union. This would of course undermine the Foreign Office's own basic assumption that a hard policy towards Germany was the way to win Soviet goodwill. As Wilson discovered, it was difficult to find other areas in which military collaboration with Russia could be promoted, notwithstanding the existence of the 1942 alliance. In September the Foreign Office decided to withdraw from the PHPS. At the beginning of October Eden tried to clear the air by having a meeting with the Chiefs of Staff. For the latter Portal argued the need to consider the worst possible case. Eden admitted that there might be differences with Russia but thought that the PHPS was going too far in that direction. It was agreed that the Chiefs of Staff would restrict the circulation and discussion of papers in which Russia was mentioned as a potential enemy. But the question of what assumptions might be made about Soviet aims and policy in such papers was left un-resolved. In effect, the Chiefs of Staff were saying that the PHPS could think of Russia as hostile but should not say it aloud; the Foreign Office regarded it as dangerous even to have such thoughts. This did not prevent the PHPS from continuing until the summer of 1945 to produce strategic assessments in which the Soviet Union figures prominently, although she was not portrayed as automatically hostile to British interests (Documents 27 and 28).[21]

7 From Yalta to Potsdam

At the beginning of 1945 Churchill's attention turned again to Soviet aims in the Far East. By now he had forgotten the disquiet he expressed over the ending of the Sakhalin concessions. Ismay put before him the views of the Chiefs of Staff, who were not unduly worried by the prospect of Russia regaining a naval base at Port Arthur. This would help in maintaining control over Japan, something in which Britain and the Soviet Union had a common interest. Eden had doubts about this optimistic conclusion; it seemed to him that Russian ambitions in Manchuria and Korea were likely to produce friction with China, and the latter was likely to look to both America and Britain for support. He therefore warned against unnecessary concessions to the Soviet Union. Although Churchill agreed with the last point he felt that the advantages of Soviet intervention against Japan far outweighed any possible damage to Chinese susceptibilities, particularly as he assumed that the United States would be anxious to secure Russian participation; in other words the Americans would be prepared to pay a reasonable price.

It is clear, therefore, that in January 1945 Churchill was willing to condone the kind of bargain which Roosevelt and Stalin were to make in the Far Eastern Agreement signed at Yalta. Writing in 1954 Churchill admitted to supporting the Russian acquisition of Port Arthur but was careful to distance himself from the Yalta Agreement as being mainly an American concern. It is true that the British only signed the agreement without participating in the discussions, but they too had some interest in bringing the Soviet Union into the war against Japan. The atomic bomb had still to be tested; after the defeat of Germany there was the prospect of a protracted struggle in the Pacific and South-East Asia. British forces would be involved, although they were not expected to play a large part in the assault on the Japanese mainland. But nine years later the Far Eastern Agreement had acquired a bad reputation for its alleged contribution to the defeat of Chiang Kai-shek, and Churchill did not wish to emphasise that at the time he had not objected to paying Stalin's price.[1]

Remembering the disorganisation of Tehran, Eden and Cadogan were in favour of once again holding a preliminary meeting of Foreign Ministers. Unfortunately Eden did not propose this until it was too late for the idea to be fully implemented, despite his claim to have had it in mind for some time. He was stimulated into action by a minute from Cadogan on 1 January which argued the case for regular meetings between the Foreign Ministers to clear the ground on complicated and technical issues. This can be read as an implicit admission that the EAC had been a failure. It had been intended to serve much the same purpose. Following a discussion with Cadogan on 4 January, Eden put to Churchill a proposal for a meeting at least a week before the Yalta Conference began, perhaps in Egypt. Despite some doubts Churchill tried the suggestion on Roosevelt but the latter rejected it on 10 January. He claimed that Stettinius could not be out of the United States for a lengthy period just before the main conference. Churchill had made clear that Molotov would be invited, so that there was no question of an exclusively Anglo-American gathering. But Roosevelt had chosen Stettinius to succeed Hull at the beginning of the previous December precisely because the President intended to be his own Secretary of State. For that purpose he required a cheerful hard-working assistant, not someone who would negotiate independently with Eden and Molotov. Roosevelt did agree that Eden and Stettinius could meet at Malta on the way to the main conference, but this was a far cry from the original British proposal. Sargent and Harvey were left to contemplate the gloomy prospect of another chaotic meeting between the Big Three.[2]

The Foreign Office assembled a detailed and extensive list of priorities for Yalta. It particularly wanted to discuss the future of Germany, the Polish question and possible French participation in later meetings of Foreign Ministers and Heads of Government. The problem of voting in the United Nations Security Council, unsolved at the Dumbarton Oaks Conference the previous summer, was best left for others to raise. It would be useful to discuss the frontier between Italy and Yugoslavia but this was not seen as urgent; that particular view was to prove a miscalculation. Perhaps most interesting are the three questions which the Foreign Office definitely wished to avoid. Of these a preliminary peace treaty with Italy was the least significant. More important was the desire to avoid discussing the future of the Black Sea Straits. Stalin had not responded to Churchill's suggestion (made during the October visit to Moscow) that he should make specific proposals for revising the Montreux Convention and it seemed wise to let sleeping dogs lie. The same was true of Rumania and Bulgaria; if Britain complained about Soviet behaviour in those countries she would probably stir up Russian criticism over Greece. The percentages agreement presumably lay behind this argument.

In fact the question of an Italian peace treaty did not come up; little was said about Rumania and Bulgaria; revision of the Montreux Convention was again postponed to await Soviet proposals. Thus what the Foreign Office had viewed as potentially awkward topics were avoided. Nor did the conference prove to be as ill-organised as had been feared. The regular meetings of Foreign Ministers to carry out preparatory work for the plenary sessions ensured a degree of order in the proceedings and contributed to the smooth running of what the American and British delegations initially regarded as a considerable success. The Far Eastern Agreement confirmed the Soviet commitment to join in the Pacific war and seemed to hold out the prospect that Stalin would support Chiang Kai-shek rather than the Chinese communists. The question of voting in the Security Council had apparently been solved by the Russian agreement that the veto should not be used to prevent discussion of an issue. Roosevelt had also induced his partners to accept the Declaration on Liberated Europe. Although in its final version this document only required consultation among the three allies in order to promote representative governments and secure free elections, it at least implied that they would continue to observe the principles of the Atlantic Charter and would avoid dividing Europe into spheres of influence. The agreement on repatriation of prisoners was expected to speed up the return home of British and American personnel liberated by the Russians; its sinister notoriety lay in the future. Above all, the formula for reconstructing the Lublin government raised hopes that Poland would become a less significant source of tension between Russia and her Western partners.

There were also some decisions which could be seen as specifically British gains. It had been agreed that France should be given a zone of occupation in Germany and a place on the Control Council. This appeared especially important since Roosevelt repeated at Yalta that American troops were unlikely to remain in Europe in any large numbers for more than two years after the defeat of Germany. If the Americans withdrew and France was given no share in the control of Germany then Russia was likely to gain a predominant position in Europe. Moreover, Eden persuaded his colleagues to agree to regular meetings of Foreign Ministers, every three or four months. The first such meeting was to take place in London at some time after the conference to draft the Charter of the United Nations (which was arranged for late April in San Francisco) and would consider Soviet proposals for revision of the Montreux Convention.[3]

Discussion of the post-war treatment of Germany brought up two issues which left the British delegation less satisfied – reparations and dismemberment. The British argued strongly against the Russian wish to set a figure of $20,000 million of which they themselves would get half. In the British view it was dangerous to set a target before deciding what level of economic activity Germany could or should attain. As a compromise Roosevelt got agreement that the figure should only be taken as a basis for discussion. This left it open for the Russians to take the $20,000 million as a firm commitment. As it turned out, however, there was little progress on this subject before the Potsdam Conference. The three-power reparations commission agreed upon at Yalta did not meet in Moscow until June and soon ran into difficulties. There was disagreement about how definitely Roosevelt had committed himself to a fixed figure, on how reparations should be shared out, and on the vital question whether these should be a first charge on the German economy or whether reparations should only be extracted after a minimum level of exports had been achieved. The commission held a few more meetings in Moscow after the Potsdam Conference but came to an end in September.

The discussions on dismemberment brought that topic out of the limbo in which it had lingered since Tehran. There the Big Three all seemed agreed on the principle of partitioning Germany. Yet during 1944 there was little detailed study of how this was to be achieved in practice. Strang tried to introduce the topic at an early stage in the discussions of the EAC, but that body moved too slowly to allow dismemberment to be discussed. The Russians were unwilling to commit themselves and within the Foreign Office there were strong reservations. Some of the British differences surfaced in the Armistice and Post-War Committee. Chaired by Attlee, it tended to favour dismemberment in contrast to the doubts expressed by Eden. The latter came to Yalta sceptical but not yet committed to outright opposition. Molotov's pressure on the issue helped to make Eden's dislike of dismemberment more explicit, and he resisted the Russian attempt to make it obligatory (Document 33).

Why did Molotov choose to press the question so hard, given that the German communists exiled in Moscow were making their post-war plans on the basis of a single German state? He may have wished to test American and British commitment or to prepare the way for a Soviet change of policy. The London Committee agreed upon at Yalta had held only one meeting, on 7 March, when Gusev surprised the Foreign Office by informing them that Russia now regarded dismemberment as an option to be used in the last resort and not as an obligatory act. The shift in attitude was confirmed by Stalin's victory broadcast of 9 May in which he denied any intention of dismembering Germany. After a second meeting on 11 April the committee lapsed into inaction until Molotov agreed to its dissolution in August. The British government was thus saved from the problem of how to resolve its doubts and divisions on this issue.[4]

Despite the potential arguments which reparations and dismemberment seemed likely to produce, Churchill left the Crimea once again overcome by that euphoria which face to face contact with Stalin and Molotov seemed to inspire in him. The Prime Minister wrote enthusiastically to Attlee that nothing had been avoided in the discussions: 'It is a different Russian world to any I have seen hitherto.' This optimism had evaporated long before Roosevelt's death on 12 April added to the problems confronting the British government. The Soviet government appeared to have decided to consolidate its position in eastern Europe and the Balkans without going through the formalities of consultation. At the end of February Vyshinsky visited Rumania and forced King Michael to appoint a communist-dominated government. In view of the percentages agreement it was difficult for Britain to complain too loudly, and Roosevelt for his part was not prepared to make the issue a test case on the Declaration on Liberated Europe. As he admitted to Churchill on 11 March the Russians had been predominant in Rumania from the beginning.

On 19 March Molotov formally denounced the 1925 treaty of friendship with Turkey. This was perhaps a preliminary warning before the Russians put forward proposals for amending the Montreux Convention. Even more serious was the rapidity with which the ambiguities of the Yalta Agreement on Poland became clear when Clark Kerr, Harriman and Molotov began on their work as a commission in Moscow on 25 February. The Russians argued that the Lublin group must form the dominant element in any new government and should have a power of veto over the choice of potential members. Molotov expressly stated that Mikolajczyk must be excluded. The United States and Britain could agree on rejecting the two latter points, but there was some difference of emphasis between them on the extent to which they were seeking a completely new government. Roosevelt pointed out to Churchill on 29 March that the Yalta formula had put more emphasis on the Lublin group but was not intended to give them a dominant position. The President therefore wanted to concentrate on opposing the claim of a veto right for the Lublin group. Molotov's rigidity made this difference of view of little significance.

There were other disquieting elements in Soviet policy. On 22 March Molotov informed Clark Kerr that he would not be leading the Soviet delegation to San Francisco. At the very least this was a snub to the United States and suggested that Russia did not attach much significance to the new international organisation. By the beginning of April there were doubts within the Foreign Office whether the San Francisco Conference could go ahead. At this point the atmosphere was worsened by Stalin's accusation on 3 April that his allies had been acting in bad faith in the negotiations in Berne designed to bring about the surrender of German forces in Italy. Instead, alleged Stalin, there had been an agreement designed to allow British and American forces an easy passage through Germany while the Red Army had to continue fighting. Stalin did offer Roosevelt a rather grudging apology, but the ease with which Soviet suspicions could be aroused horrified both Eden and Clark Kerr.[5]

British assessments of Soviet intentions therefore became increasingly gloomy. Nevertheless at the end of March Clark Kerr put the best face he could on the situation, arguing that Russia was mainly concerned to assert her position in eastern Europe and would not necessarily abandon completely co-operation with her allies (Document 34). Stimulated by discussions with Bruce Lockhart, Sargent argued the case for a diplomatic showdown just before Stalin made his accusations about the Berne negotiations (Document 35). This would require the support of the United States and on the eve of his death it was still uncertain how Roosevelt intended to proceed. He had certainly decided to play down the Berne incident. Despite the deterioration in his health which had been evident at Yalta, the President's death came as a shock to Churchill and Eden. How much support could they expect from the unknown and untested Truman?[6]

Halifax's initial impression of the new President was favourable and he did not anticipate great changes in policy. One of Truman's early decisions was that the San Francisco Conference should go ahead as planned. Harriman was able to persuade Stalin that Molotov should after all lead the Soviet delegation, somewhat to Clark Kerr's surprise. Thus the three Foreign Ministers would be seen to be demonstrating their support for the new international organisation. On questions that bore more directly on British interests, however, Truman was to prove rather a disappointment to Churchill. Roosevelt, for all his suspicions of British imperialism, had some empathy with Churchill; Truman shared the suspicions but lacked the empathy. The same could be said of Byrnes, who replaced Stettinius as Secretary of State at the beginning of July. In the second half of the year Truman was to leave Byrnes a fairly free hand in foreign policy, but before the latter took over Truman found himself subjected to conflicting advice with Joseph E. Davies supporting a continuation of America's mediating role between Britain and Russia.[7]

On the one hand, therefore, Truman showed increasing irritation towards the Soviet Union yet on the other refused to follow Churchill's recommendations for an early meeting with Stalin and for the maintenance of Anglo-American forces in their existing positions in Germany. Churchill hoped to use withdrawal to the agreed occupation zones as a bargaining counter. Having made this suggestion by implication on 11 May, the Prime Minister put it more explicitly in his 'iron curtain' telegram of 12 May. For Truman the timing of a Big Three meeting depended largely on the forthcoming test of an atomic bomb. If that were successful then America's bargaining position *vis-à-vis* Russia would be greatly strengthened, although it is not clear how far Truman had thought through the diplomatic implications of the new weapon.

On withdrawal to the occupation zones he temporised but finally informed Churchill on 12 June that he had decided to go ahead in order not to delay the beginning of four-power control in Germany. The Soviet Union could otherwise delay the entry of the Western allies into Berlin and, indeed, into Vienna. On 27 April the Russians had recognised the provisional Austrian government of Karl Renner without consulting their allies. The veteran socialist was no communist cat's-paw, but Britain and the United States were annoyed by yet another example of unilateral Russian action and refused to recognise his government.[8]

By mid-July, however, the machinery of four-power control was getting under way in both Germany and Austria. Churchill had lost one argument with Truman. He received rather more support over the Trieste crisis, but even here Truman vacillated. Implementation of the Tito–Subasich agreement of the previous October was delayed by King Peter's objections to the composition of the Regency Council. The establishment of a new united government was announced on 6 March. By now, however, Churchill was prepared to write off hopes of British influence in Yugoslavia and to support Italy against Tito's territorial claims, as he made clear in a minute to Eden on 11 March. The latter was dubious about being drawn into armed conflict over the frontier question but agreed that the Yugoslav claim to Trieste should be resisted. The issue became a live one at the beginning of May when British and Yugoslav forces both reached Trieste. Having earlier shown caution, Truman on 12 May was strongly critical of Tito's apparent intention to take over the disputed border areas unilaterally. The President mentioned 'further steps' if Yugoslav forces did not withdraw. By 16 May, however, he was beginning to have second thoughts about involving American troops in a war with Yugoslavia, and although he agreed to a demonstration of force he was clearly still unhappy about a possible conflict. A joint Anglo-American approach in Belgrade on 2 June which in effect called for Yugoslav withdrawal from the disputed areas was accepted by Tito on 9 June. The question of how far the Americans would have supported the British was thus never put to the test. Churchill was proved right in his assumption that Tito lacked the full support of Moscow. Tito's retreat did not alter the fact that his agreement with Subasich soon became a dead letter and nothing was left of the 50% influence which Britain had contemplated in October 1944.[9]

The most obvious demonstration of Truman's independence was the decision to send Harry Hopkins to Moscow at the end of May in order to break the deadlock on Poland. The idea of such a mission had been in the air for some time but the final decision seems to have been taken fairly suddenly; Truman gave Hopkins only a short briefing, telling him to sort out the Polish question. At first the Foreign Office was in the dark. As Clark Kerr began to obtain information on the course of the talks there was some concern in London. Sargent felt that Stalin had seized the initiative; Churchill's view varied. In fact the British had to acquiesce in a settlement which left the Lublin Poles clearly dominant in the new government, although Mikolajczyk was included. To add insult to injury Truman sent Joseph E. Davies to visit Churchill at the same time as Hopkins went to Moscow. Churchill's dislike of Davies was not lessened by the news that Truman was apparently contemplating a separate meeting with Stalin before the main conference. In the face of Churchill's obvious annoyance this proposal was dropped.[10]

The reserved American attitude meant that British complaints and disquiet about Russian policy in the three months or so before the Potsdam Conference opened on 17 July had little effect. Early in April Clark Kerr took Maisky to task over recent Soviet behaviour but doubted whether the latter carried much weight in the Kremlin. 'The truth is that the Russians are in a hurry to be great and that is uncomfortable.' Commenting that the Russians were only interested in UNRRA for what they could get out of it he doubted if they would release relief supplies for areas outside their control. America and Britain would be well advised to build up their own position in Western Europe. Despite this note of gloom Clark Kerr and Roberts were cautious when discussing Soviet policy towards Czechoslovakia and Yugoslavia (Documents 36 and 37). Here they saw Russia as mainly concerned to strengthen her position in eastern Europe; she would still collaborate with her allies, but on her own terms. Sargent took a gloomier view in May when he agreed with Bruce Lockhart that the Soviet Union was aiming at expansion beyond eastern Europe. He did not, however, allow others to outdo him in pessimism, and therefore rejected the hard line for which O'Malley argued (Document 38). The latter may have been reflecting the doubts and fears of the London Poles, yet the tone of his paper is not too different from the views which Churchill was expressing to Truman.[11]

Indeed Churchill went almost as far as O'Malley when he gave Gusev a dressing down after entertaining him to lunch on 18 May. The Prime Minister complained about the exclusion of America and Britain from Eastern Europe and warned that he had postponed demobilisation of the RAF. Perhaps as a result of this onslaught Gusev invited Eden to dinner on 23 May and made a point of expressing surprise at the way Churchill had spoken to him. He affected to find no reason for concern about the state of Anglo-Soviet relations. A week earlier Warner had attended a reception at the Soviet Embassy and found himself engaged in conversation by Koukin, who held the rank of Counsellor. The latter argued that it was unwise for Britain to work too closely with the Americans, since they would soon pull out of Europe. Britain should rather make clear to Russia exactly what she wanted and where her interests lay. Warner in turn complained about Soviet methods and lack of frankness. Sargent and Eden found some encouragement in this exchange despite the hint of blackmail on Koukin's part.[12]

During June two further issues confirmed Russian willingness to act unilaterally. On 7 June Molotov informed the Turkish Ambassador of the preliminary price required for a new treaty – the return of territory ceded to Turkey in 1921, the grant to Russia of bases in the Black Sea Straits, and a revision of the Montreux Convention. The projected London meeting of Foreign Ministers had not taken place so Russia now seemed anxious to put pressure on the Turks before the Big Three conference. The Turks refused to make any concessions and the issue remained in suspense until the Potsdam Conference. At the end of June came the news that Czechoslovakia had agreed to cede sub-Carpathian Ruthenia to the Soviet Union. The issue had apparently been raised in January and June and the Czechs were not prepared to resist the Russian request. They lost a troublesome Ukrainian minority; the Soviet Union gained a common border with Hungary. Clark Kerr was instructed to take up this territorial transfer which anticipated the peace settlement. Molotov did not reply until 4 September, when he argued that frontier changes made by agreement and in an atmosphere of goodwill need not await the final peace conference. There was in any case little that the British government could do about this *fait accompli*. Another worrying factor was the slow progress of the EAC. The spasm of activity which Gusev displayed towards the end of 1944 did not last long. During 1945 the EAC became bogged down over occupation zones in Austria and the question of a French zone. Between the end of January and 4 April it did not meet at all. The control agreement for Austria was finally signed on 4 July and the French sector in Berlin was agreed on 26 July.[13]

On the eve of the Potsdam Conference, therefore, the British had little reason to be optimistic. Nevertheless, Sargent's stocktaking paper in July was less gloomy than some of his earlier utterances. He reverted to the view that Stalin was mainly concerned with security and was not aiming at further territorial expansion. Britain should therefore try to maintain her influence in eastern Europe, but would clearly need American support. Sargent appended an amended version of a minute written by Bruce Lockhart in April, which at the time he had found 'full of truth', although the latter had not intended it for circulation (Document 39). A Research Department paper examined in some detail the techniques employed by the Russians to establish their influence in eastern Europe and northern Persia. These varied somewhat from country to country, but the general effect was to exclude or limit British and American influence. This did not augur well for Sargent's proposal that Britain should endeavour to maintain a foothold in at least parts of the area (Document 40). Clark Kerr writing from Moscow pointed out that the recent improvement in Soviet relations with the Western allies had not been accompanied by any major Russian concession. He too emphasised the need to obtain American support on troublesome issues and unconsciously echoed Koukin's comment that Britain must define her vital interests and decide where she stood. Warner found his dispatch in line with feeling in the Foreign Office but Eden said only that it was a good survey (Document 41).[14]

8 From Potsdam to Moscow

Two problems had receded by the time of the Potsdam Conference. At San Francisco the Russian delegation had reverted to their more restrictive formula on voting in the United Nations Security Council, but Hopkins had persuaded Stalin to agree that the veto should not be used to prevent discussion. A Preparatory Commission was now dealing with loose ends and the United Nations was expected to begin its work early in 1946. Moreover, there was a Polish government recognised by all three allies. Visiting Warsaw on his way to Potsdam, Clark Kerr found Mikolajczyk not unduly despondent about his political prospects. New difficulties, however, appeared to replace old ones. Although it had been agreed at Yalta that a final delimitation of Poland's frontiers would be made at the peace settlement, the Russians had allowed the Polish authorities to occupy German territory up to the line of the Oder and western Neisse rivers. Apart from disliking yet another example of unilateral Soviet action, the United States and Britain feared the loss of a valuable source of food for their zones of occupation. There was also the question whether they should recognise the Rumanian and Bulgarian governments. If they withheld recognition this was likely to delay the signing of peace treaties. Above all, the three powers would have to confront the problem of how they were to treat Germany.

The British delegation did not come to Potsdam in a happy frame of mind. At the beginning of July Cadogan warned Churchill of Britain's weak bargaining position. From Washington Halifax told of continuing American suspicions of British aims; Truman would be more receptive to arguments about the dangers of economic chaos in Europe than to warnings about the threat from communism. Eden expressed his own fears about Soviet intentions in a long minute to Churchill early in the conference. But the Prime Minister's attention had been distracted by the election campaign (polling took place on 5 July) and he was showing clear signs of exhaustion from the strains of war. It was not only the professional eye of Moran which detected evidence of decay; during 1944 Eden, Cadogan and Tedder had all noticed some decline in

Churchill's powers. Eden himself had been suffering from an ulcer and during the conference received confirmation that his eldest son had been killed on a flight in Burma. Over the previous three years there had been complaints from Foreign Office officials that the leadership of the House of Commons had seriously impaired his ability to deal with external relations. Eden himself admitted the strain of his dual burden yet in the last resort was unwilling to abandon it.[1]

As a result, the British found it difficult in Berlin to defend their declining influence. Truman got on well with Churchill personally but neither he nor Byrnes went out of their way to co-ordinate policy with Churchill and Eden. Labour's victory in the election meant that on 28 July the latter pair were replaced by Attlee and Bevin. The change produced little alteration in the substance of British policy but the new team found that Byrnes in particular tended to treat them very much as junior partners. He pushed ahead with his proposals for a package deal that would resolve the two most contentious issues of the conference – the Polish western frontier and reparations. The United States would drop its complaints about the Polish take-over of territory up to the Oder–Neisse line if the Russians would accept the American formula on reparations. Stalin and Molotov agreed, in order to obtain supplies of industrial equipment from the western zones, although this would involve abandoning their previous insistence on a fixed sum for reparations. The British delegation had some reservations, fearing that the agreement would undermine the principle of treating Germany as an economic unit, but in the end had little choice save to fall in with the American plan. Nevertheless, Attlee expressed his disappointment at the lack of consistent and resolute American support.[2]

Various issues were postponed for later discussion. Over the Rumanian and Bulgarian governments there was in effect an agreement to differ. Revision of the Montreux Convention was once again left over. No central government for Germany was to be set up in the meantime. This avoidance of troublesome problems was made possible by the creation of a Council of Foreign Ministers, charged with the task of drawing up peace treaties with the former European allies of Germany but also capable of dealing with any other matters that might be referred to it. The proposal for a Council came in the first instance from the United States. Britain and the Soviet Union accepted the idea, but there was some discussion about what part France and China should play. Here Byrnes made a serious tactical error; he intended that all five members should be able to participate in all discussions on the peace treaties even though decisions on drafting and content would be reserved to the individual signatories of the various terms of surrender. Unfortunately no such explicit provision was written into the agreement establishing the Council. It was agreed, however, that the provision made at Yalta for regular meetings of Foreign Ministers should remain in force. Eden was prepared to drop it, but Molotov having at first agreed came out in favour of retention. Given the general Russian desire to keep decision-making in the hands of the Big Three, it made sense to keep alive an alternative forum to the larger body. As a result of the creation of the Council of Foreign Ministers the EAC was dissolved. This rather unlucky creation of British diplomacy had never become the efficient clearing house that had been intended.

The American and British delegations do not seem to have regarded these procedural points as of great significance. They were more impressed by the news on 17 July of the successful atomic test in New Mexico. The bomb brought a quick end to the war with Japan and thus enabled the United States to establish a dominant position in the post-war control of that country. But she could not prevent the Soviet Union's occupation of Manchuria and signature of a treaty with China which gave Stalin what he had been promised at Yalta. Possession of the new weapon, however, could be expected to strengthen America's general bargaining position; Byrnes seems to have been more excited than Truman by the diplomatic possibilities of the bomb. The sudden end to the Pacific war confronted Britain with the problems of conversion to a peacetime economy much earlier than had been anticipated. Lend–Lease ended in August, and Britain spent the rest of the year negotiating a loan from the United States. Terms were agreed in December, but it has to be remembered that Foreign Office discussions on policy towards Russia in the second half of 1945 were taking place against a background of economic weakness.[3]

In the interlude between the Potsdam Conference and the first meeting of the Council of Foreign Ministers Clark Kerr speculated about the effect of the atomic bomb on Soviet policy. He foresaw possible clashes of interest between Russian and America in the Far East whereas Britain was more likely to clash with the Soviet Union in the Near and Middle East. He was not, however, unduly pessimistic (Document 42). Byrnes on the other hand arrived in London confident that he could soon get peace treaties under way. But, like others before him, he found Molotov stubborn and unyielding. The latter took a strong line; he did not merely defend Russia's claim to a sphere of influence in eastern Europe but also asserted her right as a great power to have interests elsewhere, as with the request for a trusteeship in Libya. He also showed himself prepared to defend Yugoslavia's territorial claims against Italy. As a result, the conference had made little progress, when, on 22 September, Molotov threw a procedural spanner into its machinery. At its first meeting the Council had accepted Bevin's argument that all five members should participate in all discussions. Now Molotov moved back to a strict interpretation of the Potsdam Agreement; even discussion should be limited to those states which had signed the surrender terms.

From this position he refused to budge, despite appeals by Attlee and Truman to Stalin, and despite much ill-tempered argument at the conference itself. On 29 September he introduced a further difficulty by insisting on separate protocols depending on whether decisions affected two, three, four, or all five members of the Council. Molotov did indicate a willingness to compromise if he obtained recognition of the Rumanian and Bulgarian governments or if the United States would proceed to set up inter-allied control machinery in Japan. But his stubborn tactics antagonised the other delegations. Byrnes and Bevin were unwilling to revert to a narrow interpretation of the Potsdam formula since this would annoy France and China. There was of course the risk that Molotov would walk out. Warner did not think this was likely, but Cadogan was less sure. As it turned out, Molotov did not take such an extreme step and the conference was adjourned indefinitely without agreeing on a protocol (Document 43).[4]

During the conference Frank Roberts was reporting from Moscow on Soviet press criticism of any suggestion that Britain might try to form a group of western European states under her leadership. The Moscow Embassy received hints that Britain should copy Russia in pursuing a clear and consistent policy. This made little impression in the Foreign Office where the general feeling was that Britain was entitled to go ahead with her own plans if she so wished. In any case, that particular topic was overshadowed by speculation about Soviet intentions at the London Conference. Little weight was attached to the atomic bomb or to Soviet resentment at being excluded from Japan. British officials tended to concentrate on Russian aims in the Mediterranean and the Middle East (Document 44). The question arose whether early action should be taken to revive the Council of Foreign Ministers. Roberts argued for a clarification of Anglo-Soviet relations which would involve recognition of Russian vital interests, especially in the Balkans. Ward saw a dilemma: if Britain made such a deal with Russia she could be accused of flouting the Atlantic Charter and would alienate the United States. Yet if no deal were made the Russians might make themselves awkward in the United Nations and even wreck that body. The upshot was that Bevin decided to leave well alone and not to make an early approach in Moscow.[5]

Byrnes professed to agree with this policy and told Halifax that he had dissuaded Truman from sending a special envoy to Moscow. But he was prepared to contemplate a meeting of the Big Three alone, provided it was followed by discussions on peace treaties among the Five and the other European allies. Indeed Byrnes would have been prepared to compromise in London had he not been restrained by John Foster Dulles, who had been brought along to represent the Republican viewpoint. Ward was worried by Byrnes's attitude. Such a proposal might help to break the deadlock, but the Secretary of State seemed too anxious to make a compromise. Bevin thought that if Byrnes was in such a hurry he could be allowed to get on with it. A joint approach by Clark Kerr and Harriman to Stalin would be preferable. But joint action seemed increasingly to be a thing of the past, as Roberts gloomily commented to Sargent. He was unhappy at the thought of Britain playing the part of Lepidus in the triumvirate of the powers. In this case, too, Byrnes went ahead unilaterally. On 24 October Harriman set off to visit Stalin who was holidaying at a Crimean resort. Although friendly enough Stalin made clear his displeasure at being excluded from Japanese affairs. The peace treaties would have to be drawn up by the Big Three in the first instance and the number of participants in the peace conference should be strictly limited. Bevin wondered whether Clark Kerr should also visit Stalin but decided not to reverse the policy of inaction. In any case, Stalin's proposals did not offer a satisfactory way out of the deadlock. The Foreign Office wanted the Council to continue to operate as a body of five and disliked the idea of limiting the number of participlants in the peace conference. Harriman's visit to Stalin should be seen against the background of the assessment of Soviet policy given by Roberts at the end of October (Document 45).[6]

Evidence that the Russians were worried about the deadlock appeared in a speech by Molotov to celebrate the anniversary of the Revolution. This included the first official Soviet reference to the atomic bomb. Its secrets could not remain the monopoly of any one power, said Molotov; but he went on to make encouraging references to three-power collaboration and to the United Nations. He also held out hopes of solving the problem of control machinery in Japan. At a later function Molotov was at pains to tell Clark Kerr that the moderate tone of the speech was intentional. It did not, however, indicate how discussions were to be resumed. Halifax found Bohlen and Dunn still pessimistic in mid-November. They did not feel that Stalin's proposal to Harriman offered much of an advance on Molotov's attitude in London. Yet on 23 November Byrnes took the initiative and instructed Harriman to suggest to Molotov a meeting of the three Foreign Ministers in Moscow. To justify this retreat he reverted to the Yalta formula for regular meetings of Foreign Ministers. They had met in San Francisco and at Potsdam and now ought to meet in Moscow. He thus hoped to have the advantage of direct contact with Stalin.

The Secretary of State had not consulted Bevin or even informed him in advance. Indeed, the latter's first news of the proposed meeting came in a message from Clark Kerr. Although Bevin made his annoyance clear Byrnes was determined to press ahead whether the Foreign Secretary attended or not. Bevin reluctantly gave way; he was worried by the sudden change of policy and by the fact that the conference would be working to a deadline. It would need to finish its work before the inaugural meeting of the United Nations in January. Clark Kerr too was opposed to setting a time limit, but these views made no impression on Byrnes. It is noticeable that the British prepared for the Conference in a general atmosphere of gloom. At the Moscow Embassy there was concern about the Russian war of nerves against Turkey. Clark Kerr and his staff did not think the Soviet Union would resort to force, but were worried by Russian unpredictability. In London Sargent wondered whether mutual fear would lead to eventual agreement. Cadogan commented: 'Let us hope so. But an uneasy equilibrium is not a pleasant situation to look forward to for some years to come. However, I see no radical cure.' Nor was there much enthusiasm for provoking an argument over Rumania; Sargent was quite prepared to concede it to the Soviet Union.[7]

The conference did not prove as disastrous as the British had feared. By patching up relations among the Big Three it ensured that the United Nations would not begin its life with the handicap of an open split among the permanent members of the Security Council. Indeed, agreement was reached fairly easily on setting up a commission for the control of atomic energy consisting of the permanent members plus Canada. Molotov insisted that the commission must report to the Security Council, where the veto would apply, and not to the General Assembly. Byrnes made concessions over the Balkans in return for a Soviet retreat over Japan. The Rumanian and Bulgarian governments were each to admit two new members and in the case of Rumania early elections would follow. This would open the way for recognition of both governments by Britain and the United States. In exchange for this Russian window-dressing Byrnes secured a Far Eastern Commission in Washington and an Allied Council in Tokyo which left effective control over Japan in American hands. On the preparation of peace treaties he virtually accepted the Soviet position – the treaties would be drafted by those members of the Council who had signed surrender terms (France counting as a signatory of the Italian surrender). The Five would then summon a general conference whose recommendations would be considered by the signatories in drawing up the final texts. It is true, however, that Byrnes persuaded Stalin to accept a larger membership for the peace conference than Molotov was at first prepared to concede. The abandonment of the principle of a Council of Five annoyed the British delegation, who again found that Byrnes did not consult them or go out of his way to protect their interests. Bevin's conversations with Stalin and Molotov failed to produce clarification of Soviet intentions towards Turkey and Iran. Ward complained that Byrnes was excitable and only too ready to make concessions. Hood concluded that Britain might as well press on with plans for an Anglo-French treaty and the creation of a Western group. The Moscow Conference left the British still uncertain about Soviet aims and doubtful about American reliability (Document 46).[8]

In conclusion, something will be said about developments during 1945 over the Military Missions and trade credits. When submitting his final report in December 1944 Burrows argued that the Military Mission should be abolished and replaced by three service attachés, a proposal with which both Wilson and Warner agreed. The mission continued to function, however, with Admiral Archer as its acting head, until it was decided in May to send out General Gammell as successor to Burrows. The war against Japan was still expected to last for some time and in view of the anticipated Soviet entry it seemed worthwhile to keep the mission going. Gammell was given a cordial reception but like his predecessors found it difficult to obtain information. The Moscow Embassy, preoccupied first with the Polish question and then with the arrival of the reparations commission, could do little to help. As late as the Potsdam Conference, the Chiefs of Staff were still ready to keep the mission in being. The sudden ending of the Pacific war destroyed its *raison d'être* and at the beginning of September it was agreed that the mission, and the Soviet mission in London, would be closed down on 1 October. Thus the frustration which had dogged the mission from its inception ended in anti-climax.[9]

Following the Russian decision in January to accept virtually no civil supplies from Britain under the fourth Lend–Lease protocol, negotiations on a post-war credit remained in stalemate. A new element entered the situation in April when it became clear that the £60 million credit provided under the 1941 agreement was overdrawn. The Treasury now began to wonder if the Russians would pay up. At the end of May the latter indicated that the proposed interest rate of $2\frac{1}{4}\%$ of any new credits would be acceptable and enquired if it could also be applied to outstanding payments under the 1941 agreement. Neither the Foreign Office nor the Treasury liked this proposal which was formally rejected in July. Meanwhile Churchill had decided on 10 June that all civil supplies should be stopped in an effort to make the Russians pay up. The Labour government agreed in August to resume supplies if outstanding claims were settled. This did produce an acceleration in Soviet payments, but there were still some disputed items at the end of the year. Nothing more had been heard about the British credit offer of September 1944. Here also 1945 ended in uncertainty about Russian intentions.[10]

DOCUMENTS

---

1   **Correspondence between Eden and Cripps, January–July 1941**

A Eden to Cripps, 17 January 1941

...I share with you a keen desire to improve relations with the Soviet Government and I have also had my share of disappointment in these endeavours so that I can appreciate to some small extent the daily difficulties with which you are faced. I feel sure, however, that if anyone can bring about an improvement in relations, you will; and it is perhaps also an advantage that the Russians profess to regard me as one who has no prejudice against them.

But Russian suspicions lie so deep and Russian fears of German military might are so vivid and real that our task must be a formidable one. In the main only our own military successes can bring us certain relief, though I need hardly say that as and when there is any modification in the Russian attitude I shall be very ready to seize any opportunity that presents itself.

Meanwhile, I entirely approve the policy of reserve which we are pursuing on your advice; and the new Soviet–German agreement seems to me an additional reason for continuing it. After that, and their failure to respond to any of our various approaches, there can, I think, be no question of our making any further political or economic offers to the Soviet Government. Nor do I think that we can hope to gain anything in present circumstances by making fresh attempts to reach a settlement of the various outstanding Baltic questions. This, I understand, is your view also . . .

. . . In the Far East the Soviet Government appear to consider that it is their interest at present to encourage Japan to interest herself southward rather than to make a common front with us. If so, any approach from our side to make a joint stand against Japanese aggression would presumably only lead to a rebuff. I suppose that in this field also the Soviet Government will not be disposed to join in putting pressure upon Japan until Japan has herself been weakened by others. We have here, it is true, one common interest, in maintaining the resistance of China. Maisky assures me that the Soviet Government will continue their help to China and so shall we so far as our resources allow.

In general, I feel that we can only possess our souls in patience until such time as we have sufficient success in our military operations to inspire in the Soviet Government some of the fear and respect which they now feel for the Germans . . .

B Cripps to Eden, 26 January 1941

. . . I do not think that there has been any change in the long term out-look of the Soviet Government upon their relations with Germany, but on the other hand I believe that the recent agreements mark quite definitely a lessening of the temporary tensions and a determination by this country to avoid any armed conflict with Germany at almost any cost.

The settlement of all outstanding questions in relation to the Baltic States is, I think, a major success for Russian diplomacy. They have by this means avoided the danger of any 'incidents' in that area and have stabilised vis-a-vis Germany their occupation of Lithuania, Latvia and Estonia, in such a manner that it will be almost impossible for Germany in the future to make any trouble for this country over relationships arising in those areas . . .

. . . I therefore regard the agreements as signalising:

a a sound economic arrangement for Russia;
b a finalisation of Russo-German relations arising out of the Russian occupation of the Baltic provinces, and the elimination of the possibility of future German claims;
c An improvement in the short-term relations between the two countries to the practical elimination of the fear of armed conflict on both sides.

This I regard as the outcome of Molotov's visit to Berlin . . . I have little doubt that the Soviet policy is to push Japan to the South, to relieve Japanese pressure on the Soviet Far Eastern territories and in the hope of embroiling Japan with the United States of America. This would be the most effective way for the Soviet Government to dispose of Japanese pressure for a long time to come. It is possible that the Soviet Government might be prepared to promise and even to sign an agreement on quite broad terms with Japan on the under-standing that Japan went southwards, in the certainty that thereby Japan would be weakened and would lay herself open to very large claims by the Soviet.

For the same reason I think for the present the Soviet Government will maintain the Chinese pressure on Japan by giving China what help she needs to prolong the war.

I am quite certain that any agreement between the Soviet Government and Japan will be animated by the hostility of the Soviet Government against Japan and not by any friendship for Japan, though the desire to avoid actual hostilities might well play a part in it . . .

. . . It must never be forgotten that the whole history of Anglo-Soviet relations leads to a continued and bitter hostility against Great Britain, and that this hostility is unlikely to disappear unless some very visible signs of accomplished facts convince the Soviet Government of a change of attitude. This is why they have attached great importance to the questions arising out of their occupation of the Baltic States, and why also they did in fact attach great importance to His Majesty's Government's political offer of last October, although they decided eventually to do nothing about it . . .

. . . Given that it is right, as I believe it to be, for His Majesty's Government to exert economic pressure on the Soviet Government to change their political outlook, then I think the United States should join effectively in that pressure and should let it be known that in fact the action is a joint action, and that an improvement in Soviet–United States relations is conditional upon a more friendly attitude being adopted vis-a-vis Great Britain.

I do not imagine myself that any quick reaction will be obtained to our present pressure which cannot from the nature of things be very strong. I am however of the opinion that it will gradually have its effect and that sooner or later we shall have the opportunity of re-opening the question of Anglo-Soviet relations upon the basis of their economic needs. This will be the more likely if we can concert our action with the United States of America . . .

C Cripps to Eden, 29 July 1941

. . . The other point that I want to mention is about the length of my stay here. Fairly soon we shall have got everything going and the only really important thing will be to start considering what we can get these people to do after the war to help in the job of settling the new conditions for Europe. This question will have to be broached especially as regards the frontiers of Russia in the North and in Bessarabia. It is obviously a matter that wants the most careful consideration on our part first but also I feel that we ought at least to have some general talks with them before there is any likelihood of a peace conference actually taking place. Also if we wait until they are clearly victorious it may be much more difficult to get them to see eye to eye with us on these particular problems and also upon the general questions which will arise as to the post-war structure of Europe in those areas where they are particularly interested.

My own view therefore which I would very much like you to discuss with Winston, is that I might, in a month or so return with a view to coming back again, not as Ambassador, but as a person specially instructed to discuss with Stalin the post-war problems . . .

2   Memorandum by Orme Sargent of 26 April 1941 on Cripps's behaviour as Ambassador in Moscow

Sir S. Cripps' occasional unwillingness to carry out his instructions, combined with his tendency to take independent and unannounced action of his own, has recently caused a certain amount of confusion, thus complicating the task of the Prime Minister and the Secretary of State. When looking back over the events of the last few months one has the impression that there has been a lack of consistency in Sir S. Cripps' dealings with the Soviet Government and one cannot help feeling that he has no very definite plan or clear objective. For instance, at one moment he advocates and practises a policy of reserve and aloofness while at the next moment, although conditions have not materially changed, he is to be found addressing appeals and remonstrances to the Soviet Government which, I fear, may well produce on Stalin the impression of weakness and even panic which it ought to be our object to avoid above all else with the Soviet Government . . .

It will be recollected that the original efforts of Sir S. Cripps to negotiate a trade agreement which started last June, may be said finally to have expired in the autumn in the face of the refusal of the Soviet Government to make any response to our advances. In spite of this failure Sir S. Cripps, on his own suggestion and against our better judgement, made certain political proposals to Vyshinsky last October. These too remained unanswered and when Sir S. Cripps finally realised that no progress was possible on these lines he recommended in December that henceforth he should maintain a negative or reserved attitude until they showed signs of dealing with our offers or approaching us. With this object he recommended that we should at all costs avoid the appearance of running after the Soviet Government, which would only be interpreted as weakness, and should await advances from them.

So matters continued until the clear evidence of Germany's intention to invade Yugoslavia at an early date produced a new situation which compelled us to make an effort to establish contact with the Soviet Government. This new phase was ushered in when Sir S. Cripps was instructed on March 21st to ask the Soviet Government whether they would intervene to prevent the Yugoslav Government from signing a treaty with Germany. To this approach Sir S. Cripps received a reply from Vyshinsky to the effect that the necessary prerequisites for discussing wide political problems with H. M. Government did not exist, because of the economic pressure which H. M. Government were exercising on the Soviet Government in support of their blockade policy, and because of H. M. Government's general policy of hostility towards the Soviet Union. Sir S. Cripps was not discouraged, however, by this rebuff, which curiously enough he interpreted as evidence that the Soviet Government were 'making a considerable move in our direction'. Nevertheless he proposed to 'continue with our policy' i.e. the policy of reserve and aloofness and intimated that he would avoid seeing Vyshinsky again for a time.

Within a few days, however, Sir S. Cripps had reported that increased German pressure on the Soviet Government was to be expected shortly as a result of German activities in the Balkans and to a lesser extent Finland, and was arguing therefrom that it was necessary for us to negotiate an early settlement of the Baltic question with the Soviet Government. A lengthy correspondence ensued . . . This correspondence has for the time being ended in a long telegram from Sir S. Cripps of the 19th April in which he advocates that we should tell the Soviet Government straight away the extent of the concessions we are prepared to make and the circumstances in which we are prepared to make them, even though there may be no immediate prospects of negotiating a settlement on this basis. This proposed procedure has not been approved . . .

On April 11th he had addressed to Vyshinsky a long personal letter ' reviewing the succession of failures by the Soviet Government to counteract German encroachments in the Balkans and urging in the strongest terms that in their own interests they must now decide on an immediate vigorous policy of co-operation with countries still opposing the Axis'. He gave as his reason for this action the fact that he could not approach Stalin more directly after Vyshinsky had told him that the Soviet Government were not prepared to discuss political questions . . .

Not content with this demarche, however, Sir S. Cripps, fearing that the German Ambassador at Moscow who had left for Berlin might return with a new offer to the Soviet Government, followed it up apparently on 18th April, by handing to Vyshinsky for delivery to Molotov (who refused to see him) a document in the form of an aide-memoire recording a verbal statement, which reviewed the developments since he had last seen Molotov, went on to warn him that H. M. Government and the U. S. Government took a grave view of the fact that the Soviet Union had remained Germany's main channel of supply and to hint that if the war were protracted we might be tempted to make peace with Germany at Russian expense . . .

This document, containing the very dangerous and wholly unauthorised threat that we might be prepared to make a compromise peace with Germany was, needless to say, delivered without previous consultation with or authority from H. M. Government. As might have been expected Vyshinsky's reaction to this quasi-ultimatum was 'not at all favourable' . . .

Up till now the misunderstandings between Sir S. Cripps and H. M. Government and the vagaries of his independent actions in Moscow have had no serious results, since the Soviet Government have not been ready to alter the orientation of their general policy in our direction. But matters are moving so fast in Eastern Europe that we may soon be faced with the necessity of taking major decisions at short notice in regard to our general policy towards the Soviet Government. If this were to happen the growing inability of Sir S. Cripps to work on the same lines as H. M. Government and in consultation with them might easily have most dangerous and far-reaching results. In these circumstances it is for consideration whether it would not be wise to ask Sir S. Cripps to return home without delay for consultation and instructions.

Cadogan minute of 28 April

I confess that I have found it very difficult to follow Sir S. Cripps and I had myself wondered whether it would not be a good thing to get him back for discussion. I think on the whole it would be. The question might arise whether at this moment it would be a good thing to be without an Ambassador in Moscow and how the Russians might interpret his recall. I don't think these are real objections – because I don't think Russian policy is going to be deflected by such trifles or indeed by anything except their own view of their own particular interests.

But it cannot be to the good that we take one line while our Ambassador takes two or more others in Moscow. It is also conceivable that with Sir S. Cripps here we might be able to work out a positive line of policy. My difficulty is that I don't see what we have to offer the Russians (except unlimited supplies, with most of which they would buy off the Germans and we can't allow that). The Russians want a price and I don't see where we find it.

Eden minute of 30 April

This is a very difficult question, which requires some further consideration . . .

3   Exchanges between Eden and Cripps, October–November 1941

A Cripps to Eden, 25 October 1941

. . . There is no doubt that relations between the two countries, as reflected here, are getting worse and not better. It is clear to us here that, if we cannot relieve pressure on the Russians by action elsewhere, the only way in which we can improve matters is to send some troops to this country.

Until something is done I am reasonably certain that we shall find more and more difficulties in the way of co-operation, and it will become increasingly difficult to do anything except to make arrangements as regards supplies, which are accepted most ungraciously and without a word of thanks.

There is an obsession that we are sitting back and watching them, and nothing will dispel it except concrete action on our part to relieve pressure on Russian front. I make full allowance for the fact that Molotov and others are stressing this point for reasons of policy, but I am satisfied beyond doubt that there is also a wide-spread general obsession with this question. Officially, I am beginning to be anxious as to result of this on morale generally. If the sense of isolation continues I think it may result in a crack of morale during the winter, when conditions will inevitably be very bad throughout most of the country. Already and after harvests there are reports of serious food shortage from various sources, and so far as the Russian people as a whole are concerned, real trial of war will only come this winter. We cannot exclude the possibility that disappointment and disillusionment may even affect morale to such an extent as to count Russia out of the war altogether. I hope this aspect of the situation will receive full and immediate consideration.

I am quite confident that the Government are determined to fight on, but, should the situation continue to deteriorate without the country's feeling of isolation being countered, it is perfectly conceivable they will not be able to do so. Crisis is now at its height. We can either continue our present policy, in which case I cannot guarantee that Russia will not collapse, but I can guarantee that our relations will go from bad to worse. Or we can take military action immediately, which, in my opinion, would help definitely to tide Russia at any rate over this serious crisis.

B Eden to Cripps, 1 November 1941

For your information following is summary of note by Mr. Harriman of conversations between him, Lord Beaverbrook and Stalin during the Moscow Conference.

There was considerable discussion regarding military co-operation with Russia. Lord Beaverbrook offered strategic discussions with General Ismay during the conference and invited the Russians to send a mission to England to consider the British problem and to give advice on what might be done and, in addition, information as to what had been learnt by the Russians in their recent battles with the Germans. Lord Beaverbrook indicated that His Majesty's Government were building up divisions in Persia which might be joined up with Russian forces in the Caucasus, and that General Wavell was proceeding to Tiflis for conversation on these lines. Stalin's comment on this was that there was no war in the Caucasus but that there was one in the Ukraine. Lord Beaverbrook indicated that this question might also be taken up. Lord Beaverbrook asked Stalin if he thought the British could invade France, to which Stalin replied that he did not know enough about the situation, but had confidence in the Prime Minister's judgement. He enquired, however, why a force could not be sent to Archangel or the Ukraine.

C Cripps to Eden, 5 November 1941

I am amazed that these most important conversations should be now reported to me for the first time and that apparently little notice has been taken of them by anyone at all...

The failure to inform me of these conversations is all the more unfortunate in that, if they were accurately reported, they must obviously modify some of the views which I have expressed about the general trend of opinion of the Soviet Government...

It must be remembered that Molotov was present at all these discussions, but that at Beaverbrook's request, and since the conversations were only to concern the matters which he came out to discuss – which I understood to be questions of supply – I was not present. This has, of course, put me in an entirely false position as regards Molotov and probably explains a phrase which he used to me the other day and to which I did not then attach any significance. When I was pointing out that I had urged upon His Majesty's Government a certain course of action, he remarked that he was afraid that I had no power of persuading them. This is probably due to his quite natural view that I am now excluded by His Majesty's Government from political discussions about the U.S.S.R. and therefore have no influence when advising them on policy.

In these circumstances I can see no use in my remaining here to act as an occasional post-box (for messages to Stalin about the formulation of which I am not consulted and which I am not instructed to discuss with him) unless I can do something to contribute to winning of the war or assisting in the post-war settlement...

It would of course be necessary for His Majesty's Government to have some general idea as to the way in which the post-war situation was to be tackled if we are to arrive at an agreement with these people to work with them after the war. The first and fundamental thing to decide is that we are prepared to continue collaboration with them after the war is over for the purpose of working out terms of the new settlement of Europe.

If you agree to this, then we should be ready to discuss at once the basis for a treaty with them to that effect.

Basis should be that Great Britain, United States and U.S.S.R. will subsequently, and before the peace conference, negotiate an agreement covering broad lines of a European settlement, and that we undertake to enter consultations with the Soviet Government in this matter at an early date . . .

I am most anxious that the unfortunate circumstances described earlier in this telegram should somehow or other be made to yield good results rather than bad. I am unconcerned with the personal side of the matter, provided that I can do something useful now; but otherwise you will appreciate that my position has been such that it would be much better for you to send someone else here.

I have therefore come to quite definite conclusion that, unless I can now be of some use in negotiations of the sort described above, you will be better served by someone else in this post. If I find in the course of such negotiations that my position has been rendered such as to make me an unsuitable person to conduct them, I should, of course, let you know at once . . .

D Eden to Cripps, 10 November 1941

I much regret that you should feel that you have been put in a false position by not having been informed earlier of the political discussions between Lord Beaverbrook and Stalin.

Maybe we have now given you a false impression of their importance by extracting every item of diplomatic consequence out of conversations of fifteen hours on supply. Beaverbrook is quite sure that Stalin did not attach importance you attribute to these exchanges, and he knows that Harriman shares his view. Beaverbrook throughout made it plain that his mission was not politics but supply, and asks me to assure you that there were no serious diplomatic talks at all. I am sorry that it was not possible to make all this plain to you before the mission left Moscow, but you will be the first to make allowances for the high pressure under which the work of the mission was put through . . .

. . . I agree that we ought to begin examining the question of our post-war relations with the Soviet Government as far as it is possible to do so at the present stage of the war. We certainly are prepared, as suggested in your paragraph 15, to continue collaboration with the Soviet Government after the war is over for the purpose of working out the terms of the new settlement of Europe. I am, however, at present in some difficulty because I have not received any explanation from Stalin as to what he himself had in mind when he proposed a post-war alliance . . . This is understandable enough in present conditions when no doubt he has infinitely more urgent matters with which to deal. The important thing is surely that the Russians should know that we are prepared to carry forward our collaboration with them into the peace and beyond. This has been explained to M. Maisky and I shall be grateful if you will emphasise our general attitude in this respect to Stalin or Molotov at any convenient opportunity. When, however, we come to consider methods, the time is surely not yet ripe for us to commit ourselves to the undertaking to enter into early consultations with a view to an agreement covering the broad lines of a European settlement ... But even if we cannot embark straight away on detailed negotiations, I hope that, as the war situation improves and develops, we shall find more frequent opportunity of discussing with the Soviet Government plans for future collaboration not only during the war but also at the peace settlement. This gradual and tentative procedure, I think, will prove both safer and more profitable than if we were to attempt prematurely to define our collaboration in treaty form. In a treaty we should both have to introduce so many provisos and conditions to safeguard our position in the unforeseeable future that the result might well be to arouse suspicions and misgivings on both sides which might injure rather than improve relations between our two countries. But even if we do not embark upon definite negotiations straight away, I am convinced that your services in Russia as His Majesty's Ambassador will be of the greatest value in preparing the ground so that these negotiations can be undertaken with every prospect of success at the appropriate moment ...

E Cripps to Eden, 15 November 1941

As I have more than once pointed out, there is a long and unfortunate history of bad relationship between the two countries leading up to the present time. This, added to the Russian Georgian suspicion of Western European countries, does, in fact, predispose Stalin (and Molotov) to be excessively suspicious of our motives. In result all we do and say is most easily misconstrued. This is a basic fact and it cannot be disregarded or brushed aside.

Stalin is not convinced that we are in this war with the Russians wholeheartedly and without reservations. He has his own ideas as to tests which will convince him one way or the other or will predispose him to such ultimate conviction. These he has stated as his two conditions with complete frankness in his last message. Form of the statement is typically Stalinesque, and he is unlikely to change that manner of stating his views.

In spite of frequent warning, His Majesty's Government have so far appeared to overlook the fundamental importance of the issues, which Stalin regards as touchstones of their sincerity in all-in collaboration not only during the war when the Russian army is clearly an asset of inestimable value to us, but after the war, when our sympathetic collaboration with Russia may be thought by some to be more advantageous to the Soviet Government than to us.

The longer this state of uncertainty continues in his mind, the more will Stalin be ready to believe – and I do not doubt some of those around him (including possibly Molotov) will emphasise the point to him – that we are not prepared to go in whole-heartedly with Russia on his terms, but that our only object is to keep her fighting the Germans as long as we can ...

F Cripps to Eden, 15 November 1941

... If we regard it as important to get a better degree of collaboration, as I do myself, then I think we must make up our minds to (a) treat the Russians as in every way an equal and as important as Greece or Turkey from the point of view of discussion and the personnel we send to conduct the discussions. On this latter point they are, as I am sure you fully realise, extremely sensitive. (b) Discuss with them the question of post-war collaboration. I understand that we are prepared to undertake such collaboration. (c) Enter into staff collaboration to plan mutually the future conduct of the war on the basis of a really frank and comprehensive basis...

4   Minute by A. R. Dew on policy towards the Soviet Union, 21 November 1941

In his message to the Prime Minister dated November 8th Stalin said that the existing lack of clarity in the relations between the U.S.S.R. and Great Britain was due to two circumstances:

a that there was no definite understanding between our two countries on war aims and on plans for the post-war organisation of peace;
b that there was no agreement between the U.S.S.R. and Great Britain on mutual military assistance against Hitler in Europe.

The purpose of this paper is to discuss what progress can be made as regards (a). It will embody the results of a discussion, held in Sir A. Cadogan's room on November 18th at which were present, in addition to Sir A. Cadogan, Mr. Law, Sir O. Sargent, Mr. Strang, Mr. Harvey and Mr. Ronald.

In the first place, it is probable that Stalin's desire to secure a definite understanding on war aims and on plans for the post-war organisation of peace arises out of a suspicion that it is the desire of H. M. Government to see Russia weakened by the struggle with Germany and at the conclusion of the War to make an Anglo-American peace from which Russia will be largely excluded. (It was no doubt Stalin's hope to see Germany and Great Britain fight each other to a standstill with the result that Russia would play a predominant role in the peace.) Other causes of suspicion and mistrust of our intentions are listed in Sir S. Cripps' telegram No. 109 of November 15th. It will be recollected also that in his conversation with the Secretary of State on November 12th M. Maisky mentioned the suspicion that prevailed in Russia that there were many people in this country who advocated allowing Germany a free hand in the East and added that as we did not form a second front these suspicions had, to a certain extent, been revived . . .

In point (a) of his message to the Prime Minister on November 8th Stalin does not specifically mention his desire for the conclusion of a treaty or further written agreement, but it will be recollected that in Mr. Harriman's account of Lord Beaverbrook's conversation with Stalin on September 30th, it is said that 'Stalin asked Beaverbrook if the present military alliance and agreement for no separate peace should not be extended to a treaty, an alliance not only for war but for post-war as well. Beaverbrook answered that he personally favoured it and believed it was an opportune time to take it up. Stalin remarked that all the Soviet Government officials favoured the proposal.' We must therefore be prepared for Stalin to interpret the phrase 'definite agreement' as a suggestion for a treaty or, at any rate, a bilateral declaration . . .

Two problems have now to be considered:

i What are Russian ideas on war aims and the post-war settlement and what
   kind of an agreement to be concluded at this stage will satisfy them?
ii How far are we prepared to go?

As regards (i), the Russians have been extremely reticent in defining their ideas on war aims and the post-war settlement. When M. Maisky, in conversation with the Secretary of State on August 25th last, said that the Soviet Government felt that they might have been consulted about the Atlantic Charter Declaration, he said that it was not that they had any objection to the individual principles enunciated in the declaration, 'though they would have liked to alter the phrasing of some and to stiffen the phrasing of others'. These remarks must be remembered when we read the declaration made by M. Maisky at the Inter-Allied Conference at St. James's Palace in September last . . . In that declaration, M. Maisky, after enunciating at some length the principles which guided Soviet foreign policy, said that the Soviet Government proclaimed its agreement with the fundamental principles of the Atlantic Charter. He added that 'considering that the practical application of these principles will necessarily adapt itself to the circumstances, needs and historical peculiarities of particular countries, the Soviet Government can state that a consistent application of these principles would secure their most energetic support'. Finally, M. Maisky's declaration said 'attributing great importance to the equitable use of all material resources and food stuffs in the post-war period, the Soviet Government believes that the most imperative and most pressing task of to-day is the correct allocation of all the economic resources and war supplies with a view to an early liberation of all the European peoples now oppressed by Hitlerite slavery' . . .

It can be expected, however, that Russian objectives in any post-war settlement, and thus of their war aims, may be to ensure access to warm water ports, which is an old Russian ambition, and some scheme which will ensure the preservation of Russian interests in the Baltic and Black Seas. We may thus expect demands for Russian access to the Persian Gulf, for a revision of the Montreux Convention, possibly for the establishment of Russian bases in Norway and in Finland and the Baltic States to ensure the security of Leningrad and Kronstadt. Such demands might, however, be revised if an efficient scheme for disarmament and an international police force can be devised. The chief aim of Russian policy is security and if the threat to her from any European or Asiatic Power can be conjured by some international scheme, then Russia would not necessarily have to adopt the policy which led to the partition of Poland, the absorption of the Baltic States and the establishment of Russian bases in Finland.

It remains to consider how far we are prepared to go in discussing war aims and plans for the post-war organisation of peace and what sort of an agreement we are prepared to sign with the Russians at this stage.

The difficulty here arises that we have not made up our own minds on the questions of the economic and political post-war settlement and that we are definitely committed to the Americans not to undertake during the war commitments which would bind us at the peace and after. We are therefore at a serious disadvantage. At the same time we do not know whether the Russians, for their part, have made up their minds on these matters. It may be possible to confine any agreement with the Russians to some declaration reaffirming the intention of Great Britain and the Soviet Union to continue the war until the defeat of Germany and stating that the two countries are resolved to co-operate in making the peace settlement and to co-operate thereafter in maintaining that settlement. If the Russians press for more detailed definition of war aims and plans for the post-war settlement, it would be for them to define their ideas on the subject for our consideration and that of the Americans. At the same time it might be made clear to the Russians that they would be treated on a basis of equality in these matters with ourselves and the Americans and that in fact the peace settlement would be largely dictated by these three Powers, who would now begin to study among themselves the solution of these problems. Bringing in Russia in this way might in fact serve to help us in our dealings with the Americans on these matters . . .

5   Eden's visit to Moscow, December 1941

A Eden's summary of the talks, 5 January 1942

At my first conversation with M. Stalin and M. Molotov on the 16th December . . . M. Stalin set out in some detail what he considered should be the post-war territorial frontiers in Europe, and in particular his ideas regarding the treatment of Germany. He proposed the restoration of Austria as an independent State, the detachment of the Rhineland from Prussia as an independent State or a protectorate, and possibly the constitution of an independent State of Bavaria. He also proposed that East Prussia should be transferred to Poland and the Sudetenland returned to Czechoslovakia. He suggested that Yugoslavia should be restored and even receive certain additional territories from Italy, that Albania should be reconstituted as an independent State, and that Turkey should receive the Dodecanese, with possible adjustments in favour of Greece as regards islands in the Aegean important to Greece. Turkey might also receive certain districts in Bulgaria, and possibly also in Northern Syria. In general the occupied countries, including Czechoslovakia and Greece, should be restored to their pre-war frontiers, and M. Stalin was prepared to support any special arrangements for securing bases, etc. for the United Kingdom in Western European countries, e.g., France, Belgium, the Netherlands, Norway and Denmark. As regards the special interests of the Soviet Union, M. Stalin desired the restoration of the position in 1941, prior to the German attack, in respect of the Baltic States, Finland and Bessarabia. The 'Curzon Line' should form the basis for the future Soviet–Polish frontier, and Roumania should give special facilities for bases, etc., to the Soviet Union, receiving compensation from territory now occupied by Hungary.

In the course of this first conversation, M. Stalin generally agreed with the principle of restitution in kind by Germany to the occupied countries, more particularly in regard to machine tools, etc., and ruled out money reparations as undesirable. He showed interest in a post-war military alliance between the 'democratic countries' and stated that the Soviet Union had no objection to certain countries of Europe entering into a federal relationship, if they so desired.

In the second conversation on the 17th December . . . M. Stalin pressed for the immediate recognition by His Majesty's Government of the future frontiers of the U.S.S.R. more particularly in regard to the inclusion within the U.S.S.R. of the Baltic States and the restoration of the 1941 Finnish–Soviet frontier. He made the conclusion of an Anglo-Soviet Agreement dependent on agreement on this point. I, for my part, explained to M. Stalin that in view of our prior undertakings to the United States Government it was quite impossible for His Majesty's Government to commit themselves at this stage to any post-war frontiers in Europe, although I undertook to consult His Majesty's Government in the United Kingdom, the United States Government and His Majesty's Governments in the Dominions on my return. This question, to which M. Stalin attached fundamental importance, was further discussed at the third meeting on the 18th December . . .

At the fourth meeting, on the 20th December . . . M. Stalin agreed to my proposal that I should consult His Majesty's Government in the United Kingdom, the Dominion Governments and the United States Government on my return to the United Kingdom. He suggested that, meanwhile, the signature of any Anglo-Soviet agreements should be postponed with a view to 'signing a proper treaty, or two treaties', after I had been able to consult the 'Governments concerned . . . within the next two or three weeks'. M. Stalin said that he was sure that, whether the treaties were signed or not, Anglo-Soviet relations would improve with the progress of the war, which 'compelled many countries to discard their prejudices and preconceived views'. He did not think that 'failure to sign the treaties now (i.e. during my Moscow visit) should be regarded in too tragic a light. If the treaties were signed in London in two or three weeks' time it would come to much the same thing. Our relations would meanwhile be based on the July Agreement, and they would become closer.' At this meeting M. Stalin communicated the text of the draft communique which was eventually issued at midnight of the 28th/29th December. After this meeting M. Stalin was my host at a banquet attended by most of the leading political and military figures in the U.S.S.R. which lasted until 5 a.m. and was marked by the greatest cordiality . . .

M. Stalin expressed himself as satisfied with the course of developments in Persia, and agreed that it was in our joint interest that Turkey should remain outside the war as a buffer against further German penetration eastwards. He even advocated territorial offers to Turkey with a view to strengthening the determination of the Turkish Government to continue their present policy.

B Soviet drafts of proposed military and political treaties, 16 December 1941

Military treaty

Article 1
An Alliance is formed between the Soviet Union and Great Britain, and both the allied Powers mutually undertake to afford one another military assistance and support of all kinds in the war against Hitlerite Germany and against those who take part in Hitlerite aggression in Europe.

Article 2
Both Parties undertake not to enter into negotiations with the Hitlerite
Government of Germany or with any other German Government representing
the Nazi Imperialist regime, and not to conclude an armistice or a peace treaty
with Germany except by mutual consent.

Article 3
Both Contracting Parties undertake not to conclude any alliances and not to
take part in coalitions directed against one of the Contracting Parties.

Article 4
The present Treaty enters into force immediately after its signature, and is
subject to ratification at the earliest possible date.
    The exchange of the instruments of ratification shall take place in London.

Political treaty

Article 1
Both Parties mutually undertake that, in the solution of post-war questions
connected with the organisation of the cause of peace and security in Europe,
they will act by mutual agreement.

Article 2
Both Parties are agreed that upon the termination of the war they will take
all steps to render impossible a repetition of aggression and violation of the
peace by Germany.

Article 3
The present Treaty enters into force immediately after its signature, and is
subject to ratification at the earliest possible date.
    The exchange of the instruments of ratification shall take place in London.

C Eden's counter-proposal for an agreement, as finally amended, and proposed covering letter of intent

His Majesty's Government in the United Kingdom and the Government of the Union of Soviet Socialist Republics have concluded the following
Agreement:

Article 1
The two Contracting Parties undertake to consult together regarding the
terms of the peace settlement, including frontier questions. They will also

collaborate in the settlement of post-war questions connected with the organisation of peace and security in Europe.

Article 2
The two Contracting Parties jointly affirm their acceptance of the principles of the declaration made on the 14th August, 1941, by the President of the United States and the Prime Minister of the United Kingdom.

Article 3
The two Contracting Parties agree that after the termination of hostilities they will take all measures in their power to render impossible a repetition of aggression and violation of the peace by Germany.

Article 4
The two Contracting Parties undertake to work together for the reconstruction of Europe after the war with full regard to each other's interests.
   The objectives of this task of reconstruction will include in particular:

a The safeguarding and strengthening of the economic and political independence of all European countries either as unitary or federated States.
b The reconstruction of the industrial and economic life of those countries whose territories have been overrun by Germany or her associates.

Article 5
The two Contracting Parties agree to render one another all possible economic assistance after the war.
   My understanding is that, by the signature of the two agreements completed today, there now exists between the Government of the U.S.S.R. and His Majesty's Government a relationship similar to that created by the Atlantic Charter between His Majesty's Government and the United States Government.
   These three documents, in effect, establish the principle that His Majesty's Government will work together with your Government and the United States Government in every way, during and after the war.

D Extracts from Eden–Stalin meeting of 18 December 1941

   ... EDEN: I see that you do not like my Article 4 together with the letter as much as your own redraft of that article. My difficulty about your draft is that I am not clear what it really means. In my letter I say that we had the principles laid down in the Charter and will discuss between the three Governments the actual frontiers proposed. Your draft of Clause 4 either has no definite meaning or else it means that we bind ourselves to agree to your frontiers as they were in 1941, and that is the proposition that we have already discussed at such length. I would like to have Article 4 in the form that I have submitted together with the letter which I propose.

STALIN: That is difficult to accept.

EDEN: I do not want to be anything but completely honest and open with you. I do not want to cover up what is really a difference of opinion by words which may be misunderstood, and I do not really know what your new Article 4 is intended to cover.

STALIN: In the new clause I have first of all added the word 'Security'.

EDEN: I do not take any objection to that. That is quite all right.

STALIN: We have already discussed the necessity for the second alteration, that in Article 4. We have spoken of the possibility, for instance, of the increase of the territory of Yugoslavia, and it seemed that you were not necessarily against that. We also discussed the incorporation of East Prussia in Poland and the giving of certain islands to Greece and Turkey. And to none of these did you object. In fact, you accepted the necessity for increasing the territories of these countries. All we ask for is to restore our country to its former frontiers. We must have these for our security and safety; for instance, at Leningrad. I want to emphasise the point that, if you decline to do this, it looks as if you were creating a possibility for a dismemberment of the Soviet Union.

EDEN: That is not in the least the case. If you were to ask me now to give my signature for definite frontiers for any country, say, Greece or Yugoslavia, or even Great Britain itself, I should have to refuse in exactly the same way. I think you have probably a strong case on the ground of security, and I shall be glad to put it forward, as I said that I would do. But what I cannot do now is to put these definite frontiers into an agreement . . .

EDEN: How could I explain this clause to the Poles? They would inevitably read it as meaning that we had agreed that the U.S.S.R. should go back to the frontiers which they held immediately before the outbreak of their war with Germany.

CRIPPS: Could we know whether the phrase 'having full regard to the interests of the U.S.S.R. in the restoration of its frontiers', means the recognition by us of the U.S.S.R. frontiers of 1941?

STALIN: Yes, it does mean the recognition of the right of the U.S.S.R. to their 1941 frontiers.

EDEN: The Poles pressed me very hard at the time of their agreement with the Soviet Union to agree with them upon their Eastern frontier, but I refused. If I now agree to this Article I should, in fact, be agreeing to the Polish frontier as it was in 1941.

STALIN: This does not entail an agreement on the Polish frontier. This does not affect it and I would give a letter to make that quite clear.

EDEN: Yes, but that is how it will be read throughout the world.

STALIN: So far as the effect on public opinion is concerned, everyone would ask the question whether Hitler was right in violating our frontiers when he started the war. The British Government is apparently hesitating about this, but I have no doubts about it, nor would the public.

EDEN: I have no doubt about it either, but this agreement is an agreement upon the principles on which we would work together for peace now and after the war, and what you are now trying to do is to put into it a decision as to a particular portion of the frontiers of Europe.

STALIN: After I observed last night such an uncertain attitude on the part of the British Government as regards the situation in the Baltic States I felt bound to introduce such a clause into the agreement.

MOLOTOV: We are going to sign a treaty of mutual assistance or alliance and we must know what we are fighting for and where we stand.

EDEN: We are fighting to beat Hitler. Quite apart from the question of my right to make this agreement, if I signed it I should have any number of questions put to me as to its effect upon Poland, etc., and what was its exact meaning, and I could not, of course, disclose your private letter, but if you wanted me to put into my letter an acknowledgement of your views, I would certainly be prepared to do that.

STALIN: My letter as to the exclusion of the Polish frontiers would be sent to General Sikorski, too, and I should be prepared to have it published as well. My formula must stand.

EDEN: I am afraid I cannot possibly accept it.

STALIN: That is very regrettable.

EDEN: I have tried very hard to meet you on this and I am prepared to do anything except to agree to definite frontiers, and I cannot do that without breaking pledges I have already made to other people, and I am not going to break pledges.

6 Orme Sargent's memorandum of 5 February 1942 on the possible development of the Russo-German war

... There are in particular two contingencies which cannot be ruled out and which for us would be very disconcerting.

If the Soviet Govt. found the going easy and political conditions favourable they might very well combine their military operations against German territory with a political offensive and set about to create a series of autonomous Soviet Socialist Republics in different parts of Germany. The Soviet

Govt. would thus conveniently achieve not only its ideological objective but also give practical effect to Stalin's avowed policy of 'breaking up' Germany.

Or else a military deadlock might ensue and give rise to pourparlers for a separate peace. If the German people and army had no longer the strength or cohesion to launch a counter-offensive, and if Stalin found that the will to fight of the Russian soldier was flagging once the enemy had been driven out of Russia, and if the difficulties of transport and supplies had, with the ever-lengthening lines of communication, become too great, then he might decide that it would be good tactics to make such a peace, if only in order to give time to reorganise his resources and rest his troops. Both dictators would realise that it would be only a truce until one or other was ready to renew the struggle. But Stalin on his side might well argue that he stood to gain most by such a truce, since Russia would as long as it lasted, be left at peace to lick her wounds, whereas Germany would continue to be harassed by Great Britain and the U.S.A. In fact, such a truce would create for the Soviet Govt. the situation for which Stalin had always hoped and which the course of the war has hitherto denied to him, namely, that Germany and the Western Democracies should exhaust themselves in an inconclusive struggle to the ultimate benefit of the Soviet Government.

We may comfort ourselves that it is most unlikely that the conditions conducive to such action by the Soviet Govt. will occur, and that if they did occur Stalin would not necessarily adopt the courses foreshadowed. It is indeed fortunate that this is so, for the termination of the war in Europe after this fashion could not but be highly detrimental to our interests. It would mean in effect that the peace as far as the European continent was concerned, would be made by the Soviet Union alone and uncontrolled. How far we and the U.S. Govt. would be allowed to participate would depend on three factors: (1) the amount of mutual confidence and good will with which we had beforehand been able to surround our relations with the Soviet Govt.; (2) the extent to which the Soviet Govt. would have to rely on Gt. Britain and the U.S.A. for the means to restore her economy and make good the havoc of the war; (3) the presence on the continent of Europe of British and U.S. forces. (The fact that we can withhold supplies to the Soviet Govt. might serve as a lever in certain circumstances for bringing pressure to bear on the Soviet Govt., but in the cases which we are now considering it would be of little or no avail.)

It is hardly possible to suppose that British or U.S. troops could appear in Europe in time and in sufficient force to affect Soviet actions and policy if matters were to move as fast as we are now supposing. We would have, therefore, to make shift as best we could with the two other and lesser instruments of policy at our disposal.

It is by no means clear how far we should in practice be able to withhold economic and financial assistance after the war from the Soviet Union without at the same time damaging our own interests, and how far the Soviet Govt. would be intimidated by such a threat on our part. A whole series of technical questions is involved as well as various politico-economic issues. It would be useful to have these examined so that we may know what value to set on this instrument of policy and in what circumstances, if any, we should be able to use it to good effect . . .

. . . we ought clearly to begin at once to seek all the means open to us of improving our relations with the Soviet Govt. while the conditions are still easy, so that if the moment of strain were to come we should at any rate start with Anglo-Soviet relations in a healthy state, unencumbered as far as possible by misunderstandings and suspicions on major issues of policy.

By this it is not meant that we should try to propitiate Stalin by one-sided sacrifices and surrenders. But it does mean that we should try to create a sound basis for our future relations, which would be honourable and beneficial to both parties, by negotiating a Treaty of Alliance to cover not only the war but the peacemaking and the post-war reconstruction of Europe. To achieve such a treaty it is obvious that we shall have to make concessions not only on the Baltic issue but probably in other matters. But if we want to prepare our relations with the Soviet Govt. against the more difficult period ahead of us, such concessions will be well worth while, so long as they are balanced by corresponding concessions on the part of Stalin and thus form a sound foundation on which to build up a system of Anglo-Russian co-operation.

Cadogan minute of 7 February

. . . If the Russians have not made any decisive advance beyond where they are now, they might hold the Germans there. If, on the other hand, they had reached more or less the 1940 western frontier . . . I should be very much afraid of being double-crossed by Stalin. *That I regard as the great danger.* So that one ought to hope for continued pressure by the Soviet, with erosion of further manpower and material and not *too* great a geographical advance! . . .

Eden minute of 8 February

This is a most useful paper. I have had something of this sort in mind. Personally I think it unlikely that the Russians will get further in the next few months than they have in the last. The further they advance the greater their difficulties. The rate will have to be increased if Germany is to be prevented from launching a counter-offensive. But it remains broadly true that a German collapse this year will be an exclusively Soviet victory with all that implies. Therefore clearly we must do all in our power to lessen grievances and come to terms with him for the future. This may not prevent him from double-crossing us, but it will at least lessen pretexts. He has them now.

7   Discussions on how to handle the Russians, February 1942

A Baggallay's telegrams of 12 and 13 February

Telegram, 12 February

... 3 Soviet Government are only interested in us as allies to the extent to which they think our activities will assist:

a their own victory in the war
b their own security after the war.

4 As regards (a) they are disappointed as we have not been able to send forces to the Eastern Front or achieve success elsewhere. Our material aid is important but not decisive. They accept the explanations politely, but they are not interested in the reasons or motives. We move up and down their chart by results alone and at present we are not very high.

5 As regards (b) they are suspicious. They await our decision about their territorial claims aiming at military security. If we do not accept them they may be confirmed in their belief in our utterly innate ill-will, but they will not necessarily become more difficult to deal with perhaps the contrary. Meanwhile our day to day political relations are reasonably cordial over secondary matters ...

7 For the rest – the Soviet Government are supremely self-centred and so long as they get all they want or all we can give (I do not mean only 'give' material things but collaboration in every field) will give not more than they have to in return. They are no different in this from other people but they are more thorough and consistent in their egotism and they do not realise that generosity is sometimes the best policy.

Telegram, 13 February

Our own technique though possibly not our basic motive is very different. So far as I know we do everything possible to meet requests of Soviet representatives in the United Kingdom and to interest British public in comments on the war effort of the workers, at the same time we applaud without stint the unquestionably magnificent performances of the Soviet forces and try to show some appreciation when others applaud us: finally press and public are free to criticise any failure, real or apparent, to support Soviet Government.

2 In the ordinary way, I believe this technique to be in our own best interests. It is imperative that the eastern front should hold and that we should make every effort in our power to help it hold and in the long run our technique conduces to this main object better than others to which we are less accustomed.

3 But this means in effect that the Soviet Government get all they want (or can) unconditionally and so long as they do this they will not trouble to fulfil their obligations to ourselves even in small matters which mean little to them and a great deal to us . . .

B Warner minutes of 16 February

i The analysis of the Soviet attitude to our assistance and collaboration, contained in Mr. Baggallay's telegram No. 186, is very interesting and I am convinced correct . . .

Mr. Baggallay's telegrams raise the extremely interesting and important question of the general tactics for handling matters, both big and small, with the Russians. I have felt for some time that we have not got this right and that we should attempt to reach an agreed doctrine, which would be applied by all Departments and Missions who deal direct with the Russians. But this is a big question and I am submitting a separate minute upon it . . .

ii I have felt for some time past that it is important that we should make up our minds what is the right course of tactics for dealing with the Russians and should get the method adopted by all the British Departments, Missions etc. which have direct dealings with them. It would be excellent if we could take the opportunity of the present telegrams to achieve this. For I have felt more than a suspicion that our tactics, in so far as they have been consistent at all, have been wrong, and have not only failed to achieve the results we want in specific cases, but (which is obviously of great importance) have given the Russians a completely wrong impression of ourselves.

2 What I take it Mr. Baggallay is advocating is a less sentimental approach, a more matter of fact and businesslike one. By this, I think, he means that we should moderate our adulation of the Russian effort, not offer them assistance that they have not asked for, examine any requests for assistance and give a straight answer based on reasonable and fully explained grounds; and occasionally, when we have reason to feel that we are not getting a satisfactory deal from them, show our displeasure not by complaints or threats or (I think Mr. Baggallay would add) attempts to drive bargains, but merely by not responding on some Russian desideratum, without talking or making a fuss about it.

3 This seems, from all I can learn from those who know the Russians well, extremely good counsel. Mr. Baggallay does not make the point, but it is made by many who know the Russians, that the Russians resent being singled

out for special methods of treatment as if they were something peculiar. [Here Eden minuted: 'I agree'.] They would wish to be treated in a normal way and not cajoled nor treated to fine complimentary phrases, but taken into our full confidence, and told what we can do and what we cannot do on a reasonable and collaborative basis of examination. (The fact that they are peculiar does not alter the force of the argument that they should not be openly treated as though they were.)

4 There would, however, be a corollary to the adoption of what I may call the 'normal, businesslike' method of treating the Russians, viz. that we should also be careful not to treat them as in a 'peculiar' category of allies, with whom we only take contact on day-to-day matters of direct and immediate mutual concern, but who are not consulted on matters concerning the wider conduct of the war and the peace. I am perfectly aware that this would be a counsel of perfection and that in practice consultation with the Russians on many of these wider matters would be difficult, if not impossible. [Here Cadogan minuted: 'It is they who make it so'.] At the same time we should, I think, do our best to overcome the difficulties, or at least minimise the bad effect, of not consulting the Russians by keeping them informed and explaining why they were not consulted. Take, for instance, the setting up of the Anglo-American supply and production machinery. I have little doubt that the Russians are aggrieved at the whole matter being dealt with purely as an Anglo-American concern (although they have given no overt indication) and have noted it as further evidence that we think of this war as primarily an Anglo-American concern leading up to an Anglo-American peace. I think there are excellent reasons against bringing the Russians in; but we should, I believe, always consider how we can minimise the effect upon the Russians of leaving them out of such matters, e.g. by informing them immediately of what has been done and why it has been done in that way . . .

Comments on Warner's second minute

Bruce Lockhart, 20 February

I agree with Mr. Warner's minute and should like to emphasise the importance of paragraphs four and five.

Suspicion has always been deep-rooted in the Russian mind. It is partly a social characteristic and partly the inevitable consequence of centuries of despotism. Even in the full flush of 'westernisation' there was always a xenophobe party in Russia. The Western lamp was extinguished in 1918, since then xenophobia has developed in a remarkable degree.

As far as the present rulers of Russia are concerned, their suspicion of all foreigners has been embittered by harsh memories of the humiliations suffered during the last twenty-four years. In my own dealings with the Bolsheviks I always found that if they were treated normally they made at least some attempt to behave as normal human beings. If they were treated as criminals, they behaved worse than bandits. I believe that this is axiomatic to-day.

The proper course to adopt towards the Russians is one of polite but firm directness. Any attempt to engage in a duel of dialectics is certain to lead to failure. To carry the matter into the realm of policy, I should like to see us come to some arrangement with the Russians now. 'Stalling' will merely augment their suspicions and provoke at a later date greater and more embarrassing demands. We must also realise that, even if Mr. Warner's suggestions are adopted, we cannot expect quick results but will have to show considerable patience.

Strang, 20 February

I am sure that Mr. Baggallay's telegrams and Mr. Warner's minute are on the right lines.

It is essential to treat the Russians as though we thought that they were reasonable human beings. But as they are not, in fact, reasonable human beings, but dominated by an almost insane suspicion, we have to combine this treatment with infinite patience. The things to avoid are:

1 any indication that we distrust them;
2 threats;
3 flattery, adulation and the sentimental approach.

They are pursuing their own interests and they expect us to pursue ours. The more successful we are in our part of the war, the more they will respect us: even if we are not successful they will still respect us if we put up a good fight. What they have come to doubt (in spite of the exploits of the Air Force and the fortitude of the civil population in 1940) is our will and power to fight. This, with the rather hysterical magnification of their successes by our press and public, has aroused in them something akin to contempt. [Here Eden minuted: 'I agree. This is good sense'.] They, like the Germans, regard the Western Powers as soft and decadent. We have not yet convinced them, so far as we are concerned, that this is not true ...

Orme Sargent, 28 February

Mr. Warner has called attention to a very important matter which certainly deserves further investigation. I doubt whether we shall even be able to reach a final agreed doctrine as to how to deal with the Russians, but we may at any rate be able to lay down certain rules as to how not to treat them. For instance I feel certain that we are too prone to think that if we have nothing tangible to offer the Soviet Government we can make up for the deficiency by frequent administrations of flattery and congratulations in the form of messages and telegrams. I have no doubt that this treatment has its uses when applied in addition to definite actions on our part, but taken in isolation this sort of treatment is merely a minor form of appeasement and is open to the same objections and dangers which are the inevitable consequences of appeasement, whatever form it may take . . .

Cadogan, 28 February

One point seems to me to have been rather overlooked by the minute-writers. They write as if we had made no attempt to consult with the Russians or treat them as normal allies. But we *have* done so, again and again. However, I am all for patience, if a bit short of that quality myself.

The other difficulty – of proving to the Russians our toughness and ability to wage war – is not one that the F.O. can help to overcome. We can only hope that in the fullness of time proof will be forthcoming.

But by all means let the Dept. put up a draft . . .

Eden, 1 March

I agree.

Let us see a draft. Meanwhile I will try to live up to Mr. Warner's maxims as Chairman of Allied Supplies Executive. I should find my task easier, if we could occasionally have a military success, but this is to ask much – in the next few months.

Warner, undated hand-written minute

It was later decided not to proceed with this.

8   Eden to Clark Kerr, 13 April and 1 May 1942. British and Soviet drafts of proposed political and military treaties

A British drafts with commentary

Political treaty

Article 1

. . . The High Contracting Parties jointly affirm their acceptance of the purposes and principles of the Declaration made on the 14th August, 1941, by the President of the United States of America and the Prime Minister of the United Kingdom of Great Britain and Northern Ireland.

The High Contracting Parties undertake that, in the settlement of post-war questions connected with the organisation of peace and security in Europe, they will act by mutual agreement and in concert with the other States concerned.

Article 2
The High Contracting Parties agree that after the termination of hostilities they will take all the measures in their power to render impossible a repetition of aggression and violation of the peace by Germany or the Powers associated with her acts of aggression in Europe.

Article 3
The High Contracting Parties undertake to work for the reconstruction of Europe after the war in accordance with the two principles of not seeking territorial aggrandisement for themselves and of non-interference in the internal affairs of European peoples. In so doing, they will take account of the interests of both parties in their security, and will have full regard to the desire of the Union of Soviet Socialist Republics for the restoration of its frontiers violated by the Hitlerite aggression and of the Government of the United Kingdom for the recovery of British territory occupied by enemy forces.

It is understood that the reference to the frontiers of the Union of Soviet Socialist Republics in the first paragraph of the present article does not affect the frontier with Poland. The position of the two High Contracting Parties in this regard remains as stated respectively in the agreement between the Government of the U.S.S.R. and the Polish Government signed on the 30th July, 1941, and in the communication made by His Majesty's Government in the United Kingdom to the Polish Government on the same date.

Article 4
In the case of European territories which now are or in consequence of the peace settlement may be placed under a sovereignty other than that under which they were on the 1st January, 1938, the High Contracting Parties recognise the desirability of making appropriate provision in the peace settlement to ensure to inhabitants of such territories who may wish to do so the right to leave such territories without hindrance and to carry their movable property with them.

Article 5
The objectives of the High Contracting Parties in the work of reconstruction include in particular:

a The encouragement of regional understandings and confederations among States in Central, Eastern and South-Eastern Europe where such understandings or confederations are desirable in order to safeguard and strengthen the political, military and economic security of such States;

b Full collaboration in inter-Allied plans of assistance in rebuilding the economic life of the Allied territories overrun by enemy forces.

Article 6

Each High Contracting Party undertakes not to conclude any alliance and not to take part in any coalition directed against the other High Contracting Party.

Article 7

The High Contracting Parties agree to render one another all possible economic assistance after the war.

Article 8

The present Treaty shall be ratified and the ratifications shall be exchanged in London as soon as possible.

It shall come into force on the exchange of ratifications and shall remain in force for a period of years.

Thereafter, unless twelve months' notice has been given by either Party to terminate the Treaty at the end of the said period of years, it shall continue in force until either High Contracting Party shall have given twelve months' notice to the other in writing of his intention to terminate it . . .

Commentary

. . . It is important from the standpoint of relations with the Allies that the Treaty should not give the impression of exclusive co-operation with the U.S.S.R. after the war.

Article 1

Paragraph 1 reproduces the first paragraph of Article 1 of the Moscow draft, and adds the words 'purposes and' between the words 'acceptance of the' and the word 'principles' in the Moscow draft. The inclusion of these words brings the phraseology into line with that employed in the United Nations Declaration.

The second paragraph is the same as the second paragraph of Article 1 of the Moscow draft except that the words 'in concert with the other States concerned' have been added at the end to take account of the interests of the United States and the other common Allies of the U.S.S.R. and Great Britain, who will act 'by mutual agreement'.

Article 2

Identical with the Moscow draft except that the words 'or the Powers associated with her acts of aggression in Europe' have been added to bring the Article into line with the terminology of the Military Treaty.

Article 3

The first part is substantially the same as the first part of the Moscow draft and follows M. Stalin's wording closely, though the sentence in the Moscow draft has been shortened by putting in a full stop, and by turning it round slightly. The phrase 'desire ... of the Government of the United Kingdom for the recovery of British territory occupied by enemy forces' has been inserted in the London draft to serve as a counterpart to His Majesty's Government's recognition of the desire of the U.S.S.R. for the restoration of its frontiers by the Hitlerite aggression.

The second part contains the reservation clause about Poland to which it is hoped that the Soviet Government will agree. The exchange of notes between the Secretary of State and the Polish Prime Minister was made simultaneously with the signature of the agreement between the Soviet and Polish Governments, and with the knowledge and assent of the Soviet Government.

Article 4

His Majesty's Government understand that it would greatly assist the President of the United States and United States public opinion if the Soviet Government could agree to the inclusion of a provision on these lines in the Treaty. The 1st January, 1938, has been chosen as the most suitable date preceding the German invasion of Austria.

Article 5

Article 5 is a redraft of the second part of Article 3 of the Moscow draft. (a) has been drafted to cover the point about Federated States in the Moscow draft and has been so worded as not to read as though encouragement was given to confederation between Germany and/or Italy and other Powers contrary to the wishes of His Majesty's Government and the Soviet Government. (b) is a redraft of the same section in Article 3 of the Moscow draft, but the wording is such as to bring it more into line with the Atlantic Charter, the Washington Declaration and the resolution passed at the Inter-Allied Meeting at St. James's Palace on the 24th September, 1941.

Article 6

This reproduces Article 3 of the Moscow draft of the Military Treaty.

Article 7
This reproduces Article 4 of the Moscow draft of the Political Treaty . . .

Military treaty

Article 1
. . . In virtue of the Alliance established between them and in accordance with the Declaration by the United Nations, signed at Washington on the 1st January, 1942, the High Contracting Parties mutually undertake to afford one another assistance and support of all kinds in the war against Germany and those associated with her acts of aggression in Europe.

Article 2
The High Contracting Parties undertake not to enter into negotiations with the Hitlerite Government or any other Government of Germany that does not clearly renounce all aggressive intentions, and not to negotiate or conclude except by mutual consent any armistice or peace treaty with Germany, or any Power associated with her acts of aggression in Europe.

Article 3
The present Treaty shall be ratified and the ratifications shall be exchanged in London as soon as possible.
   It shall come into force on the exchange of ratifications and shall thereupon replace the Agreement between the Government of the Union of Soviet Socialist Republics and His Majesty's Government in the United Kingdom, signed at Moscow on the 12th July, 1941.
   The present Treaty shall remain in force until the re-establishment of peace between the High Contracting Parties and Germany and the Powers associated with her acts of aggression in Europe . . .

Commentary

Article 1
   . . . Article 1 of the Moscow draft reads: 'An alliance is hereby established between the Soviet Union and Great Britain'. The draft of Article 1 now proposed reads: 'In virtue of the alliance established between . . . the high contracting parties'. The alliance between the Soviet Union and the United Kingdom already exists, so that in our view it is incorrect to state that 'an alliance is hereby established'.

The proposed draft contains a reference to the declaration of the United Nations signed at Washington on the 1st January, 1942. This declaration, which was subscribed to both by the Soviet Government and by His Majesty's Government, was signed after the Moscow conversations in December 1941, and it seems useful that reference to it should be made in the Treaty, especially as this might help with American and world public opinion.

The Moscow draft stated that the two Powers 'mutually undertake to afford one another military assistance and support of all kinds in the war against Germany and those associated with her acts of aggression in Europe'. The revised draft drops the word 'military', which has the effect of making the provision narrower than it was in the Agreement of the 12th July, 1941. The assistance and support promised is to be 'of all kinds' and not merely 'military'.

Article 2

The words 'negotiate or' have been inserted between the words 'and not to' and 'conclude' in the Moscow draft. This strengthens the effect of the article. The words 'or any Power associated with her acts of aggression in Europe' have also been added to the draft to bring Article 2 into line with Article 1.

Article 3

A Treaty cannot enter into force immediately if it is subject to ratification as stated in the Moscow draft. Article 3 of the London draft therefore provides for entry into force after ratification, the Agreement of the 12th July, 1941, remaining in force in the meanwhile. The London draft also provides that the Treaty shall remain in force until the re-establishment of peace between the high contracting parties and Germany and the Powers associated with her acts of aggression in Europe. It is obvious that the Treaty should expire when peace has been re-established, after which time the position will be governed by the Political Treaty.

[Article 3 of the Moscow draft would seem better placed in the Political Treaty, and appears, therefore, as Article 6 of the revised London draft of that Treaty.]

B Soviet drafts

Political treaty

Article 1

... The high contracting parties, jointly affirming their acceptance of the principles of the declaration made on the 14th August, 1941, by the President of the United States of America and the Prime Minister of the United

Kingdom of Great Britain and Northern Ireland, undertake that in the settlement of post-war questions connected with the organisation of peace and security in Europe they will act by mutual agreement.

Article 2
The high contracting parties agree that after the termination of hostilities they will take all the measures in their power to render impossible a repetition of aggression and violation of peace by Germany and the States associated with her in acts of aggression in Europe.

Article 3
The high contracting parties undertake to work for the reconstruction of Europe after the war with full regard to the interests of each in their security as well as to the interests of the U.S.S.R. in the restoration of its frontiers violated by the aggression of the Hitlerite Germany and her European Allies and to the interests of Great Britain in the recovery of her European territory occupied by enemy forces, and in accordance with the two principles of not seeking territorial aggrandisement for themselves in Europe and of non-interference in the internal affairs of European peoples.
    The objectives of this reconstruction shall include in particular:

a The safeguarding and strengthening of the economic and political independence of all European countries.
b The reconstruction of the industrial and economic life of the countries occupied by Germany or her European Allies.

Article 4
Each high contracting party undertakes not to conclude any alliance and not to take part in any coalition directed against the other high contracting party.

Article 5
The high contracting parties agree to render one another all possible economic assistance after the war.

Article 6
The present treaty is subject to ratification in the shortest possible time and the instruments of ratification shall be exchanged in Moscow as soon as possible.

Annex
        The Draft Note from the Soviet Plenipotentiary to Mr. Eden
        Sir,
    On the occasion of the signature today of the treaty between U.S.S.R. and Great Britain concerning settlement of the post-war problems and their

joint activities for the guaranty of security in Europe after the termination of the war against Germany and her European allies, I have to declare on behalf of the Government of the U.S.S.R. as follows:

The Soviet Government considers it as self-evident that the question of the post-war frontiers between the U.S.S.R. and the Polish Republic will form the subject of a special agreement between the Polish and the Soviet Governments in accordance with the understanding reached some time ago between the chairman of the Council of People's Commissars, I. V. Stalin, and the Prime Minister of the Polish Republic, General W. Sikorski. In this connexion the Soviet Government expresses its confidence that the said question will be settled by mutual agreement between the two countries . . .

Military treaty

Article 1
The high contracting parties in virtue of the alliance established between them mutually undertake to afford one another military assistance and support of all kinds in the war against Germany and all those States which are associated with her in acts of aggression in Europe.

Article 2
The high contracting parties undertake not to enter into negotiations with the Hitlerite Government or any other Government in Germany that does not clearly renounce all aggressive intentions, and not to negotiate or conclude, except by mutual consent of the Signatories to this treaty, any armistice or peace treaty with Germany, or any other State associated with her in acts of aggression in Europe . . .

Eden's comments to Clark Kerr, 1 May 1942

The Soviet Ambassador came to see me this afternoon and handed me the Soviet Government's proposals for the draft treaties. As regards the draft military treaty, there was only one change from our text. The Soviet Government did not wish to refer expressly to the declaration of the United Nations in article 1. His Government were not against that declaration, but they thought that our military treaty went further, and they would, therefore, prefer not to make any reference to it.

2 As regards the political treaty, article 1 was the same as our text except that his Government thought it sufficient to affirm their acceptance of the principles of the Atlantic Charter. They saw no need to add the words 'and purposes', which we had included. Nor did the Soviet Government wish to

include the words at the end of the article 'in concert with the other States concerned'. They thought that these words were superfluous.

3 Article 2 was accepted as it stood.

4 In article 3 they did not wish to include a reference to the Polish position, which they would prefer to deal with by an exchange of notes. The draft Soviet note I would see was attached as an annex. I remarked that article 3 seemed to call for a further undertaking on our part. In the Moscow draft we had spoken of the Soviet desire for the restoration of its frontiers. Here we spoke of Soviet interests. The Ambassador admitted the change. I said that I would study this and communicate with the Ambassador further on the subject.

5 In respect of article 4 the Ambassador said that the Soviet Government wished to omit altogether our proposal which would allow the inhabitants of such territories who may wish to do so the right to leave such territories without hindrance and to carry their movable property with them. He said that, so far as the Baltic States were concerned, this matter had already been dealt with and plebiscites had already been held. I said that this was most disappointing. I had explained to him my desire to put in some article which would meet American susceptibilities. It was as important for the Soviet Government as for ourselves to take account of American opinion, and there was also a large section of opinion here which would have found satisfaction in such an article. I must tell his Excellency that we should almost certainly be compelled to return to this issue.

6 We then spoke of the duration of the treaty, and the Soviet Ambassador said that his Government were willing to leave this matter to us. They thought that the period should be not less than five years. If we so desired, they were willing to agree to it being not less than ten years. I said that I would study this and communicate with the Ambassador further.

7 I then asked his Excellency whether he had received any reply from his Government to my suggestion that at the time of the signature they should make some declaration making it clear that the Baltic States would have certain rights of local autonomy. The Ambassador appeared, however, to have had no instructions from his Government on this point. I told M. Maisky that these texts clearly did not give us any help in trying to present our treaty in the form most acceptable to American opinion and our own. That was most disappointing. I could only now say that I would examine the documents further and see his Excellency again within the next few days . . .

9 Discussions with Molotov on the Anglo-Soviet treaty, May 1942

Second meeting, 3.30 p.m., 21 May

... With regard to Article 3, M. MOLOTOV stated that his Government had been somewhat surprised at the British draft. M. Stalin and he himself had had the impression that it was agreed that the Soviet Government and the Polish Government would reach direct agreement as between allies. This draft Article, however, raised a new question. His Government had been under the impression that the question of the Polish–Soviet frontier was left open for future discussion: they wished so to leave it, and did not desire that Great Britain or Poland should be committed more than they were already committed. He was prepared to give a letter to the Polish Government, which should not, however, be mentioned in the Treaty.

THE SECRETARY OF STATE said that he quite understood that the question of the Polish frontier should be left open for discussion. Our difficulty was, however, that His Majesty's Government had certain commitments to Poland to which reference was expressly made when the Soviet–Polish Agreement was signed last year. His Majesty's Government only wished by this Article to indicate that that position was maintained, and he thought that this was the easiest way of meeting any Polish doubt as to whether the attitude of His Majesty's Government had changed or not. He saw no objection to dealing with the matter outside the Treaty by means of an exchange of letters ...

THE SECRETARY OF STATE recalled that when he was in Moscow he had no authority to agree to the Soviet proposals concerning the Baltic States. Now on that point His Majesty's Government were prepared to agree: they had made this concession, and they were prepared to agree to the phrase proposed by the Soviet Government. The only thing they wished to do was to safeguard their position with Poland as it was at the time of the signature of the Soviet–Polish Treaty. Therefore, if M. Molotov were to address him in the terms of the draft letter he might perhaps reply on the lines of the second sentence of the second paragraph of the British Article 3.

MOLOTOV replied that this would present great difficulty as it would give rise to doubt about the position in the future. The Soviet point of view was that Poland should be compensated at the expense of Germany by receiving East Prussia. That would be entirely justifiable but it was not suitable that that should be included in the present Treaty. The effect of the British draft would be that the British Government were supporting one side in the Soviet–Polish frontier discussion. He could give every assurance that his Government wished to discuss the matter with the Polish Government in the most friendly manner, but Poland should settle the matter direct with the U.S.S.R. Molotov hoped that His Majesty's Government would undertake the Soviet point of view as stated in his letter; they did not ask His Majesty's Government to confirm the position . . .

. . . In regard to the second paragraph of Article 3, the SECRETARY OF STATE enquired whether Molotov would agree to insert any reference to federation as had appeared in the Moscow draft.

MOLOTOV agreed that this question had been discussed in Moscow. The Soviet Government had certain information to show that some federations might be directed against the Soviet Union. The question was one for the future and he thought it might be better to deal with it when it was raised in definite form.

THE SECRETARY OF STATE said that His Majesty's Government would never, of course, be parties to any scheme directed against the Soviet Union; that was the very opposite of their policy. They were only interested in the formation of federations as a defence against Germany.

It was agreed to endeavour to find some form of words that would meet this point.

Third meeting, 4 p.m., 22 May

THE SECRETARY OF STATE pointed out that there remained Article IV of the British draft, which found no place in the Soviet draft. He recalled that the Prime Minister had explained yesterday that this had been inserted to meet an express request from President Roosevelt. The United States Administration had expressed disapproval of the treaty, and it would help us with them, and with American opinion generally, if something of this kind could be inserted. His Majesty's Government themselves attached importance to this principle: for instance, if it were agreed eventually to transfer E. Prussia to Poland, it would certainly be desirable that arrangements be made enabling the German population to be removed.

MOLOTOV said that he quite agreed that this principle should be applied in the case of E. Prussia, but he did not indicate that he could accept this Article in the treaty. He said that it introduced a new and complicated question, and to include it in the treaty would encourage all kinds of propaganda on the part of dissatisfied elements . . .

Fourth meeting, 3 p.m., 23 May

. . . MOLOTOV turned to the British draft article 4 regarding the transfer of populations. This raised a new question, and he would prefer that it should not figure in the treaty itself, though it could doubtless be discussed apart from the treaty.

THE SECRETARY OF STATE referred to the fact that the Prime Minister had already explained to Molotov the origin of this article, which was, indeed, a suggestion made by President Roosevelt himself. He must frankly say that the Cabinet attached great importance to it. If the actual text caused any difficulty, he would willingly consider any modification. If the new alternative draft were to be adopted there would be no need for an article of this kind, but in any treaty dealing with frontier questions he was sure that His Majesty's Government would require something on these lines.

MOLOTOV said that he had already explained the attitude of the Soviet Government in this matter. An article on these lines would inevitably incite the inhabitants of the territories in question to make claims against the Soviet Government. He suggested that it might be possible to find a rather more restricted formula, and he would be prepared to make a proposal to that effect. He did not consider that any real difficulties would arise even if no such article were included in the treaty. If, for instance, a Pole wished to leave Lithuania for Poland, no objection would be raised by the Soviet Government. In point of fact, he did not think that such cases would arise, but if it were considered important from the point of view of American public opinion, it might be possible to find a more restricted formula . . .

Fifth meeting, 4 p.m., 24 May

THE SECRETARY OF STATE begged Molotov to look again at the new alternative draft treaty which he had submitted to him yesterday, and which actually made a bigger offer than His Majesty's Government had ever made in the course of history. It was an offer which they could make now, and an agreement on those lines could be signed now and no one in the world could have the slightest grounds for objection. It would be a buttress of the future peace of Europe and would not exclude discussion between us as allies, not only of the problems presented by Finland and Roumania, but of the future map of Europe and the economic problems of the post-war period. The Treaty which he had offered would afford a strong foundation on which lasting friendship between the two countries could be built . . .

Sixth meeting, 3 p.m., 25 May

MOLOTOV said that he had informed his Government of the terms of the new alternative treaty and had reported that Mr. Eden had considered it would be more suitable and correct to adopt a treaty on these lines rather than continue discussion of the former drafts. He had reported that the Prime Minister was also in favour of this course. Moreover, he had told his Government that, according to the information at the disposal of the Prime Minister and the

Secretary of State for Foreign Affairs, the United States Government and President Roosevelt himself would favour the new draft and would deprecate a treaty containing the controversial points which had already caused difficulty.

Molotov added that he had had a conversation yesterday with Mr. Winant, who had confirmed that President Roosevelt's opinion was as indicated.

Molotov said that he had reported his own opinion that the new treaty would have great importance both for the period of the war and for the period after the war, and he had asked for instructions with regard to it . . .

10   Foreign Office comments on Soviet aims in Eastern Europe, May 1942

Makins, 7 May

. . . Dr. Benes' views fit in very well with what I take to be the general trend of Soviet policy as disclosed in recent negotiations. This is an extension of exclusive Russian influence over the whole of Eastern Europe, to be effected by the occupation of Finland, the Baltic States and Roumania, the closest possible association with Czechoslovakia and Yugoslavia, the crushing of Hungary and the encirclement of Poland. So ambitious a programme is probably even more unwelcome to Dr. Benes than it is to ourselves, and he therefore wishes to avert it as far as he is able by playing up to the Russians and at the same time securing from ourselves adequate guarantees, not only for his country but also for Poland, at the expense of Germany and Hungary. Such assurances, though not necessarily contrary to the policy which we may eventually adopt towards Germany, would certainly be contrary to our propaganda policy, and it would be a mistake to give them and to make them public at the present moment.

It need hardly be added that this manoeuvring of Dr. Benes will have little or no effect on Russian policy, though it may well be an embarrassment to ourselves . . .

Dew, 9 May

. . . It may be argued that by concluding a treaty we tacitly approve this Soviet programme and, at the same time, appear to abandon our interest in Eastern Europe to the Russians, but on the other hand if we have no treaty at all and the Soviet Government have a free hand at the end of the war, will not the position be worse then . . . For if the Russians started to realise their programme at the end of the war we would have no *locus standi* for opposing it.

The Scandinavian countries would be nervous about undefined Russian encroachment in Finland and along the southern shores of the Baltic. The Poles, to whom we have given no guarantee about restoring the integrity of their territory, would be left to face the Russians alone. The Roumanians would collapse; the Turks would be anxious about Soviet encroachments to the South. All these countries would be turning to us and to the Americans to save them from the Russian danger. We would not be able to take any action to oppose the Russians and, as stated above, we should have no *locus standi* for intervening with the Soviet Government on the diplomatic level.

Strang, 12 May

It will not be long, I think, before Dr. Benes is called upon by the Russians to choose between Russia and Poland: in other words, to conclude a treaty with Russia which will make any Polish–Czechoslovak federal scheme empty of meaning, or even stand in the way of its conclusion. The Russians certainly intend to isolate and encircle Poland and to prevent the formation of a Baltic–Adriatic bloc, based on Poland in the north.

Sargent, 13 May

Assuming this to be the Soviet policy how would Mr. Strang propose that we should counter it either now when it is still only an aspiration or later or when it becomes a reality?

Strang, 14 May

I do not think we can counter the establishment of Russian predominance in Eastern Europe if Germany is crushed and disarmed and Russia participates in the final victory.

Sargent, 14 May

In that case the worst fears of the Poles, Yugoslavs, Greeks and Turks are justified and their only hope for the future lies in a Germany strong enough to countenance Soviet predominance. But I should be very sorry to have to reach such a distressing conclusion. [Eden saw these minutes but made no written comment.]

11   Orme Sargent's memorandum of 1 June 1942 on confederations in Eastern Europe

... 5 No form of confederation of the Balkan States could hope to be satisfactory, either from the point of view of the members of the confederation, or of its utility first as a deterrent to a revival of the German aggressive spirit and then, if this failed, as a barrier to German aggression, unless it contained provisions for defence. For this purpose it is highly desirable that the constituent units should abandon as far as possible the old collective sovereignty. This could, as a minimum, seem to require some executive machinery whereby the will of the confederation as a whole could be enforced on its members. This in its turn would seem to involve (a) a common system of defence; (b) a customs union and common currency; (c) a common foreign policy. Although it would be foolish to think that the highly individualistic States which would form a Balkan confederation would willingly agree to any derogation of their national sovereignty, these are certain material considerations which might weigh with the Greek and Yugoslav Governments. It is very much to their advantage that Bulgaria should be sterilised. It is equally to their advantage to have a share in the oil of Roumania. Fear in the first case and greed in the second might therefore lead the Greek and Yugoslav Governments to acquiesce in some form of centralised control under which they would obtain their share in the riches of Roumania and ensure that the Bulgarian military spirit were kept down.

6 The second question is whether the proposed confederations should be capable of resistance both to Germany and to Russia or to Germany alone. It is fairly evident that no combination capable of standing up to both of these Great Powers for any length of time is within the range of practical politics, and it is therefore to Germany rather than to Russia that the confederations should be resistant ...

... The attitude of the Soviet Government towards the whole idea of confederation in Central Europe is dubious. They pretend to think that such confederations would be directed against the legitimate interests of Russia. It will therefore be necessary to reassure them on this point, in order to obtain at least their acquiescence, if not active support. But it must be recognised that, assuming a victorious Russia, any combination of States in South Eastern Europe would have to rely on Russian goodwill, and that if durable political and economic units are to be established a moderate risk of Russian expansion westwards will have to be taken. Special treaty relations, therefore, between the two confederations and the Soviet Union would seem necessary. In this connexion the point mentioned in paragraph 9 below about the Soviet Union's interests in Roumania and Bulgaria must be borne in mind.

7 The third question is the optimum composition of the| confederative units. It appears necessary to visualise two groups of States, a Central European confederation and a South-Eastern European confederation . . . In regard to Yugoslavia, it may prove the best solution for Serbs, Croats and Slovenes each to form a separate unit in the confederation, the experiment of uniting into one kingdom three peoples joined by racial and linguistic affinities, but separated by divergent interests and outlooks, having proved a conspicuous failure. In the case of Roumania, it will be necessary to settle the status of Bessarabia and Northern Bukovina, which the Soviet Government will presumably wish to reoccupy. The Soviet Union may also demand for her own security that she should occupy certain strategic bases on the Roumanian and possibly the Bulgarian coast, and may also want to have for the same reason special treaty relations with Roumania. It may be difficult to reconcile these Russian demands with the absorption of these two countries into a Balkan confederation which would be independent of any outside control. In regard to Bulgaria, some readjustments of territory in favour of Greece and Yugoslavia may be necessary, and, as in the case of Hungary, it may be found necessary to use force to compel Bulgaria to enter the confederation and prevent her from leaving it. As for Albania, it would seem that the only way that it could maintain its national identity after the war would be as a constituent member of a Balkan confederation. The experiment of an independent Albania has not been encouraging, and rather than see it repeated Yugoslavia and Greece might well argue that their security required the partition of that country between them . . .

12 Rumours of a separate Russo-German peace, July 1942

A Telegram from Mallet in Stockholm, 19 July

Following is a report from a Swedish informant of statements recently made to him by German official visiting Sweden.

Journalists regard source as entirely reliable. Possibilities of a separate Russo-German peace are greater now than last winter (when there were rumours that the former German Ambassador at Moscow was conducting negotiations) because Hitler is ready to sacrifice anything even the Ukraine to free himself from war in the East . . .

Stories of Russo-German peace appear to be circulating fairly extensively in conservative circles in Stockholm. *Socialist Demokraten* of July 15th also suggests that if the second front is not set up in time, Russia's only alternative will be separate peace.

B Minutes on the above

Wilson, 20 July

This all sounds pretty phoney to me. A Soviet–German peace which left the U.S.S.R. with the Ukraine (and therefore presumably the Caucasus) and with her army intact would be a German defeat, and the U.S.S.R. is certainly not going to pull out of this war if Germany shows marked signs of weakening. The U.S.S.R. will not make a separate peace, and so leave us and the U.S.A. with the honours and fruits of victory, unless she is pretty certain that the Germans will win anyway and that her chances of resisting have dwindled to nothing. The last para. of the Tel. says there are rumours of a separate peace on the basis of Russian exhaustion, in which case she would certainly not be allowed to retain the Ukraine. The two rumours just about cancel each other out . . .

Sargent, 22 July

We can safely assume that Hitler will want to bring about the termination of hostilities in Russia before the winter sets in. If he cannot achieve this by defeating the Russian armies in the field, he may well try to achieve it by means of a separate peace.

There are, of course, limits to the terms which Hitler could offer and he clearly could not abandon the Ukraine and leave the Soviet armies more or less intact unless he could at the same time recoup himself by the speedy conquest of the Middle East. But if he saw a prospect of such a conquest on easy terms, can we be sure that he would not make Stalin an offer of peace plus the Ukraine? It would be a big gamble and a difficult *volte face* to explain to the German people but, knowing Hitler as we do, we cannot rule it out on those grounds.

Such an offer could not fail to have great attractions for Stalin and I doubt whether he would reject it, as suggested by Mr. Wilson, merely because such an offer would show that Hitler was weakening and because he – Stalin – does not intend to leave to us and the U.S.A. the fruits of ultimate victory. Stalin might well take his decision on a short-term view and might prefer an immediate, though uncertain, truce in which he could lick his wounds and prepare for the next round rather than the continuance of the present war of attrition which may leave the Soviet state so exhausted at the end as to be in no position to reap the fruits of the common victory. In a word, Stalin will have to be convinced, if and when the time of temptation comes, that the danger to his country and his regime will be greater if he makes peace with Hitler this autumn than if he continues to struggle throughout the winter and that means that his decision will depend on a number of factors, the relative importance of which it is impossible at present to foresee.

Cadogan, 22 July

If Stalin could get anything like the terms here hinted at, I should be decidedly apprehensive, for the reasons Sir O. Sargent gives. The immediate menace to Stalin is the possible severance of his north–south rail and river communications. If Hitler withdrew that threat (as is implied here), that would give the Russians a wonderful breathing space. But in the present military situation, I should have thought there would be no chance of Hitler offering it, and we may perhaps take comfort from that reflexion.

C Dew memorandum of 20 July

The following note records certain recent instances in which Soviet spokesmen, when urging the early formation of a Second Front in Western Europe, have accompanied their remarks under this head with hints that if the relief of an Allied invasion of Europe is not afforded in the near future the situation may become desperate in the U.S.S.R., and that the Red Army and the Soviet Government may be forced to give up the struggle:

1 On July 14th the Soviet Ambassador, in conversation with the Secretary of State, took a pessimistic view of the military situation in the U.S.S.R., which he described as very serious. He said that Soviet man-power was not inexhaustible and feared that if our convoys to North Russian ports were suspended on top of our inability to open a Second Front, and an apparent relaxation in our bombing efforts, the effect on Soviet resistance at this time must be very serious.

2 On July 16th President Benes informed Mr. Bruce Lockhart that the Czechoslovak Minister in the U.S.S.R. had telegraphed on July 15th that for the first time he had noticed signs of alarm among the higher Soviet officials, and that there was considerable criticism of the British for not implementing their pledge to form a Second Front this year. President Benes expressed the view that we might today have to consider the possibility of a complete collapse of Soviet resistance, and that he had been perturbed by the attitude of the Soviet Ambassador and M. Bogomolov, who had indulged in thinly veiled criticisms of British policy. President Benes feared that we might wake up one morning to find that the U.S.S.R. and Germany had concluded a separate peace. His instinct told him that our good relations with the Soviet Union were in danger. The Soviet Government would consider their own interests with complete disregard of ours. If they thought that we were holding

back either from a fixed purpose or on account of weakness they would not hesitate to betray us.

3 In a recent conversation with His Majesty's representative to La France Combattante M. Bogomolov had spoken very pessimistically about the military situation in the Soviet Union and in urging the immediate formation of a Second Front in Western Europe had hinted that Russian resistance might not be able to continue indefinitely.

4 As reported in his telegrams Nos 1025 and 1026 Sir A. Clark Kerr had a conversation with M. Vyshinski about the military situation of July 16th, during the course of which the latter, remarking that what would ease a clearly dangerous situation best would be the immediate establishment of a Second Front, added that while the Red Army could of course be counted upon to fight on to the death the time might come when they could not go on and then a Second Front would be too late.

13   Possible post-war federations in Eastern Europe, September–October 1942

Wilson minute of 23 September and comments on it

Soviet policy towards federations in Europe

Apart from Stalin's remark to the Secretary of State in Moscow last December, that 'if certain of the countries of Europe wish to federate then the Soviet Union will have no objection to such a course' (N 109, p. 11), there is little evidence that the Soviet Union will be prepared to agree to federations in Eastern Europe after the war. The reasons for this attitude is their fear lest such federations might be directed against themselves. Thus, when the Anglo-Soviet Treaty was under discussion in April, a draft was sent to Moscow in which the idea of federation figured fairly prominently. The Moscow counter-draft omitted federation altogether and, on being questioned about this in London, Molotov said that 'The Soviet Government had certain information to show that some federations might be directed against the Soviet Union' (N 2902). During the negotiations in London he only consented to the in-clusion of the federation idea in the draft of the then proposed treaty, on condition that a clause was added to the effect that any such federations should be 'on the basis of friendly relations towards the Union of Soviet Socialist Republics and Great Britain'.

2 Molotov made his position equally clear in his conversation with Dr. Benes. He showed his suspicion that a Czecho-Polish confederation might be directed against the Soviet Union (C 6122) and asked whether, if the

confederation came into existence, Czechoslovakia would be supporting Poland against the Soviet Union. On being told 'No', he said that the Union of Soviet Socialist Republics was prepared to accept the confederation provided it was not directed against themselves (C 6483), and he asked for, and was given by Dr. Benes, an assurance that Czechoslovakia would not join any 'larger European confederation' without previous consultation with the Union of Soviet Socialist Republics.

3 Bogomolov has been equally emphatic. He told Ripka that, now that the Union of the Soviet Socialist Republics had come into the war, confederation was unnecessary and that, if Germany was beaten, there was no reason for confederation (C 7636). At the time of the Yugoslav–Greek agreement he had adopted a very chilling attitude to the whole policy of the pact, and at the same time Vyshinski had indicated to the Greek Minister in Kuibyshev that the Soviet Government regarded the whole development with suspicion and distaste (R 712).

4 It seems clear therefore that, while the Soviet Government is not prepared at the moment to veto these embryo federations entirely, it regards them as both unnecessary and undesirable. This cannot be because of any fear of the federations as such – they cannot conceivably, in any foreseeable future, either singly or in combination be strong enough to menace the Union of Soviet Socialist Republics. Her dislike of them must therefore be based on either a fear that they will prevent her 'getting into Europe', or a fear that they will be used by other powers against her interests, in much the way that Finland was used by Germany. The first alternative is inherently improbable in as much as the Soviet Union will probably have neither the wish nor the strength in the immediate post-war period to interfere in Europe beyond the limitrophe states, and the second alternative seems much the more probable. In that case, the only powers that she can contemplate as 'using' the federations are ourselves and the Americans . . .

9 The Russian argument would be that, if Germany is defeated, Russia can look after her perfectly well so far as the east is concerned and the strengthening of Germany's eastern or south-eastern neighbours by federation is unnecessary. They would expect that proposition to be equally obvious to us and, arguing again from their own practice, would say that our interest in eastern European federation was not purely philanthropic and disinterested but was designed to further some British interest. As that interest could not, *ex hypothesi*, be *merely* the holding down of Germany or the good of the countries concerned, it must in some way be directed against Russia. Therefore the safest thing would be to try and exclude Great Britain from the continent altogether, and to concentrate on a more pliable partner.

10 Unless the Union of Soviet Socialist Republics is so weakened by the war that she can exert no influence at all outside her own frontiers (which is

unlikely) no federation can come into existence in Eastern Europe and probably the Balkans too without at least her tacit goodwill. Unless therefore we are fairly certain that she will not discourage federations, we are in danger of irritating her to no useful purpose if we go out of our way to encourage them, and where any of the countries concerned consult us about the idea of federation, our safest course is surely to make it abundantly clear that they will only have our full support provided they can secure the goodwill of the Russians. If we adopt any other course, the Russian tendency will be to oppose our plans not only in Eastern Europe but in Western Europe as well . . .

Dew, 27 September

. . . I agree with his conclusions in paras. 9, 10 and 11 though I don't think H.M.G. can, at the moment, be described as going out of its way to encourage confederations, so that we are not likely to be arousing much irritation at the moment. The Polish attitude towards the U.S.S.R. and the views the Poles have of the Polish–Czech Confederation and of the place of Poland in Eastern Europe after the war are really the cause of most of the Soviet Gvt's hesitations over the idea of confederations. H.M.G. will be judged to a great extent by the support which it gives to those Polish schemes and plans. And here we have to watch our step because of American plans for a vast federation of Eastern Europe which for Mr. Berle at any rate, is to serve as a sort of barrier against the U.S.S.R. (see Mr. Law's report on his conversation in the U.S.A.) . . .

Roberts, 1 October

It is, of course, obvious that the proposed confederations can only function with a modicum of Soviet goodwill, and to that extent the advice in paragraph 10 of Mr. Wilson's memo is clearly sound. But we should be making a great mistake to regard this purely from the Soviet angle. We are fighting this war to prevent German domination of Europe, and we have found Allies among the smaller nations of Europe because:

1 they prize their national independence,
and
2 they expect our victory to produce a better Europe than the present German dominated Europe.

I am fairly confident that no European nation would in the long run regard a Europe dominated by Russia as preferable to a Europe dominated by Germany. Therefore, unless we encourage the minor Allies to strengthen their own position, to some extent independently of ourselves and of Russia, we shall make it much easier for Germany to rise again after the war as a sort of patron for the minor European States fearful of Russia, and we shall risk finding European unity recreated around Germany before very long.

Finally, I do not think that we can adopt quite so detached an attitude as is suggested by Mr. Wilson. We have after all made several public pronouncements welcoming the Polish–Czech and Greek–Yugoslav proposals. The last of these statements was that made by the Secretary of State at Leamington on September 26th. These confederations are delicate growths requiring all the encouragement we can discreetly give them. They will wither away all too easily if we withdraw such encouragement for fear of Soviet susceptibilities.

Warner, 2 October

. . . I think, therefore, that Mr. Wilson goes a little too far at the end of paragraph 10 of his memorandum; for, if we, whenever approached about confederations by one of the countries concerned, 'make it abundantly clear that they will only have our full support provided they can secure the goodwill of the Russians', they will certainly be discouraged, since the Russians can be counted upon not to give positive assurances of good-will. But I agree that the Russians will regard our attitude on the subject of confederations as one of the tests of our real intentions towards them and we must therefore always handle the matter very carefully . . .

Sargent, 3 October

I agree with Mr. Warner. I am not sure the time has not come for us to have a talk with the Americans 'off the record' as to how we see this question of confederations in Eastern Europe and how we think it ought to be handled.

14   Clark Kerr on Soviet policy. Dispatch to Eden of 25 November 1942, received in London on 5 January 1943

It may be desirable to touch on the Soviet Government's attitude – if they can as yet be said to have one – towards post-war problems and political and economic reconstruction.

A clear distinction can and obviously must be made between 'post-war relief' and 'post-war reconstruction'. The former is, relatively speaking, a simple, short-term problem, in which the Soviet Government's collaboration is likely to be readily secured (so far as they are physically able to collaborate) and in regard to which their policy is unlikely to raise serious complications.

When, however, it becomes a matter of the political and economic re-organisation of Europe after the war, the attitude of the Soviet Government is, so far as one can see, a good deal more negative . . .

I do not use the word 'negative' in any pejorative sense. I merely mean that the Soviet Government, as hard-headed realists, are not going to be carried away, or levitated off the ground, by any long-term reconstruction plan which does not bear tangible relation to the conditions existing in Europe at the end of the war . . . All the thought and energy of this country is bent to the immediate task of winning the war. In this respect the Soviet Government, who are at present in the thick of the fight against Germany, are in quite a different position from that of the eight exiled Governments in London, who – it is no disparagement of them to say so – necessarily have more time to devote to post-war problems than has the Kremlin.

What will be the trend of the Soviet Government's thoughts when the war is over is quite another matter. If form is any guide, they will occupy themselves first and foremost – and quite rightly – with the reconstruction of their own devastated areas . . .

So far as they are concerned, economic will be subordinated to political considerations. What are these political considerations? In the first place, territorial claims. The Baltic States, a strip of Eastern Poland, Bessarabia; these, at least, the Soviet Union will aim at assimilating to herself in order to secure strategic frontiers in the west. How much further south and west she will be able to go, either in frontiers or in spheres of influence, depends on the conditions existing at the end of the war, on what her other Allies do, and to some extent on what the populations of the Axis-occupied territories do. She may claim a sort of undefined protectorate over the other Slav people of Europe, and a somewhat more tangible influence over the destinies of 'Slav-civilised' Bulgaria. Further it would at present be idle to speculate . . .

Her economic interests will, of course, follow her political interests. But in this connexion it must be remembered that Soviet Russia's own industrialisa-tion is by no means complete. The greater part of it, even that part which was impeded by the necessity of preparing against military attack, may still be to come. The question seems to be: will she continue it *pari passu* with the interest she will possibly develop in the light or consumption industries of Eastern and Central Europe – will she, that is, use these industries to supple-ment her own – or will she, on the other hand, decide to do without such things until she can provide them for herself? Here, again, much must depend on the conditions existing at the end of the war and on the ability of her other Allies to supply her with the capital goods which the process of industrialisa-tion requires.

One thing can be said: Soviet Russia, after the war, will probably be pre-pared to take things quietly for a considerable period of time. There will, so

far as this country is concerned, be a general desire on the part of the population at large for a greater degree of comfort and happiness than was granted
them before the war. Most observers agree about that . . .

15 Discussion on Soviet policy in the Balkans, December 1942–January 1943

A Rendel (Ambassador to Yugoslavia) to Eden, 19 December 1942

. . . the problem, of which the conflict between General Mihailovich
and the Partisans and its repercussions on Anglo-Yugoslav relations are one
aspect, is by no means a purely Yugoslav one. On closer analysis it seems
clear that the real centre of gravity of the communist movement in the Balkans
is to be found in Bulgaria, and that, without first considering probable developments in that country, no true estimate can be made of future prospects
in Yugoslavia. Indeed to approach any Balkan problem without taking
Bulgaria into account is merely to deal with the periphery and to ignore what
has so often proved in the past to be the central core. . .

. . . In any case, once the defeat of the Axis becomes certain, Russia
victorious will surely exercise an even greater mesmeric influence over the
Bulgarian people than she did in the days of her eclipse. It is therefore hardly
a rash prophecy to assume that in the hour of Russian victory the pro-
Russian and pro-communist forces in Bulgaria will carry everything before
them, will eliminate King Boris and the pro-German groups at present in
control, will eclipse or displace all other party organisations and will establish
a native communist regime.

But, for two reasons, the question is not a purely internal one: (a) Bulgarian
communism will lean on Russia, and (b) it is likely to prove infectious . . .

. . . With Soviet republics to the north in Hungary and to the south east in
Bulgaria, it is difficult to see how the communists of Yugoslavia, who have
already enjoyed so much Soviet support, could fail to establish themselves
firmly in the southern Slav countries which have hitherto formed Yugoslavia,
or how the establishment of a chain of Associated Socialist and Soviet
Republics from Burgas to Trieste and from the Dobruja to Montenegro, could
be avoided.

Inevitably it is easier to see dangers than their remedies. Moreover the mere
fact of the danger itself may be exaggerated. There is a large and responsible
body of opinion in England which would no doubt see many real advantages
in the establishment of such a chain of republics in south east Europe. Such a
group might for instance form a kind of Union among themselves, presenting

many of the advantages of the Balkan Confederation which we have hitherto been inclined to regard as the most hopeful scheme for the post war reorganisation of this area . . .

As against this, however, it may be considered optimistic to regard Russian imperialism as wholly dead. Stalin has been described as a 'Red Peter the Great', and the aspirations of Moscow for an outlet on the Mediterranean are founded on motives too solid to be lightly abandoned or ignored. It may be therefore that the establishment of a chain of Soviet Republics in the Balkans and in the Danube basin might prove not so much a solution of their problems to those countries themselves as a decisive acquisition of power for an Empire which has not yet completely abandoned expansionist dreams. The history of the Baltic States, though not wholly parallel, is perhaps not wholly without significance in this connexion.

In any case the immediate international repercussions of what may be termed the 'sovietisation' of south eastern Europe might be dangerous and far reaching, particularly in the neighbouring countries. In the first place it could hardly leave Turkey unaffected or unmoved. The extension of Soviet influence over the Balkan area would constitute a formidable threat to what Turkey has long regarded as one of her most vital interests. If this were accompanied by the establishment of Russian military power in Varna and Burgas, and thus in south eastern Bulgaria, immediately behind the Straits and within 20 miles of the Aegean coast, Turkey might well feel that she had been dealt a formidable blow . . .

B Minutes on Rendel's dispatch

Rose, 30 December 1942

. . . I have no doubt that the Soviet Government, as at present minded, is likely to be a serious obstacle to the post-war organisation of a peaceful and prosperous European comity of nations. Stalin's mind, as he showed it to the Secretary of State during the latter's visit to Moscow, is bent on prevention and not on cure: not on assuring for the future the peaceful development of the peoples of Europe, but on strengthening Russia and binding Germany in a purely military sense and to the complete exclusion of all other considerations, whether of natural justice, organic growth, popular feeling or economic need. It is, moreover, the universal opinion of all countries bordering on Russia and having experience of Russian rule that the German jackboot, however horrible, is the lesser evil compared with the kindly domination of Mother Russia . . .

. . . Once we allow that the break-up of the former pre-war Balkan states is in certain cases desirable, not only have we ready to hand a solution to all the more vexed Balkan problems, Transylvania, Macedonia and Albania, not only are we in a position to exploit those separatist tendencies which are a main prop of Soviet propaganda: we are also taking a step towards the ultimate establishment of a strong cohesive and effective Balkan confederation . . .

Howard, 1 January 1943

. . . The obvious and easiest solution would of course be that we and the Americans by an invasion of the Balkans should be on the spot and in a position to police that part of the world and thus prevent an immediate collapse and opening for Communist risings. It is important, however, to have alternative ideas for coping with the situation, should we not be on the spot at the right moment . . .

Warner, 2 January 1943

. . . I personally think that (assuming Russia is not reduced to a state of impotence before the end of the war), our only chance of preventing the Balkans from falling completely under Russian control will be by securing Russian agreement to Anglo-Russo-American collaboration there . . .

I should have thought it would be found very difficult to concert with the Turks' plans, the real object of which is to get Turkish co-operation in keeping the Russians out of Bulgaria; without it becoming quite obvious to the Russians and the Turks that this *is* our real object; in which case one would surely have done incalculably more harm than good. Further would Turkish presence and co-operation in policing Bulgaria really be of much help? . . .

Sargent, 11 January 1943

There is no doubt a good deal of foundation for Mr. Rendel's fears, and the Russians would be more than human if they did not attempt to turn to their own advantage any developments in the Balkans favourable to themselves. This, of course, applies especially to Bulgaria, which has always been a special Russian preserve. On the other hand, I am not convinced that the Soviet Government are consciously planning to dominate the Balkans by means either of Bolshevisation or Pan-Slavism. The Soviet Government have publicly endorsed on many occasions the principle of non-intervention. As regards the Balkans, their territorial ambitions, as disclosed in the Secretary of State's conversation with Stalin in Moscow and with Molotov here, were confined to Bessarabia and Northern Bukovina and bases in Roumania. It is, of course, very possible that they would propose to reconcile wider territorial ambitions with these statements by engineering 'spontaneous' applications on the part of Communist Governments in the Balkan States for incorporation in, or some other term of association with, the Soviet Union. But the present trend of Soviet policy, so far as one can judge, appears to be against unlimited expansion. But, of course, this does not necessarily preclude the possibility that one or other of the Balkan States (and Hungary ought also to be included in this category) may at the end of the war collapse into Communism merely as the result of the economic conditions then prevailing, and this is most likely to happen, as Mr. Rendel points out, in Bulgaria, owing to the traditional admiration of the Bulgarians for all things Russian.

There is, I am afraid, no cut and dried way of guarding against these unpleasant possibilities, but I agree that we ought to take steps so to direct our present policy as to lessen the chances of our losing control of the general situation in Central and S. E. Europe at the critical moment. For I assume that H. M. Government are definitely opposed to the policy advocated by Professor Carr in *The Times* that we should tacitly disinterest ourselves from Central and S. E. Europe, and that now and at the peace settlement we should recognise all this part of Europe as falling within the exclusive Russian sphere of influence . . . [Eden minuted: 'Yes'.]

. . . The alternative, of course, would be for us to start discussions with the Soviet Government and try to convince them that it was in the general interest to prevent this part of Europe from collapsing into chaos, and that for this purpose we should begin to organise the existing forces of law and order and lay down certain basic plans which would enable the various authorised Governments to assume control at the earliest possible moment. [Eden minuted: 'I prefer this'. Sargent in his previous paragraph had repeated Warner's arguments against involving the Turks in Bulgaria.]

. . . It is difficult to foresee how the Soviet Government would respond to such an approach, and it is for this reason that I think it would be useful that Sir A. Clark Kerr should, on his return to Moscow, take soundings as to the present attitude of Stalin on the whole question of the post-war reconstruction of Europe.

We must always remember, however, that even though the Soviet Government are as regards the Balkans in a strong position to dictate their terms and to refuse collaboration, we also may have a card or two to play, of which the three most important would be: (1) the possibility that at the end of the war there will be British and American armies in the Balkans; (2) that Turkey may be a belligerent with an army also in the Balkans; and (3) the fact that we and the Americans will control the relief organisation which will have to feed the starving populations throughout the Balkans for an indefinite period after the withdrawal of the Axis forces.

16   The approach to the Russians about post-war problems, February–March 1943

A Eden's instructions to Clark Kerr, 4 February 1943

I have for some time been considering what measures can be taken now to facilitate and encourage Societ co-operation in the post-war settlement. If this co-operation is to be obtained, it is essential that His Majesty's Government should on all possible occasions treat the Soviet Government as partners, and make a habit of discussing plans and views with them as a matter of course. Only in this way will it be possible to break through the crust of suspicion which results from the previous relations between the two countries and our widely differing institutions. We should not be unduly deterred by the fact that on many major questions which must arise in talks with our Allies we have not yet reached any settled policy. Although it may often be necessary, for various reasons, to discuss matters of policy with the United States Government before broaching them with the Soviet Government, by so doing we may risk giving offence to the latter. I propose, therefore, so far as possible to consult both Governments simultaneously and, where it is necessary to consult the United States Government first, to do so informally. It may also help to assuage the Soviet Government's susceptibilities if we on some occasions consult them before the United States Government. For instance, in questions relating to Eastern Europe or to reparation, it may well be desirable to open discussions with the Soviet Government first.

With this in mind, I consider that the improved atmosphere occasioned by M. Stalin's speech of the 6th November, which seems the signal for greater co-operation in all spheres by the Soviet Government, the extensive victories which the Allies have recently gained and your Excellency's return to Moscow after consultation in London afford a suitable opportunity to review with the Soviet Government our plans and hopes for the future, and the possibilities of co-operation between the major Allied Powers. I shall therefore be glad if your Excellency will seek an interview with M. Molotov on your return and speak to him along the following lines . . .

. . . You should suggest that there seems to be general agreement that the 'Anglo–American–Soviet' coalition must be continued after the war if possible. In the maintenance of this coalition lies the main hope of securing a durable peace. Moreover, both Mr. Welles and myself have stated publicly that our Governments attach the greatest importance to the main lines of the peace settlement being agreed to by the United Kingdom, the United States and the Soviet Union in advance of the Armistice. Though M. Stalin has not said this publicly, it seems to be implicit in his speech of the 6th November.

You should then turn to the progress which has been made in considering the main lines of the peace settlement. You should make it clear that, owing to our preoccupation with the prosecution of the war, we have not yet had time to arrive at definite conclusions on the major problems involved . . .

. . . After these explanations your Excellency might then enquire of M. Molotov what preparatory studies the Soviet Government have engaged in, to supplement the indications given to me by M. Stalin in Moscow in December 1941 and those arising out of the negotiations in London in May last leading to the conclusion of the Anglo-Soviet Treaty . . .

Your Excellency should then go on to discuss the two extracts from M. Stalin's speech of the 6th November given in enclosure No. 2 to this despatch, which seem to call for further elucidation. Commenting on the first extract, you might say that it seems not only good propaganda but very sensible. On the other hand, you are not quite clear whether, in the light of this statement, Mr. Stalin has modified the views he expressed to me on the 16th December, 1941, when he proposed the restoration of Austria as an independent State, the detachment of the Rhineland from Prussia as an independent State or a protectorate, and possibly the constitution of an independent State of Bavaria, in addition to the transfer of East Prussia to Poland and the return of the Sudetenland to Czechoslovakia. Commenting on the second extract, you might say that there is at least a superficial difficulty in reconciling this with Section 6 of the Atlantic Charter, to which the Soviet Union has subscribed, and which provides for the disarmament of aggressor nations. It is to be presumed that M. Stalin's speech was at least partly made with a view to the propaganda effect upon Germans in general and the German army in particular, and that he is not in fact, in favour of Germany retaining armed forces other than those necessary for police work and the maintenance of public order . . .

. . . At this point you might suitably introduce the main substance of your *démarche*, namely, the desirability of the three major Allies pursuing an agreed policy in regard to Europe as a whole. His Majesty's Government would, in fact, propose that Three-Power consultations should in due course take place on post-war arrangements alike in Western, Central and Eastern Europe. Only if this principle is accepted will there be any hope of getting some real European order established when Germany collapses, and it should be excluded that any one of the three Great Powers should run a policy of its own in opposition to, or behind the backs of, the others. Moreover, only if it is accepted will any joint planning be either possible or desirable. Some assurance from M. Molotov that the principle is accepted by the Soviet Union will accordingly be of great value as a first step towards real Three-Power collaboration . . .

. . . Your conversation on the subject may also afford a means of finding out how far, and, if so, for what reasons, the Soviet Government are opposed to the Polish–Czechoslovak and Graeco-Yugoslav confederations, despite several statements made on behalf of the Soviet Government favouring such confederations in principle . . .

. . . the Soviet Government have, however, conveyed the impression to the Allied Governments concerned in London that they are in fact opposed, if not to the principle of confederations, at least to the two units now in question. For your own information, M. Bogomolov was asked by the Czechoslovak Government to give them a clear indication of Soviet views when he returned recently from Moscow, but he has confined himself on his return to taking the line that 'les milieux sovietiques', to use his own words, are not at present ready to commit themselves over the plan for a Polish–Czechoslovak confederation, that the situation is not yet sufficiently clear, and that they would prefer to wait possibly until the end of the war. This is clearly an unsatisfactory situation, which is imposing considerable strain upon the relations between the various Governments concerned with these confederation schemes, and in particular upon the Polish and Czechoslovak Governments . . .

Extracts from M. Stalin's speech of 6 *November* 1942

i Hitler said 'We shall destroy Russia and it will never rise again'. That is perfectly clear but it is rather silly. We are not burdened with the problem of destroying Germany, because it is no more possible to destroy Germany than it is possible to destroy Russia. But to destroy the Hitlerite State is possible and necessary. Our first aim is the destruction of the Hitlerite State and the men who inspire it.

ii Hitler went on to say: 'We shall prosecute the war until no organised armed force remains in Russia'. Clear is it not? But not convincing. It is not our aim to destroy all organised military force in Germany, for every literate person will understand that it is not only impossible in regard to Germany as it is in regard to Russia, but is also inexpedient from the point of view of the future. But Hitler's army can and should be destroyed.

B Extracts from F.O. memorandum enclosed for Clark Kerr's guidance, also dated 4 February

. . . quite apart from the problem created by the entry of Soviet armies into Central Europe, there remains the question of how to enforce the authority of the newly-established Allied Governments in the previously occupied countries. They may well be in need of military assistance to defend themselves against the local enemy State or to suppress rival Governments in their own country, and unless there are at the time British and United States armies on the Continent it is evident that they will look for assistance to the

Soviet Government. Similarly, it is not excluded that they may, if left uncontrolled, attempt to recover those of their former territories still in possession of the enemy, and, indeed, to stake out further claims at the expense of either Germany, Italy, Hungary, Bulgaria or Albania, as the case may be. This can only be prevented by the intervention of the major Allies, who would have to impose provisional frontiers within which the authority of the various Governments would be limited pending the peace settlement. But here again Great Britain and the United States will only be able to speak with authority and be able to impose their wishes if their armies are on the Continent. If this is not the case, then the Soviet Government will alone be in a position to prevent such fighting and to impose some provisional regime throughout this part of Europe.

It is, however, clearly not in our interests, or in the interests of Europe as a whole, that the Soviet Government should undertake the task of thus policing Central Europe. But if, as is probable, we have to acquiesce in their doing so, it is most desirable that some sort of arrangement should be made beforehand whereby the Soviet Government would undertake towards us and the United States to accept and conform to some general scheme whereby the various Allied Governments were established and confined within certain territorial limits and were enabled within those frontiers to establish and assert their authority as quickly as possible after the withdrawal of the enemy ...

... We are not yet in a position to predict what will be the circumstances attending the collapse of the Central Powers, and predictions as to the course of a war seldom turn out to be well founded. In particular, it is impossible to say where the remnants of the German armies will be or what will be the position of the Soviet armies and the state of mind of the Soviet Government when the collapse sets in. Any agreement negotiated with the Soviet Government now must therefore be based on hypotheses which may be falsified by events ...

C Clark Kerr to Eden, 21 February

I spent two hours with Molotov last night. He was in friendly and jocular mood ...

... but he confessed that, in the midst of their urgent military pre-occupations the Soviet Government had not yet got beyond the merest preliminary study ... They certainly had not cleared their own minds, but, when they had, they would be ready to open serious discussions ...

... Thus far things had gone well and easily, but when I referred to the first extract from Stalin's speech he showed discomfort and seemed to be unable or unwilling to understand the nature of our enquiry ...

... As the conversation went on his discomfort increased and he said that he would tell Stalin that His Majesty's Government had raised this point. I got the strong impression that he was afraid to commit himself without consulting his Chief and that this was the cause of his malaise . . .

. . . Meanwhile, in order that there should be no room for misunderstanding about the nature of our enquiry I said that I would put it to him in a private and personal letter. I am doing so today . . . [Eden minuted: 'Clark Kerr seems to have made rather heavy weather'. Orme Sargent: 'That is what I thought too on reading this telegram'.]

D Clark Kerr to Eden, telegrams of 26 February

First telegram

As I was leaving him last night, M. Stalin referred to the question of extracts from his speech of November 6th and produced a letter from himself to me in reply to private personal communication I had made to Molotov . . .

Second telegram

. . . I am of opinion that in order to clear up questions which refer to disarmament of Germany and methods of restraining the latter, as well as for reaching unity in this matter (and other matters likewise) only one correct method exists, namely that of a meeting between official representatives of both countries and the reaching of an agreement which would be binding on both parties. It was just this method which was proposed to British Government during Mr. Eden's visit to Moscow in December 1941, but British Government did not then respond, having no wish to become bound by any sort of agreement. Should, however, the British Government now consider it necessary to arrange such a meeting and to come to agreement with the Soviet Government on question of the fate of Germany or of other countries, the Soviet Government are prepared to meet them half way. [Churchill minuted: 'Foreign Secretary, please tell me what has happened to bring all this stuff up?']

E Minutes on a meeting between Orme Sargent, Ronald, Dew and Jebb

Jebb, 27 February

. . . It was agreed that Sir A. Clark Kerr had possibly been in error in writing a detailed letter to M. Molotov, but that Stalin's reaction, though vigorous, was not necessarily unpromising.

The real point was whether or not the Soviet Government would agree to

Three Power talks. The suggestion that they should so agree had been one of the central features of our instructions to the Ambassador . . .

Unfortunately Stalin in his letter had said that his idea would be 'a meeting between official representatives of both countries and the reaching of an agreement *which would be binding on both parties'*. Even if he could be persuaded therefore to agree to tripartite as opposed to bipartite conversations, there was reason to suppose that he would like to have some kind of formal conference the decisions of which would engage the three Governments. This was as at present advised *not* our idea, which was rather that experts from the three countries should meet together to see whether they were in a position to recommend any agreed policy to their respective Governments . . .

Sargent, 27 February

Although it is no use crying over spilt milk, it is a pity that Sir A. Clark Kerr should have got himself into the position of writing letters about Stalin's speech. We had merely intended that he should use the speech as a gambit for discussing post-war questions generally, and for this purpose it would have been clearly better that he should have played the gambit not with Molotov but with Stalin himself. When he saw that the move was not going to succeed with Molotov, it would have been better if he had played another move instead of writing a letter as he did . . .

F Eden to Churchill, 1 March

It seemed clear to me that our Ambassador on his return from leave ought to make some response to the allusion made by Stalin in his speech of last November regarding future Anglo–American–Soviet collaboration, and that he ought to use this opportunity to discuss with Stalin various specific questions of common interest, e.g. the situation in Yugoslavia, policy towards Roumania, the idea of Confederations in eastern and south-eastern Europe, in respect of which Soviet policy seems recently to have been uncertain.

It was, I confess, never my intention that our Ambassador should hand any written document to Molotov or to Stalin about the future of Germany . . . [Churchill initialled this minute on 4 March without comment.]

G Eden to Clark Kerr, 1 March

. . . It ought not to be necessary for you to continue a written correspondence with Stalin or Molotov on the subject of reference to Germany's future in Stalin's speech on November 6th. Reference to this part of the speech was only intended for you to use as an opening gambit and need not be pressed further . . .

... You have explored the Soviet attitude sufficiently for present purposes, and if the Soviet Government wish to know the attitude of the United States Government I presume that they will approach them direct.

As regards Stalin's suggestion for a meeting between official representatives of Great Britain and the Soviet Union with the object of reaching an agreement which would be binding on both parties, I should prefer to leave this question unanswered if possible since such a meeting in the present circumstances be clearly premature, but you can, if necessary, assure Stalin that having regard to Article 5 of the Anglo-Soviet Treaty we are always at his disposal to discuss matters of common interest affecting Europe. We do not want to pin Stalin down at this stage on any particular post-war question any more than we want to be pinned down ourselves, but we would always welcome a frank exchange of views in order to clear our own minds and avoid future misunderstandings.

17 Dispatch by O'Malley criticising the idea of post-war federations in Eastern Europe, 30 April 1943

... no pressure or persuasion from Britain is likely to induce the lesser Powers to unite in an effective confederation and to pool any part of their individual sovereignties unless they are assured that their individual aspirations and grievances are going to be considered by us on their merits rather than as subsidiary features of the terrain on which the forces of the Great Powers are deployed diplomatically or militarily against each other. If Germany is disarmed and if Russia emerges from the war as a military power of the first order, there will be one Great Power, namely Russia, which Britain will have to consider before all others in relation to events in Eastern Europe, and all the lesser States know it. They also surmise that we shall have strong inducements to acquiesce in Russia's wishes and very limited means of restraining her even if we wished to do so. Therefore, and so far as there might be any question of all or some of them uniting into one or more confederations, it is more than anything else by the view which each individually takes of communism and of Russian policy that their decision for or against union would be determined ...

... In general I would certainly not put it beyond the power of a victorious and dynamic Russia to lay a heavy hand upon all the peoples I have enumerated, and, having done so, and having carried her influence to the borders of Germany, to keep our great enemy at bay. But this prospect raises the important question of whether such a situation would be consonant with British interests or the interests of the world at large? ...

... I make no apology for the critical and destructive intention of this despatch, for believing that confederations cannot be made and would not work in the way and for the purposes which would suit us, I am bound to attack what seems to me illusory schemes. But to be sceptical about confederations is not to despair of making a modest advance towards an 'integrated Europe' if we not only deploy our military strength, and more particularly our financial and economic strength, but also exert to the full our moral authority. We are immensely powerful and may be more powerful at the conclusion of the war. We shall have the opportunity to exert great moral authority on the continent of Europe, because we are the only European Great Power that has no wish to annex or dominate or even create a new 'sphere of influence', because we alone are feared by none except those with whom we are at war, because we alone can hold the balance between despotism and chaos, and because, without us nothing can ensure freedom, justice and security to all . . .

Minutes on O'Malley's dispatch

Roberts, 13 May

. . . I agree with him, however, that it is just as well to face the possibility that circumstances may change and that the Russians may not play the part in the post-war world which we should wish. After all no previous war-time alliances have proved eternal and history is full of examples of great powers falling out after victory has been achieved. It therefore seems to me just as well that we should from time to time be reminded, as Mr. O'Malley has reminded us in this despatch, of the difficulties confronting us and of the view taken in many parts of Europe regarding Russia, whatever the form of government may be in Russia.

To sum up I think, therefore, that Mr. O'Malley's despatch should be regarded mainly as a warning note from a sceptic against putting too much confidence in a 'Brave New World' emerging from this war . . .

Dew, 17 May

. . . Mr. O'Malley considers quite rightly that Soviet policy is dictated by self-interest, but personally I doubt whether self-interest would lead the Soviet Government to follow the policy foreshadowed by him. Without going into the point in detail it seems to me that self-interest would only lead the Soviet Government to the policy in question (1) if it were felt that the independence of the countries in question threatened the security of the Soviet Union, or (2) because after the war Soviet policy becomes one of territorial aggrandisement not only in Europe but in Asia. In the first case, however, it seems to me that if after the war Germany is deprived of all power to repeat her policy of aggression, at least for a considerable number of years, the countries of Central and South-Eastern Europe which will have suffered greatly during the war will not be in a position either singly or in combination to offer any serious threat to the security of the U.S.S.R. While the Soviet Government may be preparing for all eventualities they cannot expect that an anti-Soviet policy on the part of these countries would be supported by the countries in Western Europe including Great Britain. Furthermore, from the point of view of the security argument would not a Soviet attempt to bring about the Sovietisation of Central and Eastern Europe be the one policy calculated to bring about such a revulsion of feeling among those countries which could offer a threat to the Soviet Union as to negative the value of such a policy from the point of view of Soviet interests?

If we assume that Soviet policy after the war will be one of aggrandisement the same arguments apply in that such a policy would merely promote a reaction from just those countries which are likely to offer a threat to the Soviet Union not only in Europe but in Asia, and would bring this country and the U.S. together with considerable backing against the U.S.S.R. Leaving aside the question of whether the sovietisation of European countries would really benefit the U.S.S.R. would this not be a dangerous policy to follow while the Soviet Government will have so much to do in the way of re-construction within the Soviet Union proper? . . .

Ronald, 25 May

. . . Personally I think that the way in which the Soviet Union will behave towards us and those in whom we profess to be interested after the war will, anyhow to some extent, be conditioned by how we behave towards her between now and then and by the habits of co-operation that we mutually contract towards one another and the extent to which the Soviet Govt. come to appreciate the value to them of those habits of co-operation. I continue to think therefore that in the interests of the countries in Central and South Eastern Europe the sooner we begin to exchange ideas with the Russians the better, about the roles which we two think those countries ought to play in their own interest and in that of those by whose exertions they will have been saved from absorption by Germany.

Strang, 29 May

. . . Unless the 80,000,000 aggressive Germans can be contained or tamed, our very existence, not only as a world power, but as an independent state, will be again threatened. In order to contain Germany we need Russian collabor-ation. The conclusion of the Anglo-Soviet Treaty last year marks our decision that this must be our policy now and after the war. No one can say what Russia's future policy will be. There is a respectable and well-informed opinion that Russia will not, either now or for some years after the war, aim at the bolshevisation of Eastern and Central Europe or adopt an aggressive policy elsewhere. But even if Mr. O'Malley's fears are justified and 'a victorious and dynamic Russia lays a heavy hand' upon the peoples of Eastern, Central and South-Eastern Europe, I should not like to say that this would be to our disadvantage provided that the German menace to our own existence continued to be mastered. It is better that Russia should dominate Eastern Europe than that Germany should dominate Western Europe. Nor would the domination of Eastern Europe by Russia be as easy as all that. And however strong Russia may become she is unlikely ever to be so grim a menace to us as Germany could again be within a few years were her aggressive tendencies once again to revive and to be given liberty to prepare and to act.

The time may come when Russia will take the place of Germany as a threat to our world power or to our existence. But there are no signs that this will occur in any immediate future. And if ever things turn that way, we shall, it is to be hoped, adjust our policy accordingly, and in time.

Cadogan, 4 July

Sir O. O'Malley's despatch is interesting reading, but I do not regard it as a helpful contribution . . .

18   Foreign Office reactions to the recall of Maisky, July–August 1943

Wilson, 27 July

. . . It is difficult to understand the motives behind this appointment, which seems rather like a slight to us. It will certainly make any kind of free exchange of views in London virtually impossible, and will concentrate things more and more in Moscow. I have no doubt that M. Maisky will be most valuable in Moscow, but they might have found us something better than M. Gusev.

Dew, 27 July

. . . It certainly seems very odd to appoint as Ambassador to your principal ally a man who has had so little experience, who has never before been an Ambassador, and who indeed at Ottawa is only a 2nd Class Minister lower in rank than M. Sobelev who is a 1st Class Minister. Admittedly suitable men for the post are difficult to find in Russia but really M. Gusev is one of the least suitable though he is probably one of the few who speak English and has specialised in British affairs . . .

. . . I must confess that I do not like this move at all and it will not look well if M. Litvinov returns to Washington while M. Maisky leaves London. If both Messrs. Maisky and Litvinov are to remain in Moscow then I should fear some unpleasant development in Soviet policy . . .

Warner, 28 July

It is certainly extremely strange that at this juncture the Soviet Government should replace M. Maisky by so inexperienced and junior an official as M. Gusev. If M. Litvinov was also replaced I agree that these changes would look rather sinister. I am not informed of the latest exchanges of personal telegrams between the Prime Minister and Marshal Stalin, if any, and I do not therefore know whether any deductions can be drawn from them as regards the Soviet Government's reaction to the latest developments. Their press and wireless publicity has, in spite of Sicily, been harping on the theme that it is a direct attack on Germany that is required from ourselves and the Americans. It may well be that the Soviet Government now see before them the possibility of Anglo-American troops getting into south-eastern Europe and even perhaps into Germany before Soviet troops are able to break right through on the Eastern Front. And it might be that this has revived in full strength all the old suspicion of an Anglo-American *cordon sanitaire* policy and an Anglo-American desire to deprive the Soviet Union of the fruits of victory.

On the other hand, it seems to me hardly likely that the substitution of M. Gusev for M. Maisky should be the result of a change of attitude which could only have taken place in the last few days. It is also I think quite possible that the explanation is an entirely different one viz. that the Soviet Government cannot get on in Moscow with events in Europe about to move so rapidly as at present appears likely, without the help of someone like M. Maisky and perhaps even M. Litvinov as well, and that M. Gusev, strange as it may seem to us, may genuinely appear to the Soviet Government the best appointment they can make, having regard to the fact that he has dealt with British affairs throughout his career . . .

Sargent, 28 July

I hope that Mr. Warner's interpretation in paragraph 2 of his minute is the right one, for frankly at first sight these changes do not make a good impression. M. Maisky is being demoted, being placed under Molotov in the Moscow Foreign Office, and he is being replaced in London by a man who obviously is quite unable to replace him for the purpose of any serious political discussions.

No doubt the Soviet Government are, as Mr. Warner says, alarmed at the possibility of Anglo-American troops getting into the Balkans and even into Germany before Russian troops do. But that in itself would not be a reason for reducing their contacts with H. M. Government. May not Stalin be moved by another consideration? May he not have convinced himself that H.M.G. are not going seriously to discuss any political issues arising out of the present war situation; and that since M. Maisky has never been able to get down to any concrete discussions on these matters, he may as well abandon the idea of working through the Soviet Embassy in London.

If this is really the case it has alarming possibilities, for it means that the Soviet Government, when we eventually do decide on negotiating with them and invite their collaboration, will have by that time made up their minds to plough a lonely furrow. It makes it all the more necessary, to my mind, that we should without delay put our cards on the table and show that we are ready to discuss with them questions such as the Polono-Russian frontier, the future of Germany, the handling of the States of Central Europe, the Balkans, etc.

Cadogan, 28 July

This is all rather sinister, to me.

If M. Gusev is the man I remember, I should say he was *not* a good choice. His English was sparse and peculiar. But he may have improved this in Canada.

Eden, 28 July

I agree. The business is difficult to understand and has a disquieting note about it. In any event we cannot refuse an agreement and should ask Sir A. Clark Kerr for his view of it all.

Clark Kerr to the Foreign Office, 3 August 1943

My impression is that it is poverty more than anything else that has obliged the Soviet Government to make this inadequate appointment. There is in fact only a handful of men of the calibre required . . .

I feel that you are reading too much into the appointment. It is not, in fact, out of harmony with Soviet habit. My colleague in Chungking was jumped from Trade Delegate to Ambassador on the spot at the age of about 55 and the present Soviet Ambassador in Tokyo was, I think, a promoted counsellor. M. Gusev is probably the best the Soviet can now do unless they draw on the list I have referred to: and I think it would be a mistake to assume that they propose to pursue a lone policy from Moscow. It is possible however that until M. Gusev gets into his stride (and I foresee that this will take some time) the Soviet may tend to handle important business through this Embassy rather than through London.

On the whole therefore I am averse from taking the matter up with Molotov. First we have allowed a whole week to go by and then the British Broadcasting Corporation yesterday announced M. Gusev's appointment. If there had been any chance of taking effective action, which I am disposed to doubt, it should have been taken at once . . .

19   Eden to Churchill on the need to improve three-power consultation, 12 July 1943

I have been considering whether there is anything we can do to facilitate Anglo-U.S.–Soviet consultation, more particularly in the political field, and so improve collaboration.

You have often met President Roosevelt, and we have both met Stalin, but there have as yet been no triangular meetings, and there is no machinery for quick and effective exchange of ideas. There has been a tendency for us to agree matters with the Americans first, and to present the results to the Russians, and there are signs that the Russians resent this procedure.

The ideal, of having a 3-Power directing body established at some point, is unattainable. The three principals cannot remain in joint session, they have not so far even met together anywhere. But I wonder whether we should not try to erect some machinery, somewhere, to start work on an amount of material that has to be dealt with. Neither Stalin, nor perhaps even the President, would be prepared to delegate full powers to a representative to take important decisions on vital questions in a 3-Power meeting, but I am inclined to think that the preliminary stages of discussion could be expedited by a simultaneous exchange of views on a lower level and, if necessary, only on a provisional basis. There are quite a number of questions, to cite one example, War Criminals, on which at present we have successive telegraphic exchanges with the United States and the Soviet Governments – which might, it seems to me, be quicker dealt with if we could centralize discussion.

Would you think it possible to suggest to the President that we might have periodical meetings here of Winant, Maisky and myself?

I believe we could clear a deal of detail out of the way and put proposals to our respective Governments in a provisionally agreed form that would greatly simplify consideration and decision.

Even if this proved of no very great practical value, I should think that we might gain some advantage from letting the Russians feel that they were admitted to discussion at an early stage. We want to work with them not only during the war but after. With however little justification the Russians appear to feel that they are only brought in perfunctorily after Anglo-American agreement. I know that Stalin has so far refused meetings with you and the President; we must accept that he would probably have great difficulty in accepting. Even though he may one day accept, I feel that it might help to have some more or less permanent form of triangular contact.

We could only aspire to deal with political questions. Inter-Allied machinery for dealing with operational questions was set up in Washington shortly after Japan attacked America. It was necessarily devised largely to meet Japanese aggression, and for that reason the Russians have no part nor lot in it. Gradually it has assumed control over operations in Europe in which the Russians, though not direct participants, are directly interested, and they probably do feel that they are excluded from our counsels, though you have hitherto kept Stalin informed of all major decisions.

I am not suggesting that this can be changed at present, though I think that occasional meetings with Winant and Maisky might give the latter an opportunity to raise operational questions and ventilate them before the pressure of resentment blows out the safety-valve.

I would not propose regular meetings, but I think I could find a subject, say once a fortnight or so, that requires discussion between us three, and I believe that some practical, as well as psychological, advantages could be derived from a discussion à trois.

If you think there is anything in this, I suppose the first step would be to sound the President . . .

20   Wilson to Clark Kerr on dealing with the Russians, 8 August 1943

. . . Russian matters are pretty tricky at the moment. [Churchill] is the real snag. His statement the other day about consulting the Americans and informing the Russians was no slip of the tongue. It's his deliberate policy and it's going to land us in one hell of a mess. He's been told so often enough, but FDR is much more of a buddy than Joe and now that he can see the end of the war in sight my impression is that he does not care two hoots about the Russians. If they come to tag along with us, well and good; if not, they can go and boil themselves. The pity of it is that it's the Russians themselves who are so responsible for all this. Their general bloodiness about visas, the treatment of personnel in North Russia, wives, etc. and their general ungraciousness have made people here get the impression that it's impossible to deal with them, and as I can see this Office is the only place where it is realized that, in spite of all these things, we just *have* to get along with them or Europe will be a ghastly place for a long time. These things that the Russians are bloody about don't really matter fundamentally, and are intelligible enough to anybody who comes to look dispassionately at their history. But they are things which have to be dealt with day by day and they just put people's backs up . . .

As it is there has been no special high-powered contact with the Russians since the P.M. was in Moscow – there has been constant toing and froing with the Americans. The talks you started successfully in February were abandoned through a bad case of cold feet and nothing has happened since. The Russians will draw their own conclusions from all this, and they will not be helpful ones. But they will be correct, damn it . . .

21 Warner to Clark Kerr on dealing with the Russians, 28 September 1943

. . . we have tried to indicate to the Russians that we are prepared to discuss pretty well all the big things except the Second Front and have also tried to give ourselves the opportunity of eliciting Russian thoughts on the future . . .

Everything they do seems to me to be equally susceptible of two interpretations (A) the more optimistic one that they will collaborate and can learn to do so, if they are convinced that they will get a fair deal from us, (B) that they have not changed at all, that they have been at pains to get as much out of us as possible while they needed it, and for that purpose have gone in for a lot of window dressing . . .

Apart from the question whether they wish to collaborate, there is the question whether they can collaborate, or whether their whole background and mind does not make it impossible to collaborate with them, because their idea of collaboration is all take and no give.

22 Extracts from the proceedings of the Foreign Ministers' Conference in Moscow 19–30 October 1943

A Fourth meeting, 22 October

Item 3. Politico-Military Commission

MR. EDEN, after emphasising that his remarks were preliminary in character, made the following statement:

I have always thought it would be desirable to set up permanent machinery for consultation between the three Powers. There is great need for such machinery, and if at this Conference we can set it up, we shall have made a further and important contribution to closer collaboration between us. I attach urgent importance to this question and I therefore welcome the original Soviet proposal for a Politico-Military Commission.

I have already circulated to the Conference a paper suggesting terms of reference for the Commission (see Annex 4). Since circulating it, I have been reflecting further on the question and would like to modify my proposals.

In your original conception, the Commission was to turn its attention first to Italian problems and it was to be located only in Algiers. Our idea was, that if, as we hoped, its scope was widened, it might move, say, to London.

In making this suggestion I do not overlook two suggestions made by the Soviet Government.

These two suggestions of the Soviet Government were first, that the Commission should also deal with negotiations with other Axis satellites who might dissociate themselves from Germany, and second, with the question of liberated territory; and also that the Commission should actually direct and co-ordinate the work of the various organs of control in Italy.

As regards the first point, the more I think of it, the more I am convinced that the Commission should have very wide terms of reference. Indeed, I think that it might be entrusted with the study of any European questions, other than military operational questions, which our three Governments might agree to refer to it. It would have an advisory character and its members would make recommendations either collectively or individually to their Governments. We should thus have a permanent body which would act as a clearing house for European problems of common interest connected with the war. This might be of the greatest service to us all.

A body with such comprehensive terms of reference could not, I think, conveniently meet at Algiers or in Italy. It would be essential that it should meet in one of the three capitals, and I should be happy if my colleagues would agree to London, which would be a convenient central place. We should be ready to welcome it there at any time.

I now come to the second Soviet proposal, namely, that the Commission should take executive charge of the control machinery in Italy.

This raises one or two points.

The first is a constitutional point. In view of our own system of government, we should not be able to agree that a Commission of this character should itself decide questions of major policy or have executive functions. In our conception the Commission would be advisory. It would make recommendations to Governments but the Governments would decide.

The second is a practical point. If the Commission undertook to direct the work of control in Italy, it would become local in character and would be absorbed in day to day affairs and would be tied to the Mediterranean area. It could not in these circumstances fulfil the wider functions which we have in mind for it.

There is a third practical point. Other machinery of an international character is in contemplation which would provide for the association of our three Governments, with some others, to operate the control machinery in Italy. This would not, of course, preclude the Commission in London from concerning itself with the Italian question in its broader aspects if it were desired . . .

B Seventh meeting, 25 October

Permanent status of Germany

MR. EDEN said that after the war the British Government would like to see a united Germany give way to a number of separate States. They would particularly like to see the separation of Prussia from the rest of Germany and thought that they should do whatever they could to encourage separatist movements. The British Government found it impossible at present to assess the prospects of imposing such a solution by force. They therefore kept an open mind on the subject but did not exclude the possibility. He would be glad to know the Soviet Government's views as to what was a desirable goal to work for and how it should be done.

M. MOLOTOV said that, in all measures calculated to make Germany harmless as an aggressor State, the Soviet Government gave full support to the British and American Governments, and he repeated the words 'in all measures' by way of emphasis. Was that enough or not?

MR. EDEN said that he would like to know M. Molotov's mind on this point. The Prime Minister had specially asked him to enquire about the breaking up of Germany after the war. The British view was that, if separatist movements existed, they should be encouraged, but if it was necessary to force them they had not made up their minds. What did the Soviet Government think?

M. MOLOTOV said that, so far as the American paper was concerned, it seemed to him that Mr. Hull had put it forward as a minimum programme which might be found insufficient on further study. The Soviet Government had so far received no proposals from Great Britain. They had the impression that the United States Government were prepared to go further than the British Government, but this had not found expression in the document presented by Mr. Hull.

MR. EDEN said that he had nothing to add to what he had already said, namely, that the British Government wanted to encourage separatist movements and had an open mind on the enforced splitting up of Germany, and that the Prime Minister would be very much influenced if he knew the Soviet Government's view.

M. MOLOTOV said that he would reply to Mr. Eden's question, but wanted some information first. Was he correct in thinking that the British Government approached this problem with less resolution and with plans less broad than those of the United States Government?

MR. EDEN replied that it was for the Americans to state their position. His Cabinet had taken no decision. Some were in favour of the forcible splitting up of Germany, others were doubtful whether it was practicable. The Prime Minister had asked him to find out what his Soviet colleagues thought.

MR. HULL said he could not say more than was in his document. They had sought to make this contribution as a sound and suitable basis for discussion When they approached this question they found widely divergent views among the Allied Governments and very cogent reasons advanced in support of the different views. Members of his Government had started with a definite inclination in favour of the dismemberment of Germany. As discussions had proceeded, the trend had still been in that direction, but less strongly so, and they were determined to keep an open mind so as to consider all ideas and opinions which might determine the matter in one way or the other. The subject should be fully exhausted so that they might find out what was practicable.

M. MOLOTOV said that the Soviet Government was somewhat backward in the study of this question, probably because of the military pre-occupations of their leaders. He noted the fact that the United States Government had the honour of having tackled this question and of having submitted this document. The Soviet attitude to it was favourable. They thought that the programme submitted by Mr. Hull correctly illuminated the main questions. He noted, too, that the programme was a minimum rather than a maximum one, and he thought that Mr. Eden was quite right to put his question. Of course, further study must be given to the question, and he would give some indication of the opinions that prevailed upon it in the Soviet Union. He said frankly that people would be found who would be prepared to go further than Mr. Hull and would think his proposals insufficient. He did not doubt that any voice raised in favour of dismemberment by force would carry great weight. The Soviet Government paid attention to these feelings. They would continue to study the whole question in the light of Soviet public opinion and of the views of their Allies, and also from the point of view of whether this or any other solution was politically advisable. But at present he could not say that the Soviet Government had come to any definite conclusion as the matter was still under consideration. He hoped that the Conference would be helpful in studying this matter and in preparing the way for a decision by the Governments. He wanted to make it clear that the Soviet

Government did not think that the forcible dismemberment of Germany was excluded.

MR. EDEN said that the Soviet position seemed to be the same as our own and therefore no reply was needed and no remarks called for about the activities of their respective leaders in connexion with military operations.

(After a short interval)

M. MOLOTOV remarked that not much was said about the future frontiers of Germany, and asked whether Mr. Hull contemplated the restoration of territory captured by Germany.

MR. HULL replied that his Government had not yet come to that point in their study of the German question. They had made no effort at this stage to come to any decisions on these questions.

MR. EDEN said that surely it could be agreed that Germany should at least revert to her pre-Anschluss frontiers.

M. MOLOTOV agreed and said that there could be no second opinion about it . . .

C Eighth meeting, 26 October, and Annex

M. MOLOTOV said that he had a statement to make on the proposal as regards confederations, and he then read the statement of which a translation is given in Annex 7 to the Secret Protocol of the Conference.

MR. EDEN thanked M. Molotov for his statement and said that the discussion on this subject had been very useful. His Government was not interested in the cordon sanitaire against Russia, but was deeply interested in it against Germany. There was great force in what M. Molotov had said about the difficulty of making progress until Governments unmistakably representative of their people could speak for them in the smaller countries. He did not, therefore, press for any statement by the Conference now on paragraphs 2 and 3, especially as, after what M. Molotov had said, he felt that their points of view were fundamentally very close together.

MR. HULL said that, without going into a recital of the principles applicable to small nations, his Government had for some years sought to set forth and keep alive the principles relating to the rights of small nations in the war and post-war situations. M. Molotov's statement in the main was in harmony with the principles enunciated by his Government for several years, and there would be no difficulty in harmonising them in principle.

M. MOLOTOV said that, as his statement met with no objection from Mr. Eden and Mr. Hull, the question of confederations could now be put forward in a different form.

MR. EDEN said it was largely a question of timing. M. Molotov had said he did not think this was a proper moment, and he thought that was probably right. He did not think we need do anything now. There had been a good discussion and they could all consider the matter later, nearer the time.

This view was generally accepted . . .

Annex 7. The future of Poland and Danubian and Balkan countries, including the question of federations
The Soviet Government consider the liberation of small countries and the restoration of their independence and sovereignty as one of the most important tasks in the post-war arrangement of Europe and in the creation of lasting peace. For this purpose the defeat of aggressive force, as a result of the victory of the Allies and the removal of the threat of new aggression, at any rate in the first years after the war, will create favourable conditions. The Soviet Government consider that the small countries will require some time, which cannot yet be definitely calculated and which will not be the same for all of them, to enable them fully to orientate themselves in the new situation created as a result of the war and in the re-created relationships with neighbouring and other States, without being subjected to any outside pressure to join this or that new grouping of States. The premature and possibly artificial attachment of these countries to theoretically planned groupings would be full of danger both for the small countries themselves as well as for the future peaceful development of Europe. Such an important step as federation with other States and the possible renunciation of part of their sovereignty is admissible only as a result of a free, peaceful and well-considered expression of the will of the people. It is to be feared that neither the existing *émigré* Governments nor even the Governments which will be set up immediately after the conclusion of peace under conditions still not sufficiently normal will be able fully to ensure the expression of the real will and permanent aspirations of their people. The creation of such federations by the decisions of *émigré* Governments which, in virtue of their special situation, cannot be closely bound with their people, might be interpreted as imposing on the people decisions not in conformity with their wishes. It would be particularly unjust if countries which had become satellites of Hitlerite Germany should at once be placed as equal members of any such federation in conditions as favourable as those of other small States, which had been the victims of attack and occupation, at the hands, among others, of those same satellites, and thus freed from the consequences of their part in the Hitler–Mussolini crises.

Moreover, some of the plans for federations remind the Soviet people of the policy of the 'cordon sanitaire', directed, as is known, against the Soviet Union and therefore viewed unfavourably by the Soviet people.

For these reasons, the Soviet Government consider it premature, from the point of view of the interests both of the small countries themselves and of the general post-war settlement of Europe, now to plan and thus artificially to encourage combinations of any States in the form of federations and so forth. They will in due course be ready to re-examine this question in the light of the experience of post-war co-operation with other United Nations and of the circumstances which may arise after the war.

D Tenth meeting, 28 October

... It was agreed that the proposals regarding Turkey and Sweden should be dealt with separately.

Turkey

MR. EDEN stated that His Majesty's Government entirely shared the Soviet view as to the desirability of Turkey being brought into the war at the earliest possible date. The question was one of ways and means. He did not believe that Turkey would be prepared to come into the war of her own volition. If pressure was brought to bear on her he considered it certain that she would require guarantees to help in her defence against any action the Germans might be able to take against her. Our own commitments in the Mediterranean made it quite impossible for us to give any such guarantee. Indeed, we should not be able to provide Turkey with the 25 squadrons of aircraft which we were committed to supply in the event of a German attack against that country. He therefore suggested that possibly the best way of bringing Turkey into the war was by stages to bring her from neutrality, through non-belligerency, to active participation.

MR. HULL did not dissent from the view expressed that it was desirable that Turkey should rapidly be brought into the war, but did not think that any steps should be taken in this direction to induce her to do so in view of the other pressing claims on Allied resources in men, material and transportation. Mr. Hull did suggest, however, that an approach might be made to Turkey for the lease of air bases and transportation facilities upon the basis of Turkey remaining neutral.

M. MOLOTOV said that it appeared to him that on this question the three Powers were a long way apart. He himself considered that for Turkey to be brought into the war at the present stage would unquestionably involve the enemy in great difficulties, and he was not satisfied that a joint approach by the three Powers, coupled with the threat of withholding further supplies of arms to the Turks, would not meet with success. If it were decided to postpone such an approach, he failed to understand what case there was for continuing to supply arms to Turkey at all. Against whom were these arms to be used?

MR. EDEN pointed out that, in fact, we were a long way behind in the supply of arms and munitions to Turkey to which we were committed. We had diverted a considerable part of the resources allocated to Turkey to our own more pressing needs.

M. MOLOTOV proposed, and it was agreed, that the Delegations should report the above exchange of views to their Governments with a view to the Soviet proposals being re-examined and further consideration being given to them at a later date.

MR. EDEN stated that if His Majesty's Government decided to ask for the use of airfields in Turkish territory, they would, of course, inform the other two Governments beforehand.

Sweden

MR. EDEN stated that, while he was advised that the use of air bases in Sweden would not be of advantage to us in our bomber offensive against Germany, he did not, on that account, oppose the Soviet proposal if our Allies were likely to derive advantage from it. In this case also, however, Sweden would be unlikely to agree to grant bases to the Allies without guarantees of assistance in her defence. Our commitments did not at present permit of such guarantees being given.

MR. HULL expressed the opinion that the moment was not opportune for making such a request of Sweden, but proposed that consideration should be given to the matter at a later date.

M. MOLOTOV explained that he had not put forward the proposal on account of any direct advantage that the Soviet Government expected to obtain from the use of airfields in Sweden. He went on to point out that the two proposals the Soviet Government had put forward for shortening the war against Germany appeared to receive little support from the British and American Delegations. He therefore enquired whether anyone had any other proposals to put forward with a view to this end . . .

23   PHPS paper on military occupation in south-eastern Europe, 10 February 1944

The objectives of the Three Powers

. . . 4 When the enemy States in South-Eastern Europe surrender, and the Allied States are liberated, the main objects of the Three Powers will be to maintain their ability to impose their will on each defeated nation, to see that the terms of surrender are speedily and completely carried out, and to ensure that, as far as possible, political and economic developments in the Balkans conform to their interests.

5 There are substantial political reasons in favour of the presence of British forces of occupation in this area, although it may well be that the Three

Powers will not see altogether eye to eye on this question. The principal political arguments are:

a The Four-Power Declaration, to which the United Kingdom is a party, clearly contemplates that action taken for such purposes as re-establishing conditions of peace and order in South-Eastern Europe should be joint action.
b Even apart from this aspect, if South-Eastern Europe is left entirely to its own devices after this war, it is likely that the resultant anarchy will, in the long run, entail action by some Great Power, and that if this means uni-lateral action by the Soviet Union there might be grave danger of a dis-ruption of the Anglo-American–Soviet front.
c In any event, the possibility of a physical occupation of the whole area by Russia is not one which, on the whole, the United Kingdom could contem-plate with equanimity.

6 From the military point of view occupation by Allied forces is also desirable. Not only is it the most effective means of impressing the peoples of the conquered States with the reality of their defeat, but the maintenance of order is a prerequisite to the carrying into effect of the various relief schemes and the restoration of normal daily life, and it is most improbable that in the absence of Allied forces of occupation such conditions will exist. Moreover, experience shows that Control Commissions and other Allied bodies will need the backing of forces of occupation if they are to carry out their duties effectively.

Liberated countries

7 All our information points to the probability of serious disorder, amounting perhaps to civil war, existing in Greece, Yugoslavia and Albania when the enemy withdraw. It may well be inadvisable for the Three Powers to intervene in the internal affairs of these countries, but they cannot remain entirely indifferent. We suggest that they must be prepared to undertake at least the following tasks:

i to protect lines of communication;
ii to protect United Nations Agencies, such as those for relief and re-habilitation, and
iii to maintain order in disputed or disturbed frontier areas . . .

Bulgaria

. . . 18 Should Russia obtain control of Bulgaria she would be in a position to establish airfields within 100 miles of the Straits. Moreover, the Russians have a traditional connection with Bulgaria and occupation by them might lead to permanent control. Occupation by British forces would tend to strengthen British influence, not only in Bulgaria, but also in Greece and Turkey. Moreover, the Soviet Union is not at war with Bulgaria, whereas the United Kingdom is . . .

24   Dispatch from Dana Wilgress, Canadian Ambassador in Moscow, 9 March 1944, and later Foreign Office comments

. . . 6 From now on we may expect the Soviet Union to act as any other national state concerned chiefly with looking after its own interests rather than being concerned with spreading its own ideology by means of a Marxian crusade. This does not mean that the Soviet Union may not attempt to bring about the establishment of communist regimes in other countries if this would further its own interests, but a strong case can be made out for the view that this would be contrary to the interests of the Soviet Union in the post-war period. More than any other country, except perhaps China, the Soviet Union will require a long period of peace and security and this will only be possible if the communist bogy is allayed and other countries are satisfied that the Soviet Government is not interested in interfering in their internal affairs. The history of the period between the wars showed that the communist bogy can be used for promoting the formation of anti-Soviet blocks and for establishing reactionary regimes in other countries, all of which is antagonistic to peace and security. Stalin is said to be sincerely desirous of disproving Hitler's contention that the Soviet Union is out to bolshevize Europe. No doubt this is true because it is consistent with his chief ambition to go down in history as the man who not only made the Soviet Union strong but also made it possible for the Soviet peoples to benefit from Soviet socialism through a plentiful supply of consumers' goods . . .

The interests of the Soviet Union in peace and security, therefore, are very great and real. Until the ravages of the war are repaired and until the Soviet Union becomes a country which is actually, and not merely potentially, strong economically, it is reasonable to assume that the Soviet Government will concentrate on a pacific policy of internal development and will take care to avoid any actions in the external sphere which might disturb the system of peace and security which will be so necessary to the Soviet Union . . .

9 This assumes, of course, that a satisfactory and workable system of general security will be established after the war. It assumes also that the Soviet Union will not be frustrated in the attainment of what she considers to be her just minimum demands. These include the recognition of the incorporation in the Union of the Baltic States, the fixing of a frontier with Poland

which is ethnographically just and strategically satisfactory to the Soviet Union, the securing of adequate reparations from Germany for the damage inflicted by the invaders on Soviet territory, disarmament of Germany and other measures to prevent the recurrence of German aggression until the Soviet Union is strong enough economically to fear no longer the threat of such aggression, and the avoidance by the United Kingdom and the United States of a rapprochement with Germany that appears aimed against the Soviet Union.

10 Given these conditions the Soviet Union may be expected to cooperate wholeheartedly in a system of collective security. The Soviet Government may also be expected to avoid scrupulously interference in the internal affairs of democratic countries and especially the appearance of supporting communist parties in these countries, because to do so would immediately align other countries against the Soviet Union and disturb the system of security she so badly needs for internal reasons. This does not mean that in the immediate period of the restoration of the liberated territories the Soviet Union will be indifferent to the regimes which will be established in these territories. On the contrary she will continue to follow a most forward and progressive policy as she has already shown in regard to France, Italy, Poland and Yugoslavia. That policy will be to make possible the coming to power of regimes likely to have the broadest possible base of popular support and to remove from Europe the last vestiges of fascist-minded regimes. Particularly the policy will aim at preventing in countries strategically placed like Poland the establishment of regimes motivated by hostility to the Soviet Union, because then such a country would be a base for anti-Soviet intrigues and for the formation of anti-Soviet blocks. This, however, is not the same as endeavouring to establish communist regimes in other countries. I believe that the Soviet Government would be embarrassed if the communists should come to power in any European country. This would justify Hitler's ominous predictions of the Bolshevik menace and would align other countries against the Soviet Union to the prejudice of the system of general security . . .

Warner, 2 July

. . . Even if Russian suspicions, which are almost pathologically acute, can be allayed – in spite of probable differences of outlook on the degree of harshness to be employed against Germany – the Kremlin is by nature and tradition 'anti-right-wing' and Soviet Russia has an attraction for the more radical left-wing elements in most countries. They will, almost inevitably favour such elements in any country, where there is no good 'raison d'etat' for refraining . . . unless the Kremlin becomes a good deal more sensitive to feeling in this country and the U.S.A. than they are at present and find in collaboration with this country or the U.S.A. sufficient reason for conducting themselves very carefully in this matter, their support of the more extreme left-wing elements in European (and perhaps S-American countries) will arouse immense suspicion, I fear, among moderates and right-wingers here and in the U.S.A. This will make any real degree of collaboration difficult.

Cadogan, 4 July

. . . But as Mr. Warner points out, there are many difficulties in the way of wholehearted collaboration between the Soviet and the countries of the West, not all of them of the latters' making. However, there is no doubt that our own policy must be directed to cooperation: if it fails, it must not be through our fault.

Eden, 6 July

That is so. It is all very difficult, but at least we are convinced that we are trying to operate the right policy. The Russians may make it impossible. If we fail it should not be through our fault, nor through an undue display of weakness on our part towards Russia.

Warner, 29 July

. . . But it is pretty clear that, while taking account of our close relations with the U.S.A., they are 'suspicious' of a British–American line up against them. Particularly where Europe is concerned, they are at pains to indicate that they are everywhere (e.g. France, Norway, Italy) entitled to be consulted and apt to resent too great a tendency for H.M.G. and the U.S.G. to settle major matters in principle between themselves and then inform or consult the Soviet Govt. after – more or less as a matter of form. (Conversely when H.M.G. recently suggested to the Kremlin that we shd. take the lead in Greece and they in Roumania, they immediately enquired the views of the U.S. Govt.)

If the Americans 'pull out' of Europe, the Russians wd. then, I think, consider that they and we shd. principally collaborate on European affairs and wd. be apt to react badly if we still made the U.S. Govt. our principle consultants on Europe . . .

25 Foreign Office paper on post-war Soviet policy, 29 April 1944

Probable post-war tendencies in Soviet foreign policy as affecting British interests

Part I

The probable long-term impact of Russian strategic policy on British interests depends upon Russia's power, her major interests and her general outlook on world affairs. Of her power, and her capacity to use it, if she wishes, there can be little doubt. In, say, ten years, in man-power, in economic resources, in industrial capacity she will be immensely strong and, almost certainly, well organised.

2 Of her major interests and outlook in ten years' time it is far more difficult to predict. But certain fixed points can be discerned. Internally, the fixed points are that the U.S.S.R. will remain a highly-centralised federation where all the means of production are publicly owned and centrally planned and controlled; and that Russia's major interest will be to devote her main energies for many years to come to the colossal task of post-war rehabilitation and the further development of her own territories. Externally the fixed point will be in the future, as it has been in the past (at any rate, since Stalin's victory over Trotsky), the search for security against any Power or combination of Powers which might threaten her while she was organising and developing her own domain. In particular, after her narrow escape and tremendous losses she will fear a German recovery.

3 The result of Germany's attack upon the Soviet Union has been (a) to consolidate the regime; (b) to retard her internal development; (c) to face her with a vast task of rehabilitation in the occupied areas which must take her, one would suppose, at least five years; (d) to cause her an enormous loss of manpower in the younger generation; (e) to give her the chance of exorcising for an indefinite time her fear of Germany and Japan; (f) to give her the chance of getting on to terms of equality, confidence and co-operation with the remaining principal world Powers. In other words, the war has complicated or at any rate retarded her task of internal organisation and development, but will have given her the opportunity of devoting herself to it without fear either of aggression from without or of counter-revolution from within.

4 The logical deduction seems to be that, provided the British Commonwealth and the United States do not appear to the Soviet authorities to wish to deprive Russia of the means of eliminating the menace from Germany (and Japan), do not appear to be supporting a combination against her and give reasonable consideration to her views, Russia will welcome a prolonged period

of peaceful relations with the British Commonwealth and the United States. She will need at least five years for rehabilitation, and many further years for the development of her internal resources and for industrialisation and social development. During this period it is unlikely that she would be prepared to risk the interruption of a major war, whether during that period she had adopted a policy of co-operation or had decided to play a lone hand.

5 But this prediction is based on the assumption that the Russians do not suspect us of having designs hostile to her security, and that largely depends on whether she is satisfied with the measures taken to render Germany (and Japan) innocuous. Should she not be so satisfied (and her demands are likely to be high and her methods perhaps very drastic to British and American eyes), she will always be in fear of an eventual combination with Germany against her, her attitude to this country will be suspicious and potentially antagonistic, she will be more preoccupied with her own security and will take her own measures to provide for it. She would then probably become an intensely disruptive force in Europe. She would be unlikely, save as a last resort and in exceptional circumstances (see paragraph 37 below), to combine with Germany, for this would lead to a German revival and would thus be dangerous to herself. But she would be constantly manoeuvring to increase the strength of her own position in Europe by establishing her influence in European countries through Left-wing Governments and by interfering in their internal affairs both through intrigue and through power politics. Outside Europe, too, she would no doubt follow a similar policy.

6 One may predict, then, with some confidence, that, during a period of at least five years after the termination of the war with Germany, Russia will be preoccupied with her post-war rehabilitation and will constitute no menace to British strategic interests. During this period she almost certainly will experiment with the policy of co-operation with the British Commonwealth and the United States in whatever world organisation may be set up after the war. If this gives satisfactory results from the Russian point of view and in particular if she is satisfied that we have no intention of allowing Germany's power to be restored, this experiment may become an established feature of her foreign policy and the period during which she would constitute no threat to major British strategic interests may be indefinitely prolonged, while she continues her internal development. Even if through the withdrawal of the United States or any other reason post-war schemes for a world organisation should fail, the Soviet Union would not necessarily withdraw from co-operation with Great Britain. If, on the other hand, she finds the experiment of co-operation a failure, she will almost certainly seek to weaken British and American influence, but she will not necessarily become expansionist and her policy may well still not directly threaten British strategic interests, especially if the British Commonwealth can rely on American support. Russia, however,

will almost certainly keep herself immensely strong on land and in the air. So far as can be judged at present she is most unlikely to be troubled by internal disorders. Her influence throughout the Eastern hemisphere is likely to be great and she could develop an overwhelming threat to our position in the Middle East.

7 Part II of this paper elaborates the argument of the preceding paragraphs. Part III deals with Russian interests in particular areas ... The Russians are going to dread the recovery of Germany in a way in which we have never done, even in our blackest moments. This may take two forms, either they will set themselves the task of keeping Germany indefinitely in a state of abject subjection, or, if they find that they are obstructed by the other world Powers from applying this policy, they may decide that the best course is to make friends of their enemy while they are still in the way with them. In that case we may see a close German–Russian collaboration growing up against the rest of Europe and Asia ...

24 But without looking so far ahead as that we may expect that from the peace settlement onwards any friction there is between us and Russia will not arise so much out of ideological disagreement but chiefly, if not solely, because we and the Russians may take different views as to the post-war treatment of Germany. There is good evidence that Russia desires the most drastic measures to keep Germany in a permanent state of weakness and wishes to see the complete defeat of Japan. Stalin is an advocate of the complete dismemberment of Germany, and there is little doubt that the Soviet Government propose both to exact from German war criminals, from the highest to the lowest, a terrible punishment and to make Germany render, both in labour and in goods, the fullest possible contribution to the rapid restoration of the devastation she has caused in Russia. In other words, Soviet foreign policy is still based on the search for absolute security until she can render herself impregnable. Nor will the Soviet Government take any chances (such is not their habit) of any strong Power or combination of Powers growing up on her western frontier which might themselves, or in combination with a revived Germany, constitute a preoccupation to the Soviet Union. The Soviet Government have up to the recent past at any rate suspected that the United States and Great Britain wanted to husband their strength while Germany and Russia weakened each other, and that many circles in the United States and this country still desired a barrier between Western Russia and the rest of Europe. It seems to be the Soviet Government's way to apply simple but somewhat drastic tests to the real intentions of foreign countries, even of her Allies. It is very likely that the final test they will apply to these suspicions is the attitude taken up by this country and the United States on the question of the post-war treatment of Germany and the States that lie between Germany and the Soviet Union, and in the post-war period on the

zeal with which we enforce the letter of the treaty on Germany and show ourselves ready to knock Germany on the head every time she shows any sign of recovery either military or economic – Russia is likely to view with grave suspicion the argument that a prosperous Germany is necessary if Europe as a whole, and Great Britain in particular, is to be prosperous. Russia's post-war attitude is likely also in the same way to be influenced by the effect upon her own security of our post-war treatment of Japan and the post-war settlement we advocate for the Far East generally.

25 On the other hand, the war has given the Soviet Union the opportunity of transforming themselves from a revolutionary Power, to a great extent isolated from and suspected by the other Great Powers – something of a pariah – into one of the four leaders of the world. If she can achieve a satisfactory co-operation with the other three in ordering the post-war system, this would give her a better assurance than any other of freedom from external pre-occupations, while she was carrying out her own internal industrial and social development. It would also open to her a position of respect and even of admiration throughout the world. There are signs that such a transformation from their previous role has some attraction for them.

26 The Soviet Government is now clearly ready to give co-operation with the United States and Great Britain a trial. If the post-war settlement in Europe gives her sufficient reassurance against a German revival and sufficient satisfaction to her desires in other directions, she is likely to continue the trial for at least the five or more years required for the rehabilitation of Soviet territory. If reasonably successful, the experiment might well be further prolonged. Soviet ideas are not rigid and it is possible that, with the lapse of time, with the success of her own internal developments and the successful operation of international organisations in which Russia will be playing a leading part, international co-operation might have become something of a habit with the Soviet Government.

27 But in the initial stages at any rate, the Soviet Government will not be easy to satisfy. They certainly require, in the first place, that their western frontiers should be along the lines of those of 1941. In the second place, a settlement in regard to Germany which will 'completely exclude the possibility of fresh aggression on the part of Germany' (Stalin, the 6th November, 1943). In the third place, Russia will wish to be satisfied that nearby European countries are not in a position or in the mood to threaten her territory either alone or in combination or to prevent her getting at Germany, if the Soviet Government think it necessary at any time to employ force to keep her in a state of docility. This latter consideration dictates the whole of her Polish policy. The Declaration of the Moscow Conference on Italy, which originated with the Soviet delegation, may be taken as an indication of Soviet desires elsewhere. The Soviet Government will no doubt continue to suspect Right-

wing Governments. But in their conversations with His Majesty's Government they have drawn a distinction between the countries to the east of Germany, which they consider should, in friendly relations with the Soviet Government, form the eastern bulwark against the possibility of a German revival, and the countries of Western Europe who should, led by Great Britain, form the western bulwark . . .

33 With their internal preoccupations the Soviet Government would be most unlikely to follow a purely expansionist policy. They would more probably be passively unco-operative and work steadily against schemes of international co-operation favoured by this country, rather than be adventurous and provocative where British interests are concerned. More especially would this be the case if Anglo-American relations were good and the United States had not withdrawn into isolation but seemed likely to support the British Commonwealth. Even when it became clear – and it might not become clear for a considerable time – that Russia had finally decided against a policy of co-operation, Anglo-Soviet relations would not necessarily undergo an immediate and violent reversal. It is, perhaps, more likely that the deterioration would extend over a number of years as instances of Soviet action antagonistic to the interests of this country gradually accumulated. We should probably little by little fall back into a prolonged period of uneasy relations poisoned by mutual suspicions, which would spread to and divide other countries and would hinder the progress of settlement and recovery in war-devastated Europe. This might well lead to very serious divisions of opinion in this country, to which the Soviet Union would not hesitate to contribute.

34 No doubt the Soviet Union's policy towards British interests will be affected to a major degree by the attitude of the United States both towards this country and towards the U.S.S.R., supposing the United States withdraws from international co-operation in the political sphere. But here it becomes unprofitable to speculate owing to the multitude of factors, internal and external, which would come into play in the United States. Popular feeling towards the Soviet Union is far less favourable now than in our own country, irrespective of anti-Soviet pressure groups such as the Roman Catholics and the Poles. For many ordinary Americans the Soviet Union remains the apostle of communism, and to American organised labour even socialism is regarded as a danger to the American way of life. In the United States, therefore, the Bolshevik bogy is very much alive. This is balanced to some extent by the American respect for Russia's mere size and for her proved but unsuspected industrial capacity . . .

37 The Soviet Union's main immediate interest will be to extract – through compulsory labour and deliveries in kind – as full reparation as possible for the enormous damage inflicted by the Germans. Russia's long-term policy towards Germany is that she should be so completely weakened that she will

no longer be a potential menace. To this end Stalin has suggested that Germany should be split up into a number of separate units, which should be kept separate, by force if necessary, and that Germany east of the Oder should go to Poland. Provided the Russians can secure this dismemberment of Germany the complexion of the Governments of the resulting States would be a secondary consideration. The Free German Committee can safely be regarded as a mere propaganda weapon and its doctrines as no indication of the Soviet Government's real intentions towards Germany. It is to be observed, however, that the Soviet Government, at least in their formal official pronouncements, still qualify the Germans and Germany as 'Hitlerite' or 'Fascist'. It looks as if this were done in case the Soviet Government at some time might wish to reverse their policy and come to terms with Germany when the latter has rid itself of Hitlerism. Such, however, is Russia's dread of a German recovery that such an eventuality seems highly unlikely. However, the Soviet Government might take the risk and seek Germany's friendship if they were to convince themselves that Great Britain and the United States had reversed their present policy and were building up Germany as a defence against the Soviet Union, and if they felt confident of Russia's recovery of strength and her ability to remain the dominant partner. Unless these conditions obtained, it seems very improbable that Russia would welcome even a Communist Germany, for she might well develop into a dangerous rival. Indeed, as the Soviet Union moves further from communism, the danger to her position as leader of the extreme Left in the world from a Communist Germany would clearly grow. This consideration, combined with Russia's healthy fear of German powers of organisation and of the German capacity for a unified effort under strong rule would almost certainly make Russia fear communism in Germany; it would not be surprising to find that German communism would be stigmatised as Trotskyite. All the same, if Germany were spontaneously to go Communist the Soviet Government would be under severe pressure from the ideologists, as distinct from the realists, to abandon their policy of repression and to befriend the new proselyte, even at the risk of the Communist rulers in Germany proving too strong for the Soviet Government to keep under control. Needless to say, this pressure would be all the greater if at the time the Soviet Government felt that the policy of co-operation with the Western Powers was not going to succeed. If, however, it was working satisfactorily, the realists in Moscow would, it is to be hoped, be able to keep the upper hand.

38 It would be unwise to assume that in Soviet–German affairs the role of Germany is going to be an entirely passive one. Germany will be on the lookout for any weakening in the policy of Anglo-Soviet co-operation after the war and will be quick to offer herself as occasion requires to either party as soon as she sees any sign of a quarrel. To the Soviet Government she will present

herself as the Socialist partner ready to help to keep the capitalist Western Powers from meddling in Central and Eastern Europe. To the Western Powers she will pose as the champion of European culture ready to join in resisting Russian penetration of Europe from the East. Against these manoeuvres the only effective weapon will be a continuance of close Anglo-Soviet co-operation.

Poland

39 As regards Poland, the Soviet Government's latest statement is to the effect that they are in favour of a strong and independent Poland in good relations with the Soviet Union, with its eastern frontier running approximately along the Curzon Line; if desired there could be an alliance for mutual aid against Germany, and Poland could adhere to the recent Soviet–Czechoslovak Treaty. It appears from the discussions at the Tehran Conference that the Soviet Government wish to have Lvov, but that they agree that East Prussia should go to Poland (possibly less Konigsberg, which the Russians may want for themselves), and that Poland's western frontier might be moved westward even as far as the Oder. It is clear that Poland will not succeed in getting a settlement on more favourable lines. A large extension of Polish territory at the expense of Germany would probably so embitter Polish–German relations that Poland would be forced into close association with the Soviet Union. In any case, the Soviet Government is certainly determined not to tolerate a hostile Poland. If satisfied on this score they may well be content that Poland should retain a real independence. But Soviet–Polish hostility has behind it four centuries of deeply charged history, and it must be doubtful, whatever the final settlement, how far the Poles and Russians can overcome their deep-seated hatred of each other and how far the Poles can abandon their historic, almost mystical, conception of Poland's 'eastern mission'. Russia is concerned to ensure that her forces will always be able to pass through Poland, if necessary, in order to nip a threat from Germany in the bud. This latter consideration dictates the whole of her Polish policy . . .

Confederations in Central Europe and the Balkans

45 Soviet opposition to confederations between the Baltic and the Aegean was stated at the Moscow Conference to be founded (i) on a rooted suspicion of the Poles and of a *cordon sanitaire*; (ii) on the belief that the antagonisms, divisions and uncertainties in the countries concerned make confederations immediately impracticable; and (iii) on the idea that such confederations might prove over favourable to the satellites of Germany. It is no doubt in reality Russia's determination to take no risk of a strong combination of countries on her western frontiers which might, out of fear of

herself, turn to Germany for support that accounts for her opposition. The Soviet Government's attitude is unlikely to change, at least until they have reached satisfactory settlements with the individual States, especially Poland. In the case of Czechoslovakia, they have reached such a settlement in the recent Soviet–Czechoslovak Treaty. As regards Roumania and Bulgaria, they no doubt prefer that these countries should be independent but wholly under their influence, rather than members of a confederation.

The Balkans and Turkey

46 It is a vital Soviet interest that no strong Power should be able to threaten the Black Sea or to draw on Roumanian oil for aggression against the Soviet Union.

47 The Soviet Government are determined to regain Bessarabia and Northern Bukovina, and in exchange will probably advocate the return of Transylvania to Roumania. They may also want a share in Roumanian oil resources, the right to maintain naval and military bases in Roumania and the conclusion of some sort of mutual assistance treaty, in return for which they might be prepared to guarantee Roumania's new frontiers . . .

51 The Soviet Union probably has no major territorial claims against Turkey. It is extremely improbable that any Soviet statesman would advocate physical control by Russia of either the Straits or Constantinople. The only possible claim that might be made in certain circumstances is one for the annexation of the Soviet Union of the Province of Kars, ceded to Turkey after the first world war. The Soviet military authorities may feel that this is necessary for the security of Baku and it must not be forgotten that the Soviet Government, thanks to the disclosures of the Germans, are perfectly aware of Turkish participation in conversations with ourselves and the French regarding the bombing of Baku and the Caucasian oil wells.

52 Russia's real desiderata regarding Turkey are, however, focussed on two points: the Straits and Turkey's relations with other Great Powers. As regards the Straits, traditional object of Soviet as of Imperial Russian policy is to secure unlimited right of egress for Russia's Black Sea fleet and complete denial of ingress to non-Black Sea Powers. The Montreux Convention gave a degree of satisfaction to these aims which no previous convention had given, but the Turco-Soviet negotiations of 1939 showed that it was not enough. What worried the Soviet Government was the fact that in certain circumstances even if Turkey was not at war the Turkish Government had discretion to open the Straits to non-Black Sea Powers. The ideal arrangement in Russian eyes is probably that this discretion should not be exercised without Russian consent. As regards Turkey's relations with other Great Powers it is probably true that the Soviet Government have never relished Turkey's alliance with Great Britain. A hostile Turkey is a threat to two vital Russian

interests, her communications between the Black Sea and the Mediterranean and the security of the Caucasian oilfields. Turkey in isolation is a manageable proposition, but any alliance with a Great Power such as Great Britain puts a different complexion on the situation. The Turkish Minister for Foreign Affairs, in unofficial conversation with His Majesty's Ambassador, has probably summed up the position fairly well in saying that Russia does not want to absorb Turkey, but would like to see her in the same position as Belgium after 1830, an independent Power with no ties of alliance to any Great Power. Russia's attitude on this, however, as on so many other points, depends upon the degree of confidence she feels in British policy . . .

63 It may be taken for granted that Russia will claim a voice in any Pacific settlement, and in any organisation for maintaining the peace in the Pacific area. As she is one of the largest Pacific Powers, we should have no justification for attempting to oppose this. But her most direct interests will be in the North Manchuria, Korea, Saghalien and the Kuriles, and, if we adopt an understanding attitude regarding her wishes there, she seems unlikely to make trouble for us in the southerly regions where our own interests lie. We could not effectively oppose any measures which Russia might decide to take in the north for her own security, and we should therefore be ill-advised to try. If we did try, she might retaliate by holding out a helping hand to Japan, which the latter would be only too ready to seize.

64 The likeliest ground of conflict within the Four-Power system in the Far East lies in Russo-Chinese relations. The Russians concurred in the declaration made at Cairo in respect of Korea and Manchuria. Even if we assume that this means complete Russo-Chinese agreement on these points (a very large assumption indeed), there remain the questions of Outer Mongolia, Sinkiang and the eventual attitude and behaviour of the Kuomintang towards the Chinese Communists. None of these matters as such is likely to affect British strategic interests. It is, however, conceivable that we might become embroiled with Russia as a result of a Russian policy in regard to these matters violently opposed to Chinese and United States interests and to British and American sentiment.

26 Paper by W. H. Young on Soviet policy in Persia and what this suggests about possible Russian behaviour in Germany, 1 May 1944

. . . 2 . . . In Persia the Russians have certainly been obstructive and difficult in their attitude to us and the Americans. There can be little doubt that this is in part the outcome of settled policy and specific instructions from Moscow. But in a great number of cases, perhaps in the majority, the basic trouble has most probably been the fact that the Kremlin has had other things to think about and that in the absence of any directive the local Russians have preferred to keep us at arm's length just to be on the safe side. Russian policy in Germany, on the other hand, is likely to be a major preoccupation of the Soviet Government, and to this extent the same considerations may not apply. This is not to say that the Russians are likely to be nicer to us in Germany than in Persia, only that if they are nasty, it will be for rather different reasons. And 'Captain Ivanov who hasn't received any orders' will doubtless turn up in Germany as elsewhere!

3 This much said, there does seem to be a certain potential similarity between the two cases, especially on the economic side. To take your points in the order in your letter:

a The Russians at first denied that the areas under their occupation in Persia produced a surplus of grain, and said that Tehran was in normal times fed mainly from the centre and south. Later, the Russians admitted in principle that the northern provinces have grain surpluses and ought to contribute to feeding deficit areas, such as Tehran, and they promised to help the Persians to collect the grain and send it to Tehran. But the fact remains that grain from the northern provinces has reached Tehran only in minute quantities. Similarly, the Russians prevent the export of dried fruits from Azerbaijan to the South: as soon as this ban has produced a gratifying drop in prices, the Russians buy up what they want at prices of their own choosing: the rest they leave to rot without any regard to needs of the Allies or of the rest of Persia. They are equally difficult about rice.

b The Russians have always placed their own needs of cereals etc. first and have taken what they wanted from the northern provinces, relying on us and the Americans to make up any deficit in the rest of Persia.

Our chief complaint against them here was not that they took the grain (since their needs were unquestionably urgent), but that they would never inform us or the Persians in advance of their intentions. The result has been famine conditions in at least one winter in Tehran and great political complications.

In so far as their behaviour in Persia is any guide, the Russians may be expected either to deny that the areas of Germany which they occupy produce a surplus; or, if they admit that much, to help themselves as they find convenient and at the same time to give undertakings to send supplies to other areas, but to be very leisurely about carrying out their promises. They may of course say as in Persia that they need the food for their own people more than the Germans do. In that case we shall no doubt try to insist on advance information of what they are going to take away, but Persian experience does not encourage one to hope for much result ... If it is the case that the

Russians will occupy the main surplus-producing areas of Germany, and that 'running German economy on a national basis' would mean in practice that the Russians would be expected to part with some of their surpluses for the benefit of other parts of Germany, then, on their form in Persia, I should say that there was very little chance of their playing. If, on the other hand, it is possible to bring home to them, in some way that hurts, that their own immediate practical interests are best served by collaboration, then the prospects might be rather brighter. But all appeals to Allied co-operation, united front etc., *as such*, have never in my experience had the slightest effect, except to arouse suspicion. Even highly plausible appeals to Russian and Allied general interests have been equally unsuccessful. In Persia, the only thing that has ever moved the Russians to take common action with us has been a direct and immediate threat to the functioning of the supply route. (You will remember the two occasions for that is all there have been: (a) when the Persians tried to withhold local currency and (b) when Axis agents had to be rounded up.) But so far we have never got anywhere with such arguments as that a total collapse of the Persian administration or famine and disorder in Tehran would in time endanger the supply route and that it was therefore in the Russian interest to join us in helping to run Persia as a single whole.

My guess then would be that the Russians will co-operate if and only if it is possible to demonstrate in some practical and, if necessary, painful way, that they will lose by failure to do so . . .

27 Post-war collaboration with Russia. Disagreement between the Foreign Office and the Services, June–October 1944

Jebb, 15 June

1 I told you the other day that the P.H.P. Staff were going to have an oral discussion 'off the record' with the Vice-Chiefs of Staff on this subject (it would have been impossible for me to prevent this even if I had wanted to since at least two Directors were determined to air the matter). The discussion took place today and lasted about an hour.

2 I started the ball rolling by saying that we had naturally had much discussion as between ourselves as to how to construct the strategic papers which we had been told to write and that we had provisionally agreed on two assumptions (the original A and B) which we thought would provide the necessary background. I then explained that assumption B had had an un-favourable reception in the Foreign Office, who had pointed out that it had

seemed to indicate the Soviet Union as the sole potential enemy (apart from Germany and Japan). I also said that there had also been criticism on the grounds that it was difficult, if not impossible, to go on such all-inclusive assumptions as these; that we could not say for certain, in the event of any disruption of the Three Power alliance, who our enemy or enemies were likely to be; and that in any case the threat to our interests (if any) would presumably vary in accordance with the geographical area considered.

3 For these reasons (I continued) it was most unlikely that the Foreign Office would agree to assumption B, as drafted, and that if we were to have any assumption at all something more general would have to be put up, such as:

4 'That the British Commonwealth continues to dispose of armed forces, bases and other facilities sufficient to provide the necessary minimum of security in the event of any breakdown of the tripartite alliance' . . .

5 In any case in my view the proof of the pudding lay in the eating. It was obvious for instance that we could not, in the sort of paper which we had been ordered to produce, disregard British interests as such nor fail to make any allusions to what (if anything) might be done to guard against the risk that the relations of the Great Powers between themselves might not be all that we hoped they would be at the moment. For this reason we should in any case have to construct our papers in three parts, the first contemplating the part we ought ourselves to play in any world security organisation or as the result of a tripartite alliance, the second indicating the sort of risks with which we might be faced if the world organisation failed to materialise or alternatively the three power alliance did not continue, and the third summing up the situation and indicating what (if any) insurance from the military point of view was necessary or desirable to guard against such risks. For all these reasons I strongly urged the Vice-Chiefs to agree to our not attempting to formulate any general assumptions but to wait and see how they liked the papers which we should eventually produce.

6 My Air and Naval colleagues then made speeches saying they did not agree with my thesis; that in their view it was 'unrealistic' not to contemplate what measures should be taken to secure our interests against attempts to undermine them on the part of the Soviet Union in the event of things going wrong; and that purely strategical planning ought not to be unduly influenced by political considerations.

7 After some discussion, the Vice-Chiefs (very sensibly as I think) directed the P.H.P. Staff *not* to attempt to formulate any assumptions, but at the same time so to construct their papers as not to ignore any potential risks, which would no doubt vary as between area and area.

8 I may say that the Vice-Chiefs themselves showed no disposition to want to plan operations against the Soviet Union but were merely concerned lest

economy and popular outcry might in the long run succeed in reducing our armed forces below what was required for the protection of our vital interests, including of course in the first instance the control of Germany and Japan.

Sargent, 28 June

. . . the Foreign Office should state, for the information of the Chiefs of Staff, the general lines of foreign policy which the Foreign Secretary was following and hoped to be able to follow during the ensuing period of, say, two years. This statement would thus serve as a basic political assumption for the Chiefs of Staff in their plans covering this period. Moreover, as foreign policy has to be modified and adapted according to changing circumstances, I suggested that this statement should be reviewed every six months in order to ensure that it still held good, and, if not, to replace it by a fresh one.

Cadogan, 28 June

The value of Sir O. Sargent's proposals is that there would be a review of the situation every six months, and I think we might all agree on that. When he asks for 'the general lines of foreign policy which the Foreign Secretary hoped to be able to follow for the next two years', I answer him quite easily: 'We hope to maintain co-operation with the U.S. and the U.S.S.R. for the defeat and holding down of Germany and Japan, with the assistance, as we hope, of a World Organisation'. The whole point is, how are we to plan if the 3 Power co-operation breaks down and if the World Organisation fails to materialise or won't work? The wretched P.H.P. are asked to plan on the 'assumption' of either or both of these failures. I maintain that they *can't*, and that you can't even formulate the assumptions . . .

Warner, 17 July

. . . the most important point in securing Russian collaboration after the war will be to convince Russia of our determination to go with her in holding Germany down and only in the event of our appearing to play with Germany against Russia is Russia likely to try to get in first with Germany. Instead of that we have a paper which barely conceals that it is thought Russia is just as likely to be an enemy as Germany and is quite likely (circumstances unspecified) to join with Germany against us . . .

Warner, 24 July

. . . But I fear some damage may have been done, since the vague idea of a Russia overrunning Europe (quite soon? or 15 years hence? – nothing is said on this point) and of our building up Germany is endorsed by the F.O. to the *Chiefs of Staff*. The distance to the next step – 'we had better start building up Germany pretty soon and so we had better not knock her down too completely' – is a very short one, particularly for the military mind and for those who suffer from the anti-Bolshevik complex . . .

Jebb, 28 July

. . . The Chiefs of Staff start from the assumption that Germany will be knocked out as the result of the present war and for a time at least reduced to impotence. They further believe that no conflict between ourselves and the U.S. is possible and they therefore argue that there is only one power which would be in a position to menace our security after the war and that is Russia. Consequently they draw the conclusion that all our military plans for the post-war period should be based on a *potentially* hostile Russia.

The Chiefs of Staff, as I understand it, do not dispute that it would be in our interest to achieve a World Organisation, or anyhow an alliance between the three Great Powers, but they are it seems 'profoundly sceptical' of a World Organisation ever coming into being and, I regret to say, of the United States ever coming to our assistance in time if we should get into serious trouble on the continent . . .

Mason, 28 July

. . . The Chiefs of Staff may or may not be right in thinking that the U.S. would never come to our assistance *in time* if we got into serious trouble in Europe, or in being profoundly sceptical about the creation of a World Organisation. Again, it is undoubtedly true that there is much anti-Russian feeling in Middle West circles in the U.S. and there have certainly been indications that American military authorities think of Russia as the next enemy. On the other hand it seems clear that, if the Chiefs of Staff really embark on a policy of building up Germany as a support against potential Russian aggression, the Americans will be frightened right out of any participation in a World Organisation: and if they do not participate in a World Organisation it is more than probable that American assistance to us, in the event of our getting into serious trouble in Europe, would not be in time. The Chiefs of Staff thus seem to me to be arguing in what is literally a vicious circle.

Warner, 29 July

Two vicious circles, of course, because the policy of building up Germany must mean that the Soviet Union will bend its efforts *immediately* to eliminating the danger to themselves which they would consider this constituted. If necessary, they can devote themselves to this task without having to worry much about their own people's war-weariness and desire for better conditions; they can even, if necessary, cut down the amount of effort they devote to post-war rehabilitation – although it would probably not be essential for them to do so. Against this we should be, I think, practically non-starters.

Wilson, 10 August

... The military say, quite rightly, that the only power in Europe which can, in the foreseeable future, be a danger to us is the Union of Soviet Socialist Republics. They go on to argue that the only way to meet that potential danger is to organise against it now, and in pursuance of that policy they have recently advanced as an argument in favour of the dismemberment of Germany the theory that we might then be able to use the man-power and resources of north-west Germany in an eventual war against the Russians. In a number of other ways also it has been apparent that, in considering post-war plans, the Russian danger has been at the forefront of their minds.

The view taken in the Foreign Office has been that, in planning along these lines, the military will make inevitable the very danger they are trying to avoid. The implementation of some of their plans could not be concealed from the Russians, who would retaliate in kind and could do so much more quickly and effectively and ruthlessly than we possibly could. Any chance of co-operation with the Russians would then disappear completely. In any case, the Anglo-Soviet Treaty is one of the corner-stones of our whole foreign policy, and it is not possible to strain every nerve to make the Treaty work and at the same time to base our military plans on the assumption that the next war will be fought against the other party to that Treaty.

We and the military are on common ground (a) in acknowledging as a fact that Russia is the only power in Europe that can be a danger to our security, (b) in wanting to avoid that danger, and (c) in wanting to secure that, in any future war, we and the Russians are on the same and not on opposite sides. The difference between us is therefore one of method and not of principle, though we may take different views as to the imminence of the Russian danger. But one way of reducing that danger would be if we and the Russians were, after the war, regularly engaged in military conversations and staff talks about the security of our common, or even individual, interests. The usefulness of such talks would depend on the degree of confidence each side felt in the other, and our willingness to enter into them at all would go a long way to increase Soviet confidence in us. Conversely, a refusal on our part to enter into them would make the Russians still more mistrustful and suspicious. Such talks would give us an opportunity, which we have not yet had, of making abundantly clear to the Russians our vital interest in Middle Eastern oil and the security of our communications in the Eastern Mediterranean, and our participation in them could be made dependent on these vital interests being explicitly recognised. As a corollary we should have to recognise Russian vital interests in Eastern Europe. It is even for consideration whether it might not be good tactics, if we think that the Russians are likely to make this suggestion, for us to take a leaf out of their book and ourselves to make it first. This could be done by our saying to them in the fairly near future that, at the end of the European war, the military provisions of the Treaty will lapse and that we should then be prepared to discuss with them whether anything, and if so what, should take their place in the post-war period.

The military might take the view that their being engaged in such talks with the Russians would make it more difficult for them to make the plans they thought necessary against a potential Russian danger. That is of course true to some extent, but it would not prevent them entirely though it might direct their planning into less dangerous channels than at present.

This is, of course, all very dependent on the outcome of the World Organisation talks in Washington and the view that the Americans might take of any such proposals. But it seems to me very possible that the European allies would welcome the fact that the Anglo-Soviet Treaty was, in the post-war period, re-inforced by regular staff talks between us and the Russians.

Ward, 15 August

I agree that Mr. Wilson has made an excellent suggestion, which seems to me to offer a definite objective for our counter-attack against the Chiefs of Staff and their wild acolytes in the P.H.P.S. Hitherto, the Foreign Office representatives have been in a difficult position in trying to stifle this anti-Soviet planning because our attitude was essentially negative and we had no concrete alternative to propose. This enabled the military to answer our criticisms by the accusation that we were behaving like ostriches, as the Government did in the 1930's in respect of the German menace.

I think that Mr. Wilson's suggestion, as a means both of keeping us together with the Soviet and enabling us to watch more closely the trend of their policy, should at some stage go in a communication from the Foreign Office to the Chiefs of Staff, in which we would also make our assault upon the wild talk in the P.H.P.S. Just how and when this should be done might be discussed in relation to the general problem of the P.H.P.S.

This proposal to build up an Anglo-Soviet alliance will, of course, have to be handled very carefully from the point of view of the Americans. But I hope that we should not allow ourselves to be deterred by excessive deference to America. I do not think that the French and the small Western Allies would oppose Mr. Wilson's suggestion. On the contrary, they are scared of the Russians and would be only too glad to see us conjure the danger by working in with them more closely.

Butler, 16 August

. . . It is not really a question of due or undue deference to the Americans, but of having a policy that is intelligible to and approved by British, Dominions, and American public opinion and the Soviet Government, and of sticking to it, avoiding seductive bypaths. We have now got such a policy in the idea of the three (or four) great power system. The situation in London that has prompted Mr. Wilson's suggestion is reproduced very closely in Washington, where the State Department may expect to be under pressure from their own Chiefs of Staff, and might well welcome the application of Mr. Wilson's idea in their own case.

The solution may lie in extending that idea so as to make it tripartite and to cover Japan also, and to have it worked out in the Higher Military Organisation which, under our plan, is to subserve the new League of Nations.

Eastern Department will no doubt have views as regards bilateral discussions with the Soviet Government on the Middle East. I do not believe that such bilateral staff talks are consistent with the partnership idea underlying the three great power system, especially as regards a part of the world where the third partner has begun to take a great interest. If the Americans are not brought in as principals and equals in these big questions, they will think that the new system is a sham and quite certainly become isolationist . . .

Roberts, 18 August

I have long felt that we were adopting too negative an attitude in attempting to discourage the Chiefs of Staff from even considering the possibility of a hostile Russia. I am, therefore, very attracted by Mr. Wilson's proposal. Surely history has shown that alliances which do not provide for military staff talks are entirely useless and break down the minute their implementation becomes likely. I see the force of Mr. Butler's objections, but surely we have to persuade the Dominions Governments and the U.S. Government that military security in Europe is a primary consideration and that we can only ensure it in co-operation with Russia and that the latter will only play on the basis of precise practical commitments. Otherwise we shall, I fear, soon find ourselves back in the old Geneva atmosphere and European, and no doubt world security as well, will be nothing more than a pack of cards likely to be blown down at the first puff of wind. After all we had military talks with France before 1914 and before 1939.

Wilson's memorandum of 24 September 1944

... The Treaty imposes on both parties in the post-war period certain substantial though vague military commitments, and by that time the present military collaboration, such as it is, will to a large extent have ceased. I therefore suggest that we should remind the Russians in the fairly near future that, at the end of the European war, the military provisions of the Treaty will lapse, and say that we should then be prepared to discuss with them whether anything, and if so what, should take their place in the post-war period. Probably the most practical step would be to agree that Staff talks should be held at regular intervals.

5 This course would have the following advantages.

a Both we and the Russians have an uneasy feeling that the other party may regard the Treaty only as a temporary convenience during time of war and that, in spite of official statements to the contrary on both sides, it may not in reality be the basis of our future foreign policy. A suggestion that provision should be made for regular military conversations and staff talks would do much to remove Russian suspicions.

b The Russians are far more interested in precise practical commitments than in vague expressions of good-will. They place little or no reliance on the latter, and surely history has shown that alliances which do not provide for military staff talks are useless and tend to break down the moment their implementation becomes likely.

c It is our policy to build up, even within the framework of a World Organisation, a Western European security bloc which will involve close military collaboration with our European neighbours. There is every reason to suppose that the Russians will do the same in Eastern Europe. These two military blocs will be a danger to peace rather than otherwise unless their two leaders – the Union of Soviet Socialist Republics and ourselves – are very closely linked together not only diplomatically but also militarily.

d Military staff talks on the lines suggested would be welcomed by the smaller countries in the two blocs as they would give them a much greater sense of security. It might be possible, and would certainly be valuable, for the French to be associated as a principal in such conversations.

e It provides the only positive solution to the difference in outlook which is developing between the Foreign Office and the Service Departments on policy towards Russia ...

f It has to be admitted that, even on the most favourable hypothesis, there may.be a conflict of strategic interest between us and the Russians in the Middle East. The depth of defence which the Russians consider necessary for their Caucasian oil supplies may well overlap with the depth of defence which we consider necessary for our oil supplies in Persia and Iraq and for our communications in the Eastern Mediterranean. Unless this potential conflict of interests is frankly discussed, it will produce endless suspicion on both sides. Staff talks would provide an excellent opportunity for bringing it into the open and would give us a chance, which we have not yet had, of making abundantly clear to the Russians what we consider to be our vital interests.

g Such talks might give our military opportunities of assessing Russian intentions and capacity, and would probably enable us to get earlier notice than would otherwise be the case of any sinister Russian designs in Europe.

h It is unlikely that the Russians will at once put all their security eggs into the World Organisation basket, and any setback to that organisation will strengthen the hands of those in Russia who do not want to co-operate anyway. If they have a firm military alliance with us, they will be less likely to play an entirely lone hand in their search for security . . .

9 The usefulness of such military talks would of course depend on the degree of confidence each side felt in the other, but the fact of our suggesting them at all would go a long way to increase the Russians' confidence in us. It is the sort of proposal which they may well make themselves, if we do not make it first. If that were to happen, a refusal on our part would certainly make the Russians still more mistrustful and suspicious. We are unlikely to have a better opportunity than the present time to make our suggestion to them. I suspect that they are a good deal more impressed by our military achievements in France than they are ever likely to admit, and would now realise that we made the suggestion from strength and not from weakness. Such a positive indication by us of the importance we attached to the Anglo-Soviet Treaty in the post-war world, and of our determination not to let our two countries drift apart after this war as they have done after previous wars, would do more than anything else to get Anglo-Soviet relations on to a better basis.

Jebb, 18 October

I have discussed this with Mr. Warner.

My view for what it is worth is that it would be extremely difficult for us to propose 'staff talks' with the Russians on matters which after the conclusion of hostilities with Germany and Japan would not be in some way bound up with either regional or general security arrangements, in all of which, of course, other States would be equally concerned.

Nor do I think that it would be on the face of it desirable to have staff talks in regard to e.g. Middle Eastern problems, since it would be rather difficult to see what could come under discussion here except defence against each other and this I imagine would not be a very profitable topic for debate.

Warner, 25 October

I fear that this is so and that there is therefore no subject on which we could reasonably propose bilateral staff talks with the Russians if the World and Regional security arrangements come into being. As we cannot at this juncture make a proposal to the Russians which assumes that they will not, there is nothing, I fear, which we can do at present along the lines of Mr. Wilson's proposal. Mr. Wilson agrees.

28   Extracts from PHPS papers, June 1944–June 1945

A Effects of Soviet policy on British strategic interests, 6 June 1944

... 4 A forecast of Soviet Russia's probable long-term policy can only be based upon a survey of her present known aims and of certain territorial demands which she is either known or expected to make as a result of the present war. The survey in the following paragraphs has been based upon information contained in a Foreign Office memorandum. Account has been taken of all available evidence of Russia's post-war intentions. The survey, however, deliberately does not attempt to deal with the possibility that Soviet Russia may profit by her position in Eastern Europe to extend her influence over Western Europe and thus dominate the whole Continent. Nor does it attempt to deal with the equal possibility that the Russia of the future, as a result of the development of Siberia, might attempt to dominate the Continent of Asia. It is evident that, if either of these situations were to arise, there would be a serious threat to British interests, against which we should have to defend ourselves as best we could. But the evidence at present available does not in any way suggest that the desire for wholesale domination of this sort is in the mind of the Soviet leaders or their people.

In laying down any secure foundation for long-term planning in regard to British defence requirements, however, it is essential to realise that the U.S.S.R. will almost certainly emerge from this war the principal land Power in Europe (and in Asia). Although her present aims need not bring her into conflict with this country, the domination (actual or potential) of Europe by one Power or group of Powers has always been regarded as a menace to our vital interests. Unless therefore our security is once again to be entrusted to what are euphemistically described as 'diplomatic resources', this situation however Soviet policy may turn out, clearly calls, if only as a precautionary measure, for the maintenance of a high level of armaments by ourselves, together with France and our other natural associates in Western Europe.

This policy clearly pre-supposes the early re-emergence of France as an effective military power. Only by this means, in fact, shall we be able to prevent the establishment of some European *bloc* of which the Soviet Union would be the natural leader. It does not follow – nor, as we have said above, do we think it likely – that the establishment of such a *bloc* will be the object of Soviet policy. But if any vacuum in Western Europe appears, it is asking too much of human nature not to suppose that the Soviets would attempt to make use of it for their own purposes . . .

13 The Soviet Government are clearly determined to prevent any risk of a revival of the German menace in Central and South-Eastern Europe. It is already clear that it is their present intention to take the strongest measures to destroy the military power of Germany and to ensure that the minor States of Central and South-Eastern Europe do not again fall under German domination. It is impossible to foretell exactly the measures which the Soviet Government will seek to take to neutralise Germany in the future, e.g., whether she will insist upon a prolonged military occupation of Germany or try to carry out the political dismemberment of Germany. The enormous power of the Russian land forces in Europe after Germany is defeated will, however, give the Soviet Government the ability, if they wish, to dominate Germany for an indefinite period.

14 As regards the small States of Central and South-Eastern Europe, the satisfaction of the Soviet Union's territorial claims against Poland coupled with the driving of Poland westwards at German expense, would not only make Soviet influence dominant in Poland, but would also give the U.S.S.R. a common frontier along the Carpathians with Czechoslovakia. This, together with the Soviet–Czech Alliance of December 1943, would give her powerful influence over the restored Czechoslovak Republic. It seems likely that Russian forces will occupy Hungary, and this country is also likely to fall under the predominant influence of the Soviet Union in the period after the end of hostilities. Russian forces will certainly occupy Roumania and the Soviet Union will insist upon maintaining her 1941 frontier so that Bessarabia and the Northern Bukovina remain within the U.S.S.R. The Soviet Government has expressed to His Majesty's Government secretly a desire for bases in Roumania. While their policy towards Bulgaria has not yet been made clear, the Soviet Government are likely to take a very close interest in that country, where Russian influence has always been and is bound to be very strong. We must reckon with the possibility that the Soviet Union may also obtain bases in Bulgaria, from which she could exercise a large measure of control over the Straits. In Yugoslavia the Soviet Government are closely co-operating with the Partisans, and, although geography will probably limit the extent to which she can dominate Yugoslavia, on the long term her influence here, too, is likely to be great . . .

41 The following are vital British strategic interests which might be threatened by the U.S.S.R.:

a Middle Eastern oil supplies; for, if our oil supplies were cut off in Iraq and Persia, our position in war would be precarious. The United States have very considerable interests in this general area, however, and the fear of American intervention might act as a deterrent to the U.S.S.R.
b Mediterranean communications; by way of Turkey. Such a move would also constitute a threat to our Middle Eastern oil supplies.
c Our vital sea communications; if the U.S.S.R. were to become a first-class Naval and Air Power.
d The concentrated industrial areas of the United Kingdom; if the U.S.S.R. built up a large strategic bomber air force.

British policy

42 We conclude, therefore, that the following basic principles should govern the military advice given by the Chiefs of Staff on policy affecting the Soviet Union:

a A real endeavour to secure the full and friendly participation of the U.S.S.R. in any system of world security appears to be the best means of avoiding friction between us. Failing the establishment of such a system, we must endeavour to perpetuate and strengthen our existing Treaty of Alliance with the U.S.S.R. and our present relations with the United States and China.
b In furtherance of the above aims we should not oppose any reasonable demands of the U.S.S.R. where they do not conflict with our vital strategic interests as indicated in paragraph 41. In exchange we should expect the U.S.S.R. not to oppose our claims in areas vital to us.
c Since there exists the possibility of a threat from the U.S.S.R. to our vital oil interests and communications in the Middle East, our policy should be directed towards ensuring that the United States are on our side in the event of such a threat developing . . .

B Security in Western Europe and the North Atlantic, 9 November 1944

. . . 17 The World Organisation may never materialise, and even if it does, it may break down. For instance:

a The United States may refuse to undertake any definite commitments or, having undertaken them, may subsequently repudiate them.
b Despite the Anglo-Soviet Treaty, the U.S.S.R. may not co-operate.

18 Whatever the cause of a breakdown it is likely that there will be reluctance to admit the failure of an organisation upon which so many hopes had been based. In the period between the beginning of Allied disintegration and its final realisation by world opinion, our security will be progressively threatened, and we must, therefore, always be prepared to meet the resulting grave dangers.

19 It is essential, therefore, to seek a policy which, while calculated to produce conditions in which a World Organisation can come into being and become effective, provides us with security even if a World Organisation fails to materialise or breaks down. We believe that such a policy is to be found and that our strategic requirements need confront us with no political dilemma.

Threat from a re-armed Germany

20 When allied unity has in reality been broken but before anyone is prepared to recognise the breach, Germany may achieve some measure of rearmament by playing one ally off against another. We believe, however, that the U.S.S.R., even if she had at the time determined on an expansionist policy, would probably oppose German rearmament. It would presumably suit the U.S.S.R. better for Germany to be acquiescent rather than strong.

21 So long as the U.S.S.R. does continue to co-operate, there should be no military difficulty in preventing German rearmament reaching serious proportions even if the United States refuses to undertake any definite commitments or, having undertaken them, subsequently repudiates them . . .

31 As a means of providing some part of the necessary depth of defence against a hostile U.S.S.R., a western group of allies, if such a group could maintain its effectiveness in face of a major threat from the U.S.S.R., would be of even greater value than against a re-armed Germany. A strong and friendly France would be essential. The inclusion of Sweden, Spain, Portugal and Iceland would again be desirable.

32 Since the territory in which we have a major strategic interest includes much of Germany, we examine below the practicability of obtaining German help against the U.S.S.R. We cannot be confident of obtaining adequate assistance from this source.

33 Our own forces and those of our European allies would be utterly inadequate to limit a Soviet advance through Poland and through a disarmed Germany into Western Europe.

34 The United States is, therefore, the only country which possesses sufficient man-power and reserves to stabilise and restore the situation. Time will be the crucial factor if the Western European States are not to be overwhelmed. It is, therefore, vital that United States' help should be forthcoming with minimum delay.

Possibility of German help against a hostile U.S.S.R.

35 We have stated our opinion that no Soviet threat to this country is likely to arise until after 1955 unless the British Commonwealth and the United States fail to co-operate with her in eliminating the German menace. None the less, since at least a part of Germany is included in an area of major British strategic interest, we have examined the practicability of using German territory, man-power and armament potential.

36 Any measures originally intended for the prevention of German re-surgence, which resulted in the continued presence in Western Germany of our own armed forces or those of our allies, would help to provide depth for our defences, and would not involve any change in our declared policy to-wards Germany. It follows that we should in no circumstances agree to evacuate our zone in Germany unless the U.S.S.R. evacuated hers, and in the event of some serious breakdown in our relations with the U.S.S.R., we should have no hesitation in re-occupying our zone.

37 The defence of Western Germany against any determined Soviet attack would, however, demand the use of very large forces. Whatever policy we might adopt to secure German co-operation to this end – and experience indicates that a conciliatory policy is unlikely to win German respect – any German promise to fight on our side against an aggressive U.S.S.R. would at best be unreliable.

38 Any advantage we might gain from Germany's armament potential would depend upon the extent of its destruction during the present war, and the time which it would take to rebuild her armament factories if we changed our present policy. We cannot assess these factors, but German industry, wherever situated, will be very vulnerable to air attack from the U.S.S.R.

39 Any measures designed to secure for our benefit a revival of German power, which are inconsistent with the policy of preventing renewed German aggression, must inevitably tend to alienate our Western European allies and antagonise the U.S.S.R. In any event, we could never be sure that German support would be reliable, nor should we have any confidence that it could be made effective in time. Nevertheless, should circumstances arise which enabled us to obtain German co-operation, it would be of great value to us despite the fact that, after the defeat of the U.S.S.R., a strong Germany might again constitute a major threat to our own security.

40 We conclude that, unless and until a major clash with the U.S.S.R. is clearly unavoidable, we must adhere to the policy of eradicating German ability to wage war. This policy would limit the assistance which the U.S.S.R. could obtain from Germany. The continued presence of our armed forces and those of our allies in Western Germany would be consistent with this policy and would have advantage in the event of Soviet hostility.

Possible German co-operation with the U.S.S.R.

41 If the U.S.S.R. did obtain the full support of Germany against us, we should be menaced by the most formidable combination. We should be hard put to it to hold our own island, and even the help of the United States could hardly enable us to restore the situation. It is, therefore, vital to us that Germany and the U.S.S.R. do not make common cause, and our policy must be to ensure that the help which the Germans are in a position to give to the U.S.S.R. is as small as possible. This requirement can be fulfilled, at least in part, by the continued enforcement of measures designed to prevent the resurgence of Germany . . .

C Security of British Commonwealth and Empire interests in South-East Asia and the Pacific, 31 January 1945

. . . 18 It thus appears that a major threat to our interests could only arise if the U.S.S.R., contrary to expectations, adopted an aggressive policy in the Far East. In such circumstances she would have to exercise some degree of control over Japan in order to ensure that Japan could not be used as a base for offensive action against her.

Measures to meet the threats

19 The defence measures recommended in the following paragraphs in order to deal with a possible Soviet threat would be equally applicable against a rearmed Japan. It should thus be possible to pursue a policy of co-operation with the U.S.S.R. which would provide for the participation of the United States and ourselves in the control of Japan, and at the same time to take certain measures to insure against the potential threats from a hostile U.S.S.R.

20 The outstanding interests of the United States in the Pacific have led us to assume that she will co-operate with the British Commonwealth against a threat from a major Power. It is essential to ensure that we agree in advance on a policy for the provision of both forces and bases.

21 The geographical position of China in relation to British Commonwealth territories makes her of strategic importance. It would therefore be greatly to our advantage to secure her friendship. The spread of Soviet influence in China would not be in our long-term strategic interests. It will therefore be necessary to ensure that the United States and ourselves take a share in the development of China at least equal to that of the U.S.S.R.

22 The co-operation of France and Holland is important, particularly if there should be any delay in the full development of the United States' war effort.

23 In the period under review we should on no account attempt to enlist

the support of Japan, since to do so would antagonise the U.S.S.R. and be unacceptable to both the United States and China . . .

D The security of the British Empire, 29 June 1945

. . . 139 An effective World Organisation would contribute to our security in relation to the U.S.S.R. in that:

a Co-operation between the U.S.S.R. and the other Great Powers will be facilitated, and it should be easier to obtain recognition of our claim to primary responsibility for the maintenance of peace and security in those areas where British interests predominate. It might also help to resolve conflicting claims to predominance in those regions where both the British Empire and the U.S.S.R. have strategic interests.
b The U.S.A. might be expected to assume military commitments not only in the Pacific, but also in Europe and the Middle East, as part of her obligation to share in the maintenance of world peace. It is most unlikely that she could be persuaded by any other means to assume such obligations, owing to her aversion from 'entangling alliances'. These commitments on the part of the U.S.A. would serve as a deterrent if the U.S.S.R. were to contemplate aggression.
c Regional security systems would help us to build up defensive alliances.
    e.g., in Western Europe, which might endure even if the World Organisation broke down.
d Facilities required for the protection of British interests in certain areas,
    e.g., the Middle East and the Straits of Gibraltar, may only be obtainable through agreements under the aegis of the World Organisation.

140 The existence of a World Organisation would, however, confront us with certain potential dangers. In the first place, it will be necessary to educate British public opinion to appreciate that the existence of a World Organisation constitutes no permanent guarantee against aggression on the part of a Great Power. Misconception as to its efficacy in preventing a major threat to our security might lead to demands for the reduction of our armed forces. If such views were to prevail, the existence of the World Organisation would become a menace to our security. Secondly, it would be difficult to resist Soviet participation in regional defence systems in the Middle East and possibly in other areas in which British interests predominate. If she were to use the influence which she thus acquired for purposes of undermining our position, with a view to future aggressive action against us, our capacity to defend our interests in such areas would be seriously weakened.

29   Clark Kerr on Soviet policy, 31 August 1944

In the hope that they may usefully contribute to the present debate, the observations in the present despatch are offered by way of a supplement to the wider survey of Soviet foreign policy contained in Foreign Office memorandum of the 29th April last.

2 As a point of departure it seems safe to postulate the following three major assumptions: in the first place, complete victory over Germany will have the immediate effect of relieving the Soviet Union of any serious threat to her security in Europe. Secondly, it is evident that, having led its country to her first victory in a major war since 1812, the Soviet regime, with Marshal Stalin as its head, will feel great confidence in itself and more stable and secure against possible internal enemies than at any time since its establishment. Thirdly, everything seems to show that the regime has discarded the theory of world revolution, and that Communist parties and organisations abroad are now looked upon solely as instruments which, where appropriate, may be employed to further the interests, as they unfold themselves, of Russia as a state as distinct from Russia as a revolutionary notion.

3 Turning now, on the basis of these assumptions, to the motives which seem likely to inspire Soviet foreign policy in the period immediately after the war when the Soviet Union, having successfully emerged from a patriotic struggle of vast dimensions, occupies the position of the greatest military power on the continent. By way of introduction we must note the fact – apparent to all observers, yet of such importance that it calls for constant repetition – that in spite of the twenty-year treaty of alliance with Great Britain and the stream of hatred directed against Germany through the press and wireless, the Soviet Government retain complete freedom of manoeuvre in foreign affairs, and, in terms of their own public and of their sympathisers abroad, see to it that this liberty is maintained. With a few notable exceptions Soviet citizens are cut off from direct access to the thought and civilisation of the outside world; they hear and read nothing but what the Soviet Government consider it useful for them to know; and although they may have their moments of doubt, they have no standards by which they can compare the strategy and tactics of their own Government with those of His Majesty's Government or of the United States Government. For them there are, indeed, no standards excepting those set by the Soviet Government; and the difference between one policy and another, between a policy of friendship and a policy of hostility, is imperceptible until that difference is defined by the propaganda machine of the Soviet Government. To the Soviet citizen there is nothing paradoxical, unless the Soviet Government choose to draw attention to the paradox, in attacking 'Fascist bandits' one day, and resuming cordial relations with Marshal Badoglio on the next. There is nothing incongruous about

vilifying the Poles of the Underground movement because they refrained from an armed rising against the Germans, and yet refusing to equip those same Poles when they do rise, on the ground that their action had not been co-ordinated with the Soviet High Command . . .

7 This fluidity in Soviet policy, which places the Soviet Government in a far stronger position than His Majesty's Government, whose conduct of foreign affairs, especially in regard to the Soviet Union, is under a constant fire of criticism, makes it of the first importance to try to discover the explanation for the official attitude. Leaving aside for the purpose of the question in hand all other factors which may determine the handling of Soviet foreign policy and relations with individual states, the available surface evidence points strongly to the conclusion that the whole approach of the Soviet Government to international problems is strongly influenced by a morbidly developed sense of inferiority. Again and again Russians have shown themselves prompt to take offence at outside criticism; they are imbued with an almost desperate determination that their country should be thought no less respectable, no less cultured, no less efficient than the peoples of the West. Thus, when in 1941 General Sikorski mentioned to Marshal Stalin that public opinion abroad might react unfavourably to stories of the treatment of Polish military units in the Union, he was met with the retort: 'They think we are savages'. In a passage of words with the former Swedish Minister at an official party on the 7th November, 1943, Monsieur Molotov was seen to strike his chest whilst exclaiming loudly: 'I am proud, proud, I tell you, to be the foreign minister of this great country'. In talks with members of this Embassy high Soviet officials are apt to complain of hostile critics in the British press and to brush aside the fact that such critics are, as often as not, obscure people without honour in their own country. The exposure of foreign critics of the Soviet Union, regardless of their domestic importance, is a favourite pastime of the Soviet press which, it may be remarked in parenthesis, is equally ready to select foreign comment from however insignificant a source in order to make it appear to the public that the Kremlin policy enjoys substantial support abroad. Competent observers are of opinion that fear of unfavourable comparisons has played an important part in the difficulties experienced by foreign experts living in the Soviet Union when seeking to visit factories or military or front line areas . . .

11 In the light of the foregoing considerations it seems safe to infer that the tactics and perhaps the strategy of Soviet foreign policy will depend in no small measure upon whether the Soviet Government are satisfied that the Western democracies are treating their country with all the deference to which they now consider her entitled by virtue of her military victories and newly-found prestige and responsibility. It is no exaggeration to say that the most important thing about the Moscow Conference was that it was held in Moscow.

12 In thus drawing attention to the Janus-like character of Soviet foreign policy and to the obstinate blend of pride and sensitiveness to criticism which, with the Slav capacity for suspecting the motives of others, are apt immeasurably to complicate the task of transacting current business with our ally, I would not by any means wish to suggest that we should follow the line of least resistance when situations arise where we have reason to consider that our just requirements are being obstructed or ignored. Realists themselves, the rulers of Soviet Russia respect realism in others. Whilst never prepared to admit to an error or to give way under pressure of a direct threat, they are by no means wedded to an *a priori* approach to the problems which confront them. Pitiless in exploiting the weaknesses of others where it is expedient to do so in the higher interests of the state, the knowledge that a foreign power is tenaciously abiding by its objective may induce them to alter course wherever the balance of advantage points to the need for readjustment.

13 A Soviet foreign policy divorced from the restraining influence of enlightened public opinion and hypersensitive in all matters affecting national prestige is likely to offer serious impediments to the development of post-war inter-Allied relations in an atmosphere free from recurring tension. There are, however, important mitigating circumstances. The mere fact that the Soviet Government will find themselves directly involved as equal partners in the settlement of world problems far transcending the scope of their immediate security requirements should fortify them in the desire to demonstrate that they are worthy of international respect. Although, under the prevailing system, there seems no reason to suppose that the Soviet emissaries abroad will be given any wide latitude to depart from the framework of well defined directives close familiarity with the more flexible methods of the West may in time move the Kremlin to realise that, where controversial issues are at stake, the larger interests of their country are better served by methods of compromise and tact than by a boorish display of rigidity and brusqueness. In a minor way the enlarged field of diplomatic activity now open to the U.S.S.R. and the multiplication of its missions abroad should tend to assist the process by increasing the number of permanent officials with direct experience of the outside world and of dealings with foreign governments. The influence of this factor is, however, severely limited by the fetters which the administrative machinery lays upon personal initiative . . .

30   Churchill in Moscow, October 1944

A Meeting at the Kremlin, 9 October 1944, at 10 p.m.

. . . THE PRIME MINISTER pointed out that there were two countries in which the British had particular interest, one was Greece. He was not worrying much about Roumania. That was very much a Russian affair and the treaty the Soviet Government had proposed was reasonable and showed much state-craft in the interests of general peace in the future. But in Greece it was different. Britain must be the leading Mediterranean Power and he hoped Marshal Stalin would let him have the first say about Greece in the same way as Marshal Stalin about Roumania. Of course, the British Government would keep in touch with the Soviet Government.

MARSHAL STALIN understood that Britain had suffered very much owing to her communications in the Mediterranean having been cut by the Germans. It was a serious matter for Britain when the Mediterranean route was not in her hands. In that respect Greece was very important. He agreed with the Prime Minister that Britain should have the first say in Greece.

THE PRIME MINISTER said it was better to express these things in diplomatic terms and not to use the phrase 'dividing into spheres', because the Americans might be shocked. But as long as he and the Marshal understood each other he could explain matters to the President.

MARSHAL STALIN interrupted to say that he had received a message from President Roosevelt. The President wanted Mr. Harriman to attend their talks as an observer and that the decisions reached between them should be of a preliminary nature.

THE PRIME MINISTER agreed. He had told the President – he and the President had no secrets – that he would welcome Mr. Harriman to a good number of their talks, but he did not want this to prevent intimate talk between Marshal Stalin and himself. He would keep the President informed. Mr. Harriman might come in for any formal talks as an observer. Mr. Harriman was not quite in the same position as they were.

MARSHAL STALIN said he had only sent a reply to the effect that he did not know what questions would be discussed, but as soon as he did know he would tell the President. He had noticed some signs of alarm in the President's message about their talks and on the whole did not like the message. It seemed to demand too many rights for the United States leaving too little for the Soviet Union and Great Britain, who, after all, had a treaty of common assistance.

MARSHAL STALIN went on to say that he had no objection to Mr. Harriman's attending the formal talks.

THE PRIME MINISTER referred to the Conference at Dumbarton Oaks. The President had not wanted this to be discussed in Moscow but only when the three heads got together. The President had not said so, but he must have had in mind the coming election. The President would be more free to talk in about a month's time. It was fair to say that while at first His Majesty's Government had inclined to the American view they now saw a great deal of force in the other point of view. Supposing China asked Britain to give up Hong Kong,

China and Britain would have to leave the room while Russia and the United States settled the question. Or, if the Argentine and the United States had a quarrel they would object if England, China and Russia had to settle it. The Prime Minister pointed out that all this was off the record. The wise thing was not to refer in Moscow to this question, but to wait until the meeting of the three heads, when it could be settled.

THE PRIME MINISTER then raised the question of the interests of the two Governments in the various Balkan countries and the need to work in harmony in each of them. After some discussion it was agreed that as regards Hungary and Yugoslavia each of the two Governments was equally interested, that Russia had a major interest in Roumania and that Britain was in the same position with regard to Greece. The Prime Minister suggested that where Bulgaria was concerned the British interest was greater than it was in Roumania. This led to some discussion about the crimes committed by Bulgaria.

[Clark Kerr's original version of the above paragraph was much less discreet:

PRIME MINISTER then produced what he called a 'naughty document' showing a list of Balkan countries and the proportion of interest in them of the Great Powers. He said that the Americans would be shocked if they saw how crudely he had put it. Marshal Stalin was a realist. He himself was not sentimental while Mr. Eden was a bad man. He had not consulted his cabinet or Parliament. The Prime Minister declared that Britain had been much offended by Bulgaria. In the last war the Bulgarians had beaten back and had cruelly attacked the Roumanians. In this war they had done the same to the Yugoslavs and Greece.]

M. MOLOTOV asked whether the Turkish question related to this matter.

THE PRIME MINISTER replied that he had not touched upon Turkey. He was only saying what was in his mind. He was glad to see how near it was to the Russian mind.

M. MOLOTOV remarked that the Convention of Montreux still remained.

THE PRIME MINISTER said that was a Turkish question and not a Bulgarian.

MARSHAL STALIN replied that Turkey was also a Balkan country. According to the Convention of Montreux Japan had as much right as Russia. Everything had been adjusted to the League of Nations and the League of Nations no longer existed. If Turkey were threatened she could close the Straits and Turkey herself had to decide when she was faced with a real threat. All the paragraphs in the Montreux Convention were controlled by Turkey. This was an anachronism. Marshal Stalin had put this question in Tehran and the Prime Minister had expressed his sympathy. Now that they were discussing the

Balkan question and Turkey was a Balkan country, did the Prime Minister think it appropriate to discuss it?

THE PRIME MINISTER agreed.

MARSHAL STALIN pointed out that if Britain were interested in the Mediterranean then Russia was equally interested in the Black Sea.

THE PRIME MINISTER thought that Turkey had missed her chance after the Tehran conference. The reason she was frightened was because she had no modern weapons, she thought she had a good army, whereas nowadays an army was not everything. Turkey was not clever.

MARSHAL STALIN remarked that Turkey had 26 divisions in Thrace and asked against whom they were directed.

THE PRIME MINISTER replied they were directed against Bulgaria, because Bulgaria was armed with French weapons taken by the Germans. The Prime Minister went on to say that, taking a long view of the future of the world, it was no part of British policy to grudge Soviet Russia access to warm-water ports and to the great oceans and seas of the world. On the contrary, it was part of their friendship to help the Soviet Union. They no longer followed the policy of Disraeli or Lord Curzon. They were not going to stop Russia. They wished to help. What did Marshal Stalin think about the kind of changes required in the Montreux Convention?

MARSHAL STALIN could not say what point required amendment, but he felt the convention was unsuitable in present circumstances and the spearhead was directed against Russia. It should be dropped. If the Prime Minister agreed in principle with that point of view it might be possible to discuss the required changes. It was quite impossible for Russia to remain subject to Turkey, who could close the Straits and hamper Russian imports and exports and even her defences. What would Britain do if Spain or Egypt were given this right to close the Suez Canal, or what would the United States Government say if some South American Republic had the right to close the Panama Canal? Russia was in a worse situation. Marshal Stalin did not want to restrict Turkey's sovereignty. But at the same time he did not want Turkey to abuse her sovereignty and to grip Russian trade by the throat.

THE PRIME MINISTER replied that in principle he shared that point of view. He suggested that the Russians should let us know in due course what was required. Otherwise Turkey might be frightened that Istanbul was to be taken. When the three heads met later on there would not be the same difficulty. He was in favour of Russia's having free access to the Mediterranean for her merchant ships and ships of war. Britain hoped to work in a friendly way with the Soviet Union, but wanted to bring Turkey along by gentle steps, not to frighten her.

MARSHAL STALIN said he understood.

THE PRIME MINISTER said that, if they were sitting at the armistice table and

Marshal Stalin asked him for free passage through the Straits for merchant ships and warships, he personally would say that Britain had no objection. Britain had no ties with Turkey except the Montreux Convention, which was inadmissible to-day and obsolete.

MARSHAL STALIN said he did not want to hurry the Prime Minister, but only to point out that the question existed in their minds and he was anxious that it should be admitted that their claim was justified.

THE PRIME MINISTER thought Marshal Stalin should take the initiative and tell the United States what was in his mind. The Prime Minister thought Russia had a right and moral claim. Looking at the Balkans he thought they should do something to prevent the risk of civil war between the political ideologies in those countries. They could not allow a lot of little wars after the Great World War. They should be stopped by the authority of the three Great Powers.

MARSHAL STALIN agreed . . .

MARSHAL STALIN reverted to the Balkans and suggested that our interest in Bulgaria was not, in fact, as great as the Prime Minister had claimed.

MR. EDEN remarked that Britain wanted more in Bulgaria than in Roumania.

MARSHAL STALIN claimed that Bulgaria was a Black Sea country. Was Britain afraid of anything? Was she afraid of a Soviet campaign against Turkey? The Soviet Union had no such intention.

MR. EDEN said Britain was not afraid of anything.

MARSHAL STALIN asked whether the Prime Minister thought Bulgaria was being punished less than she deserved. Bulgaria should be punished for her two wars on the side of Germany.

MR. EDEN reminded Marshal Stalin that Britain had been at war with Bulgaria for three years and wanted a small share in the control of that country after Germany's defeat.

THE PRIME MINISTER suggested that M. Molotov and Mr. Eden should go into details. This was agreed.

B Meeting at the Kremlin, 10 October 1944, at 7.p.m.

. . . M. MOLOTOV agreed about the necessity for speed, but said he could not understand the American proposal. How would three representatives act in Bulgaria where there were no zones? Did the Americans and British contemplate stationing troops in Bulgaria? How could there be proper management in Bulgaria after the end of the war with Germany? It was obscure and might mean friction. He considered that 90/10 as proposed by Marshal Stalin was fair.

MR. EDEN replied that there was no intention to station troops in Bulgaria.

He suggested there might be a permanent Soviet chairman on the Control Commission.

M. MOLOTOV refused to consider this as the three representatives would decide affairs which would mean that the British and Americans would have 33 per cent each and the Soviet Union 1 per cent more than they because the President was a Soviet citizen. They would have 34 per cent instead of 90 per cent. He asked what was the object of the proposal.

MR. EDEN pointed out that in Roumania the British and American officers were observers. For the period of hostilities with Germany they accepted that position also in Bulgaria. But after the surrender of Germany they would like to be more than observers and have active participation. He had no views as to how to express this. Britain's share was less than the Russian because Russia had troops and administration in Bulgaria.

M. MOLOTOV thought it would be a strange kind of management where no indication was given of who was responsible.

MR. EDEN said the main responsibility would lie with the Soviet Union.

M. MOLOTOV declared that despite this responsibility the Soviet Union was asking for 90 per cent and not 100 per cent.

MR. EDEN said he did not know much about these percentages. All he wanted was a greater share than we already had in Roumania. In Roumania we had 10 per cent which was almost nothing.

M. MOLOTOV pointed out that the idea of percentages arose from the meeting on the previous day, and it was worthy of consideration. Could they not agree on the following: Bulgaria, Hungary and Yugoslavia 75/25 per cent each?

MR. EDEN said that would be worse than on the previous day.

M. MOLOTOV then suggested 90/10 for Bulgaria; 50/50 for Yugoslavia and Hungary subject to an amendment.

MR. EDEN pointed out that they had not agreed about Bulgaria.

M. MOLOTOV remarked that he thought 90/10 was an ultimatum and meant the unconditional surrender of Moscow. However something would have to be done which would be acceptable to all three.

MR. EDEN said he was ready to meet M. Molotov's wishes with regard to Hungary, but he asked for M. Molotov's help to get some participation in Bulgaria after the Germans had been beaten. Possibly some other formula would be accepted. For instance we and the Americans might each have an officer on the Control Commission who would not be as important as the Soviet representative.

M. MOLOTOV then suggested 75/25 for Hungary.

M. MOLOTOV continued that they had not finished with Bulgaria. If Hungary was 75/25 then Bulgaria should be 75/25 and Yugoslavia 60/40. This was the limit to which he could go.

MR. EDEN said he could not make this suggestion to the Prime Minister who was greatly interested in Yugoslavia. He had been at pains to champion Tito and to furnish arms. Any change in Yugoslavian percentages would upset him. Mr. Eden then suggested Hungary 75/25; Bulgaria 80/20; Yugoslavia 50/50.

M. MOLOTOV was ready to agree to 50/50 for Yugoslavia if Bulgaria were 90/10. If the figure for Bulgaria had to be amended then Yugoslavia would also have to be changed.

MR. EDEN pointed out that with regard to Hungary we had made a concession.

M. MOLOTOV repeated that Hungary bordered on Russia and not on Britain. The Russians had suffered losses in Hungary. Marshal Stalin had mentioned this to the Prime Minister. What did 60/40 for Yugoslavia mean? It meant the coast where Russia would have less interest and would not interfere, but they were to have a greater influence in the centre.

MR. EDEN repeated that Britain had been at war with Bulgaria for three years. The Bulgarians had treated us badly. They had beaten British and American prisoners. Russia had been at war with Bulgaria for 48 hours, and then Britain had been warned off Bulgaria who had received favourable treatment.

M. MOLOTOV did not agree. Russia had suffered more than Britain from the Bulgarians, to say nothing of the last war, but the Soviet Union did not want to increase its number of enemies. It had had the intention several times to declare war on Bulgaria. The harm done by Bulgaria to the Soviet Union was many times greater than that done to anyone else. Roumania and Bulgaria were Black Sea Powers. Neither of them had access to the Mediterranean so that Britain should have little interest in those countries. M. Molotov was not speaking of Greece. The Soviet Union was prepared to help Britain to be strong in the Mediterranean, but hoped that Britain would help the Soviet Union in the Black Sea. That was why they were interested in Bulgaria. Bulgaria was not Greece, Italy, Spain or even Yugoslavia.

MR. EDEN said that they had little interest in Bulgaria and they were therefore asking for very little. But we had been at war with her and the question should be looked at through British eyes. Tito happened to have been accessible and Britain had helped him with arms. He had now come to Moscow but Britain had been kept in ignorance. When the British public found this out there would be criticism and rightly so. He was making an arrangement for Bulgarian troops to stay in Yugoslavia, an arrangement between Bulgaria, Yugoslavia and Russia. A bad impression would be created and suspicion aroused as to Russian intentions.

M. MOLOTOV said he thought Marshal Stalin would agree to the following: 75/25 for Bulgaria, but 60/40 for Yugoslavia. He did not think that British sailors would call the Black Sea a 'sea' but only a lake . . .

MR. EDEN said he did not care so much about the figures. He understood Russia's interest in Bulgaria and Britain accepted it. But Britain asked for something more there than in Roumania. If M. Molotov did not like the American formula, any other proposed by the Russians would be considered. For example, instead of calling it the Allied Control Commission it might be called the Soviet Control Commission, with an American and British representative.

M. MOLOTOV asked whether they could reach agreement in regard to Yugoslavia.

MR. EDEN asked what they had to decide.

M. MOLOTOV claimed more weight for the Soviet Union. The Soviet Union had nothing to do with regard to affairs on the coast. They were ready to stay on their 'lake'.

MR. EDEN preferred to have a common policy. There were various questions to decide. When Yugoslavia was free there was the question of the relations between Tito and the Government in London. Were they to come together? Was there to be joint administration? It was desirable that the Allies should pursue the same ideas . . .

C Molotov to Eden, 15 October 1944

With reference to the new wording accepted by us on the 14th October of Article 18 of the draft Armistice Agreement with Bulgaria I consider it necessary in this letter to return to the comments made by me on the question of the direction of the work of the Allied Control Commission during the second period of its activities. Taking into account your aim and that of Mr. Winant to have such a wording of this Article which would provide the necessary diffentiation between the nature of the work of the Allied Control Commission during the first and second periods of its activities, I agree to the wording of Article 18 as proposed by you subject to the amendment with which you are acquainted. It must be repeated that this amendment, as I stated on the 14th October, must find its proper practical expression in the relative directions of the work of the Control Commission during the second period of its activities. It is for this reason, as you will remember, that I suggested to replace the words 'under the chairmanship of the Soviet Representative' by the words 'under the chairmanship of the Representative of the Allied (Soviet) High Command', which, in substance, would mean that the direction of the Allied Control Commission would belong to the Soviet High Command during the second period also. Of course, in accordance with our agreement, the leading role of the Soviet High Command in the Allied Control Commission in the second period of its activities will to some extent be restricted in favour of the British and American representatives. But one cannot agree, as I indicated on the 14th October, with the remarks contained in the British Embassy's Memorandum of the 23rd September to the effect that the Three Governments must have equal participation in the practical work and responsibility of the Commission. Such a construction, as I wrote to you on the 14th October, would in practice mean the elimination of the Soviet Command from the direction of the Control Commission which, in substance, in view of the present circumstances in Bulgaria cannot but lead to the complete elimination of all direction in the work of the Allied Control Commission as regards the exercise of control over the fulfilment by the Bulgarian Government of the Armistice Terms and which would not be in the interests of the Allied States.

In agreeing to the new wording of Article 18, as proposed by you, with the inclusion therein of the above-mentioned amendment, the Soviet Government proceeds in this case from the necessity of maintaining the leading role for the Soviet High Command, though in a somewhat different form also during the second period of the Allied Control Commission's activities, as we agreed as a result of our talks.

D Extract from the Armistice with Bulgaria, 28 October 1944

... 18 For the whole period of the Armistice there will be established in Bulgaria an Allied Control Commission which will regulate and supervise the execution of the Armistice terms under the chairmanship of the representative of the Allied (Soviet) High Command and with the participation of representatives of the United Kingdom and the United States.

During the period between the coming into force of the Armistice and the conclusion of hostilities against Germany, the Allied Control Commission will be under the general direction of the Allied (Soviet) High Command ...

31   Clark Kerr on Soviet policy, 19 November 1944

A Memorandum respecting observations on the attitude of the Soviet Government towards the possible formation of a group of Western European democracies

1 The Russians regard our post-war attitude towards Germany as the touchstone of our good faith as an ally.

2 They will look to us to collaborate closely with them in enforcing on Germany the maximum possible measures of economic disarmament.

3 At a time when the Russians themselves are concerned to build up in South-Eastern and Central Europe a bulwark of military and economic power against a renewal of German aggression, there seems to be no reason to suppose

that they would find it abnormal if we on our side were to promote security measures of our own designed to extend British military and economic power into Western Europe. Indeed, during the Moscow talks, Marshal Stalin seemed to agree with the Prime Minister when the latter remarked that it would be an advantage for British industry if German heavy industry were to be kept under control after the war. So, too, during his visit to London in 1942 M. Molotov suggested to the Secretary of State that Britain might wish to acquire bases for herself across the Channel.

4 Whilst the Russians interpret any British inclination to deal leniently with a regenerated Germany as dictated by anti-Soviet motives, they have throughout the period of our association as allies shown no jealousy of Britain's strength as a Great Power, and their propaganda has abandoned almost all criticism of us on the score of imperialist designs.

5 So long as His Majesty's Government pursue an anti-German policy in collaboration with the Soviet Government the attitude just described is likely to persist, and the Russians will welcome all evidence that Great Britain is ready to play a vigorous part in containing Germany. Indeed, throughout the Moscow talks, Marshal Stalin frequently went out of his way to stress the need for the peace-loving Powers to be constantly in readiness to assert their strength. He repeatedly argued that the weakness of these Powers, including Great Britain, had enabled the aggressors to score their initial successes in Europe and the Far East. He developed the same theme in his broadcast speech on the 6th November.

6 The Russians think of the future world order in terms of a concert of the three major Allies. They are opposed to independent regional federations of smaller States, which they expect to move in the orbit of the Great Power situated nearest to them. In so far as can at present be judged, the Russians are aiming at the creation in Central and South-Eastern Europe of a bailiwick of more or less independent countries. Their object is to build up a military and economic security zone which will make it impossible to revive any of the pre-war makeshift plans of a *cordon sanitaire* against the Soviet Union.

7 On present showing, moreover, the Soviet Government are disposed to admit that, just as they are themselves entitled to organise a continental orbit of power in regions adjacent to their borders, so His Majesty's Government are at liberty to claim the right to pursue a similar policy along the Atlantic and Mediterranean seaboards – subject always to the proviso that the primary aim is to immobilise Germany. In return for the recognition by His Majesty's Government of their special interests in Roumania and Bulgaria, the Soviet Government have done the like for us as regards Greece. During the Moscow talks they spontaneously acknowledged that the Adriatic Coast had a special importance for Britain. They have followed Anglo-American leadership in the recognition of the Provisional Government of France.

8 The readiness of the Russians to support, and even to encourage, moves on our part calculated to contain Germany, seems to be reinforced by a belief that it would not rebound to their military and economic advantage if Britain were so weak as to leave world power to be divided between the United States and the U.S.S.R. As was clearly shown during the presidential campaign, the Kremlin has deep misgivings as to whether the United States may be permanently counted upon to pursue a policy of international collaboration.

9 All present indications go to show that the Soviet Government are convinced that the future of Germany, and with it the future of European security, must be decided within the months immediately following the collapse of the Reich, whilst memories of German barbarism are still fresh in the minds of the victims. As the Russians see it, common enmity to Germany is at present the only really solid bond between the United Nations, who will tend to fall apart unless new links can be forged in the first glow of victory.

10 The Russians themselves are apparently taking time by the forelock in so far as concerns the organisation of Central and South-Eastern Europe. From the foregoing analysis of their attitude it would seem to follow that, if we on our side wish to safeguard our interests in the manner suggested, we must take action before the Russians can have ground for thinking that our policy is dictated by other than anti-Germany motives. It would incidentally seem advisable to deal with the problem whilst the political conditions in Western Europe are favourable to a closer alignment with us and, if need be, with the Americans.

11 In the absence of concerted action to stimulate closer association between ourselves and the countries of Western Europe, there is a risk that the latter will conclude that a war-weary Britain has abdicated her continental power. Left-wing elements in those countries would then inevitably be driven to place an even greater reliance than they do already on Soviet power and influence. The Soviet Government themselves, confronted with a security vacuum, would be tempted to exploit the situation to their own exclusive advantage. The resulting increase in the domestic strains and stresses of Western European countries needs no emphasis.

12 The preceding paragraphs may seem to have placed undue stress upon Germany as the predominant factor in the future of Anglo-Soviet relations. So far as concerns the immediate future, an examination of the problem certainly suggests that the initial basis for European concord must take the form of international arrangements somewhat akin to Bismarck's *Drei Kaiserbund*, a main purpose of which was to prevent the resurrection of Poland. At the same time, this initial basis of collaboration seems to offer the only practicable point of departure for that wider Anglo-Soviet understanding which is essential for the maintenance of world peace.

B Summary of Foreign Office comment on the above, 26 January 1945

This is an interesting despatch but based on the doubtful premise of a partition of Germany. The French seem to have got the impression in Moscow that Marshal Stalin is now against the policy of partition, and it now seems more likely that a policy of 'truncating' Germany's western head and eastern tail will be agreed upon.

The desirability of partition in Soviet eyes is argued in the despatch on the ground that the necessity which would result of keeping German populations in subjection would constitute the most, if not the only, effective bond of union among the victorious powers. Against this it may be suggested that if public opinion in the Anglo-Saxon countries and elsewhere did not in the long run regard the policy of partition as justified the moral effect might be to weaken the Western European group which it was designed to cement. Rather than promote this result it would seem better to accept the risk of an unattached German 'no-man's-land' between the two European power groups and trust to the latter's predominant strength and to the world security organisation to keep the position stable.

As regards the idea of a western security group, His Majesty's Ambassador seems to be right in arguing that the Russians would view this with favour as part of a wider security system and provided it were linked with a firm attitude towards Germany.

32   Soviet attitude to UNRRA, December 1944

Camps, 4 December

As far as I can judge, the relations between the Russians and U.N.R.R.A. have always been uneasy and latterly there have been further discouraging signs . . .

It may be that the Russians are anxious to keep U.N.R.R.A. out of Eastern Europe, or those parts of it which they claim an interest in. This, if true, is probably connected with the fact that U.N.R.R.A., if furnishing supplies, would expect to exercise a considerable degree of supervision over the use of them, and to be fairly strongly represented in the regions concerned.

All the above is fairly indefinite, and it may be that U.N.R.R.A. will succeed in despatching its various missions in the near future and that our own military authorities will reach a satisfactory agreement with the Yugoslavs thus opening the way to a subsequent agreement between them and U.N.R.R.A. We can therefore afford to wait a little longer and see how things move.

It seems to me however that it would on general grounds be very desirable if we ourselves and the Americans could establish closer relations with the Russians over U.N.R.R.A. matters . . .

Hoyer Millar, 6 December

Before, however, we approach the Russians we should be clearer in our own minds what we really want. It seems to me that there are two main problems to clear up, (a) Russia's attitude towards UNRRA in respect of help to Russia itself – i.e., does the Soviet Government intend to ask UNRRA to help provide supplies for Russia itself and to seek UNRRA's help in respect of Soviet displaced persons, and (b) Russia's attitude in respect of UNRRA's help to those Allied liberated countries in which Russia is specially interested – Poland, Czechoslovakia and Yugoslavia.

As regards (b) our attitude is presumably that we should like to see UNRRA helping these Allies to the greatest possible extent and that we should deprecate a different attitude on the part of the Russians or any attempt by the latter to encourage the Yugoslavs, Poles, etc. to impose conditions, such as the non-acceptance of observers, which might make it more difficult for UNRRA to help the Allied countries. The Russians will no doubt be reluctant to see foreign observers loose in Yugoslavia etc., but if it can be made clear to them (and to the Yugoslavs etc.) that no observers means no UNRRA and no UNRRA means no relief supplies (except what Russia can produce) then they might alter their line.

As regards (a), the Russian decision whether or not to seek UNRRA's help for Russia itself will no doubt depend on whether they think they can get more out of UNRRA than they can out of His Majesty's Government, the U.S.A. and Canada by a continuance of the present Protocol arrangement. From the UNRRA point of view, there is a lot to be said for relief supplies for Russia being provided outside UNRRA, since for UNRRA to provide them on the scale which the Russians would expect would deplete UNRRA's funds enormously and pretty soon break the UNRRA machine up – since there is little prospect of the Russians agreeing to go through the Resolution 23 procedure regarding capacity to pay. Nor do we want most of the benefits of UNRRA to go to Russia to the exclusion of the other allies in whose economic recovery we are, for our own selfish reasons, closely interested . . .

Wilson, 9 December

. . . 3 I think there can be little doubt that the Russians do not like U.N.R.R.A. sending observers to countries in Eastern Europe, whatever the attitude of the countries concerned may be on this point. This is partly dictated by desire to use the relief for their own purposes, partly by prestige reasons, but mainly I suspect because they would never feel quite certain that such observers were confining themselves strictly to the business in hand. I am not certain what importance we attach to this question of observers, but if we are going to insist on making acceptance of them a condition for the provision of supplies, it should be made quite clear that their purpose is to see that roughly the same standards are applied in different countries rather than to see that the supplies are equitably distributed within any particular country. If the latter is, or is made to appear to be, their purpose it can easily be represented as having political implications so that the blame for not sending supplies would fall rather on us for insisting on sending the observers than on the countries concerned for not being prepared to accept them. The Russians have already sent relief supplies into Yugoslavia with no strings attached to them, and if it suits their purpose to do so, they are probably prepared to do the same thing in other cases. If they appear to be more generous than U.N.R.R.A. the results may be unfortunate to say the least.

4 As regards Russia's own requirements I agree that it would be better for us and the Americans to put a proposition up to the Americans than merely to ask the Russians what they would like. From the Russian point of view everything will depend on the terms on which they can get supplies, and they will, not unnaturally buy in the cheapest market. We and the Americans should therefore I think clear our own minds on this aspect of the matter as soon as possible . . .

Memorandum by W. J. Hasler of the War Cabinet Offices, sent to the Foreign Office on 11 December

. . . 2 The Russian attitude towards U.N.R.R.A. is no doubt compounded of many elements; – a suspicion of the motives of the U.S.A. and ourselves in putting up money for nothing, doubt about the ability of an organization such as U.N.R.R.A. to do a real job, desire to exploit the supplies and the needs of Eastern Europe and the Balkans in her own interests and other less obvious factors probably influence her. I believe however that the largest single factor is the doubt in the minds of the Russians on whether they will themselves obtain free supplies from U.N.R.R.A. It seems to me likely that until recently the Russians have always thought that a large part of the purpose of U.N.R.R.A., if not the main one, was to provide them with supplies and services free. We on the other hand have tended to assume that U.N.R.R.A. was designed for the smaller countries and that the role of the Great Powers in U.N.R.R.A. was to contribute resources, to put drive behind the organization and to see fair play. It seems to me that most of the actions taken by Russia in connection with U.N.R.R.A. which have worried us can be explained by their feeling that they should be beneficiaries . . . we shall soon be faced with the fact either that U.N.R.R.A. can do only half a job or that it must be given considerable additional funds. It should be emphasised that we may well be faced with this awkward alternative in any case. It is certain however that we shall meet it in a more acute form and sooner than would otherwise be the case if Russia is a beneficiary of U.N.R.R.A. If therefore we still attach most importance to the essential measures of relief in Europe being undertaken it looks as though we should either see that Russian relief needs are met without U.N.R.R.A. finance or else that the way is made smooth for the provision of more funds for U.N.R.R.A. . . .

33 Extracts from the meetings of Foreign Ministers at Yalta, February 1945

A Meeting held at 12 noon on 6 February 1945

. . . 2 MR. STETTINIUS said that three topics had been referred to the Foreign Ministers as a result of yesterday's Plenary Meeting. These were:

1 The procedure for studying the dismemberment of Germany.
2 The integration of France in the control machinery for Germany if she were given a zone of occupation.
3 Reparation. In particular principles should be laid down for the guidance of the Moscow Commission on Reparation when it was set up.

Starting with the first point, he thought that an immense amount of research and study would be necessary before conclusive views on the dismemberment of Germany could be reached. He hoped, however, that we might reach agreement on general principles at this conference. He suggested that consideration should be given to the desirability of adding the word 'dismemberment' to Article 12 (a) of the Terms of Surrender for Germany (see Annex). Finally he thought that consideration should be given to whether the study of dismemberment should be assigned to the European Advisory Commission.

M. MOLOTOV said that two points arose. As regards the addition of the word 'dismemberment' to Article 12 he would accept this.

MR. EDEN proposed another possible formula, viz., that the second sentence of Article 12 (a) should read as follows:

> In the exercise of such authority they will take such steps as they deem requisite for future peace and security, including the complete disarmament and demilitarisation of Germany and measures for the dissolution of the German unitary State.

MR. STETTINIUS said that he felt it was immaterial which of the two forms of wording was used.

M. MOLOTOV proposed a formula which involved an alteration of the first sentence of Article 12. He suggested that to the end of the first sentence should be added the words 'and they will take measures for the dismemberment of Germany'.

MR. EDEN said that this formula would involve a commitment not to the principle but to the act of dismemberment.

M. MOLOTOV then suggested the insertion of a new sentence into the Article between the first and second sentences as follows:

> In order to secure peace and security they consider necessary the dismemberment of Germany.

He considered the advantage of this formula was that it set forth the reasons why the Allies considered the dismemberment of Germany essential.

MR. EDEN pointed out that this would commit us to dismemberment in all circumstances before we had made our study of the problem. This was further than he could go.

M. MOLOTOV pointed out that as a result of the previous day's Plenary Meeting we were committed to the principle of dismemberment.

MR. EDEN said that what we now had to do was to work out the implications of this principle with particular reference to its practicability.

ME. STETTINIUS suggested that perhaps what was wanted was the inclusion of the words 'right to dismemberment'.

M. MOLOTOV pointed out that unconditional surrender already included that. The important thing was that the Allies considered dismemberment necessary.

MR. EDEN said that one could not say that it was necessary until its practicability had been worked out. What we had done was to say that we considered it desirable. It was not our fault that the E.A.C. had not completed a study of dismemberment as had been agreed at Tehran.

M. MOLOTOV then asked to see Mr. Stettinius's suggested formula again. After consideration he thought that it would be acceptable. He then suggested a further amendment, namely, the addition of the words 'for future peace and security', at the beginning of the second sentence. The word 'such' should be omitted before 'steps' and the sentence would end at 'Germany'.

MR. EDEN said that this would leave us no choice. We would be bound to take all steps to secure dismemberment.

M. MOLOTOV repeated that we had already accepted dismemberment in principle. He considered the words 'as they deem requisite' must be omitted. The point of this amendment was that it made the principle of dismemberment more definite.

MR. EDEN said that the original text allowed us a certain latitude. If it were amended as suggested by M. Molotov that latitude would be denied us. He would be prepared to accept Mr. Stettinius's original suggestion of the addition of the words 'and the dismemberment' after 'demilitarisation' in the second sentence.

MR. STETTINIUS then put forward a suggestion to substitute after 'demilitarisation' the words 'and the dismemberment of Germany to the extent deemed necessary for future peace and security'.

MR. EDEN said that he was prepared to agree to the insertion of the word 'dismemberment' as originally suggested by Mr. Stettinius, but he was not prepared to do any more.

M. MOLOTOV argued that this formula would be susceptible of a double interpretation; it might mean that we accepted the principle of dismemberment now; or it might only amount to acceptance in the future. He added that his formula was more definite and gave enough latitude.

MR. EDEN said he could not accept it without reference to the Prime Minister.

M. MOLOTOV said that the discussion might be summed up as follows: All concerned thought that it was necessary to add the word 'dismemberment' to the Article. As regards the second amendment Mr. Eden would consult the Prime Minister.

MR. EDEN said that his position was quite clear. He agreed to the first amendment, namely the insertion of the word 'dismemberment', but not to the second. He would, however, consult the Prime Minister.

MR. STETTINIUS finally said that his position was as originally stated at the opening of the meeting. He thought that the best solution would be to insert the words 'and the dismemberment' after 'demilitarisation' in the second sentence of Article 12.

MR. STETTINIUS then enquired whether it was agreed that the study of the details of dismemberment should be reserved for the E.A.C.

M. MOLOTOV suggested that it would perhaps be better to have a special commission.

It was finally decided to leave this question open until the next meeting.

Article 12 (*Original*)

a The United Kingdom, the United States of America, and the Union of Soviet Socialist Republics shall possess supreme authority with respect to Germany. In the exercise of such authority they will take such steps, including the complete disarmament and de-militarisation of Germany, as they deem requisite for future peace and security.

ANNEX

Article 12 (*Amended*)

a The United Kingdom, the United States of America, and the Union of Soviet Socialist Republics shall possess supreme authority with respect to Germany. In the exercise of such authority they will take such steps, including the complete disarmament, demilitarisation and the dismemberment of Germany as they deem requisite for future peace and security.

B Meeting held at 12 noon on 7 February 1945

... M. MOLOTOV said that the second question on the Agenda concerned the setting up of a commission to study dismemberment. He proposed that a commission should be set up for this purpose in London consisting of Mr. Eden as Chairman, together with the United States and Soviet Ambassadors in London.

MR. STETTINIUS feared that if this task were not given to the European Advisory Commission, its prestige would be lessened.

MR. EDEN said that while he was touched at the suggestion that he should preside over such a commission and work with the colleagues proposed, he thought that the advantage in referring the matter to the European Advisory Commission lay in the fact that the French would be present there.

MR. STETTINIUS said that was just the point in not referring it to the European Advisory Commission. It would be agreeable to the United States Government that studies of dismemberment should be carried out in London, and that their representative on the proposed commission should be Mr. Winant.

M. MOLOTOV thought that since the body concerned would be considering the procedure to be followed in dismembering Germany, it would be better to set up a special commission. The matter might perhaps be referred later to the European Advisory Commission.

MR. EDEN hoped that the body would go further than merely the consideration of procedure. He then read out a suggested Terms of Reference (see Annex I).

MR. STETTINIUS and M. MOLOTOV both agreed with the suggested Terms of Reference.

MR. EDEN said that the point that they had to decide was whether the proposed body was to do the work of studying dismemberment, or whether it was merely to decide how that work was to be done.

After some further discussion, it was agreed that no directive had been issued at the Plenary Meeting that a special body should be set up. Nevertheless, it would be desirable for an examination of the problem to be carried out in London.

MR. EDEN said that he was worried at the idea that the French should not be brought in. The French after all were neighbours of Germany and we knew that they had ideas about the future of the Rhineland. We might or might not agree with those ideas, but if we kept the French out of these discussions, he considered that we should be making a grave mistake.

M. MOLOTOV said that the question of the participation of France might be discussed by the body studying dismemberment.

MR. STETTINIUS agreed to this, and it was finally agreed that the commission proposed by M. Molotov should carry out the study of dismemberment in London, but that, at Mr. Eden's request, the latter should be at liberty to appoint a deputy if his duties should not allow him to preside in person over the commission . . .

Annex 1. Suggested terms of reference for commission on dismemberment

1 On the assumption that Germany is to be split up, if necessary by force, into separate States to examine (a) what the boundaries of the States should be; (b) what measures would need to be taken by the occupying forces to ensure the more or less efficient functioning and survival of the States; and (c) what relationship should be allowed amongst the separate States and with other foreign Powers.

2 To submit a factual report indicating the advantages and disadvantages of the above mentioned scheme from the point of view of general security . . .

34 Clark Kerr on Soviet policy, 27 March 1945

Over a month has now passed since the signing of the Crimea Agreement, which received so warm a welcome throughout the world, and not least in the Soviet Union. It is perhaps too soon to draw up a balance sheet on the results of the conference at Yalta, but a provisional assessment is, I think, justified by developments in Soviet policy during the past month.

2 The Crimea talks covered a wide range of subjects, and the fact that agreement was reached on all of them was the more gratifying because, during the months that went before the Yalta meeting, there had been many instances of lack of consultation and here and there of actual divergence of policy between the Soviet Union on the one hand and Great Britain and the United States on the other. I fear, however, that much has happened since to trouble the harmonies established at Yalta and to fortify critics, who are included to question the value of the meeting.

3 In one all-important respect there can be no cause whatever for disappointment. Events have shown that the military decisions taken in the Crimea are being carried out so successfully that the final defeat of Germany now seems likely to be only a matter of months. The political decisions at Yalta concerning Germany were equally satisfactory and dispelled many lingering doubts on either side. They have been the subject of much comment in the Soviet press, and it is clear that they are in tune not only with the policy of the Kremlin but also with the mood of the Soviet people.

4 Elsewhere unhappily the picture becomes disappointing and even disturbing. The American delegation attached particular importance to the compromise on voting procedure, which rendered possible the calling of the United Nations Conference in San Francisco in April, and they welcomed M. Molotov's declared intention to attend in person. His sudden decision to leave the leadership of the Soviet delegation to a man of the meagre calibre of M. Gromyko marks a sharp change of mood which calls for a more convincing explanation than that which has been given.

5 The most obvious set-backs since Yalta, however, concern the declaration of liberated Europe and that on Poland, about both of which considerable satisfaction had been felt. To our vexation we have found the Soviet Government openly interpreting both these declarations to their own advantage. Their conduct in Roumania has been the sheerest power politics, entirely out of harmony with the principles enshrined in the Crimea declaration. There has been no attempt to consult with us or with the Americans and we have been expected to condone and, indeed, to associate ourselves with the decisions imposed upon King Michael by M. Vyshinski. When we quote the Yalta declaration to the Russians we meet with the reply that our arguments are not in accordance with the Statutes agreed upon for the Allied Control Commission. In other words, the Yalta declaration is being treated by the Soviet Government as little more than a sedative which cannot be allowed to interfere with what is, in the eyes of the Russians, their established right, fully admitted by us, to do as they like in Roumania. When our protests become more urgent, no time is lost in starting a minor press campaign against General Plastiras and his Administration in Greece, as if to remind us that Russian forbearance as regards that country is measured by ours in Roumania.

6 But however dissatisfied we and the Americans may be with what has happened in Roumania, the Russians know that we are unlikely to make it a real test case in their relations with the West. They must, however, be blind if they do not see that Poland might become such a test case, and their attempt to twist the Yalta communiqué to the exclusive benefit of the provisional authorities at Warsaw is therefore disquieting. My telegram will, I think, have shown you that there may have been a genuine misunderstanding as to the real meaning of the formula on Poland, and I should add that it was not only the

Russians in Moscow who interpreted it as an abandonment by us of the Polish Government in London and an important step towards recognition of the Lublin authorities. But although time is passing and the situation inside Poland is not improving, there still remains some hope of breaking the present deadlock in the Moscow Commission, and the time has therefore not yet come to dismiss the Yalta formula as mere waste paper.

7 Of the other Balkan questions raised in the Crimea, the only one which has developed on satisfactory lines is Yugoslavia. But here the Yalta communiqué only confirmed a situation which already existed and which was pleasing to the Russians. When we turn to Bulgaria and to Bulgarian relations with Greece and Yugoslavia, we find that the representations which you made to M. Molotov, and which I have since renewed more than once in Moscow, have hitherto remained fruitless. In fact, since the Yalta meeting, the Russians, regardless of our representations, have pursued their own Balkan policies, which are clearly based upon support of the Slav States of Bulgaria and Yugoslavia and upon the squeezing of Roumania into a mould of their own shaping.

8 On top of all this comes the denunciation on the 21st March of the Soviet–Turkish Treaty of Alliance. This has followed a press campaign against Turkey which has been proceeding for some months past and which continued even after the Turkish declaration of war upon Germany and Japan, a step to which the Soviet Government had given their approval at Yalta. My Turkish colleague is disposed to take a philosophic view of what has happened and, for the present at any rate, I am inclined to abide by his judgment and to see in the denunciation no more than a wish to put a little of the fear of God into the Turks before raising the question of the revision of the Montreux Agreement.

9 One of the more valuable practical results of the Crimea Conference was the agreement, concerning the repatriation of British and Soviet prisoners of war. Here again, our experiences have been anything but satisfactory, and it has now proved necessary for you and the Prime Minister to address personal messages to M. Molotov and Marshal Stalin, urging them to ensure that the agreement is carried out in the spirit as well as in the letter. While we clearly cannot accept the present position, allowances should, however, be made for the rooted Soviet objection to admit foreign military observers into forward areas; for the Soviet disinclination to show us anything which might appear discreditable to the Soviet Union, for the primitive harum-scarum conditions under which the Red Army lives and moves, and finally for the natural, although inexcusable, temptation to blackmail us into some degree of recognition of the provisional Polish authorities.

10 A further sign of the times is perhaps the attitude of the Soviet delegation at the Trades Union Congress in London. The proceedings of this congress

have received considerable publicity in this country, where it is claimed that the Soviet delegation succeeded in pushing through all of its proposals. This is a subject which calls for fuller treatment than is possible in this review, but it is enough to say here that the Russians are obviously making a serious, if not unexpected, attempt to dominate whatever new international trade union organisation emerges from the war.

11 The above developments are certainly uncomfortable. They must have provoked in you, as they have in me, fresh anxieties about future Russian intentions and the possibility of continued collaboration between the Soviet Union and the West after the war. I think, however, that while, after the flow of brotherhood at Yalta, we have every right to grumble about recent Soviet behaviour, we should make a mistake if we built up a black record from the events of the past few weeks, and if we decided that they implied that the Kremlin had turned away from the policy of co-operation with the West. You will well remember that we have suffered similar set-backs and disappointments after all the earlier three-Power meetings. Some observers maintain that it is Marshal Stalin's set policy after any such manifestation of inter-Allied unity to take steps to remind his people that the Soviet Union can still go her own way and is in no sense dependent upon her allies. There may well be something in this, but another explanation may be that the Soviet leaders come to such international meetings, as it were, to sniff the air, and to discover how far they can safely go in pushing Soviet interests in those parts of the world with which they are immediately concerned. At Yalta the Soviet leaders no doubt confirmed their impression that they could pursue their own ends in the Balkans without fear of serious opposition, provided always that they stopped short at Greece. Probably the latest development in regard to Turkey may be explained by our expressed readiness to agree to some revision of the Montreux Agreement and by our own criticism of recent Turkish policy.

12 It is safe to assume that the Soviet Government are also under special temptation, at this stage of the war, to press ahead with their plans for Eastern and South-Eastern Europe while they have a relatively free hand. They must feel pretty sure that, until Germany is finally beaten, we shall not strongly oppose Soviet action in such countries as Roumania and Bulgaria. They now have a unique opportunity, with the Red army in occupation and with the complete disruption of pre-war social systems, to bend internal developments in those countries according to their will. They realise that such an opportunity may not recur, and they are determined that, when society crystallises again in those countries bordering on the Soviet Union, the social structure, although not necessarily identical to, will be in harmony with that of the Soviet Union, and that all potential hostile influences will have been eliminated. Similar considerations no doubt guide Soviet policy in Poland, where the Russians have even more reason to fear a re-emergence of hostile and indigestible elements.

13 But this Russian policy, however distasteful it may be to us, and how-ever great a strain it may at times put upon our patience and upon our belief in the whole system of collaboration and consultation between the three Great Powers, has the air of remaining a policy of limited objectives, none of which immediately endangers essential British interests. Where these interests are at stake, and the Russians know them to be at stake, as in the case of Greece, they have refrained from intervention and have shown what is for them extreme moderation. Here it is also worth noting that, although the Soviet representatives at Yalta refused to subscribe to any new declaration on Persia, they have in fact refrained from reviving their demands for oil concessions, and they seem to have realised that the independence of Persia is a matter of vital importance to us and one in which regard must be paid to our interests and feelings. Turkey is another question where our vital interests are directly engaged. Here again, as I have said, there is no proof as yet that the Russians are going further than preparing the way for a revision of the Montreux Convention, to which we have explicitly agreed. Finally, we have not since Yalta been faced with any preposterous and blundering public accusation such as the *Pravda* peace rumour which followed the Tehran Conference.

14 There remains always the troublous question of Poland. Here the issues at stake, so far as Anglo-Soviet relations are concerned, are mainly psycho-logical. The Russians lack the niceness of feeling which we cherish about an ally for whom we went to war, and they are incapable of measuring the weight that lies behind public opinion in the west and how it bears upon us. They are chiefly bent upon getting a comfortable neighbour. To them this is a matter of the first importance. To us, who are more concerned with decencies, it is not. It may well be that they cannot understand why we should insist upon having so tight a hand upon a question in which no direct British interest is involved. It is possible that at Yalta, in spite of all our efforts, Marshal Stalin and M. Molotov may have got the impression that we might be satisfied with their interpretation of the Yalta agreement as a means of cleansing ourselves of our commitments to Poland. If so, they must be puzzled by our sustained and indeed increased interest in Polish affairs. But for us the Polish question is, and must remain, one of the utmost consequence, for upon its satisfactory solution rests a great part of our hope and belief in the possibility of a real and cordial understanding between the Soviet people and our own. Neverthe-less, Russian recalcitrance about Poland need not inevitably count as a good pointer to general Soviet policy. It is certainly not, I think, an issue which need prevent the maintenance of an alliance not quite in the form the more opti-mistic of us had foreseen, but at any rate useful to both countries – in fact, a relationship considerably closer than that which existed between Great Britain and Tsarist Russia between 1907 and 1914.

15 I would suggest, therefore, that, while we may hug our wrath and mark our displeasure, we need not be unduly discouraged by the disappointments of the past few weeks, none of which indicates any Soviet intention to impinge upon our vital interests. What has happened has probably been in many cases the result of the recent switch away from an exclusive interest in military preoccupations and of a growing concern for the international situation facing Russia after the war. The Soviet Union is now in a state of high buoyancy and utterly confident of her strength. The manifestations of this confidence are often rough and boisterous. The Soviet Union tends to disport herself like a wet retriever puppy in somebody else's drawing room, shaking herself and swishing her tail in adolescent disregard for all except herself. We must expect her thus to rampage until she feels that she is secure from any unpleasant surprises in neighbouring countries, and then we may, I think, foresee that she will emerge from her puppydom and settle down to the serious and respectable business of collaboration with her major allies, and still more to that of her relationship with Great Britain under the Anglo-Soviet Treaty, a commitment by which she sets great store. Meanwhile we need not, I think, be over nice in our approach to her. When we are shocked we may say so in all frankness. But we must always be a hundred-fold in the right. We may permit, and indeed we should encourage, franker criticism of Soviet policy and we should put a stop to the gush of propaganda at home and abroad in praise not only of the Soviet war effort, but also of the whole Soviet system, which can only have convinced the realists at the Kremlin that there is a complex of fear and inferiority in Great Britain where the Soviet Union is concerned. We shall, I am afraid, make little headway with the Kremlin so long as we conduct fruitless arguments with them over such countries as Roumania or Bulgaria. On the other hand they will, I think, respect us the more and set a higher value upon our co-operation, whenever we stand up firmly for what the Russians recognise to be our vital interests, as in Greece, in Persia and in Turkey. While memories of German aggression and fears of its revival linger in Russian minds, as they must for some years to come, these fears, together with the need for help in shouldering the heavy burden of reconstruction, should provide a solid basis for Anglo-Soviet co-operation in the major tasks of European reconstruction.

16 We must recognise however that the word 'co-operation', like the word 'democracy', has different meanings in the Soviet Union and in the West. Here it seems to mean the acceptance of something like a division of the world into spheres of interest and a tacit agreement that no one of the partners will hamper or indeed criticise the activities of the other within its own sphere. The Soviet Government will probably contribute according to their lights to the maintenance of a facade of respectability before the world, but they will judge their partners and conduct their policy towards them by their own

realistic standards. Our value as a partner will also be judged by our strength and by our readiness to stand up for our own rights and interests. Wherever and whenever we show signs of weakening we may expect to be pounced upon. We must therefore not only be strong, we must look strong and, so far as possible, we should confine our quarrels with the Russians to issues on which we are prepared to stand our ground. Even then we shall have still to make allowances for the unpredictable factor of Russian suspicions of us and of our motives. These have not yet, and, I fear, never will be, entirely dispelled. We are therefore always at the mercy of some sudden squall which at best interrupts the smooth conduct of day-to-day relations and at worst may destroy confidence in both countries in the maintenance of the Anglo-Soviet alliance after the war. For myself I do not think that we need allow recent events to lead us to fear the worst. As I see it, His Majesty's Government have never set more than sober hopes upon the alliance, or asked of it any of the intimacies or the close understanding that would dwell in a like commitment with the United States or even with France. In the circumstances in which it was concluded the alliance seemed to me to be one of those flashes of genius that from time to time light our foreign policy. In this view I remain unshaken, for I am convinced that the alliance will serve us well and pay a steady, though not spectacular, dividend.

35   Orme Sargent's minute of 2 April 1945 on the need to reconsider policy towards Russia

I wonder whether with the change in the war situation the moment has not come to change the technique of our diplomacy towards the Soviet Union.

Till our invasion of France, that is to say till the Second Front had been opened, our attitude was, and indeed had to be, defensive and almost apologetic. Even since then, during the spectacular advances of the Russian armies last year, the Soviet Union seemed in Europe to be establishing a military predominance which would show its full force at the Peace Settlement and which it would be folly to ignore. Indeed it looked until the other day that it would be the Russian armies which would invade and occupy the heart of Germany, including Berlin, before the British and Americans had penetrated the German defences in the West.

In these circumstances it was only prudent that we should in our diplomatic dealings with the Soviet Government set ourselves to propitiate our Russian Ally. On every possible occasion we tried to humour him, and the Prime Minister in particular was at pains to establish a personal friendship with Stalin. The policy was no doubt the right one at the time, and though it produced no spectacular results and indeed very little response from the Soviet Government, who can say that the situation would not have been very much worse if we had during this period asserted our rights on every occasion by the various means of pressure open to us, such as retaliation in kind, denial of material help, and isolated action in those parts of Europe where our interests and those of the Soviet Union appeared to conflict.

But with the sudden, almost unexpected, break-through in the West, involving the collapse of the German armies and the opening of the heart of Germany to invasion by British and American armies, the situation has radically changed. Instead of the Russians being in the position from Berlin to dictate their terms to their Allies, these latter are meeting them on equal terms in Germany, and indeed the terms on which they meet may end by being more favourable to the Western Allies than to the Russians.

The first sign that the Soviet Government have understood the magnitude of this change as it affects the diplomatic field is the sudden truculence they have shown in dealing with the various outstanding questions – a truculence so out of keeping with the willingness to cooperate that they showed at Yalta. The case of Poland is perhaps *sui generis,* and we might in any event have encountered the difficulties we are now encountering in trying to bring the Yalta decision to fruition. What is more significant is the Russian attitude to the lesser, every-day questions, such as their behaviour in regard to our released prisoners of war in Poland; the coup d'etat in Roumania, and their subsequent refusal to discuss the matter with us and the Americans; the passive resistance to all our efforts to get the E.A.C. to deal with the increasing mass of questions now becoming daily more urgent about the administration of Germany and Austria after the collapse. It looks as though they were resolved to give nothing away a moment sooner than they need, because they now find that in view of the sudden increase in strength of our military position they will need all the bargaining counters they can lay their hands on in the coming struggle for position in the political field.

But what is most significant among recent occurrences is the attitude which they adopted in regard to the CROSSWORD incident – Molotov's very offensive reply in which he accused us of carrying on negotiations with the German Generals for 'a fortnight behind the backs of the Soviet Government, while the Russians were bearing the brunt of the war', shows clearly the deep suspicion which they harbour as to the uses to which we may put our victories in the West. The Soviet authorities – both in the Government and Army – have in the past displayed so little interest in our plans for the present campaign, and they have so consistently belittled our efforts, our resources, and our ability, that they have quite probably been genuinely taken by surprise by the speed and magnitude of our present victories. If they still believe that they are 'bearing the brunt of the war' they may argue to themselves that the German armies have, unlike the armies of the Oder, put up no fight. If so, the suspicious Russian mind will not be slow to suggest reasons for this and find a connexion between the CROSSWORD discussions 'which have been going on for a fortnight', and the retreat of the German armies beyond the Rhine . . .

If anything like this is passing in the Russian mind, there is little we can do except to let events gradually speak for themselves and prove our honesty. But meanwhile we cannot expect any sort of confident co-operation with the Soviet Government. Indeed, if they do recognise our honesty they will by the same token have to recognise our strength. They will then not be slow to see that as a result of the present campaign the overwhelming Anglo-American Air Force, not to speak of the Allied armies, will now be able to make their influence, if not their presence, felt in countries up till now cut off from the West, such as Poland, Czechoslovakia, Austria and Hungary.

One might suppose that all this would make the Soviet Government more anxious to humour us and the Americans, but unfortunately their reaction may take quite a different form, especially if they think, as they no doubt do, that we and the Americans intend to rehabilitate Germany as we have undertaken to rehabilitate Italy so as to save her from Communism. Thus they may well decide that there is not a moment to be lost in consolidating their *cordon sanitaire*, not merely against a future German danger, but against the impending penetration by the Western Allies. In such a mood they might not stop to count, in terms of Allied co-operation, the cost of destroying the last vestiges of bourgeois rule and sovereign independence in the countries to be sacrificed for this purpose.

This may be a too gloomy view of the situation, but given the Russian character it is sufficiently possible to warrant our considering whether our present diplomatic technique in dealing with the Soviet Government is the best calculated to divert them from this policy, or at least to minimise its effects.

Has not the moment come to speak plainly to the Soviet Government, to show our resentment, and to formulate what we consider our rights? To propitiate Stalin when we were weak he would understand, but for us to do so now when we are strong would surely appear to him as a cunning manoeuvre intended to put him off his guard. He is much more likely to understand if we insist on a show-down on the ground that our respective positions in the European scene have altered.

But if so, what should we say and how? Our language will be governed largely by the outcome of the latest attempt to reach a Polish settlement on the lines of the Yalta Agreement. If it fails, the road will be clear for the plainest of plain speaking. But even if Stalin does allow the Yalta procedure to be applied, and even if a United Polish Government is eventually set up, it may

still be necessary to make it clear where we stand, and what we will not stand –
or else the Polish settlement is likely to be as short-lived as was the Czechoslovak settlement after Munich.

The subject of our shown-down would be two-fold: (a) the treatment of
Germany and Austria; and (b) the creation of the *cordon sanitaire.*

As regards (a) it is, of course, the case that we have either already stated our
views in the E.A.C. or shall shortly be doing so in the Reparation Commission
which is to meet in Moscow. But owing to the Russian refusal to act in the
E.A.C. a great mass of proposals still awaits discussion and agreement; in
particular nothing has been settled as regards the joint occupation and
administration of Austria, although the Russian armies are now almost at the
gates of Vienna. (It looks as though the Soviet Government are resolved to
discuss Austria only when they are themselves in complete military occupation
and can dictate their terms.)

A separate paper would be required to formulate the case we should wish to
state as regards Germany and Austria, but ample material is available, and
there is a real and growing need to put an end to the present state of paralysis,
which only benefits the Soviet Government and puts us at a serious disadvantage. Our new military position makes it surely unnecessary that we and the
Americans should continue to accept this position of inferiority.

As regards (b), in the early days the Soviet Government did not appear to
have decided on any definite policy as regards the satellite States of Central
and South-Eastern Europe. But gradually, first in Poland and subsequently in
Roumania and Bulgaria, their policy has taken shape and can no longer be
mistaken or disguised. The only question now is whether they will apply the
same policy to other countries where they may expect to be able to exercise
military and political control, that is to say, Yugoslavia, Hungary, Austria,
Czechoslovakia, and possibly Turkey.

It would no doubt be easy to strike a bargain with the Soviet Government
if we were prepared to recognise their exclusive interests in certain countries.
On such terms we might be able possibly to save Czechoslovakia, Yugoslavia,
Austria, and Turkey at the cost of sacrificing Poland, Roumania and Bulgaria.
But it is inconceivable that we should adopt this course. Not only would we
never be sure that the Soviet Government would observe such a bargain, but
it would appear in the eyes of the world as the cynical abandonment of the
small nations whose interest we are pledged to defend; and for ourselves it
would represent the abdication of our right as a Great Power to be concerned
with the affairs of the whole of Europe, and not merely with those parts in
which we have a special interest.

If, however, we cannot found our policy of co-operation on a system of
spheres of influence, we must confine ourselves to making it abundantly
clear to the Soviet Government that the policy of Anglo-Soviet co-operation

must apply fully in Central and South-Eastern Europe as in the rest of the world, and that indeed we are not prepared to work the policy on any other basis.

It is difficult to foresee what would be the Soviet Government's reaction to such a summons. It would largely depend on the value they attach to the continuance of co-operation with Great Britain and the United States after the war; on the extent to which they fear the prospect of Great Britain and the United States organising an anti-Russian and anti-Communist bloc in Europe; and lastly on the material difficulties they may foresee in embarking after an exhausting struggle on a policy of political expansion which might easily develop into a military occupation. In any event the Soviet Government's reaction could not very well be worse than a continuance of the present state of uncertainty and drift which is operating all the time to our disadvantage.

We should, of course, have to demonstrate that this plain-speaking was in our view necessary in order to establish in the changed circumstances of to-day a new basis on which to continue and develop Anglo-American-Soviet co-operation during the difficult times ahead of us, and we should be at pains to show that it is precisely because of the importance that we attach to this co-operation that we feel it necessary to tackle this difficult and disagreeable subject in such a frank, realistic and comprehensive manner.

Cadogan, 4 April

I share nearly all of Sir O. Sargent's apprehensions and suspicions. But I confess I am not quite clear as to the form and object of the showdown in the whole field. I agree that we must, if necessary, have a 'showdown' on Poland. If it is not clear, within a week or so, that Stalin is prepared to implement Yalta, we must so inform Parliament. We can't go on like this. Where that would lead to, I don't know. [Here Eden minuted: 'I agree emphatically although F. M. Smuts does not'.]

But Sir O. Sargent seems to imply that, even if we got a decent Polish settlement, we must still have a 'showdown'. I'm not at all sure about that. I can't look so far ahead. What I am sure of is that the Yalta Polish agreement is an acid test, and we can't afford to be fooled out of that. We shall have lost all our bearings if that happens. We should warn Stalin now – or as early as may be – that we can't carry this farce for more than a week and shall have to be quite frank with Parliament, say, next Thursday. That *may* have some effect. Even if it doesn't, it will keep the record straight and put the Soviet on the defensive. I can't see further than that.

Eden, 8 April

I agree. Since Sir A. Cadogan wrote the above there have been developments, I think all in the sense he would recommend. But we haven't yet had an answer to P.M.'s message (and F.D.R.'s) to Stalin. How long do we wait for that? . . .

Henderson minutes of 8 April

First minute

I have spoken to Sir A. Cadogan about this and passed on to the SoS his view that the next step should probably be to notify M. Stalin that, unless we hear from him in a contrary sense, we propose telling Parliament in the course of next week or two that the Russian Government are not prepared to implement Yalta so far as Poland is concerned.

Second minute

I have spoken to Sir A. Cadogan again and to Mr. Warner on the SoS's instructions. Mr. Warner will draft a tel. from the PM to the President telling him that we propose warning M. Stalin that Parliament will have to be informed of the latest position over Poland, in the next week or two.

36   Clark Kerr on Soviet relations with Czechoslovakia, 16 April 1945

Little more than a year after his visit to Moscow in order to sign the Soviet–Czechoslovak Treaty of December 1943, President Benes has come to Moscow again, this time to clarify Czechoslovak relations with the Soviet Union before his return to establish his Government in a liberated region of Czechoslovakia. Dr. Benes was accompanied to Moscow by his Prime Minister, Mgr. Sramek, by his Minister for Foreign Affairs, M. Jan Masaryk; by the chairman of the Slovak National Council, M. Srober; and by other members of the Czechoslovak Government.

2 The party arrived in Moscow on the 17th March and left for Czechoslovakia on the 31st March . . .

6 Dr. Benes must, however, have approached his Soviet hosts with very real anxieties. Some members of his party, who were perhaps less committed in public to the view that Soviet Russia could do no wrong, hardly troubled to conceal these anxieties on their arrival in Moscow. M. Masaryk, who was paying his first visit to Moscow, was expecting the worst. His admiration for the feats of the Red army was tempered by alarm concerning the use to which Russia might now put her great strength. The behaviour of the Red army in

Czechoslovak territory had been rough and was fast alienating traditional Czechoslovak sympathies for Russia. While he recognised that Czechoslovakia had no alternative but to keep in step with Russia, he feared that she might rapidly lose any real independence. In fact, he thought that Dr. Benes's personality was indispensable to Czechoslovakia during this transitional period. If he disappeared the component parts of the republic would fall apart and come separately under Russian domination. Dr. Benes's private secretary also spoke gloomily to Mr. Roberts about the position. He felt that the main hope for Czechoslovakia lay in the maintenance of unity between the three great Allies. In this respect, developments since the Crimea Conference had been most disappointing, and Czechoslovakia would be the first to suffer if the Soviet Union embarked upon power politics in Eastern and Central Europe . . .

7 The Soviet Government can hardly have been unaware of Dr. Benes's anxieties. Indeed, they would appear to have been playing skilfully upon them for some months past. It was therefore significant that from the moment of his arrival in Moscow they spared no pains to do honour to the President and to show him that he was in every way as welcome a guest as he had been in December 1943. Even M. Masaryk was given the same warm welcome. After getting over his first surprise, when he had described M. Molotov as 'too gushing', M. Masaryk informed me that he could not find any subject for complaint or, indeed, anything but warm satisfaction in the conversations he and President Benes had conducted with the Soviet Government . . . My own conclusion would be that, while the Soviet Government are likely to be suspicious of the Czech claim to act as a link between the east and the west, they are not actively hostile to the retention of such links after the war. They intend, however, to secure their own essential interests, and in particular to buttress the Russian frontiers against any possible renewal of German aggression by bilateral treaties, such as the Soviet–Czechoslovakia Treaty, which bind the minor Slav countries firmly to Russia. In fact in this, as in other matters, Soviet policy is based upon the most realistic considerations. It tends to show scant regard for our own position or for our relations with our allies in Eastern Europe. But this should not, I think, be interpreted as a sign of hostility to the west or as a danger signal for the future . . .

37   Roberts on Soviet policy in the Balkans, 21 April 1945

. . . 10 The reception given to Marshal Tito and the way in which his visit and the signing of the treaty were handled in the Soviet press suggest that the Soviet Government at present attach more importance to their relations with

Yugoslavia than to those with Czechoslovakia. This is perhaps hardly surprising in view of the much greater contribution made by Yugoslavia to the Allied war effort. Marshal Tito has also a more colourful and more sympathetic personality than President Benes. But a more substantial consideration is the fact that Soviet policy in Eastern and Central Europe, and more particularly in Slav countries, need no longer be based (as it had to be before the war) upon one relatively small State, Czechoslovakia. Hence the present Soviet preoccupation with Poland and Yugoslavia, which the Soviet Government show every sign of wishing to build up into the two main Slav outposts defending the Soviet Union against any possibility of renewed German aggression. You will recall that when you suggested that France should be given a seat upon the Reparation Commission, the Soviet reply was that Yugoslavia and Poland had equal claims and should also be given seats on the commission. It is true that in this and similar cases the Soviet Government might argue that the basis for the claim was the special suffering in the war of these two countries. I think, however, that the main motive of the Soviet Government is to ensure for themselves the support of the strongest secondary Powers in Eastern Europe to balance France in the West. Marshal Stalin had often in the past spoken of Poland in the same breath as of France as the two European Powers upon whom the Soviet Union and the United Kingdom could mainly rely in the task of keeping Germany in check. The introduction of Yugoslavia into this restricted second category of European Powers is a more recent conception, but it is, I think, one which is likely to be developed still further and to find expression in such ways as the recent Soviet insistence that Yugoslav troops should participate in the occupation of Austria and that Yugoslavia should be appointed to the Executive Committee of the San Francisco Conference in place of the Netherlands 'in view of her superior contribution to the war effort and the more representative character of her Government'.

11 It was significant that the Soviet press gave considerable space to the reactions to the Soviet–Yugoslav treaty in Poland and in Bulgaria, whereas there was relatively little if any comment reported from other countries. This in itself suggested that the Yugoslav treaty was not being presented to the Soviet public as an international Act complete in itself, but rather as a single link in a chain of similar treaties which began with the Czechoslovak treaty of 1943 and which would ultimately cover all the lesser Slav Powers. It was therefore hardly surprising that 'spontaneous' demonstrations were reported from all over Poland demanding the conclusion of a similar Polish–Soviet treaty, and that, despite the negotiations still proceeding between the three major Powers for the formation of a new Polish Provisional Government of National Unity in accordance with the Yalta Agreement, His Majesty's Ambassador was informed on the 16th April, the day after Marshal Tito's departure from

Moscow, that the Soviet Government, in deference, it was claimed, to the strong insistence of the Soviet and Polish populations, proposed to negotiate a treaty with Poland similar to those already signed with Czechoslovakia and Yugoslavia.

12 Although a Polish–Soviet treaty will complete the main pattern of bilateral treaties with Slav countries protecting Russia's frontiers from any possible renewal of German aggression, the Soviet Government may also intend to extend the system to include the remaining Slav country, Bulgaria. The Soviet propaganda machine has been working hard to convince the world that Bulgaria has completely broken with her pro-Fascist and pro-German past and to rehabilitate her as a respectable and, indeed, praiseworthy member of the European family. She had been encouraged to form closer ties with Yugoslavia, and she has been given more favourable treatment by the Soviet Union than that accorded to any other defeated enemy State or even to some Allied States such as Greece. The Soviet Government must, however, realise that there are difficulties about the signature of a treaty with an ex-enemy State still under an armistice regime. I hope, therefore, that we may expect longer notice of a Soviet–Bulgarian treaty than we have been given of the Soviet–Polish negotiations. We must also be prepared for the establishment at a later stage, and probably in some different form, of some treaty relationship between the Soviet Union and the remaining ex-enemy States, Roumania, Hungary and perhaps Austria, lying between her and Germany.

13 While the Soviet Government attach great importance to the early establishment of this system of bilateral treaties in Eastern Europe, they do not, I think, regard it as in any way incompatible with the wider system of overall co-operation between the three Great Powers, which they so obviously desire should continue in the post-war period. Provided they are satisfied about the prospects of continued three-Power collaboration, the Soviet Government are probably at heart less interested in the future international organisation which we hope will emerge from the San Francisco Conference. Indeed, they showed this clearly in their decision not to send M. Molotov to San Francisco, a decision which was only reversed as a result of President Roosevelt's death and of the necessity for conciliating President Truman and the new American Administration. The future international organisation is probably in the eyes of the Soviet Government a useful facade behind which the world will in reality be run in agreement by the three Great Powers, each of whom will be capable of ensuring peace in its own immediate sphere by its own armed strength and by practical security systems such as the bilateral pacts now being negotiated by Russia with her Slav neighbours. Any suggestion, however, such as that of Mr. Walter Lippman that two of the three major Powers should coalesce in an Atlantic system at once arouses Soviet suspicions . . .

15 In so far as these treaties are primarily directed against the danger of any revival of German aggression, and in so far as they are definitely subordinated in the Soviet view to the overriding necessity for three-Power co-operation, they need not be regarded as a menace to our own interests. On the other hand, there is no doubt that the Soviet Government, who have not abandoned their suspicions of the West, are determined that their influence shall be dominant in all Slav countries and, indeed, in all other countries within their immediate security sphere. All our present indications are that the contacts, political, economic and cultural, of the lesser Slav and other Eastern European countries with the West will be restricted to the minimum. I noted from Belgrade telegram No. 468 that Dr. Subasic, like Dr. Benes in Czechoslovakia, desired Yugoslav foreign policy to be properly balanced and even envisaged treaty relations with Great Britain and the United States of America similar to those with the Soviet Union. Quite apart from the fact that His Majesty's Government do not at present wish to contemplate such a relationship, Marshal Tito's general attitude in Moscow did not suggest that he necessarily shared Dr. Subasic's very natural desire to avoid an exclusive orientation of Yugoslav policy towards the Soviet Union. Still less would it be approved in present circumstances by the Soviet Government. I fear, therefore, that in practice we shall find increasing difficulty in maintaining in Yugoslavia anything approaching the 50–50 interest which Marshal Stalin conceded to the Prime Minister last October. The realistic rulers of Soviet Russia, who are not used to compromise or concessions, as these are understood in the West, are determined to be the masters in neighbouring countries, and to ensure that there are no rival influences which the local Governments can play off against them. We must, therefore, I fear, expect to meet with many difficulties and disappointments even in securing and maintaining normal representation, and still more in making British influence felt in any of these countries. Provided, however that we can keep the doors open to the west, even if they remain for the present only ajar, there are grounds for hope that, as Soviet Russia settles down after the war and becomes more confident of her new international position, she will find it less necessary to pursue the 'dog in the manger' policy from which we are at present suffering throughout Eastern Europe and which is particularly inexcusable in Yugoslavia, a country where we have been conceded an equal interest and to which we have given valuable material support during the war.

38   O'Malley on future policy towards Russia, 22 May 1945

... The collapse of Germany confronts us with an armed and brittle peace. Europe is divided from the Elbe through Prague and Vienna to Trieste by an impassable barrier, across which two wholly antagonistic political systems confront each other. Since the Russian sphere stretches far beyond the old dividing line between Byzantium and Rome, since it includes about 100,000,000 people to whose age-old traditions her political system is fundamentally opposed, it is on the whole unlikely that her new sphere of influence will be absorbed quickly or without disturbances. It is probable that the armed peace will mean a condition of growing tension. When we consider the arrogant and aggressive character of the Soviet system, when we reflect that its consolidation would add say 200 divisions of cannon-fodder to Russia's military strength, I think we must conclude that this tension must end in a retreat by one side or the other or in conflict with ourselves . . . The fact is that the Soviet Government have not hitherto been given any compelling reason to suppose that we should insist on it moderating its ambitions and behaviour.

Unless we go to a further meeting of the Big Three with new and sterner resolves its result will be to give the Soviet Government 'Days of Grace' in which to consolidate their position as well as to befog British and world opinion, and to prepare the means for further expansion.

When I say 'new and sterner resolves' what I mean is that we must be ready if need be to abandon a conciliatory attitude altogether and to criticize Soviet foreign policy publicly in the most massive fashion: ready also to make political difficulties for the Soviet Union in every possible way and place, realising that this might end in a rupture of relations or a clash, and prepared to take the consequences of our action. If (as in the case of Italy in 1935) we build up political resistance without being in our own minds prepared to appeal to the 'ultima ratio' of force, our bluff will be called and an armed conflict with the Soviet Union will probably follow at a time and in circumstances more unfavourable to ourselves than now.

The general line followed hitherto by His Majesty's Government suggests that they rely upon direct governmental remonstrances while at the same time keeping public opinion calm and pro-Russian; but in my opinion this is the very opposite of the strategy which should from now on be pursued . . .

It is the worst of mistakes to regard Soviet expansion as 'inevitable'. A legendary 'inevitability' is the most powerful weapon in political warfare. Contrariwise England is strong just because she 'never knows when she is beaten'. Our material strength and preparedness is greater now than it can possibly be in five or ten years time. That is why the present moment might be appropriate for taking the gloves off. In five or ten years time, however, the Soviet Union will have recovered from her fatigues, will have set all the plants and technicians in Skoda, Eastern Germany, and Silesia to work for her, and will have embodied in her military and labour forces the whole population of Eastern Europe. And there will be no Americans in Europe . . .

In general our situation and the situation of the nations of central and eastern Europe seem to me so precarious, the prospective disequilibrium of land forces between ourselves and the Soviet Union plus central Europe seem to me so alarming, that I had rather face a crisis now than in five or ten years time. If we acquiesce however reluctantly in the course on which the Soviet Union is at present set we shall get progressively weaker and the Soviet Union progressively stronger. We shall not in the long run avert by appeasement a crisis which will become more dangerous the longer it is deferred . . .

Sargent minute of 31 May

The truly desperate remedies recommended by Sir O. O'Malley will, I trust, prove unnecessary if we play our cards reasonably well.

In any case how does he think we could apply these remedies without the support of the United States Government – and of that I should say there would be no prospect whatsoever on present form. [Eden minuted here: 'I agree'.]

It may prove difficult to get their support even for our more moderate policy of standing up to the Russians when they go too far and of refusing in future to give anything for nothing merely in the hope of creating a good atmosphere, while at the same time aiming at close co-operation with the Soviet Government in world affairs.

So long as the war was on the outlines of this policy were blurred, but now she is going to make her position clear. She is not going to be dragged into a quarrel between Great Britain and the Soviet Union, and she is not going to allow Great Britain to dictate to her European policy, and in order to avoid these two dangers she is going to assume the role of an independent mediator and to be tough to *both* the Soviet Union and Great Britain until *both* become reasonable and cooperative . . .

All of which makes it very necessary that while this American mood lasts we should walk warily in our dealings with Russia and not embark lightly on adventures and experiments such as those advocated by Sir O. O'Malley.

39   Orme Sargent's paper 'Stocktaking After V.E. Day', 11 July 1945 (revised version)

The end of the war in Europe leaves us facing three main problems, none of which has any resemblance to the problems with which we were faced at the end of the last war. They are (a) the military occupation by Soviet troops of a large part of Eastern Europe, and the Soviet Government's future policy generally; (b) the economic rehabilitation of Europe so as to prevent a general economic collapse; and (c) the task of administering Germany and deciding on her future institutions in agreement with the Soviet, United States and French Governments.

2 Our own position, too, in dealing with these problems is very different from what it was at the end of the last war, when we and France shared and disputed, and eventually lost, control of Europe. This time the control is to a large degree in the hands of the Soviet Union and the United States, and neither of them is likely to consider British interests overmuch if they interfere with their own and unless we assert ourselves.

3 Thus it suits us that the principle of co-operation between the three Great Powers should be specifically accepted as the basis on which problems arising out of the war should be handled and decided. Such a co-operative system will, it is hoped, give us a position in the world which we might otherwise find it increasingly difficult to assert and maintain were the other two Great Powers to act independently. It is not that either the United States or the Soviet Union do not wish to collaborate with Great Britain. The United States certainly find it very convenient to do so in order to fortify their own position in Europe and elsewhere; and the Soviet Union recognise in Great Britain a European Power with whom they will certainly have to reckon. But the fact remains that in the minds of our big partners, especially in that of the United States, there is a feeling that Great Britain is now a secondary Power and can be treated as such, and that in the long run all will be well if they – the United States and the Soviet Union – as the two supreme World Powers of the future, understand one another. It is this misconception which it must be our policy to combat.

4 We have many cards in our hands if we choose to use them – our political maturity; our diplomatic experience; the confidence which the solidarity of our democratic institutions inspires in Western Europe; and our incomparable war record. Unlike our two great partners we are not regarded in Western Europe either as gangsters or as go-getters. But we must do something about organising our side or we shall find our friends gradually drifting away from us. Time is not necessarily on our side. For this reason and because we are numerically the weakest and geographically the smallest of the three Great Powers, it is essential that we should increase our strength in not only the diplomatic but also the economic and military spheres. This clearly can best be done by enrolling France and the lesser Western European Powers, and, of course, also the Dominions, as collaborators with us in this tripartite system. Only so shall we be able, in the long run, to compel our two big partners to treat us as an equal. Even so, our collaboration with the Soviet Union, and even with the United States, is not going to be easy in view of the wide divergence between our respective outlooks, traditions and methods.

5 To take the Soviet Union first. It is particularly dangerous to assume that the foreign policies of totalitarian governments are opportunist and fluctuating, like those of liberal governments (using the term 'liberal' not of course in its narrow meaning connecting it with the British political party, but in its widest sense as representing a system of government which stands for freedom of speech, writing, and association, and for the rule of law, and as such opposed to totalitarianism, whether to the Right or to the Left). All totalitarian governments – and Russia is certainly no exception – are able to conduct a consistent and persistent foreign policy over long periods because the government is not dependent on public opinion and changes of government. And precisely because totalitarian governments need not explain or justify their policy to their own people it is much more difficult for the foreigner to analyse the governing principles which underlie it. It is true that in the case of Nazi Germany Hitler kindly explained in *Mein Kampf* both his objectives and methods. We were thus duly warned, but did not heed the warning. Again, Mussolini, by crudely imitating Hitler, revealed to us the secrets of his long-term policy. But in the case of the Soviet Union Stalin is not likely to be as obliging. We shall have to try and find out for ourselves what is his plan of campaign and to anticipate the tactics which he intends to employ from time to time to carry it through. And this is not going to be easy, nor shall we always be able, even among ourselves in this country, to agree on the conclusions which ought to be drawn from known facts.

6 Without attempting on this occasion to analyse Russia's foreign policy and foretell its future course, it is worth calling attention to one factor in the policy of modern totalitarian governments which seems to be fairly constant, namely, their desire to obtain for their regime the maximum degree of security both at home and abroad. As a result of the defeat of 1918 the Nazis feared encirclement by the rest of Europe and sought security by means of territorial conquest. Hence their demand for Lebensraum. Mussolini resented the encirclement of the Mediterranean by France and Great Britain and tried to break out into Africa. Soviet Russia now fears a world coalition of the liberal Powers ('liberal' again being used in its widest sense), and the revival of Germany as a 'liberal' Power; for Stalin knows even better than we do that it was the material strength and wealth of the liberal Powers, combined with the belief in their own philosophy of life, which really won the war, and he probably is more convinced than we and the Americans are as to the capacity of Germany to recover first her economic, then her political, and lastly her military power in Europe. Stalin, however, does not necessarily intend to obtain his security by territorial conquest, as Hitler wanted to. He may well prefer to obtain it by creating what might be termed an ideological Lebensraum in those countries which he considers strategically important. If he eventually is convinced that the danger of a liberal coalition is not going to materialise he

may relax somewhat his search for security, or rather change its nature so as to apply only to Germany. It must be remembered, too, that, unlike Hitler, he fortunately has not the motive of revenge to spur him on.

7 At the present moment the Soviet Union has been so weakened by the war that Stalin is hardly in a position to force through ruthlessly his policy of ideological penetration against definite opposition. For instance, in the case of Greece, Venezia Giulia, and to a certain extent Poland, he has not pressed matters to extremes and has actually compromised, though it may well be that he has only made a temporary retreat. It can surely be assumed that he does not want and could not afford another war in Europe, and it is also doubtful whether he aims at further territorial expansion. At Annex I will be found a memorandum by Sir R. Bruce Lockhart on Soviet policy and the best means of reacting to it.

8 The economic strength of the United States has certainly impressed Stalin no less than the potentiality of the Western Air Forces. He has seen what has happened to Germany from the air and what is happening to Japan. No doubt Stalin feels that now before his troops have been withdrawn from the countries which they are now occupying and before their demobilisation has begun he must seize the opportunity to reap the fruits of victory to the full, since if he delays or hesitates there may be some which later on he will no longer be able to grasp. As for ourselves, though economically we shall grow stronger as time goes on, militarily our strength in Europe will soon decline from its present peak – even quicker than the Russian strength. For this reason we must take a stand in the immediate future if we are to prevent the situation crystallising to our permanent detriment. This means in practice that we must maintain our interest in Finland, Poland, Czechoslovakia, Austria, Yugoslavia and Bulgaria, even though we may have to acquiesce in Russian domination in Roumania and Hungary.

9 If there is to be a trial of strength between us – that is to say a diplomatic trial of strength – now is the time for us to take the offensive by challenging Russia in these six countries, instead of waiting until the Soviet Government threatens us further west and south in Germany, in Italy, in Greece, and in Turkey. This is what inevitably will happen if we let Stalin pocket for good these six countries which at present he controls by a combination of political force and military pressure . . .

11 We must, of course, also be prepared for the Soviet Government to use every opportunity and make every effort to mould the future political institutions of Germany in order to obtain a dominating position in that country. This may well lead to a struggle for mastery in which it is to be hoped we shall have the full support of the United States. Even so, the struggle, if it is engaged will be a hard one and the result may well be decisive for the whole of Europe. For it is not over-stating the position to say that if Europe is won over to

totalitarianism this may well decide the fate of 'liberalism' throughout the world.

12 In every country of Europe the Soviet Government will have the great advantage of being able to exploit for their own ends the economic crisis which in the coming months may well develop into a catastrophe capable of engulfing political institutions in many European countries and paralysing all orderly government in a large part of the Continent. It is the existence of this economic crisis which makes it so important to obtain the wholehearted co-operation of the United States, who alone have the material means of coping with it.

13 It should not prove impossible for us to perform the double task of holding the Soviet Government in check in Europe and, at the same time, amicably and fruitfully co-operating with the Soviet and United States Governments in the resettlement of Europe if once the United States Administration realise both the political and economic implications of the European situation. But the process of inducing the United States to support a British resistance to Russian penetration in Europe will be a tricky one, and we must contrive to demonstrate to the American public that our challenge is based on upholding the liberal idea in Europe and not upon selfish apprehensions as to our own position as a Great Power. Mr. Lippman is by no means alone in fearing that British antagonisms with Russia that filled the second half of last century will survive into the coming post-war period and embroil the much less interested United States. We shall therefore be well advised consciously and consistently to enlist American support upon some principle, and perhaps even to exercise some restraint in not pursuing cases where a principle cannot easily be shown. In particular, the diplomatic interventions in the internal affairs of other countries, which may be necessary in certain contingencies, must not seem to be motivated by personal hostility to, or support of, individuals in the State in question unless these are pretty obviously the opponents or champions of the 'liberal' idea. Such common material interests as oil development in Persia would not be an issue in which we could count on American support very far. This is not to say that United States policy is always based on principle, far from it; but it is a fact that a British policy is suspect if it is based on anything else, and particularly so at the moment in regard to Russia . . .

Annex 1

During my enforced immobilisation I have been turning my mind to the problem of Russia's future intentions. I assume that His Majesty's Government (1) are perturbed by Russia's unilateral actions in many parts of Europe, and (2) believe in the closest possible understanding with the Union of Soviet Socialist Republics as the essential condition of future peace.

I have therefore tried to define and analyse the motives which are most likely to influenc₂ Russia's policy.

1 First, we must remember that your true Bolshevik is a convinced Marxist and that Stalin regards himself, and is regarded by his supporters, as the infallible interpreter of Marxism. To Bolsheviks Marx is almost as great a hero as Lenin. The Marx–Engels Institute in Moscow is the Bolshevik temple. We should also remember (1) that Marx was the most uncompromising of all revolutionaries and (2) that he was the professed enemy of all small national states. His whole belief in the social revolution was based on the theory that the smaller must be merged in the greater. It would therefore seem foolish for us to ignore the influence of Marx on Russian policy to-day. It would be positively dangerous for us to lend a wishful ear to those sentimental pro-Russians who assure us, with more confidence than knowledge, that we have nothing to fear because Russia has ceased to be Communist. Changes, of course, there have been, but with many of our neo-Russophils I fear desire for this change outruns actual performance in Moscow.

2 Secondly, the internal history of Russia has been for centuries a fluctuating struggle between the European-minded and the Asiatic-minded schools. Or to give a better and more modern definition, between the advocates of Western Europeanisation and the Slavophils. For, although the Slavophils were resolutely opposed to every infiltration of Western European ideas, they were not wholly Asiatic-minded. Protection of the smaller Slav States of Europe filled a prominent place in their political programme. In the spiritual life of Russia, too, the same protective policy was fostered and maintained by the Orthodox Church until Peter the Great made it a temporal instrument of the state. This idea of Russia's predestined role as a mother-state is a heritage from Byzantium. Here, again, we must remember that the Bolshevik revolution has brought history to the masses. Where in 1915 80 per cent of the population was illiterate, the same percentage can now read and write and studies its own story with an eager seriousness common to most newly educated peoples. The Bolsheviks, therefore, have an historical motive or impulse for an expansionist policy. It can be and is very easily harnessed to the Marxist motive. We can be assured that at this moment, when Moscow is trying to shape the future of the Balkans, M. Molotov does not forget that the Russians were at Corfu in 1805, and in Paris in 1815.

3 Of other factors which are likely to influence a policy of expansion we should not forget the nature of the Russian himself. Like its climate, the British genius is temperate. It avoids extremes in all matters, particularly, perhaps, in religion and politics. Again like its climate, the Russian genius moves between extremes: of hot and cold, of violent energy and laziness, of cruelty and humaneness, of practical realism and visionary mysticism. At different times in their history the Russians have been inspired by a missionary

zeal to save the world – in their own way of course – and in certain moods every Russian will risk perdition to gain what we should consider an unrealisable and sometimes worthless end.

4 In addition to these more or less constant motives the rulers of Russia are to-day emboldened to go their own way, irrespective of the wishes of their Allies, by an exaggerated realisation of their own strength. The Russian people have been encouraged to believe that they have won the war single-handed and that the *bourgeois* countries, however efficient their armaments may be, lack the fighting spirit of the Russian revolutionaries. Hitherto Stalin has never told the Russian people what the United States and Great Britain have done for Russia. His silence in this connexion is dictated by the needs of internal policy and of the conservation of his own prestige. But it is also probable that until recently Stalin himself, encouraged by the adulation of the British press and radio, may well have believed: (1) that Britain had exhausted herself, and (2) that British public opinion was so strongly on his side that he could do what he liked in Europe. Moreover, to Bolsheviks hardened in the school, first of revolution and then of social ostracism, *bourgeois* flattery is a certain sign of *bourgeois* weakness.

5 All the foregoing factors supply cogent reasons why Russia's victory policy may well exceed the limits of military security. If this view is correct, it follows that, unless some curb is put on Russia's dreams of expansion, not only will co-operation between the three leading Allies become a sham but there may well be no peace in Europe after the defeat of Germany. Indeed, a prolongation of Russia's present unilateralism must sooner or later revive pro-German feelings in the United States and in Great Britain and lead inevitably to the establishment of the Sanitary Cordon which Russia presumably wishes to avoid and which she uses adroitly as an excuse for her policy of expansion.

6 There would seem to be only one way of checking Russia's political mal-feasance, and that is by bolder, but still friendly diplomatic action by Great Britain and the United States. There is one compelling reason which is favourable to boldness. Hitherto in our diplomatic negotiations with the U.S.S.R. we have had to play from weakness. To-day we can lead from strength; in point of fact, from very great strength so long as Anglo-American military power remains at its present level. In whatever state of ignorance the Russian people may have been kept, it must now be manifest to Stalin himself that Russia has little but numbers to oppose to the immense array of armour and air power at the disposal of the Allies. In short, Anglo-American military strength is at its peak; Russia's has long since passed it.

7 In 1941 we made the mistake of under-estimating Russia's military strength. We must be careful to-day to avoid the error of exaggerating it. It may be, indeed, true that no country can afford another war in Europe, but of all countries that dare not risk a prolongation of such a war Russia must be

very nearly first. Stalin is faced with great problems of reconstruction, which he cannot hope to solve without Anglo-American aid. The moment is therefore highly favourable for a bolder diplomacy.

8 If this were to take the form of a firm Anglo-American request for a clear statement of Russia's intentions, together with a strong hint that unilateral action by Russia will make impossible every form of co-operation, including economic assistance, good results would be obtained.

11th April, 1945   R. H. BRUCE LOCKHART

Cadogan, 11 July

... Sir O. Sargent, in paragraph 8, assumes that, from now on, our military strength in Europe will decline at a greater rate than that of Russia and that there is therefore no time to lose in taking a firm stand. I think this is probably right ...

It is true that Russia during the war has received enormous material aid from us, but is it not also true that her own production is proof of an astonishing rate of development which, if maintained, might lead her almost anywhere? ...

... if Sir R. Bruce Lockhart is right, there is not such great urgency about it as Sir O. Sargent would maintain, and time might be expected to work on our side. I hesitate to accept this, and therefore rather endorse Sir O. Sargent.

40   Research Department paper on developments in Soviet-occupied and Soviet-controlled territories, 20 July 1945

1 In certain Soviet-occupied and Soviet-controlled territories, there have been political developments – some of them making their appearance in two or more places – which have given discomfort and anxiety to elements in the populations of these territories – amounting in some cases, in all probability, to a considerable majority of the politically conscious part of the population – and also to the local representatives and nationals of Great Britain and the United States, and to the British and American Governments themselves. The questions arise whether these developments are evidence of aggressive or imperialist Soviet designs against (a) the self-government and independence of the peoples of these occupied and controlled territories, and (b) the interests of the Soviet Union's two principal allies. Without seeking to answer either of these questions, the present paper attempts to present the facts by which the questions are raised.

2 The territories covered in the paper are Roumania, Bulgaria and Hungary, three countries which are wholly under Soviet occupation; the Soviet-controlled zone in Northern Persia; and Finland, which, though not under Soviet occupation, is under Soviet control. In all these countries except Persia, the powers of the Soviet occupying or controlling authorities derive from an armistice agreement to which Great Britain, as well as the Soviet Union, is a party, and in virtue of which we also have our own representatives on the spot – though, at any rate before the end of hostilities with Germany, these representatives were not entitled to the status of equal partners with the Soviet authorities in the exercise of control on behalf of the United Nations. The United States has the same status and representation as Great Britain in the cases of Roumania, Bulgaria and Hungary, but not in that of Finland, with whom she was not at war and is therefore not a party to the Finnish armistice. In Persia, the situation is different. The Soviet authorities are in *de facto*, but not *de jure*, occupation of the northern provinces while in certain other areas Anglo-American influence predominates. In so far as Great Britain and the Soviet Union are concerned, this division of control is the result of the Tripartite Treaty of the 29th January 1942. This treaty gave these Powers the right to maintain troops in Persia for the purpose of safeguarding their communications. The United States Government are not a party to this treaty, and thus have no legal right to maintain their troops on Persian soil . . .

9 In *Bulgaria* – where a traditionally Russophil population has twice, within living memory, been brought, by a Germanophil ruling clique, into a disastrous general war on the German side – it is not surprising that a drastic purge should have been carried out by elements in Bulgarian political life which had previously been repressed, and that this purge should have been warmly approved and encouraged by the Soviet occupying authorities. It is the incidence and extent of the purge, the severity of the sentences, and the brutality with which the proceedings have been conducted, rather than the purge in itself, that call for remark. There have been wholesale dismissals in the officer corps, the administrative and diplomatic service and the teaching profession; there are said to have been 10,000 arrests, to the accompaniment of beatings and other excesses which have created something like a general reign of terror; and by the end of April 1945 the so-called People's Courts had passed 2,850 death sentences, for pro-Germanism and for the persecution of political opponents, which are believed to have been dictated by the central Freedom Front Committee. It has been estimated by a Bulgarian official source that between 30,000 and 40,000 persons have been put to death without trial. One result of all this, which can hardly be fortuitous, is the elimination of almost all opposition or potential opposition to the present regime.

10 In *Roumania*, on the 29th March, 1945, a new law for purging public

offices was promulgated. This law follows up a previous law on the same subject that was promulgated by General Radescu's Government, but it imposes more severe penalties. For instance, people who have served fascist interests are to be imprisoned with hard labour, and those who have co-operated with Antonescu's Legionaries are to be dismissed without notice. On the other hand, 'penitent legionaries' are offered a hope of being allowed to work their passage at the price of transferring their allegiance to the Communist Party; and it now looks as though this Roumanian purge were not going to be carried to Bulgarian lengths, notwithstanding the capital made by the leaders of the present Government, when they were engineering the overthrow of General Radescu, of his alleged failure to carry out a purge in earnest.

11 In *Hungary*, all the former parties of the Right and Centre, to the right of the Christian People's Party, have been dissolved. The Christian People's Party has been left in being, and there is good evidence that, in general, the Roman Catholic Church is being treated with respect. The Moscow broad-caster to Hungary, M. Federov, attacks Hungarian 'fascists' in general, and the Arrow Cross, the Magyar pro-Germans and the German minority in Hungary in particular, and, indeed, the only point which M. Federov has stressed vigorously, apart from the land reform, is the necessity of punishing 'fascists' sternly. In one talk, he held up the example of the Bulgarian People's Courts to Hungary as one worthy of imitation; and he treated Hungary to a lecture when a sentence was passed which seemed to him too light. He has also given a grave warning against 'professional solidarity' resulting in the smuggling of 'fascist' elements into the new army. On the other hand, high military officers occupy important posts in the new Hungarian Government that has been formed under Soviet auspices (see para. 22 below).

12 In *Finland*, where some unquestionably and impenitently anti-Soviet Finnish political leaders have continued to play a part in Finnish politics, there is no evidence that the Finnish Communists' demand for a sweeping prosecution of war criminals and purge of reactionaries has been encouraged by the Soviet authorities. The diminution in the influence of right-wing elements in Finland has been due, as far as can be seen, to the influence on Finnish public opinion of military events followed up by Soviet propaganda.

Soviet censorship and propaganda

13 In Soviet occupied countries – but not, apparently, in Finland – the Soviet censorship and propaganda have been used, without hesitation or disguise, to produce effects, desired by the Soviet authorities, on local political developments. The Soviet propaganda to *Hungary* against Hungarian reactionaries has been referred to already (see para. 11 above). In *Roumania*, the Soviet press censor has refused to pass any statements favourable to the

traditional Roumanian political parties or any unbiassed accounts of the National Defence Front demonstrations which led up to the overthrow of General Radescu's Government and its replacement by the Present N.D.F. regime (see para. 37 below). Soviet censorship has, indeed, been carried in Roumania to the length of suppressing papers unsympathetic to the Communist point of view. Quite as stringent a censorship has been imposed in Bulgaria; and here at the same time the Soviet propaganda has hammered in the points that Bulgaria's sufferings are due to her pro-German policy and that the responsibility for this policy lies with the former ruling clique and not with the people as a whole. The Soviet section of the Anglo-Soviet–Persian censorship in Tehran prevents press messages leaving Persia which report on local affairs in a way which does not suit Soviet policy. During the 1944 oil crisis the Soviet censor stopped not only press agency messages giving the Persian point of view, but also cypher telegrams from the Persian Government to its missions abroad.

14 This use of censorship and propaganda as instruments of Soviet policy in Soviet-occupied territories can hardly be appreciated except in the light of what is the practice in the Soviet Union itself. The Soviet censorship at home is closely allied to the Commissariat of Internal Affairs (N.K.V.D.) – which is the Soviet security organisation – and is, in fact, under its control in the last resort. This censorship – which is a most important instrument of political power – operates (through Glavlit, the party press bureau and the information service of the N.K.V.D.) to suppress the expression of any views not in conformity with the party line and also to popularise and support the party line – in politics, literature, science or any other field ...

16 A study of what has happened, up to date, in the countries dealt with in this paper shows that the local course of events is influenced by two distinct factors: (a) the existing state of political forces in each country, and (b) the value, to the Soviet Government, of each country's economic and military resources. There may be already in existence a native Communist Party strong enough, at any rate with Soviet support, to seize power by itself; or such a party may exist but not be strong enough, even with Soviet support, to seize and hold power without at least temporarily enlisting the co-operation of 'fellow-travellers'; or the left-most native political party of any consequence may stand somewhere to the right of Communism. Again, the Soviet Government may be interested first and foremost in seeing a Communist or near-Communist regime established in one of these countries, or alternatively its first consideration may be to tap the country's economic and military resources. Permutations and combinations of these various alternative situations tend to produce considerable local variations in the course of political events; but one step that has been taken in Bulgaria, Roumania and Hungary alike has been to secure for out-and-out Communists the two portfolios of Justice

and the Interior, which carry with them the control of the police and/or the militia . . .

32 In any conflict of policies in any of the four European countries in question, the British and United States Governments have found themselves at a disadvantage in several respects, some temporary and some permanent. At the outset (i.e., before the proposal, since the end of hostilities with Germany, of new regulations for the Bulgarian, Roumanian and Hungarian control commissions) the Soviet authorities enjoyed, by agreement between the three Powers, a decisive predominance over their British and American colleagues in the exercise of control under the terms of the armistices. This arrangement reflected the fact that these four countries had been compelled to capitulate by force of Soviet arms and that three of them were traversed by lines of communication that were of vital importance to the Red Army for the prosecution of the war against Germany, which was then still continuing; but the effects of these Soviet victories and military necessities, which might in themselves be wasting assets, are reinforced by the permanent geographical fact that these four countries all lie close to the land-frontiers of the Soviet Union and far away from the effective range of British and American sea and land power. This permanent geographical factor also operates in the case of Northern Persia.

33 The Soviet Government and its local representatives in these five occupied or controlled territories, in their relations with the British and American Governments and their local representatives, have taken advantage of their predominant position in ways that their allies have felt to be embarrassing and unwarrantable. In behaving towards their allies in this fashion, the Soviet authorities seem to have been actuated by two distinct motives: (a) a wish to keep all other Great Powers, not excluding those which are now their partners, at arm's length from territories adjacent to the Soviet Union which she considers to be of vital strategic and/or economic importance to her; (b) a wish to prevent the British and Americans from interfering with political developments in these Soviet-occupied or Soviet-controlled territories which the Soviet authorities wish to see consummated . . .

35 The strong pressure exerted by the Soviet authorities (a) to keep down the numbers of the personnel of the British and American delegations to the Control Commissions, and (b) to restrict their freedom of movement within the occupied territories, is perhaps due both to the desire to keep the English-speaking Powers at arm's length and to the desire to prevent their putting a spoke in the wheel of local Soviet policy.

36 The latter comes out transparently in the frequent and flagrant omissions, on the part of the Soviet authorities, to give their British and American colleagues the opportunity to discuss with them, in advance, intentions of theirs in which these colleagues and their Governments were legitimately and

deeply concerned; in the creation of *faits accomplis* (as, for example, the re-placement of General Radescu's by M. Grozea's regime in Roumania); and in the tactics of procrastination and evasion with which the British and American Governments' representatives have been parried when, on being confronted with some *fait accompli* about which they had been kept in the dark while it was in preparation, they have sought contact with their Soviet colleagues in the hope of inducing them not to carry their independent action further. Here again it is Roumania that provides the most flagrant examples of the complete failure of the Soviet authorities to consult or even inform their British colleagues not only about decisions relating to Roumanian internal affairs but also about decisions directly affecting British interests . . .

39 From the foregoing survey the following conclusions seem to emerge:

i In all the five territories under consideration, the Soviet Government regards it as being an important Soviet interest that a regime satisfactory to the Soviet Union should get into the saddle. (For this purpose, a satisfactory regime means one so amenable to suggestions and instructions from the Soviet Government that it can be counted upon to refuse to play the game of the Soviet Union's enemies, either actual or potential.)

ii While this is the Soviet Government's target in all five countries alike, there is a striking local diversity in the degree of pressure that the Soviet Government has been exerting in order to bring about the result that it everywhere seems to desire. In Finland and Hungary, the Soviet authorities have displayed considerable moderation and even forbearance; in Roumania and Bulgaria they have turned the screw to the third degree; while their be-haviour in Persia has oscillated somewhere between these two extremes.

iii They prefer to work, as far as they can, through native agencies.

iv Where there is a native Communist party which is too weak to serve Soviet purposes itself, they encourage it to take into partnership 'fellow travellers' as far to the right as is compatible with working under Communist leadership and for the achievement of Soviet aims. In Persia they are quite prepared to use landowners or merchants who can be cajoled by various means into following their lead.

v In so far as the Soviet authorities find themselves compelled to intervene behind the scenes in order to help their native proteges into the saddle, they sometimes take elaborate measures for veiling what is actually happening and what they themselves are doing to help bring it about.

vi In all five territories, the Soviet Government goes to great lengths in circumscribing the influence of Great Britain and the United States, both for the sake of keeping the Soviet Union's present allies out of territories of strategic and/or economic importance to the Soviet Union, and in order to prevent the English-speaking Powers from obstructing (supposing that they wish to obstruct) the developments which the Soviet Government desires to bring about in the political life of the occupied or controlled territories.

vii Though the Soviet authorities make use of native Communist parties or movements in these occupied or controlled countries, the interests which they are trying to promote by these and other means appear to be primarily those, not of Communism but of the Soviet Union.

41 Clark Kerr to Eden on Soviet policy, 10 July 1945

...5...At the end of May there was hardly one of the many vital international problems requiring urgent solution on which we were not at loggerheads with the Soviet Union. During the past month, however, the veto difficulty which threatened the San Francisco Conference with disaster has been overcome, thanks to a Soviet concession; the new World Organisation has been established with full Soviet support and is being presented to the Soviet people as a great and constructive achievement. In Germany, agreement has at last been reached on the execution of the decisions about zones of occupation and control. The British, American and French contingents are now moving into Berlin. This has been accompanied by friendly meetings and exchanges of decorations between British, American and Soviet commanders, which have been played up in the Soviet press and form a welcome change from the previous weeks of bitter invective about alleged shortcomings and tendernesss towards Fascists and war criminals on our part and on that of the Americans. The problem of Vienna seems also to be on the way to a solution. The greatest single source of friction between the Soviet Union and her western allies – the Polish question – has been disposed of on the lines of the Crimea Agreement. Even at Trieste, a provisional agreement has been reached. Here the Soviet Government clearly did not wish to be a party to a trial of strength. Although we still have cause for serious dissatisfaction over our own position and internal developments in Roumania, Bulgaria and Hungary, there has been a definite easing in the situation in recent weeks, and the Soviet Government have themselves taken the initiative in proposing a return to more normal relations. This relatively cheerful picture is completed by the beginning of the work of the Reparation Commission in Moscow and the meeting in London of representatives of the major Allies, including the Soviet Union, to settle policy in regard to war criminals.

6 It must be recognised nevertheless that the above list of happy events does not include a single instance in which the Soviet Government have given way substantially on any issue affecting their vital interests. We must, however, reckon it as a definite gain that they are gradually substituting the technique of

international negotiation for that of unilateral action, even though their methods may still be rough and ill-mannered. A great effort was needed to bring about the above results. One of the main reasons for the unaccommodating and even hostile attitude previously taken up by the Soviet Government on almost every problem of common concern was their suspicion that their British and American allies were combining to deprive them of some of the fruits of victory. The Russians had become so used to the steady stream of praise of Soviet policy and activities, more particularly in Britain, that a disproportionate importance was attributed here to signs of British displeasure and to open criticism in the British press of certain aspects of Soviet policy in Eastern Europe. At one stage the United States Government clearly took fright at what they conceived to be a widening gulf between their two allies. To bridge this gulf and to restore a happier relationship between the three major Allies, Mr. Harry Hopkins was sent to Moscow at the end of May as President Truman's personal emissary. Mr. Hopkins evidently went a long way to persuade the Soviet Government that, for the present at any rate, American policy tended to follow the lines laid down by President Roosevelt. At the same time he seems to have moved Stalin to see that the behaviour of the Soviet Government, before and after the end of the war in Europe, had seriously disturbed public opinion in America, and that a more forthcoming attitude was needed on the Soviet side if the new President were to carry the American public behind him in a policy of continued friendship between the two countries. The outstanding results of Mr. Hopkins's mission were the Soviet concession on the veto question and the agreement with Stalin on the list of persons to be invited to the Polish consultations, which enabled the Moscow Commission to get to work again. But while these were the direct results of Mr. Hopkins's talks, the indirect result was the whole improvement in the international situation during the month of June . . .

10 One lesson to be drawn from the events of the past month, and in particular from the successful solution of the Trieste crisis, is the importance of securing full and unquestioned American support on any question likely to involve trouble with the Russians. It was clear from the outset that the United States Government were prepared, if necessary, to contemplate military operations in opposition to Marshal Tito's Trieste adventure. The result, as we know, was salutary. If we are also to make the Russians pause in Greece and Turkey it is equally essential to obtain full American backing there.

11 Despite the trials of the war the Soviet Union is teeming with vitality and bent upon making her influence felt, even far from her own frontiers. The most recent example of this is the insistence upon participation in the Tangier negotiations. She remains indifferent to arguments about the unwisdom of stirring up fresh troubles in a troubled world. Her propaganda is active against countries such as Portugal, Spain, Argentina and even democratic

Switzerland, with all of whom we have certain ties, whatever the internal regimes of the moment may be. I do not suggest that in all these cases the Soviet Union is consciously opposing our interests. Her actions are, I think, mainly a symptom of a state of mind to which I have from time to time called your attention. It is of high importance and I may perhaps be forgiven if I again remind you that Russia of to-day is rejoicing in all the emotions and impulsions of very early manhood that spring from a new sense of boundless strength and from the giddiness of success. It is immense fun to her to tell herself that she has become great and that there is little or nothing to stop her making her greatness felt. Why resist therefore the temptation to put a finger into every pie? Why be patient of correction? Untroubled by the pricks of public opinion at home, she is as often as not oblivious to its influence abroad, until a sharp reaction to some major blunder brings it home to her that there are others in the world than she who have a sense of greatness. When this happens she tends, more especially of late, to lend a readier ear to voices that come from across the Atlantic than to those that reach her from the United Kingdom, for ultimately she feels safer with our people. Despite the visit of Mr. Hopkins, the Russians clearly remain in a state of doubt about the new President of the United States and his policy. Of Mr. Roosevelt they were sure, but Mr. Truman is something fresh and unknown that still calls for gingerly treatment. This uncertainty and the approach of the meeting at 'Terminal' may well explain the slight restraint which has marked Soviet policy in recent weeks. Meanwhile, it is a melancholy truth that the Russians are still uncertain about ourselves. I mean how far we are ready to go to back our friends and to stand up in good time for our principles and what we conceive to be our vital interests. About this I feel that we should leave them in no doubt, for when they are in doubt they tend to be a danger. What would therefore serve us best is a progressive forthright and clear-cut policy aimed at those areas for which we have long been primarily responsible – our colonial empire and the Middle East – and above all where our new responsibilities lie – in the British zones in Germany and Austria. Here we must be at pains to show that we are not going to fall short of our Soviet allies in the task of up-rooting fascism and punishing war criminals. This is of the utmost importance. At the same time we may base our policy in all tranquillity upon our own conception of democracy without too nice a regard for what to us may seem to be inadmissible Soviet susceptibilities. And, in doing this, it would be prudent in us to pass speedily on to enlighten our own public opinion, soberly and with forethought, about what is distasteful to us in some aspects of Russian democracy ...

42   Clark Kerr to Bevin on Soviet policy, 6 September 1945

... 5 As regards international affairs, interest remained centred upon Europe until the end of the Potsdam Conference early in August. The auguries for this conference were promising, and the decisions reached were greeted with great satisfaction. They were described as the triumph of wise statesmanship and the consolidation of the democratic forces in Europe. From the Soviet point of view the most important decisions were those concerning Germany and Poland and the exclusion of Franco Spain from the United Nations Organisations. All these decisions were fully in harmony with Russian requirements, and the Potsdam Conference therefore appeared as a major success of Soviet diplomacy, which invited favourable comparison with the earlier conferences at Yalta and Tehran. In so far as the Soviet Government set great store by immediate tangible advantages and are, indeed, in great need of prompt material assistance for their economic reconstruction, the Potsdam decisions regarding reparations and the disposal of the German fleet must have been particularly welcome. But, above all, the Soviet people were delighted at the reaffirmation of the unity of the 'Big Three' and the consolidation of good relations with the new American Administration. Certain aspects of the Potsdam decisions, more particularly those concerning the Balkans, were perhaps less welcome to our Soviet Allies but attention was not at first directed to them, and it was not until a later stage that certain doubts began to appear about the reception of the Potsdam decisions in the United Kingdom and America ... It has hitherto been a traditional feature of Russian policy to concentrate mainly either upon the East or the West. It may be that the Soviet Union now feels herself strong enough to pursue a vigorous policy simultaneously in both spheres, but it is worth noting that the sudden shift of interest to the Far East in August has been accompanied by a certain relaxation in the Soviet grasp over Eastern and Central Europe, where during the past month we have seen slight easing of the situation to the advantage of Western democratic influence. Already at Potsdam the Soviet Government had agreed to an improvement in the position of the British and American representatives on the Allied Control Commissions in Roumania, Bulgaria and Hungary. The position of the Western democracies has improved in Poland and Czechoslovakia, and agreement has been reached on the entry of journalists from the West into Eastern Europe and upon the improvement of transport facilities with the West. The less extreme democratic forces in Eastern Europe who do not look exclusively to Moscow have regained courage, with the result that in recent weeks the Bulgarian Government and their Soviet masters have been compelled to postpone elections which would have been bound to produce an unrepresentative Government, and there have even been some slender signs of a reconstitution of the Roumanian Government on a broader basis. The Soviet Government have reacted to these develop-ments with surprising moderation. They have at the same time shown themselves accommodating in the Tangier negotiations in Paris and in their dealings with Switzerland in connexion with the repatriation of liberated Soviet prisoners of war . . .

8 It is not unnatural that we should look for the causes of this welcome change. A not unimportant one may well have been the atomic bomb. The Soviet rulers understand and appreciate strength. They must have been quick to see that the Western democracies now had in their hands a weapon with which, for some years at least, they themselves could not compete. Hence perhaps a new respect for their Western, and, in particular, for their American, Allies, and a new mood of compromise and reasonableness in their dealings with us, even in those parts of Eastern Europe where the Soviet writ still runs. The significance which the Soviet Government attach to this new development is shown in the scant and cursory way in which they have hitherto presented it to their own people. It has never been admitted that the atomic bomb had any real influence upon the Japanese capitulation and Stalin did not refer to it in his final victory broadcast. But so revolutionary a development cannot be entirely hidden, and there must surely be growing understanding among the Russian people and, no doubt, also among those of the countries within the Soviet sphere in Europe, of the change, however temporary, in the balance of power represented by this invention. Nevertheless, while they may be realistic enough to adjust their policy for the moment to the new balance, the Soviet Government cannot for long be perturbed by the present Anglo-American control of this weapon, for they must tell themselves that sooner or later its secret will be theirs too.

9 The combined effect of the atomic bomb and of the British elections seem to have placed the Soviet Government on the defensive in Europe for the first time since they were taken by surprise by the rapid Anglo-American advance into Germany last spring. It is, I think, an encouraging sign that their reaction to this new situation has thus far been so mild. We have as yet seen no attacks upon ourselves for our failure to impart to them the formula of the atomic bomb which can imply nothing but a lack of confidence in our Soviet Allies. Nor has there been any reversion to the display of suspicion, which we so rightly resented last May.

10 There is, of course, much more in this change than the fugitive influences that I have mentioned, and for it we must, I think, look mainly to the Far East, where it will be prudent to harmonise the interests of the Soviet Union with those of the United States. The Russians are clearly still uncertain and a little anxious about the future of their relations with the Americans, and this probably explains their growing preoccupation with the United States, their

unwonted restraint in dealing with the new administration and, indeed, the present show of something like good humour in somewhat trying circumstances. At the same time, it may well be that this is the good humour of repletion. The Soviet Union has now achieved the security for which she was striving in Europe and seems, since Potsdam, to be reassured about the good faith and co-operation of her principal Allies in handling Germany. Her ambitions in the Far East have been satisfied. She is full of glory and her material profit has been by no means meagre. She may well afford therefore to relax and to mull a little the sour wine which she serves her Allies.

11 The danger-spots in Anglo-Soviet relations remain in the Near and Middle East. The Soviet Union has not renounced her claims upon Turkey and the Straights ahd she is embarrassingly active in Persia. Greece remains a stick with which to beat whatever British Government is in office. The return of Dmitrov to Bulgaria is proof enough that the Russians, despite their present show of mildness, do not intend to allow the Balkan situation to get out of hand. We must also expect a fresh attempt to fish in troubled political waters in Western Europe, more particularly in France, in the hope of frightening us out of what seems a reasonable and logical policy of strengthening the ties uniting us with the other democratic States of the West. But we are now in a much stronger position than we were before the 26th July to give a firm progressive lead in Western Europe, as in the Near East and in occupied Germany. Provided all our policies, however strong and decisive, be kept within the spirit of the Anglo-Soviet alliance and of the Great-Power collaboration, to which the Soviet Government continue to attach the highest importance, we need not allow ourselves to be deflected from them by the gusts and cross-currents which will no doubt come our way from Moscow.

43   Extracts from the proceedings of the London Conference of Foreign Ministers, 11 September–2 October 1945

A Protocol of the Potsdam Conference

... 1 There shall be established a Council composed of the Foreign Ministers of the United Kingdom, the Union of Soviet Socialist Republics, China, France and the United States.

2 i The Council shall normally meet in London, which shall be the permanent seat of the joint Secretariat which the Council will form. Each of the Foreign Ministers will be accompanied by a high-ranking Deputy, duly

authorised to carry on the work of the Council in the absence of his Foreign Minister, and by a small staff of technical advisers.

ii The first meeting of the Councill shall be held in London not later than the 1st September 1945. Meetings may be held by common agreement in other capitals as may be agreed from time to time.

3 i As its immediate important task, the Council shall be authorised to draw up, with a view to their submission to the United Nations, treaties of peace with Italy, Roumania, Bulgaria, Hungary and Finland, and to propose settlements of territorial questions outstanding on the termination of the war in Europe. The Council shall be utilised for the preparation of a peace settlement for Germany to be accepted by the Government of Germany when a Government adequate for the purpose is established.

ii For the discharge of each of these tasks the Council will be composed of the Members representing those States which were signatory to the terms of surrender imposed upon the enemy State concerned. For the purposes of the peace settlement for Italy, France shall be regarded as a signatory to the terms of surrender for Italy. Other Members will be invited to participate when matters directly concerning them are under discussion.

iii Other matters may from time to time be referred to the Council by agreement between the Member Governments.

4 i Whenever the Council is considering a question of direct interest to a State not represented thereon, such State should be invited to send representatives to participate in the discussion and study of that question.

ii The Council may adapt its procedure to the particular problem under consideration. In some cases it may hold its own preliminary discussions prior to the participation of other interested States. In other cases the Council may convoke a formal conference of the States chiefly interested in seeking a solution of the particular problem . . .

B First and thirteenth meetings of the Council

First meeting of the Council, 11 September, 4 p.m.

MR. BEVIN asked whether it was a correct interpretation of the terms of reference of the Council that, while all five members might attend all meetings and take part in all discussions, in questions concerning peace settlements the representatives of States which were not signatories to the relevant Armistices should not vote.

After some discussion –

It was agreed that all five members of the Council should have the right to attend all meetings and take part in all discussions, but that in matters concerning peace settlements members whose Governments had not been signatories to the relevant Terms of Surrender should not be entitled to vote.

Thirteenth meeting of the Council, 20 September, 11 a.m.

In the course of a discussion on the Peace Treaty with Finland:

M. MOLOTOV recalled that at their first meeting the Council, departing somewhat from the terms of reference laid down at the Berlin Conference, had agreed that all five members of the Council should participate in all discussions, whether or not they were all directly concerned. The present discussion concerned only two members of the Council and the other three members had not in fact taken part in it. This suggested that the best procedure for dealing with those matters requiring further study would be to refer them, not to the Deputies as a whole, but to a special committee comprising representatives of the British and Soviet Governments only, whose function would be to examine in the light of the discussion which had just taken place the proposals put forward in the memoranda by the British and Soviet Delegations, and to make recommendations to the Council of Foreign Ministers.

MR. BEVIN said that this proposal would establish a precedent for the Treaties with the other ex-enemy Satellite States, and he was not prepared to accept it . . .

M. MOLOTOV thought, however, that his proposal for future procedure was the most practical one. If Mr. Bevin was not prepared to accept it now, he would revert to it again at a later meeting . . .

C Fourth meeting of the Council, 14 September, 4 p.m.

. . . M. MOLOTOV said that, before he put forward the proposals of the Soviet Government, he would like to mention a point of principle on which he and Mr. Byrnes were united. From what had been said that afternoon it appeared that all the States members of the Council recognised the principle of trusteeship as the appropriate method of dealing with all the Italian Colonies. Apart from the reservation made by M. Bidault, they all agreed that these Colonies should not be left to Italy. They also agreed that they should be placed under the trusteeship of the United Nations in accordance with the San Francisco decisions.

Further, they were all interested in the method by which the general principle of trusteeship should be applied in individual cases, and that was of particular importance here because this was the first practical application of the principle. He fully appreciated Mr. Bevin's warning that they should be careful in its application in the initial stages. Mr. Byrnes had put forward a very interesting proposal which was worthy of careful study, particularly his suggestion that collective trusteeship should be combined with individual responsibility in the person of a permanent administrator. But he was not certain what was involved in the principle of a permanent administrator with wide authority, and the difficulty would be to find such a person who would be acceptable to all the members of the Trusteeship Council.

What then were the proposals of the Soviet Delegation? They took the view that the principle of trusteeship might be applied to some of the Italian Colonies on the basis of individual trusteeship by a single Power and that, for others, the administration might be entrusted to a number of Powers on the basis of collective responsibility. If there was doubt about the feasibility of collective responsibility, the Soviet Government would have no objection to placing each of the Italian Colonies under the individual trusteeship of a particular Power. The Soviet Government favoured individual trusteeship by one Allied nation chosen by the United Nations.

The Soviet Government itself had certain claims. Those claims were based on the fact that Italy had attacked the Soviet Union, with ten divisions and three brigades of Blackshirts, who had devastated large areas of the Soviet Union penetrating as far as Stalingrad, the Northern Caucasus and the Crimea. The Soviet people could not ignore what they had done. It was possible to be kindhearted, but one should first be kind-hearted on one's own account and not on account of other countries. M. Molotov asked M. Bidault to appreciate the feelings and interests of the people of the Soviet Union. The Soviet newspapers had published the previous day particulars of the damage done to Soviet property during the war. This amounted to no less than 269 billion roubles, and a considerable part of it had been caused by Italian troops. It would, therefore, give satisfaction to the feelings of the Soviet Union if Italy were to be deprived of her privileges in territories where she had proved unequal to her responsibilities.

Another important reason for the Soviet claim was that the Soviet Government had wide experience in establishing friendly relations between different nationalities. This experience could be used to advantage in one of the Italian Colonies, and the Soviet Government would undertake to use the authority given them by the United Nations in such a way as not merely to maintain, but to enhance, the prestige of the United Nations.

The Soviet Government accordingly proposed that they should be made responsible for the trusteeship of Tripolitania. He could assure the Conference that the ten-year trusteeship period proposed by Mr. Byrnes would be sufficient to accomplish the task entrusted to the trustee Power by the United Nations, namely, to prepare the territory for an independent existence.

MR. BYRNES, referring to what Mr. Bevin had said, said it was important that the Council should discuss this question themselves before referring it to the Deputies, since the discussion had revealed that there were questions of policy that must be determined before the Deputies could consider the details . . .

M. MOLOTOV said that he had put forward two arguments for his present proposal – the moral rights of the Soviet Union, and the experience of the Soviet Government in nationality matters.

On the first point, he agreed that rights in this matter were not confined to the Soviet Union: the British Commonwealth had no less a right. He need not dwell at length on the sacrifices and contribution of the Soviet Union in the war against Germany and Italy because the part that she had played was well known. He did, however, want to emphasise that the Soviet Union, thanks to the part she had played in the war, had a right to play a more active part in the fate of the Italian Colonies than any rank and file member of the United Nations, and he stressed the role of the Soviet Government in deciding the destinies of Europe, of which Italy formed an important part.

As regards the experience of the Soviet Union in dealing with relationships between various nationalities, he thought that this could be usefully applied in Tripolitania and could yield fruitful results. He excluded any possibility of using Tripolitania to make good the damage which the Soviet Union had suffered or of using it for military purposes, since it was self-evident that no armaments could be tolerated in a former Italian Colony.

As regards Mr. Byrnes's statement that it was easier to choose individuals to administer the Colonies than to choose States, M. Molotov argued that an individual must be a national of some State and would therefore be, not merely an individual, but the representative of a nation. In either case, therefore, it was impossible to get away from the question of particular States. As it was not possible to avoid the question what States should be closest to the administration of a particular Italian Colony, was it not simpler to make a State rather than an individual responsible for the administration?

MR. BYRNES pointed out that an international trusteeship did not exclude the possibility of using the experience of the Soviet Government in administering the Italian Colonies. The Soviet Government would provide a representative on the Advisory Committee to give guidance on the spot to the administrator. The United States Government also had some experience in controlling territories; but they would be content to apply that experience through their representative on the Advisory Committee. He did not share M. Molotov's view that it was impossible to ignore the citizenship of the administrator. The United States Government would vote for an administrator who had the necessary qualifications, were he a citizen of the Soviet Republic, of the British Empire, or of France. They would know that such a man would have no power to harm any of the other States, but would have the power to improve the lot of the inhabitants of the country which he was to administer.

MR. BEVIN said that, if these matters were to be decided by reference to the war effort of the various nations in particular parts of the world, then indeed the British Commonwealth would have strong claims in respect of the Italian Colonies. In 1940 Ethiopia and Eritrea were liberated by the force of British arms, though the task was a hard one, and much of this was done in the years when Britain stood alone in the war against Fascism. This was a memory which was deeply burned into the hearts of the British people. But the British Commonwealth asked for no territorial accessions: they asked only for the assurance of a lasting peace. And the immediate problem was to find the best method of applying the principle of trusteeship to these territories.

He thought that the difficulty with regard to the nationality of an administrator had been over-emphasised. Such a man would have to have an international rather than a national outlook, once he had been appointed to his position.

It would be wrong for the Council to attempt to decide at once, before the matter had been fully considered in all its aspects, that one State or another should assume trusteeship in respect of these territories. A hasty decision in a matter of this importance would rightly shock the conscience of the world. This was a very difficult problem which should be given full consideration. He would like the Council to adjourn the discussion until the following day, when he hoped to be in a position to give the considered views of the British Government.

M. BIDAULT associated himself with Mr. Bevin's concluding remarks. The French Government were deeply interested in the future of the Italian Colonies, not only from the security aspect, but also bearing in mind the battles in which the French forces had joined their British comrades in these territories. His observations on this matter must for the present be regarded as provisional, and he, too, required further time to reflect on the problem. M. Molotov had suggested that he was being kind-hearted to Italy. France had suffered much at Italy's hands – in President Roosevelt's phrase, she had been stabbed in the back by Italy. He was influenced, not by kindness to Italy, but by principles of public policy. He would like, finally, to make it clear that the French Government made no reservations with regard to the principle of trusteeship. They had subscribed to that principle at San Francisco.

D Fifth meeting of the Council, 15 September, 3 p.m.

... MR. BEVIN said that the British Government had given further consideration to this question in the light of the views expressed at the last meeting of the Council. They could not agree to the proposal that the Soviet Government should assume trusteeship of Tripolitania. As he understood it, the Soviet Delegation had based their claim on the number of Italian divisions which had fought in Russia and the damage which they had inflicted there. But long before that time the British Commonwealth had been at war with Italy. South Africa had a vital interest in the future of the Italian Colonies. In the last war the South African people had joined in driving the Germans out of Africa. In this war again they had had to join in driving Italy from Africa. They could not look with favour on any arrangement which might place them in a similar position in the future. The British Government had supported the Soviet Government in its claims for adjustments of her western frontier, and in other settlements which had since been made. In view of the vital interest of the British Government in the North African area, he was very much surprised that the Soviet Delegation had put forward this claim in respect of Tripolitania. The British claims in that area had been put forward on the same basis as had Russian claims in Eastern Europe, namely, security – a perfectly legitimate basis. All that the British Delegation proposed was that Italy should renounce all her possessions in Africa and that she should accept the arrangements made for the disposal of these territories, including questions of nationality, and that, finally, she should recognise in the Treaty the right of the four Powers to be responsible for the administration of those territories pending their final disposal . . .

M. MOLOTOV hoped that the Council would give to this problem the same close attention as it had received from the Soviet Government. He wished to comment both on the specific question most closely affecting the Soviet Union – the administration of Tripolitania – and also on the general principles of the trusteeship. The Soviet Government considered the future of Tripolitania as of primary importance to the Soviet people, and they must press their request to assume the trusteeship of that territory. The Soviet Government claimed a right to active participation in the disposal of the Italian Colonies, because Italy had attacked, and had inflicted enormous damage upon, the Soviet Union. No member of the Council considered that the Italian Colonies should be left to her on the pre-war basis. The territory of the Soviet Union was vast, stretching from the extreme east far into the west. It had a sea outlet in the north; it must also have the use of ports in the south, especially since it now had the right to use Dairen and Port Arthur in the Far East. The Soviet Government had no intention of restricting in any way the facilities available to the British Commonwealth for maintaining communications with all parts of the world. But Britain should not hold a monopoly of communications in the Mediterranean. Russia was anxious to have bases in the Mediterranean for her merchant fleet. World trade would develop and the Soviet Union wished to take her share in it. Further, as he had stated the previous day, the

Soviet Government possessed wide experience in establishing friendly relations between various nationalities and was anxious to use that experience
in Tripolitania. They would not propose to introduce the Soviet system into
Tripolitania. They would take steps to promote a system of democratic
government – though not, he added, on the lines which had recently been
followed in Greece.

The purpose of trusteeship was, he believed, to ensure the development of a
smaller territory by a large State. Such a large State could play a most useful
role; but if it lacked a proper sense of responsibility there was a danger that
the economic development of the territory would be hindered.

The Soviet Delegation adhered to the decisions taken at San Francisco,
both on collective trusteeship and individual trusteeship under the control of
the Trusteeship Council. It was necessary, however, to use caution in the first
experiments in applying trusteeship. Mr. Byrnes had counselled caution at the
previous meetings, but to-day appeared to be convinced of the practicability
of international trusteeship and had urged rapid action. The Soviet Delegation,
on the other hand, was very mindful of the need for care in these early stages.
If the results of the early experiments were unfavourable, it would affect all
future arrangements made under the trusteeship system. The United States
proposals contained the elements both of individual trusteeship and of
collective responsibility. They provided for a single administrator and an
Advisory Committee. There was, however, a Russian saying that: 'If a child
has seven nurses it won't be looked after at all.'

The United States Delegation seemed to like the principle of collective
trusteeship, but would this principle be applied elsewhere? Was there any
example of its having been applied before in some Colony or Mandated
territory? If there were a good example, the Russians would try to follow it,
but in the absence of such an example they had to be careful.

In conclusion, M. Molotov said that he was prepared to agree to the
question being referred to the Deputies, but he made the same reservation as
M. Bidault, namely, that the Deputies should not be bound by any particular
scheme . . .

E Meeting in Molotov's room at Lancaster House, 22 September, 12 noon

M. MOLOTOV said that the progress of the Conference was slow. The
reason for this was that the Conference was not properly organized. We had
departed from the procedure laid down at the Berlin Conference under A.4(ii)
of the agreement for the establishment of a Council of Foreign Ministers
(item I of the Protocol). It was there agreed that France should only participate in connection with Italy. It was improper that she should be brought into

discussions on the Balkans. Moreover, China had nothing to do with Finland or the Balkan countries. Much time had been wasted over procedure, and he suggested that the work of the Conference should now be reviewed and a decision reached as to which subjects should be discussed by Russia, the United States, Great Britain alone, which by the latter Powers with the addition of France and which by all five Powers.

MR. BEVIN said that he could not accept the procedure proposed by M. Molotov, or that France should be excluded from discussion of the Balkans.

MR. BYRNES said that he had reviewed the problem in the light of the discussions leading up to the decisions reached at Berlin. He thought that the spirit of these discussions was that France would not be allowed to vote on peace treaty questions other than Italy, but on other questions would be allowed to 'remain in the room' in the same way as the United States participated in discussions on Finland (to the latter point M. Molotov interjected that there was no objection). Continuing Mr. Byrnes said that the sense of the Berlin decision seemed to be that Powers should participate in matters of direct concern to them. The problem was to determine which were the matters of direct concern.

MR. BEVIN felt that there could be no reasonable dispute about the meaning of the Berlin Protocol. Moreover, how could it be said that the Balkan question did not affect France?

M. MOLOTOV indicated that he could not continue to participate in the discussion in London unless an interpretation of the Berlin Protocol were adopted which met his point of view.

MR. BEVIN said that arguments of this kind regarding procedure were an evasion of the real issue. What really was holding up the Conference was the philosophy and attitude of the Soviet Government. In these circumstances it was impossible to make progress.

MR. BYRNES dissented and thought that some headway had already been made, and that it should be possible to make more . . .

F Meeting in Molotov's room at Lancaster House, 22 September, 3 p.m.

THE SECRETARY OF STATE said that his understanding was that the five members of the Council should be present all the time.

M. MOLOTOV interjected that this was incorrect.

THE SECRETARY OF STATE continued that he had tried to find a compromise between his point of view and M. Molotov's. His proposal was that the Council should sit as a Council and that those representatives who were not interested in the subject under discussion should not vote. The same would apply at meetings of Deputies but that the Sub-Committees set up to prepare the satellite peace treaties should have a limited membership. He said that he recognised M. Molotov's difficulties but he had his own, e.g., the Dominions, and he had gone as far as he could to meet M. Molotov and thought that his proposal met the suggestion which M. Molotov had made about procedure for handling the Finnish Treaty.

MR. BYRNES said that he accepted the Secretary of State's formula.

M. MOLOTOV said that the procedure for dealing with peace treaties was specifically laid down in the Potsdam Protocol, which made it clear in paragraph 3(ii) that only certain Governments should take part. The addition of any other Governments could only take place by agreement between the United Kingdom, United States and U.S.S.R. If this interpretation was not accepted, he had nothing more to say.

MR. BYRNES said that the Potsdam Protocol was open to two interpretations. He was influenced by the discussion which took place at Potsdam but was not recorded in the Protocol. He asked whether M. Molotov could not agree that France should take part in the discussion of the Balkan Peace Treaties without a vote.

M. MOLOTOV said he could not agree. He could not violate the Potsdam decision.

MR. BYRNES said that even on M. Molotov's interpretation it was still possible to invite France or China to come in. Would not the right course be to find out whether France or China were interested and would wish to come in.

MR. MOLOTOV replied that it was not for those countries to decide. In his view it was unsatisfactory to have representatives present who could not vote. If the 'Big Three' agreed to invite another member to come in then that member should have full and equal rights: the right to vote as well as the right to speak. There was no reference in the Berlin Protocol to the idea of certain members taking part in the discussion without the right to vote and he thought that the present arrangements were unpractical.

THE SECRETARY OF STATE pointed out that the effect of M. Molotov's proposals was to shut out France.

M. MOLOTOV said this applied only to certain treaties, though he added that France had no interest in questions such as Persia.

THE SECRETARY OF STATE said that in the eyes of the world a Council of Five had been established and the proposal to turn it now into a Council of Three would never be understood. In his opinion the governing words in the Berlin Protocol were paragraphs A and A(1) establishing a Council of Five to prepare the peace settlements, and he therefore considered that the Council's decision of the 11th September was perfectly correct.

MR. BYRNES said that this was also his understanding of the Potsdam discussions, though he admitted this was not brought out in the Protocol. He suggested that the way out of the difficulty would be to refer the matter to the Heads of Governments and ask them to state which of the two interpretations was correct.

M. MOLOTOV said that there was no doubt in Marshal Stalin's mind as he had just received a telegram stating that the Marshal regarded the Council's decision of the 11th September as a violation of the Potsdam agreement, and attributed to this violation the difficulties which had arisen over the procedure for handling peace treaties and the idea of majority and minority reports.

THE SECRETARY OF STATE said that if the procedure for handling the peace treaties was the difficulty he would accept M. Molotov's proposals for Anglo-Russian and Anglo-American-Russian commissions to handle the preparation of the peace treaties with Finland and the Balkan satellites respectively, if M. Molotov on his side would agree to allow the Council's decision of the 11th September to stand.

M. MOLOTOV said that his proposals were different: the only questions which should be raised in the Council of Five were those which affected all Five Member Governments. The peace treaties should be handled as set out in the Berlin Protocol and all other questions which did not concern all Five Governments could be dealt with by special consultation between the Three Foreign Secretaries . . .

G Conversation between Bevin and Molotov at the Soviet Embassy on the afternoon of 23 September

THE SECRETARY OF STATE began by saying that it seemed to him that our relationship with the Russians about the whole European problem was drifting into the same condition as that which we had found ourselves in with Hitler. He was most anxious to avoid any trouble about our respective policies in Europe. He wanted to get into a position in which there was not the slightest room for suspicion about each other's motives. M. Molotov had quite rightly said that he wanted friendly neighbours and security in the east of Europe. Everyone who spoke to the Secretary of State about the West suggested that the Soviet Union was suspicious about a *bloc* directed against Russia. All that His Majesty's Government wanted was to collaborate with their neighbours without any offensive intention anywhere in Europe and to recover the rights which they had enjoyed before Hitler and for which they had fought. His Majesty's Government would do nothing secret or enter into any arrangement against the U.S.S.R. with any offensive design of any kind. What the Secretary of State wanted was frankness and friendliness. He wanted to know precisely what was the Soviet policy in Europe so that every move made by His Majesty's Government need not provoke suspicion. If we made a treaty with France as a neighbour we did not want to be accused of creating a western bloc against Russia. We wanted both our neighbours and ourselves to be prosperous.

THE SECRETARY OF STATE then turned to the question of *Tripolitania* and said that he had been told by Mr. Churchill that Marshal Stalin had said that Russia had no interest in the Mediterranean. He understood that there was no agreement to this effect but that Stalin had made some such statement. If His Majesty's Government knew what the U.S.S.R. wanted, the Russians would be told frankly whether or not it was acceptable to us and we would do our best to fit our policy into it.

THE SECRETARY OF STATE then made two points to illustrate the kind of doubts he felt. He could not understand why M. Molotov could not be frank about the *Dodecanese*. About the *inland waterways* all he wanted was that we should get back what we had lost, i.e., our international rights. He ended by saying that he was not willing, indeed he would not go on with a conference in which it was impossible to deal frankly and in a friendly way with each other. If M. Molotov would tell him frankly what was in his mind, what we were expected to agree to, the Secretary of State would lay all his cards on the table with equal frankness.

M. MOLOTOV said that he would begin by referring to what the Secretary of State had said about Hitler, perhaps rightly or perhaps wrongly.

THE SECRETARY OF STATE broke in to say that he did not wish the talk to start with a misunderstanding. He had not wanted to suggest that the U.S.S.R. in any way resembled Hitler. All he had wished to suggest was that absence of frankness led to situations which became irretrievable.

M. MOLOTOV said that he understood. Hitler had looked on the U.S.S.R. as an inferior country, as no more than a geographical conception. The Russians took a different view. They thought themselves as good as anyone else. They did not wish to be regarded as an inferior race. He would ask the Secretary of State to remember that our relations with the Soviet Union must be based upon the principle of equality. Things seemed to him to be like this: there was the war. During the war we had argued but we had managed to come to terms, while the Soviet Union were suffering immense losses. At that time the Soviet Union was needed. But when the war was over His Majesty's Government had seemed to change their attitude. Was that because we no longer needed the Soviet Union? If this were so it was obvious that such a policy, far from bringing us together, would separate us and end in serious trouble.

M. MOLOTOV then turned to the *Dodecanese* and said it was an issue of no importance. He felt sure that there was room for agreement and that Greece would get the islands. But what about the *bases in Constantinople* which the Russians had suggested? When this question had been raised in Berlin their proposals had been flatly rejected. But during the last war we had offered Constantinople to the Czar. We need not assume that his Government had

had or had now any claims on Constantinople. This was not so. Why were we so concerned about the Straits which were the entrance to an inland Soviet sea and an area of the highest importance to the security of the Soviet Union? Turkey could not defend the Straits alone and we did not want the Russians to come to terms with the Turks. Our present attitude was 'far worse' than the treatment we had given the Czar during the last war. We wanted the Turks to hold Russia by the throat and when the Russians had asked for one trusteeship in the Mediterranean we had felt that she was encroaching on our rights. But we could not go on holding a monopoly in the Mediterranean. Italy was no longer a great Power. France had dropped into the background. We were alone in the Mediterranean. Could we not at least find a corner for the Soviet merchant fleet? It was very hard to understand.

M. MOLOTOV then turned to the *inland waterways* 'as a purely European affair.' It seemed to him much better to regard it in the light of a temporary situation to persist only during the period of occupation and until the peace treaties were signed with the satellites. If it were settled on this basis the supreme authorities should be the appropriate Commanders-in-Chief. Otherwise authority would be divided and friction would occur and things would become damaging alike to us, the Russians, the French and the Americans.

M. MOLOTOV's next point was about our policy in the *Balkans*. It seemed to him that an offensive was being conducted against the Soviet Union in order to 'unleash antagonism in the Balkans'.

M. MOLOTOV then said that we persisted in declining to recognise *White Russians and Ukranians* as citizens of the U.S.S.R. although we had agreed to the Curzon Line. He did not want to dwell upon these questions, but about Germany, our common foe, instead of helping them with *reparations* we were putting difficulties in the way. We did not want any reparations. He wished that we did. At the same time we were not allowing the Russians to take any, even in the present case, where our common foe was in question . . .

H Twenty-third meeting of the Council, 26 September, 5 p.m.

. . . MR. BEVIN, continuing, said that he still could not see the need for the Soviet proposals for international control of the Ruhr. This area was in the Zones of Germany controlled by the United Kingdom, the United States and France, and was under the same kind of control as an area in the Soviet Zone. It had been agreed that in the interim period it should be subject, like all other parts of Germany, to control by the Allied Control Council. If, therefore, the French Government would serve on that Council within the terms of the understanding reached at the Berlin Conference, interim control of this area by the four Powers could continue without prejudice to the long-term settlement, which should be brought about at a later stage. He could not agree to different treatment of an area in the British Zone from the treatment of similar areas in zones for which other Governments were responsible.

No one recognised more clearly than the British the importance of these issues to France. The British war cemeteries along this frontier should be evidence enough of British desire to assist France to prevent further aggression from the east; and the British Government regarded the Ruhr and the Rhineland as affecting their security almost as closely as that of France. He was not, however, prepared to engage in a full discussion of these issues at the present time. The Governments responsible for this area of occupation should consider these questions very fully; and when the time arrived for the settlement of the German question as a whole proposals could be put forward.

M. BIDAULT thanked Mr. Bevin for what he had said about France. There was no country represented at this Council which had not been seriously affected during the past three-quarters of a century by the fact that the Ruhr had served as an arsenal for Germany. The Germans had fought against the French three times during that period, and against the others twice. This question was of vital importance to France, and they therefore did not wish any decision to be taken lightly. In the east, German territory had been restricted to the line of the Oder and to this the French had no objection. But they did not see why German territory should be pruned in the east and not pruned in the west at the same time, and they therefore could not accept a position in which a central German authority should be able to give orders in the territory on the French frontier but not in areas in the east which were in a similar position. For instance, the German railway administration was unable at present to give orders to people in Breslau and Stettin, but could give orders in Mainz and the Saar.

It was perhaps natural that this question, which was so essential, should be taken at the end of their meetings, and the French Delegation would be glad to have it settled now. But they realised that that was not possible and he was prepared to agree that, on the basis of what he had said, the question should be referred to the Deputies to prepare a report for the five Governments concerned, which could be presented at the next Conference of the Council.

MR. BEVIN and MR. BYRNES said that they agreed.

M. MOLOTOV said that he did not regard this as a question for the Deputies. He did not see what progress they could make with it.

M. BIDAULT said that he was surprised to hear this view. Had he, perhaps, misunderstood the function of the Deputies? He had thought of them as a body of able and experienced officials who would meet together regularly and consider these problems in the light of instructions given to each by the Foreign Secretary to whom he was responsible. Each would have at his disposal all the resources and information of his Foreign Office, and they could bring to the study of these intricate problems more continuous time and attention than the Foreign Ministers themselves could give; but they could not themselves take decisions except by the express authority of their Ministers. The purpose of referring this particular question to the Deputies would be, not to give them any authority to take decisions on behalf of the Council, but to enable them to undertake preparatory studies of the complex issues involved and to formulate recommendations for the consideration of the Foreign Ministers at the next Conference of the Council.

M. MOLOTOV suggested that it would be preferable, in view of its complexity, that at the present stage this question should be dealt with through the diplomatic channel . . .

I Twenty-eighth meeting of the Council, 29 September, 3 p.m.

. . . M. MOLOTOV put forward the following draft resolution:

> Nothwithstanding the decision of the Council of Foreign Ministers regarding the participation of the members of the Council, adopted on the 11th September, in the drawing up by the Council of treaties of peace with Italy, Roumania, Bulgaria, Hungary and Finland, only members of the Council who are, or under the Berlin Agreement are deemed to be, signatories of the surrender terms will participate, unless and until the Council takes further action under the Berlin Agreement to invite other members on questions directly concerning them.

MR. BYRNES proposed the following as an amendment of M. Molotov's draft resolution:

> The Council will convoke a Conference under the provisions of II, 4(ii) of the Berlin Agreement for the purpose of considering treaties of peace with Italy, Roumania, Bulgaria, Hungary and Finland. The Conference will consist of the five members of the Council, which also constituted the five permanent members of the United Nations Security Council, together with all European members of the United Nations and all non-European members of the United Nations which supplied substantial military contingents against European members of the Axis. The Conference will be held in London and will begin its proceedings not later than 1945. It will take as the bases for its discussion reports of the Deputies with any modifications agreed upon by the Governments of the Deputies in question.
>
> After full hearing and discussion by the invited States, the final approval of the terms of the treaties of peace will be made by those of the invited States which were at war with the enemy State in question.

M. MOLOTOV said that he must have time to consider Mr. Byrnes's amendment and asked that the Soviet draft should first be discussed.

MR. BYRNES said that he had communicated M. Molotov on the previous day all but the last four lines of his amendment. It should be regarded as an amendment to the Soviet proposal and both should be considered together. If M. Molotov was not ready, then the matter might be discussed on some day in the following week.

M. MOLOTOV said that it would be necessary for him to communicate with his Government . . .

M. MOLOTOV said that he had no objection to the convoking of a Conference to discuss the Peace Treaties, since this was in accord with paragraph 4 of the Berlin Agreement; but the detailed application of this decision as proposed by Mr. Byrnes was in his view in conflict with paragraph 3 of the Berlin Agreement which entrusted the preparation of particular Peace Treaties to the States signatories of the Armistice Terms. The Soviet Delegation maintained that the question of inviting States to a Conference on a Peace Treaty could be decided only by the States which were signatory to the Armistice with the enemy State concerned. Unless Mr. Byrnes agreed that invitations to Governments to take part in a conference on any Peace Treaty should be issued only by agreement of the States which had signed the Armistice with the enemy State concerned, then the Soviet Delegation could not agree with Mr. Byrnes's proposals and would suggest that they should be withdrawn . . .

J Thirtieth meeting of the Council, 30 September, 9.30 p.m.

. . . At the outset of the discussion M. MOLOTOV recalled that at their meeting that afternoon the Council had agreed to consider at the present meeting his draft resolution (C.F.M.(45) 83) on future procedure for the discussion of Peace Treaties. He asked that this resolution should be discussed before the Council proceeded further with consideration of the Protocols. After Mr. Byrnes had pointed out that the recommendations in the report of the Protocol Committee had been agreed by all Delegations, M. Molotov said that he was willing to agree that the Council should consider the terms of the First Protocol, to be signed by all Members of the Council, if they would then discuss his draft resolution before proceeding to consideration of the remaining Protocols. He was prepared to discuss in full Council only the Protocol which was to be signed on behalf of the five Powers: he was not prepared to participate in any discussion in full Council of questions not concerning all five Powers. If his colleagues were unable to accept this view, he suggested that the meeting should be brought to a close.

M. BIDAULT said that, while he was prepared to consider the content of the First Protocol, he would not be able finally to approve it until the Council had considered how all the four Protocols were to be signed. On this point he had suggested a formula at the preceding meeting of the Council; and two further alternatives were put forward in the report of the Protocol Committee. The position of the French Delegation was that the preamble formed part of the Protocol and they could not finally approve the content of these Protocols unless the preamble was in a form acceptable to them. He had suggested that afternoon a formula to the effect that the provisions set out in the Protocol were discussed by the Council of Ministers, and were signed by the Foreign Ministers of the States enumerated.

M. MOLOTOV said that he had another suggestion to make. The Soviet Delegation would not sign any Protocol unless the Council adopted the draft resolution which he had put forward regarding the procedure for the preparation of Peace Treaties. As he had already said, the Soviet Delegation withdrew their agreement to the Council's decision of 11th September. If one of the parties to a decision withdrew from it, that decision ceased to exist. The Council's decision of 11th September was a mistake, and the Council could not force him to sign any Protocol embodying that mistake. The Protocol should not contain anything with which any Member of the Council disagreed.

MR. BYRNES pointed out that the draft of the First Protocol put forward by the Soviet Delegation contained a record of the Council's decision of 11th September. The form of Protocol favoured by the Soviet Delegation was a chronological record of decisions taken: it was, therefore, a factual record, and it was a fact that this decision had been taken by the Council on 11th September. It was true that at the 17th Meeting of the Council on 22nd September M. Molotov had expressed his view that the decision of 11th September was mistaken, and that he could no longer adhere to it. The proper remedy was, therefore – not to delete the record of the decision of 11th September – but to modify the record of the Meeting on 22nd September so as to indicate more clearly the attitude subsequently taken by M. Molotov towards that decision.

M. MOLOTOV said that he was not prepared to sign any Protocol which did not either (a) omit all reference to the decision of 11th September; or (b) include a record of a subsequent decision rescinding the decision of 11th September.

MR. BYRNES pointed out that for sixteen meetings the Council had proceeded on the basis of their decision of 11th September. That decision could not, therefore, be excluded from the Protocol, though the record could be made to show ·more clearly that at the 17th Meeting on 22nd September the Soviet Delegation had proposed that it should be modified.

M. MOLOTOV said that unless the decision of the 11th September was revoked he would not sign a single Protocol. In reply to questions by Mr.

Byrnes, M. Molotov said that unless a Protocol was signed there could be no Communique: that in the circumstances, there appeared to be nothing for the Deputies to do: and that the Council should be adjourned.

MR. BEVIN said that in his view it should be recorded that on 22nd September M. Molotov had withdrawn his agreement to the decision of 11th September and that thereafter no further discussion of the Peace Treaties by the full Council was possible. It should also be recorded that he, Mr. Bevin, had then asked that the Council should consider how the Peace Treaties should be dealt with in the light of M. Molotov's statement. In spite of his readiness to discuss that question, he had been met with the ultimatum that no Protocols could be signed by the Soviet Delegation and no action of the Council could proceed unless the decision of 11th September was cancelled. In his view a little further consideration of the difficulties might well have enabled them to have been overcome.

M. MOLOTOV said that the position of the Soviet Delegation was clear. The full Council of the five Ministers could not discuss the Peace Treaties with Italy or the satellite countries, as that would conflict with the Berlin decisions . . .

MR. BEVIN said that the United Kingdom Government were parties to the Berlin Agreement and honoured it. They were also parties to the decision of the Council of 11th September and would honour that also. They could not accept the view that a decision of the Council was rendered null and void simply by the desire of a single member to go back on it. Decisions taken in common could be altered only in common. If, as Secretary of State for Foreign Affairs for the United Kingdom, he submitted to any other procedure, he would forfeit the confidence of the British Parliament and public . . .

M. MOLOTOV said that when he had stated that a decision adopted at one of the Council's meetings might be revised later, he was referring to decisions which had not been formally approved and entered into by the Governments. Further, he had stated to the Council on more than one occasion his view that the decision of the 11th September conflicted with the constitution of the Council laid down by the Berlin Conference, and he had thought this would lead to a revision of the decision. Such revisions of the Council's decisions had taken place more than once. A recent example was the amendment of the decision on the repatriation of Soviet nationals.

He was, however, grateful to Mr. Bevin for his frankness. Mr. Bevin had now made clear the reasons for the proposal which he had put forward on 11th September. It was, it seemed, a first step towards the revision of the Berlin decisions. The Soviet Government now learned for the first time that the United Kingdom Government favoured such a revision. For this to be announced at a full meeting of the Council in the presence of representatives of Governments who were not parties to the Berlin agreement, constituted a blow to that agreement which could only serve to weaken the unity of the three Powers – a unit which had been preserved at the Berlin Conference, in continuation of the course which had been pursued for the last four years.

MR. BEVIN said that the United Kingdom Government adhered to the Berlin decisions and would continue to do so. Had M. Molotov's desire to revise the decision of 11th September been put forward on the basis that the decision had been ill-advised and should be reconsidered, the situation would not have become so difficult. It was quite another thing to demand its immediate revocation . . .

K Meeting between Bevin and Molotov in the latter's room at Lancaster House on the afternoon of 1 October

. . . M. MOLOTOV then began on the present position of Bulgaria and Roumania and said that it was the main cause of difficulty. If we and the Americans were not ready at once to recognise the Governments of these countries the Russians did not want us to hurry. They were quite willing to wait for the moment at which we and the Americans would be ready to recognise.

M. MOLOTOV went on to talk about France and declared that he could do nothing that did not give effect to the decisions of the Berlin Conference: so long as they stood he had no authority to change them. THE SECRETARY OF STATE asked whether M. Molotov would be ready to recommend with him that these decisions should be reconsidered. He did not want France to be the tool of a Western *bloc* or an Eastern *bloc*. He wanted her to have full voting power. This would give great satisfaction in this country and would remove many misunderstandings. He would urge M. Molotov very strongly to co-operate with him in this, for it was in this that we were mainly interested. Just as the Soviet Union wanted to have good neighbours, Great Britain wanted good neighbours too, but did not want such neighbours as might make the Russians feel that we were doing something wrong. If France, therefore, were admitted as a full member to the Council of Foreign Secretaries all suspicions would be dispelled. He could assure M. Molotov that so long as he was in office His Majesty's Government would do nothing consciously to injure Russia, but they would expect the same treatment from the Soviet Union. M. MOLOTOV replied that Russia made no claims to any of the rights of Great Britain or to those of any State in which we were interested. Russia interfered in none of our plans. She was not intervening in the Greek affair although great pressure to do so had been put upon the Soviet Government, nor indeed in Italy, although here the pressure had been equally strong. As to France, the Soviet attitude was favourable. He wanted good relations. Russia had recently made a political treaty with France and was in no sense opposed to the making of a similar treaty between ourselves and the French or between any other democratic State and France. It was in no way the fault of Russia if France had got herself into a mess, if the Government of Petain and Laval had helped Hitler. The Soviet Government had always supported de Gaulle and had been the first to sign a treaty with him. France was recovering rapidly, but she would take some time to do so completely. He was convinced that she would, but he thought it wise to wait to see that happen. It seemed to him that His Majesty's Government were getting ahead of the facts. We must be patient and so must France. THE FOREIGN SECRETARY interjected that he was being patient. This provoked from M. MOLOTOV a statement to the effect that France had not helped in the beating of Germany or Italy. Sooner or later she would have to be admitted to equality, but patience was required. THE SECRETARY OF STATE replied that if France were let in now it would help to restore her. On this M. MOLOTOV harped upon the word patience and explained that France had no army, she must be given time to recover and to get stronger. THE SECRETARY OF STATE again urged that M. Molotov should recommend a reconsideration of the Berlin decision and said that it would be a great thing if this were done by all three Governments. M. MOLOTOV said that this would be difficult in view of the Berlin decision, to which the Secretary of State replied that it was M. Molotov's and his job to get out of difficulties. M. MOLOTOV again suggested that all three Foreign Ministers were bound by the decision of the Heads of the Governments, but that when he got to Moscow he would report what the Secretary of State had said . . .

In conclusion THE SECRETARY OF STATE asked if in the event of an agreement on the question about the headings of the 'Protocol' it would mean that the matter could be finished? M. MOLOTOV replied, 'Yes, if we make a change about the resolution of the 11th September.' THE SECRETARY OF STATE said: 'Do you mean a change in form?' To this M. MOLOTOV said: 'That is the only way.' On leaving M. Molotov, THE SECRETARY OF STATE said that he regretted that so little progress had been made. M. MOLOTOV made some incomprehensible noise in reply.

L Meeting between Bevin, Byrnes and Molotov in Bevin's room at Lancaster House in the early evening of 1 October

M. MOLOTOV began by saying that he had seen Mr. Byrnes's plan. Mr. Byrnes had said that M. Molotov and Mr. Bevin had invited France and China to attend the meetings of the Council. That was right and therefore the decision of the 11th September should be recorded in a proper manner. He suggested that one of the four protocols should be taken as an example. Great Britain, the United States, the U.S.S.R. and France would invite China. The protocol of the 11th September would show that China had been so invited.

As a guest, China did not participate and had no right to vote. He went on to describe how the protocols about Italy and Finland would look and said that the record of the 30th September on the Italian question would contain a statement to the effect that the decision of the 11th September was cancelled in so far as the Balkans were concerned.

MR. BYRNES said that he had two protocols, No. 66 and No. 72. Had the Committee worked on No. 72? M. MOLOTOV remarked that there was no reference to the resolution of the 11th September in No. 72 and, in any case, he had not yet had time to study that document.

MR. BYRNES said that the time had come to look into the future and to agree what the deputies would do. Would they be allowed to do what the Council had done? Should the system of invitation persist? Would the Chinese be allowed to stay in the room? M. MOLOTOV said no, he could not consent to this. Three of the deputies would have to get together to discuss the Balkans and four to discuss the Italian Treaty. MR. BYRNES replied that that would be awkward and that the best way would be to ask the Chinese to stay but not to vote. M. Molotov here became impatient and said that he would not be induced to act in violation of the Berlin decision. Unless his colleagues agreed, it was no use wasting any more time. MR. BYRNES continued to press him and said that if the Council had the right to invite the Chinese to attend the debates why should the deputies not have the same right? M. MOLOTOV, with growing impatience, said that he had made a mistake on the 11th September and he was determined not to see it perpetuated. He had explained that already often enough; he had admitted his fault and he could not act on the basis of a mistaken decision. If this was not clear to his colleagues it would be possible to hold a fresh conference to discuss the matter. MR. BYRNES reiterated his explanation and received the same reply.

THE SECRETARY OF STATE intervened on this point to explain the two protocols in question. He said that No. 66 was a full record, while No. 72 was compressed into the actual decisions and subjects had been put under different headings. M. MOLOTOV replied that he regretted the importance which had been attached to this question and all the arguing it had involved. It was a mistake and not to denounce it was a still greater mistake. No more time should be wasted. If agreement could not be reached it should be frankly admitted and an end should be put to the talks. On the 11th September several 'erroneous proposals' had been made because the three delegates (himself, the Secretary of State and Mr. Byrnes) had not had a quiet talk beforehand. They had had time to put several things right, but not the particular one about the resolution. They had not discussed beforehand the way they should set about their business. He confessed to one-third of the blame, and said that, if quiet talks had taken place at the beginning, the absurd mistake of the 11th September would not have been made. 'We must all learn.' THE SECRETARY

OF STATE said that he was not talking about procedure. He only wanted to know how best the four protocols could be presented. The protocol of Saturday night was in chronological order and that made the question of signing difficult. On the other hand, No. 72 had not yet been checked, but it seemed to him to be all right and he thought that, if the matter were presented in this way, each protocol would be signed separately. For instance, Italy under one head, and so on, with Bulgaria, Finland and Roumania. There would be four separate sections to the protocols and four separate signatures. M. MOLOTOV said that this should be done and that he had no objection, but that he had not had time to study No. 72. MR. BYRNES asked if the protocols were in a shape to be signed, and was told by the Secretary of State that they were not. M. MOLOTOV broke in to say that it was time to take a decision. He assumed that there were to be four protocols and if there were the simplest proposal would be not to mention the decision of the 11th September in any of them. If agreement was reached, he would have no objection to their being signed in the presence of the Chinese Minister. It should be stated that the Chinese were present at a number of meetings. Otherwise, he could not sign (this was said with great impatience). THE SECRETARY OF STATE asked him not to use threats, to which M. MOLOTOV replied that he was not Mr. Bevin's subordinate and that he had no more time to waste.

M Thirty-third (and final) meeting of the Council, 2 October, 11 a.m.

MR. BYRNES said that the two questions which M. Molotov proposed should be discussed on the following day had already been exhaustively discussed over the last three days, and he saw little hope that on either of them agreement would be reached on the following morning. M. Molotov was apparently proposing that the Protocols to be signed forthwith should not include any reference to the invitation of the 11th September. This was not a new proposal but had already been considered and rejected by the Council. On the proposal for calling a Conference, M. Molotov had stated at the previous meeting that he could not express any views until he had personally consulted his Government. In the circumstances there seemed little point in discussing it further, unless M. Molotov had now received the views of his Government and could indicate that they were favourable to the proposal.

M. MOLOTOV said that he could not be expected to announce that he would accept a proposal before it had been discussed; he would say, however, that the Soviet Delegation earnestly desired to continue to work with their colleagues in a spirit of goodwill, in order to find a compromise solution. The purpose of his first proposal was to provide a way out of the difficulty in which the Council found itself, and produce a better atmosphere in which discussion of the disputed questions would be more likely to prove successful.

MR. BEVIN said that before the Council could agree to M. Molotov's proposals they must understand exactly what he had in mind. He himself was not clear whether the proposals involved the withdrawal of the invitation of the 11th September or not, and whether the meeting of the Council proposed for the following day would take place under the procedure followed hitherto or under that advocated by M. Molotov. Further, he was reluctant to agree to sign any Protocols before the Council had completed their consideration of all questions before them. While, therefore, he was as anxious as anyone to obtain harmony, he doubted whether M. Molotov's proposals would in fact produce it.

M. BIDAULT said that he agreed with M. Molotov on the desirability of reaching agreement. France would never reject an appeal to international friendship and co-operation, and the French Delegation recognised the necessity of not disappointing the world. M. Molotov's proposals, however, concerned the Protocols. On this he must repeat that, while he had agreed that the Protocols should be signed as M. Molotov had suggested, he must insist first, that all of them be submitted simultaneously to all members of the Council and secondly, that a formal assurance be given that the invitation of the 11th September would not be withdrawn.

DR. WANG SHIH-CHIEH said that before the Council reassembled he had feared that the prolongation of the session had been fruitless. Now, however, he thought he saw some possibility of reaching agreement. M. Molotov had asked that the session be prolonged for another day. He would like the opinion of his colleagues on this proposal. If they agreed to it, he would ask M. Molotov not to insist that the Protocols be signed at once, but to agree that all outstanding business, including the signing of the Protocols, be left until the following day.

MR. BYRNES said that it must be realised that no progress had been made in the last two days and that no progress would be made by prolonging the session for another day. M. Molotov had said that he must refer to his Government the proposal for a Conference. Until he had done so, it was useless to discuss that matter further. On the question of the invitation of the 11th September, it was evident that the attitude of the Soviet Delegation had not changed. If, however, his colleagues thought that any further discussion of these questions would be useful, he was willing to proceed with it at once.

M. MOLOTOV said that he was not prepared to discuss this question at once, since it was not on the Agenda for the present meeting. It was apparent from the discussion that his colleagues would not accept his new proposals. They had been devised in the hope of securing a friendly agreement, but had met with objection, and he could not force his colleagues to discuss them further.

MR. BEVIN suggested that the present meeting be adjourned and the Council meet again early the following morning to consider Mr. Byrne's proposal for a Conference.

MR. BYRNES said that he was unable to agree. If his proposal was to be discussed any further, he must ask that it be discussed that evening. He suggested that the Council should adjourn until 10 p.m. and that his proposal should be considered then.

M. MOLOTOV then said that the Soviet Delegation regarded the proposal for the calling of a Conference to discuss Peace Treaties as one which could properly be considered only by those States which were signatories to the Terms of Surrender corresponding with the Treaties in question.

MR. BYRNES said that this made it clear that the second part of M. Molotov's proposal meant that, when the Council met on the following day to consider the outstanding questions, some of its members would be excluded. Such a proceeding, at the last meeting of the Council on the last day of the Conference, would not contribute to a peaceful settlement and he could not possibly accept it. He submitted that it would be preferable to wind up the Conference at once, and to invite the five Governments to consider what possibilities there were for enabling the Council to work in the future.

DR. WANG SHIH-CHIEH said that as Chairman of the meeting, it was his duty to establish the position which had now been reached. He understood that there was no agreement that a further meeting should be held the following day. If that were so, it was his duty to declare the Conference adjourned.

No objection was raised, and the First Conference of the Council of Foreign Ministers was adjourned.

44 British reactions to the breakdown of the London Conference, September–December 1945

A Dixon's memorandum of 24 September and minutes thereon

The following is a possible interpretation of the Russian aims and tactics at this Conference.

1 The main objective of the Russians is access to and a base in the Mediterranean. The Mediterranean is therefore the real Russian challenge at this Conference.

2 The Russian tactics are to get all their desiderata put on the table, and to stall over the various items on the agenda until they see their way clear to obtaining their desiderata. These are the characteristic Russian bargaining tactics which have been adopted at earlier conferences. The Russians have

applied them much more obstinately here, because the issues at stake in the present Conference are much more vital than those in the war-time conferences. This is the opportunity for a Power on the make to grab territory and stake out interests beyond the limit of war-time conquests; the opportunity will not recur without war, when once the Peace Settlements have been made and sealed. Therefore we should be wary of Molotov's argument that while the war was on and Russia was useful to us we were prepared to meet Russian demands, but that now the war is over and we have no further use for Russia, we are unwilling to meet her demands.

3 The Russians see that the war has left us financially and economically weak and dependent upon the United States. They also know the American phobia about the British Empire and calculate that we cannot count fully on American support when defending our Imperial interests. The present Conference is therefore a good forum, and the present a good time, to press their demands.

4 The point of procedure regarding the composition of the Council when dealing with Peace Treaties has been skilfully chosen. The Russian calculation is that if we accept their proposals we shall forfeit the sympathy of France and be discredited in the eyes of the smaller nations. The object of the manoeuvre, apart from the desire to stand out for 'stooge' Governments in Roumania and Bulgaria, is therefore primarily to drive a wedge between us and the French. The Russians can safely say that they do not object to a treaty between us and the French because the object of their manoeuvre is to make such a treaty impossible. Equally, they can safely say that they are not perturbed by a 'Western Bloc' because if their manoeuvre succeeds we shall never be able to form one.

Conclusion

If this diagnosis is anywhere near correct, the conclusion is that even at a risk of a breakdown of the Conference we ought (a) to stand out against the Russian demands regarding the Straits and Tripolitania, and (b) refuse any compromise on the procedural point which would be interpreted by the French as excluding them from participation in European matters of concern to them.

Sargent, 24 September

I should agree with this diagnosis except that I doubt whether a base in the Mediterranean could be described as the Russians' main objective at this Conference. I should have thought it was put forward in order to strengthen their bargaining position in other directions. I can hardly believe they set out in the hope of ever being able to obtain Tripolitania.

Cadogan, 25 September

I agree entirely with Mr. Dixon's §4.

I am not so sure about his first 3 paragraphs. I am inclined to suggest that the Russian Mediterranean claims may be a retort to Anglo-American claims to interfere in Russian interests nearer home (Balkans). At Potsdam the retort was counter-accusative concerning Greece. Russian claims in the Mediterranean may be only an extension of this tactic.

I agree with Mr. Dixon's conclusions: we must absolutely stand out against Russian claims in Tripolitania, though I doubt whether we can refuse to consider any modification of the Straits regime. But what I am absolutely sure of is that we must lend no countenance to the exclusion of the French from the Conference. It is true that we have not a very good legalistic case, but Stalin has put himself in a not very good position by insisting on legalistic niceties. And we can make out (as we did in the message to Stalin) quite a respectable case.

Anyhow, we're not in a position to lose more friends, and even though France may not be a very strong one at the moment, our resistance to any move to restrict the Conference to 3 will command pretty wide support.

B Dixon's memorandum of 2 October and minutes thereon

In a minute of September 24th, written after Molotov had first raised the procedural point, I suggested that the Mediterranean was the real Russian challenge at this conference; and that in pursuance of this objective, the manoeuvre about procedure aimed at driving a wedge between us and the French and neutralising any development of a 'western bloc'.

2 The Secretary of State's conversation with Molotov on October 1st throws further light on the Russian hidden objectives. That conversation was held after it had been decided, the night before in the conference, that the day should be spent in attempting to find a solution of the procedural problem. Molotov towards the end of the conversation revealed his hand when he openly admitted that the Russians were bargaining our request for the cession of the Dodecanese to Greece against the Russian desire for a base in Tripolitania. But the new point which seems to me to emerge, although Molotov has touched on it before during the present meeting in London, is the intensity of Russian jealousy of our position in the Mediterranean now that France and Italy have ceased to be first-class powers.

3 Perhaps the Russian line of thought is something like this: before the war the British position in the Mediterranean was challenged by Italy and shared with France. Now the Russians see that Italy is reduced to the status of a third-class power for many years to come, probably for ever, and are possibly

sincere in believing, as Molotov said in the conversation of October 1st, that it will be long before France regains her position. The Russians therefore see us as the unchallenged master of the Mediterranean and the possible leader of a group of countries stretching from Iraq to Egypt, along both shores of the Mediterranean and up the Atlantic seaboard to Scandinavia. Such a position of strength by one power would be a potential threat to Russian security, and should therefore be sapped. If they wished to assail this position the two obvious points at which to strike would be (1) the Mediterranean, by establishing themselves there, and (2) France, by preventing closer Anglo-French relations on which the formation of a western group of peoples must be founded.

4 There has been a singular bitterness in Molotov's attitude at this conference. This is no doubt partly due to frustration at failure to make any progress towards his hidden objectives and at the failure of the procedural manoeuvre. Another thing which may account for Molotov's attitude is that from all they had been led to believe, and certainly from one electoral speech in particular, the Russians may well have expected that a Socialist Government in this country would be more accommodating towards them than its predecessors. This has not proved to be so.

Warner, 3 October

. . . it looked as if the Russians were being careful to choose the issue likely to divide ourselves from the Americans. But then, when the Balkan issue came up M. Molotov, instead of side-stepping it, made the most of it by attacking the Americans in terms that were little short of insulting and then went on to reject the Americans' pet project on International European Waterways. Thereafter, so far as I can see, Molotov resorted almost entirely to 'procedural' stalling tactics. Again, as regards Tripolitania and the Mediterranean, unless I am mistaken, Molotov seemed at one moment ready to drop the Russian request for a trusteeship in Tripolitania; but in his conversation with the Secretary of State on the 1st October, he revived it and, as Mr. Dixon points out in the attached memorandum, seemed to show intense jealousy of our position in the Mediterranean, although it is not clear from the record whether he would not have been ready to bargain the Russian claim to trusteeship in Tripolitania against our dropping the handing over of the Dodecanese to Greece.

Perhaps the most important question to ask ourselves is whether Molotov's behaviour has been based on purely tactical grounds or on long term political strategy. Was it merely a question of following the classic Russian nuisance tactics, expecting that the Americans, as so often before, would toward the end of the conference start 'formula-hunting' in order to prevent a breakdown?

On this theory, the Russians, faced with the unexpected failure of their tactics and not being ready themselves to compromise (M. Molotov may well have not been able to get authority from the Politburo by telegram) will now review the whole situation afresh. Alternatively, was M. Molotov sent here to see if Russia could get her own way as regards Tripolitania, Roumania and Bulgaria and everything else, and with instructions to build up a case for withdrawing from consultation on the affairs of Europe, if the other Powers were not sufficiently amenable? On this theory we may expect to be told that the Council of Foreign Ministers clearly is not a practicable bit of machinery and that Russia prefers in future to discuss matters through the diplomatic channel, in which case no agreed solutions of major European matters are likely to be reached, and Russia will take her own measures to bring about the solutions which she wants in Eastern Europe and in her own zone of Germany and will do what she can to prevent the other Powers settling and organising the rest of Europe.

Personally, I should guess that the first alternative was the more likely. It has always seemed to me since San Francisco that Russia attaches importance to maintaining the appearance, at any rate, of collaboration in post-war consultative arrangements. I think it is valuable for the Soviet Government to appear, to uninstructed opinion in other countries, as a benevolent and enlightened Great Power striving for the general betterment of the world and it would not do for her from this point of view to sabotage the machinery for consultation and cooperation for reasons which she would be very hard put to it to make appear adequate or even respectable. M. Molotov's 'procedural' tactics were the worst possible preparation for putting this case across.

On the whole, therefore, I think it most likely that the Russian counsels have been thrown into such confusion by their first experience of being in a minority of one and not getting their own way at the Conference that the Soviet Government require time in which to adapt themselves. They have probably been disconcerted also by the plentiful publicity which their behaviour at this Conference has received, which is a novel and upsetting experience for them. If this interpretation of the situation is correct, the Conference may have a very salutary effect. It will be extremely interesting to see whether there is a marked change, in one direction or the other, in the behaviour of Russian representatives on the Control Commissions and other international bodies.

Sargent, 6 October

I agree with Mr. Warner's analysis, expecially with his view that the Soviet Government still wish to collaborate with the Western Powers in the post-war problems.

I suspect that M. Molotov miscalculated the temper of the British and American Governments. He hoped that if he pressed hard enough the U.S. for the sake of American–Russian relations, would cease to support Great Britain in the fight to re-establish France as a Great Power and to exclude Russia from the Mediterranean. In the first of these issues he must have been terribly disappointed, especially as he committed himself so far that in the end he was unable to withdraw without loss of face.

As regards the Mediterranean, the Soviet Government may still hope to be able to isolate us on this question from America, and we may expect them therefore to persevere in their present tactics demanding bases in the Straits and the Dodecanese and a mandate in Tripolitania. Not that I suppose that they really expect ever to get Tripolitania, but they hope by masking the demand to be able to force us to a compromise by which we would agree to their obtaining control of the Straits with a base in the Aegean (possibly but not necessarily in the Dodecanese). Similarly, I do not think they are interested in the Dodecanese as such, but merely consider it as a bargaining counter in order to extract out of us the best possible settlement as regards the Straits and the Aegean.

C Roberts's telegram to Foreign Office of 28 September and Warner's minute of 6 October

...4 My impression therefore is that, although there are many frankly 'imperialist' aspects of Soviet policy, recent intransigence is mainly the result of genuine suspicions, while press outbursts are more than a tactical move in the game of power-politics or a passing phase of irritation. I have been told on good authority that it is believed in party circles that we are encouraging the ' *Western bloc*' in order to disrupt the Franco-Soviet Alliance. The Russians are seriously alarmed by the possibility of a large Western European organisation using the industrial strength of the Ruhr and relying upon American support. They feel, however unjustifiably, that this would soon become a combination hostile to the Soviet Union and that they would thus lose many of the fruits of victory. Before the atomic bomb and the end of the Japanese war the Russians had immense self-confidence. This has been shaken, although by no means shattered, and they fear that foreign machinations may yet deprive them of the place in the post-war world to which they consider their war effort entitles them. Hence the urge expressed so frankly by Ermashev (my telegram No. 4261) to take advantage of the present European situation to safeguard Russia's vital interests and incidentally to pocket whatever may be going before the general world situation crystallises. Hence also a renewed obsession with Russian security, and touchiness about outside interference in areas where Soviet vital interests are considered to be at stake, e.g. the Balkans. The result is a dangerous mixture of suspicion with a temporarily uncertain sense of power. The Russians are therefore driven to put forward extravagant requests (e.g. over Tripolitania), in which there is also no doubt an element of blackmail, and to attribute outrageous anti-Soviet motives to their allies, without perhaps realising that to the outside observer the border line between the protection of Soviet vital interests and the achievement of imperialist ambitions is becoming rather hazy. In their self-righteous mood the Russians go back to the Berlin decisions as they went back to the Yalta decisions as a bible which admits of no modification or even interpretation and continue to preach the virtues of Big Three collaboration.

5 Despite recent disquieting developments in Soviet policy, I see no reason to dissent from the view expressed by the former Turkish Ambassador here (Washington telegram No. 6374) that Russia needs world peace to enable her to recover from the exhaustion of the war. Stalin has said as much recently and further demobilisation measures just announced, although still leaving the Red Army very strong, also point in this direction. The moral drawn by the Ambassador that there is little risk in maintaining a firm front against unreasonable Russian demands seems equally sound, provided we take steps to dispel the suspicions set out above and to explain our policies in positive terms, e.g. in Western Europe where the present vague conceptions for closer groupings canvassed in the press must seem dangerous to the Russians. At present we seem to be in some danger of drifting into an atmosphere of mutual distrust and irritation, which will strengthen present Soviet tendency to play up to the Americans at our expense and to concentrate their attentions in a misguided policy of self-defence upon areas of special importance to us.

6 This is a situation which bears some resemblance to that last May when the deadlock was broken by Mr. Hopkins' visit to Moscow to explain not only the American desire for good relations but also the limits to American forbearance. It seems to call for a general clarification of British relations with the Soviet Union in order to provide a solid foundation for the alliance after the collapse of Germany. This would mean responding to Dekanosov's hint (my telegram No. 4355) that we should state our policy and our vital interests as clearly as the Soviet Government claim to have stated theirs. They will then know, as they do not seem to know now, the point beyond which they cannot safely go. Despite their great strength, the Russians fear the unknown and readily attribute the most sinister motives to us, if we talk to them in terms of general principles rather than of vital interests. These should however if possible be presented not only as British requirements but also as part of a wider world pattern, to which the Americans also subscribe. This would remove the very real risks of the Russians endeavouring to isolate us from the

Americans and of the latter slipping into the tempting position of mediating, probably at our expense.

7 A general clarification on the above lines would of course involve a recognition of Soviet vital interests, more especially in the Balkans and for this alone preliminary consultations would presumably be necessary with the United States Government to ensure that they do not launch us without full consideration of the long-term effects upon policies which we have not the means to enforce, which arouse the maximum Soviet suspicions and provoke reactions elsewhere from which we and not the Americans are likely to suffer. Nothing could have a more salutary effect here than obvious agreement between us and the Americans on concrete questions of direct interest to the Russians. But this need not prevent us impressing upon the Americans the necessity in their interest as such as in our own of making the British position quite clear to our Russian allies. I do not suggest that we should approve or condone undemocratic procedures and there is a chance, to put it no higher, that we may satisfy the Russians as to our motives and so enable us to improve our present position in Eastern Europe. But even if we fail in this it would be better, so far as Anglo-Soviet relations are concerned, frankly to reach agreement with the Russians upon our respective interests in Europe than to let matters continue to drift. This would at least dispel the present misunderstandings which endanger the whole world organisation as much as the future of the Anglo-Soviet alliance.

Warner

This is an interesting telegram on the situation as seen from Moscow. But I think Mr. Roberts' analysis might have been rather different if he had known in more detail what passed at the recent Council of Foreign Ministers. For instance, Mr. Roberts thinks that the Russians are concentrating their attacks on ourselves and the Western bloc and playing up to the Americans. The strange thing is that having started at the Conference on these lines, M. Molotov went out of his way to make vicious attacks upon the Americans in connexion with the Balkans and to torpedo the pet American project for the control of International Waterways. As a consequence, controversies in the latter part of the Conference over procedure etc. were carried on mainly, I understand, between M. Molotov and Mr. Byrnes.

It may well be, of course, that the Americans will recover from their present ill-humour with the Russians and enable the latter to resume their earlier tactics; but for the moment at least they have succeeded in antagonising the Americans quite as much as ourselves.

Nor did the events of the Conference quite bear out what Mr. Roberts says about the Western bloc and Tripolitania, I think. M. Molotov seems to have responded quite well to the Secretary of State's explanation in regard to the Western bloc and as regards Tripolitania seemed at one moment at least ready to drop the Russian claim, which suggests that, contrary to what Mr. Roberts says towards the end of paragraph 4 of this telegram, it was mainly put forward for blackmailing or bargaining purposes.

I would add, with some diffidence, that my own impression is that there is a good deal less real suspicion behind the Russian attitude than Mr. Roberts suggests at the beginning of paragraph 4.

I had a word, before the receipt of this telegram, with Sir A. Clark Kerr on the very important point whether Russian suspicions were real or put forward to extract concessions and cover their own aggressive tactics. The Ambassador said that he thought that the latter was so, but there was a strain of real suspicion as well.

As regards paragraph 6, I understood yesterday from Sir A. Clark Kerr that the Secretary of State had agreed in conversation with him that our tactics at the present juncture should be to leave the Russians alone and not as Mr. Roberts suggests to take the initiative in discussing with them our essential and vital interests. As has often been pointed out before, it would be very hard to prevent a discussion with the Russians on the basis of respecting each others vital interests not to result in an agreement on spheres of interest.

In any case, it seems to me that it would be very bad tactics at the present time to initiate bi-lateral discussions with the Russians, just when M. Molotov's behaviour at the Conference has aligned the other four Powers represented there in opposition to Russian aims. We should be hard put to it to explain ourselves to the Americans and French, if we initiated bi-lateral conversations – although we must not exclude the possibility that the Americans may do so after a short time, when (a) the pro-Russian element in American public opinion, (b) the U.S. Government departments and other circles which are pre-occupied with the necessity of finding a big export market as a solution to American labour problems will have made their weight felt.

D Wilgress dispatch of 9 October and minutes thereon

... 7 The process of deduction would seem to point to the fact that when the Session of the Council of Foreign Ministers convened on September 11th in a spirit of general good-will and co-operation Mr. Molotov agreed without hesitation to the proposal that all members of the Council participate in the discussions on peace settlements. Later when Moscow heard of this decision and when it became obvious that Mr. Byrnes intended to make a determined and frontal attack on the Soviet supported regimes in Roumania and Bulgaria, it would seem that Generalissimo Stalin sent unequivocal instructions to Mr. Molotov not to depart to any degree from the narrow and literal interpretation of section II, paragraph 3(ii) of the Potsdam Communique. Mr. Molotov thus placed on the defensive and in the position of having exceeded his instructions, also finding that things were going badly in respect of the Soviet defence of the governments in Roumania and Bulgaria and that France and China tended to side with the two Anglo-Saxon powers, became increasingly intransigent. He seized upon the procedural question as the best means of torpedoing the Session of the Council and thus retrieving the Soviet delegation from the almost irretrievable position in which they had found themselves through Stalin's refusal to countenance any departure from the narrow interpretation of the provisions of the Potsdam communique. By basing the Soviet case entirely on that communique Mr. Molotov, no doubt, thought he had uncontestable arguments on his side which would put the Soviet delegation right with world opinion. He did not realise the extent of the reaction against what the world had come to regard as tactics of obstruction by the Soviet delegation . . .

9 While on the face of it the London meeting broke up over an irreconcilable dispute on a matter of procedure, there are deeper causes than this to be sought for this so blatant a failure to achieve the cooperation which is essential to world peace. There probably were a number of factors but I believe the most important single one was the determined United States attack, supported actively by the United Kingdom and sympathetically acquiesced in by France and China, against the Soviet-sponsored regimes in Roumania and Bulgaria. The advisers in the State Department who are now dominant are mostly men with understandably strong views against the establishment of police regimes in European countries and they are convinced of the intention of the Soviet Government to spread Communism throughout Eastern Europe. They hold the view that the only means of averting this trend is to talk and act tough with Soviet representatives. The new Secretary of State is a man without deep knowledge of Europe and with great faith in the wisdom of the late President Roosevelt in securing acceptance at the Yalta Conference of his draft of the Declaration of Liberated Europe. This has led United States policy to concentrate on securing implementation of that declaration.

10 The Soviet Government is none too happy over their sponsored regimes in Roumania and Bulgaria, particularly that in the former country. When the Roumanian delegation was in Moscow last month Generalissimo Stalin made plain his distrust of Premier Groza, so much so that when the Roumanian delegation returned to Bucharest the Foreign Minister, Mr. Tatarescu, immediately began intrigues in the hope that he could secure the premiership as a man more acceptable to the Soviet leaders. The Russians have a deep-seated mistrust of the Roumanians whom they regard as unprincipled and untrustworthy. They greatly fear that the Roumanians could be a ready tool of any other foreign power seeking to build up counter-influence to the Soviet

Union in the Balkans. They are completely distrustful of the ordinary democratic processes of government being made to work in Roumania as they feel they may be made to work in Hungary without that country becoming a tool of a foreign power. In other words the Russians are unable to repose in the Roumanians that confidence for an independent and straightforward policy that they are willing to repose in the Hungarians and other more politically-mature peoples. Finally and most important of all its geographic position places Roumania in the order of strategic importance to the Soviet Union second only to Poland. The country lies on the southern flank of the Soviet Union and astride one of the Soviet pathways to the Dardanelles . . .

14 While, therefore, we cannot condone Soviet actions in Roumania and their policy towards that country and Bulgaria, we have to base our thinking on the knowledge that it is not the Soviet Union alone that has brought about the division of Europe into zones of influence. In one sense the tendency towards this division into zones first was manifested when the United Kingdom showed herself unable or unwilling to give up that historic insistence on the paramouncy of British influence in the Mediterranean owing to the importance of that body of water as a channel of imperial communications. The point that is relevant here is that Mr. Byrnes in starting his drive to implement the Yalta declaration should have done so without fear or favour, applying universally and not just locally the principles embodied in that declaration. Instead he chose to use that instrument to check the spread of Communism and he sought and obtained the support of the United Kingdom, the chief ally of the country subject to this attack and herself a perpetrator of actions not dissimilar from those which are the object of attack . . .

. . . The Anglo-Saxon powers, however, refuse to consider the peace settlements with Roumania and Bulgaria until there are established in power in each of these two countries an interim governmental authority which they can recognise. This is the first of the impasses which arose at the London meeting. Obviously the next step is to do everything possible to resolve this impasse by early discussions through the diplomatic channels looking for a basis of common understanding about the extent to which the Roumanian and Bulgarian Governments require to be broadened to make them acceptable to the United Kingdom and United States, so that these countries can accord recognition and proceed actively with the conclusion of the peace settlements . . .

19 Such conversations through the diplomatic channels appear to be necessary before there can be any further talk of another meeting of the heads of the Big Three. Obviously Generalissimo Stalin would not agree to a meeting of the Big Three to resolve the impasse over the procedural issue, because this would mean amending what was agreed to in writing at the Potsdam Conference. The Soviet Government have publicly taken the position that the

provisions of the Potsdam Conference must stand. Hence they only could be amended with loss of face by the Soviet Union. That is what makes this dispute over procedure so difficult to resolve. Inevitably it is linked with the whole question of great power dominance and the carrying over to the peace of the methods of consultation that were necessary to the effective prosecution of the war. The United States Government, though belatedly, have shown a most encouraging recognition of this fact by putting forward at the meeting of the Council of Foreign Ministers the excellent proposal for a peace conference to be held this year to discuss the peace settlements with Italy and the four European former satellites of Germany. It is so typical of the hit and miss statesmanship of this era and of the lack of any well thought-out plan for the making of the peace that this proposal should be put forward not so much on its own merits but as a means of resolving difficulties which had arisen with the Soviet Union over a not so very important point of procedure . . .

22 If the breakdown of the first session of the Council of Foreign Ministers has created little apparent concern in the Soviet Union, it is obvious from press reports that the same is not true of other countries. There is no question that in acting as he did Mr. Molotov has dissipated in what appears to be a reckless manner most of that goodwill which the Soviet Union had acquired through her achievements in the war. The chances of securing that economic assistance so greatly desired from the United States have been prejudiced. It is said that the Chinese, who hoped so to play the role of mediator between the Anglo-Saxon powers and the Soviet Union, are thoroughly disgusted at the behaviour of Mr. Molotov. The French, seeing him in action for the first time at a conference confined to the powers, are completely disillusioned about the possibility of getting along amicably with the Soviet Union. The events in London have brought nearer the inevitable drawing together of the United Kingdom and France. We have witnessed there not so much the beginning of a Western European bloc, as some commentators believe, as the birth of the Atlantic Community, because Soviet intransigence has revealed the need for continued close cooperation between Western Europe and the United States. Whatever the interpretation, much regarding which the Soviet press has been expressing fears was definitely stimulated by the very actions of the Soviet representatives in London. It is so typical of Soviet psychology that they have been willing to risk all the results outlined in this paragraph in order to prevent being pushed around in the Balkans . . .

Brimelow, 20 November

Mr. Wilgress has no liking for the policies of the United Kingdom, and shows it in his analysis of our handling of the situation in Greece (paras 12–14). But he is no less critical of the policy of toughness followed by Mr. Byrnes (paras. 9 and 14). He is perhaps too optimistic in his trust that a policy of impartial support of the Yalta declaration on liberated Europe (para. 14) and 'reasonable persuasion' (para. 16) would have produced better results and, as Mr. Balfour points out in his covering letter, he underestimates the extent to which Soviet policy in the Balkans springs from Soviet initiative, and does not merely represent a reaction to British and American policies for the same area. In spite of these shortcomings, his analysis of the breakdown of the Council of Foreign Ministers (paras. 7–9) is illuminating, and his comments on Roumania bring out the difficulties experienced by the Soviet Government, difficulties to which we tend to pay too little attention . . .

Ward, 8 December

The Canadian 'mentalite petite puissance' comes out in para 19 where Mr. W. favours big peace conferences. This mentality has been a good deal in evidence at the UNO conferences at Church House, though less offensively than that of Australia.

Note in para 20 Mr. W. develops the heresy of using U.N.O. for making peace treaties . . .

45 Roberts on Soviet policy, 26 and 31 October 1945

A 26 October 1945

. . . 2 All available evidence of reactions here has already been reported to you. It leaves the following impressions:

a The Soviet Government do not wish to admit that the bomb played any significant role in securing Japanese capitulation;

b The bomb cannot solve national or international problems; reactionaries who think it has changed the balance of power against the Soviet Union or who wish to use it as a means of intimidating her are playing a dangerous game;

c A continuance of Anglo-Saxon monopoly is intensifying Soviet suspicions of anti-Soviet tendency, in capitalist countries;

d Western scientists supported by progressive opinion seem only too anxious to have the bomb placed under international control.

3 While the Soviet Government are probably too proud to ask for the 'Know-How' they are realistic enough not to expect to receive it as a free gift. They must, however, be vitally interested in peace time as well as military uses of atomic energy and Anglo-Saxon attitude on this question must therefore be a factor in determining the general Soviet policy towards their

major allies. But I see no reason to suppose that the atomic bomb has influenced current international problems one way or the other. Soviet suspicions, which had decreased as a result of Big Three collaboration during the war, have, for a variety of reasons revived since it ended and more particularly since we and the Americans embarked upon a vigorous policy in Eastern Europe, followed by unilateral American action in the Far East, and apparent Anglo-Saxon preference for wide international co-operation instead of the Big Three procedure favoured by the Russians. All this is more than enough to account for the recent stiffening in Soviet policy and to make the Kremlin regret Roosevelt and Churchill who had become familiar figures to them.

4 Soviet foreign policy has since Tehran been based upon Big Three co-operation more particularly in regard to international security arrangements. The London deadlock was publicly, and I think sincerely, attributed here to the apparent Anglo-American departure from this fundamental principle and I have seen no evidence to support Mr. Werth's views that a gesture about the atomic bomb would in itself have affected the Soviet attitude one way or the other. Soviet policy is not, in fact, deflected by gestures of this kind. Nor has our attitude 'prevented Soviet leaders from taking the next step' since they seem pretty confident that the initiative will in fact come from the United States Government.

5 But although I doubt whether the atomic bomb has had much effect in regard to current problems it has touched the Soviet leaders on the tender spots of national and party pride and of Soviet security, about which they remain abnormally sensitive. An immediate effect may have been the determination not only to consolidate the Soviet position in Eastern Europe before the Anglo-Saxon democratic counter-offensive gathers strength, but also to avoid anything which might be construed as a weakening in their attitude under the threat of the new weapon. If friction continues on other major issues between the Soviet Union and the Anglo-Saxon democracies, the atomic bomb will probably also contribute to strengthen the traditional tendency here to hold in reserve an alternative course of action, to which the Soviet Government could swing over if they lost faith in the efficacy and value of Big Three co-operation, more particularly over security questions. But even the Soviet leaders would probably want to maintain at least a facade of collaboration if only to enable them to perfect their defence measures.

6 Even if the atomic bomb has made Soviet leaders more sceptical of long-term co-operation with the Anglo-Saxon democracies it could however hardly modify their conduct very substantially. The Soviet Union is already committed to a big military programme and has shown no signs of economising on guns beyond the safety margin to provide increased butter for the Soviet people. The Soviet plan to turn Russia in fifty years into the most prosperous

country in the world does not preclude it also being turned into the strongest military power . . .

B 31 October 1945

. . . 8 The major crisis in the Soviet Union's foreign relations came however at the meeting of the Council of Foreign Ministers in London. With the breakdown of the London Council as a result of M. Molotov's intransigence the Soviet Union suddenly found herself the subject of greater criticism and condemnation than at any period since she was attacked by Germany in 1941, and her relations with her major allies became even more difficult than in the early summer at the time of the deadlock over the Poland Commission and over M. Molotov's refusal to attend the United Nations Conference at San Francisco.

9 The failure in London plainly came as a shock to the Soviet Government. Although during September the Soviet press had made no attempt to conceal the existence of deep divergencies of view among the allies, it was confidently expected here that these would be bridged over and that the unity of the Big Three would be restored as at previous international conferences. In their first public outburst in *Izvestiya* of the 5th October the Soviet authorities showed that their main requirement was that there should be a return to the 'fundamentalist' Soviet interpretation of the Berlin agreements and to the narrow practice of Big Three consultation, extended only on certain clearly defined principles and in stated cases to other countries. The *Izvestiya* article also contained a clear threat that, if the British and American governments maintained their attitude, the prospect of continued co-operation between the Great Powers would be endangered. Subsequent press comment has been rather more restrained, but the Soviet Government have not backed down from this attitude.

10 The Soviet Government were probably not entirely surprised by the firm stand which you took up in London, since it had become clear during the preceding weeks, and more particularly after your speech of the 20th August, that there were many questions on which London and Moscow did not see eye to eye. They were, however, much taken aback by the firm stand of Mr. Byrnes, as they had been at great pains for some months past to play up to the United States Government and counted upon a more forthcoming attitude from the American representative if only as a reward for Soviet forbearance over Far Eastern questions. No doubt because the Russians are concerned over American military power, more particularly since the advent of the atomic bomb, and are anxious to obtain American economic assistance, they are still handling the Americans with some care, although there has been an increase in the attention devoted here recently to American internal troubles

and the hand of American reactionaries and of Big Business is now seen behind certain manifestations of American policy. In fact, although they are not criticised personally, Mr. Truman and Mr. Byrnes have not yet earned the same degree of Soviet confidence as President Roosevelt and they are now very much on trial here.

11 These revived Russian suspicions of the United States are largely centred around the American attitude in the Far East. Although the Russians have been ready to concede to the Americans the leading role in Japan they certainly expect to have an effective voice in the future of a country which is closer to the Soviet Union than it is to America. While Mr. Byrnes' attitude over Roumania and over the procedure of settling peace treaties in Europe may have provoked Russian intransigence in London, his refusal to admit the Russians to any effective share in the Japanese control machinery became at least an equal stumbling block to any accommodation. During the past month the Soviet press, which had previously maintained the utmost reserve about developments in the Far East, has become increasingly critical of the alleged toleration of Fascists and reactionaries in Japan. As a sign of displeasure M. Stalin has withdrawn to Moscow his military representative, General Derevyanka. So far, Soviet criticism has not extended to developments in China, although there have recently been one or two premonitory warnings and there are many indications that the Russians are consolidating their position in Manchuria, Northern Korea and, of course, in Outer Mongolia. Although there has been no hint from Moscow that the Soviet Government do not still intend to abide by the spirit and the letter of the Sino-Soviet agreement of last August, it is clear that they are well placed to exercise a strong nuisance value throughout Asia if they do not receive some satisfaction in Japan . . .

16 The solution to the immediate deadlock probably lies with the Americans, more particularly with regard to current Far Eastern problems. But there is a growing danger that if we leave major negotiations, more particularly with Stalin, too much to the Americans, we may tend to drop increasingly out of the Soviet picture and thus strengthen the tendency here to substitute a Big Two conception of the world for that of the Big Three. We are in many respects too vulnerable to Soviet material and ideological pressure to be able to risk the Russians regarding us as of little account. In so far as Germany no longer seems to be a menace and is in danger of becoming a source of quarrels, rather than of unity, between us and the Russians, there may even be a real need to find other and equally solid foundations for the Anglo-Soviet Alliance. In considering Soviet intentions and the future of Anglo-Soviet relations, it remains, I think, true that, however obstreporously the Russians may behave and however dangerous to our interests are many of their apparent objectives, these objectives at all events under Stalin's control are likely to remain limited.

There is no reason to doubt M. Stalin's sincerity when he stated recently that the Soviet Union needed fifty years of peace to restore the ravages of war and to bring her economy up to the level of the Western world. This need for peace is particularly great at a moment when the Soviet State is faced with many awkward, even if transitory, problems. We can also bear in mind the Soviet conviction, based on Russian national traditions as well as upon Marxist historical teaching and strengthened by a survey of the capitalist world as seen from Russia, that the Soviet Union will within the next fifty, or perhaps a hundred years, inevitably become the most powerful, the richest, and the best ordered country in the world. This long-term conviction, coupled with the immediate internal problems now facing the Soviet Union, suggest that she is unlikely to embark upon adventurous foreign policies in the near future, or to relapse readily into isolation. Her desire to get back to the Big Three procedure which worked so well from her point of view at Tehran, Yalta and Berlin, is genuine enough, and if we can find some means to satisfy this desire without abandoning any of our own basic principles, we may hope to survive the present crisis in our relations with the Soviet Union as we have survived other awkward crises in the past. Indeed, in showing clearly where we stand and that there are limits to our forbearance where these principles and our vital interests are involved, we may also hope to have created a more solid foundation for Anglo-Soviet relations in the future . . .

46 Extracts from the proceedings of the Moscow Conference of Foreign Ministers, 16–26 December 1945

A Meeting between Bevin and Byrnes, 17 December, 2.45 p.m.– 3.45 p.m.

Soviet Policy

MR. BEVIN said that Soviet policy was disturbing. It looked as if the Russians were attempting to undermine the British position in the Middle East. This could be seen in their attitude towards Greece, Turkey and Persia, all three points where the U.S.S.R. rubbed with the British Empire. The Soviet Government were maintaining large numbers of troops in Bulgaria and in Hungary, and there were also national armies in Bulgaria and Yugoslavia.

The world seemed to be drifting into the 'three Monroes'. The United States already had their 'Monroe' on the American continent and were extending it to the Pacific. (MR. BYRNES interjected that in the Pacific the United States only wished to establish bases for security purpose in islands many of which were uninhabited.) Russia seemed to be aiming at the formation of a 'Monroe' area from the Baltic to the Adriatic on the west, to Port Arthur or beyond on the east.

Greece

As regards Greece, if we withdrew our troops the result would be increased pressure from the Soviet Government on Greece or some manufactured incident between Bulgaria and Greece. Even if agreement were reached to withdraw Soviet troops from Bulgaria, the threat of the Bulgar army to Greece would remain. Greece had been overrun by two enemies, her economy had completely run down and everything had to be reconstructed. We were doing our best.

Dodecanese

MR. BEVIN recalled that it had been impossible to reach agreement on the cession of the Dodecanese to Greece at the London Conference. We were anxious to withdraw our troops and had thought of handing the administration of the islands over to the Greeks *de facto*. We had, however, hesitated to do this because of the Russian threat.

Turkey

His Majesty's Government could not be indifferent to a Russian threat to Turkey and would stand by her. We could not agree to the Soviet request for a base in the Straits and for the return of Kars and Ardahan. MR. BEVIN asked if Mr. Byrnes intended to raise the question of the Straits at the present meeting.

MR. BYRNES replied that he did not.

Persia

MR. BEVIN suggested that possibly a desire for oil was at the bottom of the Soviet attitude towards Persia.

MR. BYRNES doubted this since the Soviet Union had enough oil.

MR. BEVIN agreed and thought that Soviet intentions were probably to turn the province of Azerbaijan into a subservient area.

MR. BYRNES said that according to information received from the United States Representative at Tehran it was not necessary for the Soviet Government, in order to achieve their aims in Azerbaijan, to retain troops beyond the treaty date, since they would hope to control the province by underground methods after the troops had been withdrawn. He was also informed that the inhabitants of the province had a real grievance and that they had not been given the measure of provincial autonomy for which they had asked.

MR. BEVIN agreed that there was something in this and said that we had been urging the Persian Government to consider taking steps to meet the provincial demands.

MR. BYRNES thought that it would help if the British and American Governments could recommend to the Persian Government that they should grant the necessary provincial freedom; this would cut the ground from under the Soviet Government, who were posing as the defender of democracy in Persia, which offended American sensibilities.

MR. BEVIN agreed that consideration might be given to the three Powers sending representatives to Azerbaijan to report on the position.

Summing up, MR. BEVIN said that he proposed to have a frank talk with M. Molotov and tell him how uneasy Soviet intentions made us. He would ask M. Molotov what the Soviet intentions were. Just as a British admiral, when he saw an island, instinctively wanted to grab it so the Soviet Government, if they saw a piece of land, wanted to acquire it. If these were the Soviet intentions we should like to be told in order to know where we stood.

MR. BYRNES approved the idea of a frank talk by Mr. Bevin with M. Molotov, and said that he also intended to see M. Molotov and to raise with him in particular the report of Mr. Ethridge which revealed that the Bulgarian elections had been a farce and that there was a deplorable economic state of affairs in Bulgaria and Roumania. He suggested that Mr. Bevin might see M. Molotov to-morrow morning, that he himself might see M. Molotov late in the day and that the three of them should meet for an informal discussion the following day. This was agreed . . .

B Meeting between Bevin and Molotov on the afternoon of 18 December

. . . MOLOTOV began with the Balkans, and claimed that the conditions in Greece were completely different from those in Roumania and Bulgaria. Greece had been an ally. Bulgaria and Roumania were defeated enemies. In the first instance the presence of foreign troops in Greece had been justified by the necessity for military operations, but when the military situation had been stabilised there was no further need for foreign troops. The Foreign Secretary might claim that Poland was also an ally and that there was no need for Soviet troops there. But the difference between Greece and Poland was obvious. The presence of the Red Army in Poland had been discussed at Berlin and the Soviet Government had faithfully fulfilled their promise to reduce the numbers of their troops to a figure needed to safeguard the lines of communication to Germany which had to pass through Poland, for there was no other road. Most of the Soviet troops in Poland were in the former German territories which were now in Polish hands. This could not be said for Greece, which did not lie on the lines of communication to a defeated country. Here he reminded the Foreign Secretary that the Red Army had withdrawn from Czechoslovakia because no lines of communication lay through that country. The withdrawal had taken place on Soviet initiative because the Soviet Government had felt that it was no longer necessary to keep troops in an allied country. It was wrong to jumble all the Balkans together. In the course of the present discussion mention had been made of Bulgaria, Roumania and Hungary, which were occupied in virtue of armistices which had been signed with these countries. At the London Conference in connexion with the peace treaties, the Americans had even suggested that the Red Army should remain in Roumania in order to ensure the line of communications with Austria. This had been agreed to. As to Austria, the proposal for the reduction of the Allied armies was now being studied by the Soviet military authorities.

Here MOLOTOV said that he wished to call the Foreign Secretary's attention to the situation in the various countries occupied by the Red Army. It would be seen that the presence of the Red Army in these countries in no way hampered the expression of prevailing popular opinion. This had been true of Iran as it had also been true of Austria. The aloofness of the Red Army from the internal affairs in both these countries had been proved by the results of the elections. This had also been true in respect of Bulgaria and Hungary where elections had been held without any pressure from the Red Army. The results in these two countries had been entirely different. The elections had expressed the wishes of the respective local populations. It had also been so in Finland, where there had been no kind of intervention, although Finland had been a conquered country. The Russians had made no attempt to intervene because the policy of the Finnish Government had been friendly. To sum up, in Bulgaria, Hungary, Austria, Finland and Persia the people had been left to settle their own affairs . . .

C Third meeting of the Conference, 18 December, 4 p.m.

. . . M. MOLOTOV referred to the rights of permanent members of the Security Council. The conclusion of peace treaties was not within the province of the United Nations Organisation. Mr. Byrnes had correctly said so; and Mr. Bevin doubtless agreed. It was therefore also not the responsibility of the Security Council. The principle of what countries might discuss peace treaties must be laid down apart from the United Nations Organisation. Therefore the Soviet Delegation suggested that besides the States which had signed the Armistice terms (and France for the Italian Treaty) those States should be invited who actually provided substantial military forces against the country in question. They should adopt this principle which Mr. Byrnes had correctly stated, and not depart from it; and they should find out who actually participated in the war against each enemy State.

MR. BYRNES said he wished to avoid misunderstanding. He had said 'United Nations which had waged war with substantial military force against European members of the Axis'.

M. MOLOTOV said it would be more correct to say 'against the Axis country in question'.

MR. BYRNES said that he proposed that when it was a question of hearing views, States in this category should have the right to appear if they waged war against any one European member of the Axis. Thus the United States could express an opinion of the Finnish treaty but not sign it. They ought to consider the granting of a hearing on the basis of 'one war'. China had agreed that her Allies should wage war in Europe at the expense of the war against Japan. China should only make her views heard. After those who wished to be heard had been heard came the important task of drawing up the final text of the treaties by those entitled to do this.

MR. BEVIN said that war was an alliance, and waged according to geography and the best use of forces. It was largely chance whether a contingent from any country fought in one area or another. What was to happen to the peace treaties after they had been drawn up? If the United Nations concerned had a chance to be heard, they could be expected to ensure that the treaties were observed afterwards; was it therefore wise to exclude them from any voice in the peace making? Consultation over the widest area possible implied acceptance and an obligation to enforce. The United States proposals offered a middle course, without injustice to anyone.

As he saw it the United States proposals left the preparation of the treaties in the hands of those named in the Soviet paper. The next stage provided for wider consultation. The final stage returned to the original powers designated in the Soviet paper.

MR. BYRNES pointed out, while Mr. Bevin had stated the first two stages of the United States proposal correctly, its last stage provided that each treaty should be finally made by those of the invited States who were at war with the enemy State in question, while the Soviet proposal limited it to those who had signed the relevant armistice. He was willing to discuss this important question further with his colleagues.

He pointed out that the Potsdam Conference instructed the Council of Foreign Ministers to draw up treaties 'for submission to the United Nations'. If the smaller United Nations were excluded even from comment they could claim that the Potsdam Agreement by the three Heads of Governments was not being carried out; there should therefore be provision at least for discussion. Their justification for not inviting all the United Nations could be that it was more practical to limit it to those who waged war, as the United States proposal provided.

M. MOLOTOV said that as he had explained the day before there was no intention of excluding the United States from discussing the Finnish treaty. Everyone would appreciate this exception to the general rule.

China had not fought in Europe. If Mr. Byrnes did not base her inclusion on the Security Council, that altered the question; he could not see what the Security Council had to do with it. If the criterion was waging war with substantial military force in Europe, it was clear that China was not covered.

The Soviet draft presupposed convoking a Conference of the United Nations. M. Molotov then compared the last paragraphs of the American and Soviet proposals. Paragraph 4 of the Soviet proposal said that the peace treaties should be signed not only by the States who had signed the Armistice terms but also by those States who had supplied substantial military contingents against the Axis country in question; whereas paragraph 3 of the United States proposal said that final approval should be given by those of the United Nations who had waged war on these States. He was not clear about the difference. He understood that Mr. Bevin saw no difference between the two proposals.

MR. BEVIN said that neither was quite clear to him.

M. MOLOTOV said that paragraph 2 of the Soviet proposal explicitly listed which States should participate in the discussion of any given peace treaty, and those States should sign. For example, Yugoslavia would sign the treaties with Bulgaria, Hungary and Italy. Greece would sign the treaties with Italy and Bulgaria. In the case of the Italian treaty, in addition to the three Allies and France, Canada, Australia, New Zealand, South Africa, Brazil and Ethiopia would participate in the discussion and sign. The Hungarian treaty would be signed by the three Allies and Czechoslovakia. The Roumanian treaty would be signed by the three signatories to the surrender terms. The Finnish treaty would be discussed by the three Allies but signed only by the United Kingdom and the Soviet Union.

MR. BEVIN said that he was in some difficulty. He could understand the three or four States approving a given treaty, but if any other States had actually declared war, they would still be at war unless they signed the treaty also.

M. MOLOTOV said that Czechoslovakia had declared war on Finland; but he wondered what peace treaty they could have between them. He would propose to leave it to Czechoslovakia to dispose of the matter after the United Kingdom and Soviet Union had signed their treaty with Finland. The signature of Czechoslovakia was really not needed. The Soviet Union did not require it, nor could he believe that the United Kingdom would require it either.

MR. BEVIN said that if a country had declared war some action must be taken to bring the state of war to an end.

M. MOLOTOV expressed the view that this was a technicality which the country in question could decide for herself. He alleged that Costa Rica had declared war on Roumania; but he hoped that she would regard her war with Roumania as over once the peace treaty with Roumania had been signed by the three signatories to the surrender terms.

MR. BYRNES said that he was satisfied that when at Potsdam the Heads of States had agreed that treaties should be drawn up with a view to submission to the United Nations their intention had certainly been that the treaties when finally drafted must be submitted to those who had been at war in each case for them to agree to or not. They must be given an opportunity to agree to the treaties arrived at.

M. MOLOTOV asked whether it was Mr. Byrnes' view that Costa Rica should sign the peace treaty with Roumania.

MR. BYRNES replied that if Costa Rica had declared war on Roumania she must be given the opportunity to sign or not as she pleased. But since she had not been actively engaged in war against Roumania she would not have to be invited to draft the treaty. Paragraph 3 of the Soviet paper contemplated in fact what was set out in paragraph 3 of the United States proposal. The United States paper contained no paragraph on formal signature because the United States Government thought it was a matter of course that all States who had been at war would have to sign. The difference between the two proposals was that in paragraph 3 of the Soviet paper it was provided that, after the conclusion of what one might call the public hearing the signatories to the Armistice terms should draw up the final text of the peace treaty. In the United States proposal paragraph 3 provided that final approval should be given by those of the invited States who had been at war with the enemy in question. By final approval the United States Government meant the drawing up of the final text.

MR. BEVIN said that the question which he had raised was not exactly a technicality. In the case of Finland, Roumania and Hungary, all four of the Dominions had been at war. In the case of Bulgaria, Australia, New Zealand and South Africa had been at war, and Canada had not declared war. All kinds of questions concerned with trade, and shipping, etc., must be settled in order to put an end to the situation created by the existence of a state of war. In the case of countries indulging in overseas trade it was important that such questions should be cleared up and settled. He wondered whether it would not be possible to devise some means of bringing in as signatories countries which had been at war without altering the master treaty.

M. MOLOTOV recalled that in the case of the Armistice with Finland the British Ambassador had acted on behalf of the whole British Commonwealth, including the Dominions. He asked whether the same procedure could not be followed as regards the peace treaty with Finland. Czechoslovakia had declared war on Finland and she had not been represented at the signing of the Armistice terms. Therefore Czechoslovakia was the only country which would be likely to claim that she should sign the Finnish peace treaty.

MR. BEVIN said that it might be possible for the members of the British Commonwealth to agree to authorise one person to sign for them. But it was not possible for him to agree to this without consultation; otherwise the signatory might be repudiated.

At Versailles each Dominion had insisted on signing for itself and it could not be assumed that at a future peace conference the British representative would be given authority to sign on behalf of the Dominions. Each of the Dominions had an independent Parliament and might decide that they wished to sign for themselves. In the case of the Italian treaty this was covered; but not in the other cases. There was another point. Notwithstanding what might be thought to the contrary, India always insisted on signing for herself . . .

D Meeting between Bevin and Stalin, 19 December, 10 p.m.

. . . MR. BEVIN said that it was important to bring out into the light of day the misgivings which either side might have. He himself was quite ready to tell the Generalissimo what was feared in England. It was thought there that the Soviet Government were following a policy aiming at the incorporation of Azerbaijan, or making it into a satellite State. He did not say that the Government were taking that view, but it was held in the House of Commons and in the country at large. Generalissimo Stalin must realise what a sensitive point Iran was to both Governments. He had observed to M. Molotov the day before that, if there was any point of friction between their Governments, it was important at once to try to remove it at an early stage. His Majesty's Government had interests in Iraq and in Mosul and the oil of those regions. If only His Majesty's Government could know what it was exactly that the Soviet Government wanted it might be possible to co-operate.

GENERALISSIMO STALIN said that, frankly and honestly, he had no claims against Iran, that was to say, he had no idea of incorporating any part of Iran into the Soviet Union and no intention of impairing the sovereignty of Iran. But he wished to safeguard the oil of Baku against diversionary activities. There were many extreme nationalists in the Iranian Government who wished to damage the Baku oil industry and who had plans of long standing for the incorporation of Baku in Iran. As to this, he had little fear but there was a real danger of diversionary activities. He had no territorial claim against Iran or any intention of infringing Iranian sovereignty.

MR. BEVIN said that we could assume then that Azerbaijan would remain in Iran, to which GENERALISSIMO STALIN replied that Azerbaijan in fact consisted of two different regions, only one of which was genuinely Persian.

MR. BEVIN said that, at any rate, the Persian part would remain in Iran and GENERALISSIMO STALIN indicated his assent.

MR. BEVIN said that he had taken an interest in the proposal for the establishment of provincial councils throughout Iran. His Majesty's Government had suggested to the Iranian Government that that ought to be done. Could we not set up a tripartite commission to advise and assist them. The Iranians did not seem capable of carrying out reform by themselves. This reform seemed to be necessary and might effect a settlement of Persia. If this suggestion appealed to the Generalissimo, his personal opinion was that, if the latter favoured it, he (Mr. Bevin) might advocate it with the United States Government.

GENERALISSIMO STALIN said that he might support this idea, but he must know exactly what was intended.

MR. BEVIN explained that the measure had been provided for in the Iranian constitution but had never been carried out. He thought it was essential to carry it out but he feared that the Iranian Government would be unable to do it without assistance.

GENERALISSIMO STALIN thought that that was probably the case and said that he would study the matter and then discuss it further. He thought it possible that agreement might be reached on this point.

MR. BEVIN said that he wished to put a further question. What was the difficulty in regard to Turkey? He did not want the term to be misunderstood but it seemed that a war of nerves was being conducted. He had the impression that there was a difficulty about the Soviet–Turkish frontier and, as His Majesty's Government were allied with Turkey, he was very anxious to understand this question.

GENERALISSIMO STALIN replied that there were two questions.

First, the Straits. Under the Montreux Convention it was left to Turkey to decide whether there was a threat of war and whether to close the Straits and to control them. That was a difficult situation for Russia because Turkey thus had a right to hem her in and the Soviet Government wished to safeguard their liberty.

Secondly, there were certain provinces in Turkey inhabited by Georgians and Armenians which had been seized by Turkey, and it was necessary to restore, at least to some extent, the old frontier which existed in the time of the Czars because the Georgians and Armenians were putting forward claims against the Turkish Government. All talk of war against Turkey was rubbish.

In reply to MR. BEVIN's question as to how the matter could be settled GENERALISSIMO STALIN said it should be settled by negotiation either with Turkey or with the Allies.

In reply to MR. BEVIN's question as to what exactly the Soviet Government wanted, GENERALISSIMO STALIN said that the Soviet Government wished to regain the Georgian and Armenian portions of the provinces in question: they claimed, in fact, the old frontier which existed before the Treaty of 1921.

MR. BEVIN said that he understood that Russia had not then been in possession of these provinces for a very long period.

GENERALISSIMO STALIN said that it was true that this position dated only from 1870, but the population was Georgian and Armenian and had always been so.

MR. BEVIN then asked the Generalissimo to state what exactly he wanted in the Straits. There had originally been talk of a Soviet base there.

GENERALISSIMO STALIN said that this claim still stood.

MR. BEVIN asked whether that did not put Turkey in a difficulty, as the Soviet Government would be able to close the Straits.

GENERALISSIMO STALIN said that the Soviet Government would not have that right. Turkey was unable to defend herself and had shown during the war that she was afraid of everyone.

MR. BEVIN asked whether the Soviet intention was that all ships might pass through the Straits both in peace and in war.

GENERALISSIMO STALIN replied that that was so as regards merchant ships. The important thing to-day was to limit Turkey's right to close the Straits on her own authority.

MR. BEVIN asked what would be the situation if Turkey were at war, to which GENERALISSIMO STALIN replied that Turkey's interests should be placed first.

MR. BEVIN asked whether she could close the Straits, and GENERALISSIMO STALIN replied that she could and that those interested in the defence of the Straits should come to her aid.

MR. BEVIN said that he would be very interested to see definite proposals formulated by the Soviet Government so that he could consider whether there would be an advantage in calling a conference. He was anxious not to destroy Turkey's free and independent position.

M. MOLOTOV raised the point whether the question could be settled at the present Conference, and after some discussion it was agreed that that would probably not be possible, but MR. BEVIN expressed the hope that the Soviet Government would not necessitate the continuance of Turkish mobilisation.

GENERALISSIMO STALIN said that this mobilisation had been undertaken by Turkey on her own initiative, and when MR. BEVIN said that that was because Turkey was frightened of the Soviet Union, Generalissimo Stalin said that she need not be frightened.

MR. BEVIN then said he would like to raise the question of the Dodecanese. The Soviet Government had no interest there and His Majesty's Government would like to transfer the administration to Greece and to withdraw British troops. His Majesty's Government had no designs of any of the Dodecanese Islands.

GENERALISSIMO STALIN said that he would like time to think the matter over . . .

E Tenth meeting of the Conference, 23 December, 12 noon

... MR. BYRNES said that he agreed that the Commission's reports should be made to the Security Council but he believed that the formula proposed by M. Molotov was unwise. It would mean that a commission of eleven men representing eleven States would have to work under the direction of eleven other men representing the same States. The words in M. Molotov's amendment 'work under its direction' would cause misunderstanding. To avoid confusion, he thought it better that it should be left that the Commission would be directed to report to the Security Council once it had been set up, but that all possibility of doubt should be removed about the ability of the Commission to proceed with their work without waiting for directions from another body. As he saw it the Commission would be charged not only with providing a plan for the preservation of peace and security but also with providing a plan for the use of atomic energy for peaceful purposes. Whatever recommendations the Commission might make would in any case be reviewed by the Security Council in the light of the latter's function as guardian of peace and security. The Commission's work would in fact be limited to the making of recommendations to the Security Council.

M. MOLOTOV said that it went without saying that the United Nations Organisation and every country represented on it would be interested above all in knowing whether the interests of peace and security would be taken fully into account. Section II of his text provided that in appropriate cases the Security Council would transmit the reports of the Commission to the Assembly. Provision was also made for the publication of these reports in appropriate cases. But the establishment of the Commission independently of the Security Council would not be understood by the United Nations. Their task was to make every effort to ensure that atomic energy was used for humanitarian purposes. It was a difficult task but one worth working at. The attention of the United Nations would be chiefly focussed on the methods by which atomic energy could be used in the interests of peace and security and matters affecting peace and security were the responsibility of the Security Council. He accepted Mr. Byrnes's proposal that the Commission should be elected by the Assembly, since this would give satisfaction to the latter body. But it would not be understood if we failed to ensure that its work lay within the province of the Security Council. Such a failure would furthermore be in conflict with the terms of the Charter and would undermine the authority of the Security Council. Mr. Byrnes had said that the Commission would under the Soviet proposal have the same membership as would the Security Council. But it could be argued that there were many bodies set up under the United Nations Charter composed of all members of the United Nations and yet this fact was not an obstacle to their work. Moreover, there were other bodies which could be set up with the same membership as that of the Security Council. The actual personnel of the Commission might very well differ from that of the Security Council.

MR. BYRNES said that the United States proposal had provided that the Commission should be appointed by and should report to the Assembly, and the Soviet proposal had provided that reports should be made to the Security Council. He had surrendered his position and had agreed to the Soviet proposal. The difference between them therefore lay in the words in the second sentence of the Soviet proposal: 'The Commission should be attached to the Security Council and work under its direction.' He thought it wiser that the Commission should be established as he had originally proposed to do its work on its own, but with a requirement to report to the Security Council. So long as this requirement was included in the text Soviet wishes would be met.

MR. BEVIN said that they were all agreed that the Commission should be established by the Assembly. Part of its work would, however, be military and part would be industrial. If it was attached to the Security Council in the manner proposed by the Soviet Delegation, public opinion would think that it was only concerned with security. Of course, there might be matters affecting security about which the Security Council would want a special investigation to be made. He therefore had a preliminary suggestion to advance which he thought might solve the problem and meet the arguments advanced on both sides. He suggested that at the end of Section II it might be said that 'The Security Council shall have the power in appropriate cases to issue directions to the Commission on matters affecting security.' Section II might not be the right place in which to insert this phrase. He only advanced the suggestion as an attempt to solve the difficulty. It seemed to him that under the Soviet proposal, the Commission became a monopoly of the Security Council. No other body could issue directions to it at all. The phrase he proposed would leave it open to the Assembly to issue directions to the Commission on matters of industrial interest. The balance would be held between the two bodies and both claims would be satisfied . . .

M. MOLOTOV said it was not a question of reports but a question of the source from which the Commission would receive its directives. The Soviet Delegation believed that unless this responsibility was confided to the Security Council it would be impossible to settle the question. On no other basis would it be possible to give satisfactory answers to the questions which the Assembly would ask. It should be clearly shown from what quarter the Commission would receive its instructions. He hoped that it would be possible to find a formula to meet both points of view.

MR. BEVIN said that the phrase which he had suggested was precisely designed to that end.

M. MOLOTOV asked whether Mr. Bevin's phrase was designed to make it clear that on questions affecting security the Commission received its directions from the Security Council. If this was what Mr. Bevin had in mind it would not be difficult to agree on a formula.

MR. BEVIN said that the functions of the Security Council were clearly laid down in the Charter.

MR. BYRNES said that he thought they were all agreed that the Security Council had the primary responsibility on all matters affecting security. In the proposed terms of reference of the Commission all the types of directive were set forth which it might be necessary for the Commission to receive. The only work the Commission had to do was to make reports on the subjects there enumerated. He thought that if Mr. Bevin's proposal was adopted they would not be bothered by questions from the Assembly. The Assembly would in fact be more than satisfied. The Security Council would have a perfect right to issue directives to the Commission on certain types of question. But if they asked the Assembly to agree to establish the Commission in such a way as to work only under the direction of the Security Council they would have trouble. But in a further endeavour to meet M. Molotov's point of view he suggested that some such phrase as the following should be inserted in the text:

> In view of the responsibility of the Security Council for maintaining peace the Security Council shall issue directions to the Commission in matters affecting security.

M. MOLOTOV said that security was the aspect of atomic energy with which the whole of the United Nations were particularly concerned, and that security was the province of the Security Council. It was for this reason that the Commission should be firmly attached to the Security Council. It would still be able to make reports to other bodies on matters not affecting security, but he thought it right to put the security aspect in the forefront. Could they not agree in principle on this?

MR. BEVIN said that the phrase just read out by Mr. Byrnes did exactly this and he agreed with Mr. Byrnes's suggestion. Moreover he was doubtful whether it would be possible to provide that one organ of the United Nations should be 'attached' to another organ. There seemed to him to be two different approaches to the subject. He and Mr. Byrnes were prepared to agree that all reports should go to the Security Council and this met M. Molotov's point. But in view of the non-military aspect of atomic energy it would be difficult for the Assembly to accept a phraseology which 'attached' the Commission to the Security Council. He and Mr. Byrnes were trying to give M. Molotov what he wanted in the best manner that they could. He wished to be frank. There had been considerable feeling in the United Kingdom for attaching the Commission to the Assembly. He himself had opposed this and had taken the line that the first thing to be considered was the effect of the new discovery on the question of security. He had therefore obtained the agreement of His Majesty's Government to the idea that all reports of the Commission should go first to the Security Council. He had now gone further than this and had agreed that, in view of the duty of the Security Council to keep the peace, it should also be expressly recognised as responsible for issuing directions to the Commission on all matters affecting security. He was also very grateful to the United States Delegation for going so far also. He now wanted the Soviet Delegation, in a good international spirit, to come a little closer to their British and American colleagues.

MR. BYRNES said that he thought that the Assembly would never agree to 'attach' the Commission to the Security Council. There would be a natural feeling that the Assembly should be recognised as an important body and they would be interested in the humanitarian aspect of atomic energy. It might be possible to get the Assembly to agree to the Commission being required to report to the Security Council instead of to themselves and to make the Commission subject to the direction of the Security Council when matters affecting security arose. But it would be a lot to ask of them that they should agree to the Commission being attached to the Security Council. He was not willing to take a step which would be unacceptable to the Assembly.

M. MOLOTOV said that they were all anxious that not only the Security Council but also the Assembly should have a hand in the matter, but he was sure that the United Nations were considerably interested in the security aspect, although he did not wish to be a prophet and try to speak for other members of the United Nations. The Charter provided a special position for the Security Council, and this should be recognised in the text. The text could be discussed further, but meanwhile he thought it would be a good idea to deal with the next item . . .

F Meeting between Bevin and Stalin, 24 December, 7 p.m.

. . . GENERALISSIMO STALIN said that he noted that the British were not prepared to trust the Soviet in Tripolitania, to which Mr. Bevin replied that there was no question of lack of trust but a desire to avoid competition.

GENERALISSIMO STALIN said that, as he saw the situation, the United Kingdom had India and her possessions in the Indian Ocean in her sphere of interest: the United States had China and Japan, but the Soviet had nothing.

MR. BEVIN pointed out that the Russian sphere extended from Lubeck to Port Arthur.

As regards Indonesia, His Majesty's Government were determined to withdraw from there as soon as possible. British troops were due to leave Indo-China this week, their task there was finished and the Japanese had been completely disarmed. If a settlement could be reached between the Dutch and the Indonesians, British troops would be withdrawn also from there. British intentions were not so reprehensible as Generalissimo Stalin might think.

GENERALISSIMO STALIN said he was not particularly anxious to see the British leave certain territories. That might, indeed, be to the disadvantage of everyone. For instance, the presence of the British in Egypt during the war had been of considerable value.

MR. BEVIN said that His Majesty's Government had certain responsibilities in that region and must devise means for the defence of Egypt. But in matters of trade, &c., Egypt must be open to all the world. When we came to deal with that part of the world, seeing that Generalissimo Stalin recognised that the British had a duty to police it, he hoped that His Majesty's Government could count on the Generalissimo's sympathetic consideration.

GENERALISSIMO STALIN indicated assent.

Notes on selected British and Soviet diplomats

The following notes concentrate on the main posts held during the war

A. British

Baggallay, H. L.	Head of Eastern Department in 1940. Moved to Moscow Embassy in January 1941 and served there until his death in July 1943
Balfour, J. (later Sir John)	Head of American Department 1940-1. Served in Moscow Embassy 1943-5 with local rank of Minister, then moved to Washington
Brimelow, T. (later Lord Brimelow)	Served in Moscow Embassy 1942-5 with local rank of Third Secretary
Butler, N. (later Sir Nevile)	At Washington Embassy 1939-41. Head of North American Department 1941-4, then promoted Assistant Under-Secretary
Cadogan, Sir Alexander	Permanent Under-Secretary January 1938 - February 1946
Cavendish-Bentinck, V. (later Duke of Portland)	Head of Dominions Intelligence 1941-3; Head of Services Liaison Department 1944-5. Chairman of Joint Intelligence Committee 1944
Collier, Sir Laurence	Head of Northern Department 1937 - May 1941. Then Minister to Norwegian government-in-exile. Raised to Ambassador in May 1942
Coote, E. O.	Chargé d'Affaires in Moscow 1933-4. Served in Northern Department 1942-4
Coulson, J. E.	Seconded to War Cabinet Offices 1941-2. Returned to Foreign Office in August 1942. Head of Economic Relations Department 1945
Crosthwaite, M.	Served in Moscow Embassy 1943-6
Dean, P. (later Sir Patrick)	Joined Foreign Office in 1939. Became Assistant Legal Adviser. Made Head of German Department in 1946

Dew, A.	Served in Moscow Embassy 1938–40. Belgrade 1940–1. Northern Department 1941–5. Killed in air crash on way to Yalta Conference
Dixon, P. (later Sir Pierson)	Private Secretary to Eden and Bevin. November 1943 – December 1947
Harvey, O. (later Lord Harvey of Tasburgh)	Private Secretary to Eden 1941–3, then Assistant Under-Secretary 1943–6
Hasler, W. J.	Head of Relief Department 1945
Hood, Viscount Samuel	Transferred from Ministry of Information in September 1942. Served in Economic and Reconstruction Department until 1946
Howard, D. F.	Head of Southern Department 1941–5
Jebb, Gladwyn (later Lord Gladwyn)	Head of Economic and Reconstruction Department 1942–5. Chaired PHPS 1943–4. Executive Secretary of UN Preparatory Commission August – December 1945
Kerr, Sir Archibald Clark (later Lord Inverchapel)	Ambassador to China 1938–42. Ambassador in Moscow February 1942 – January 1946
Lockhart, Sir Robert Bruce	Served in Political Intelligence Department 1939–41. Liaison office with Czech government-in-exile 1940–1. Director-General of the Political Warfare Executive 1942–5
Malkin, Sir William	Legal Adviser to the Foreign Office 1929–45. Killed in air crash while returning from San Francisco Conference
Mallet, Sir Victor	Minister in Stockholm 1940–5
Millar, F. R. Hoyer (later Lord Inchyra)	Served in Washington Embassy 1939–44. Head of Western Department 1945–7
Nichols, P.	Head of Southern Department 1939–41. Minister, then Ambassador, to Czech government-in-exile 1941–8
O'Malley, Sir Owen	Minister in Budapest 1939–41. Ambassador to London Poles 1943–5
Rendel, Sir George	Minister, then Ambassador, to Yugoslav government-in-exile 1941–3. Attached to UNRRA February 1944 – January 1945
Roberts, Sir Frank	Head of Central Department 1943–5. Minister at Moscow Embassy 1945–8
Rose, E. M.	In Southern Department 1941–5. With French Committee of National Liberation June – November 1944
Sargent, Sir Orme	Deputy Under-Secretary September 1939 – February 1946. Succeeded Cadogan as Permanent Under-Secretary
Seeds, Sir William	Ambassador in Moscow, January – December 1939

Strang, Sir William (later Lord Strang)	British representative on the European Advisory Commission November 1943 – June 1945
Troutbeck, Sir J. M.	First Head of German Department 1945–6
Vansittart, Sir Robert (later Lord Vansittart)	Permanent Under-Secretary 1930–7. Chief Diplomatic Adviser 1938–41
Ward, J. G. (later Sir John)	Central Department 1941–2. General Department 1942–3. Economic and Reconstruction Department 1943–6
Warner, Christopher (later Sir Christopher)	Head of Northern Department 1941–6 in succession to Collier. Previously in Political Intelligence Department of which he was head for a short time
Wilson, Geoffrey (later Sir Geoffrey)	Northern Department 1942–6
Young, W. H.	Held various consular posts in Iran. Served in Eastern Department of the Foreign Office December 1941 – November 1945

B. Soviet

Bogomolov, A. Y.	Ambassador to Allied governments in London 1941–43, to French Committee of National Liberation 1943–4, to France 1944–50
Gromyko, A. A.	Counsellor at Washington Embassy 1939–43. Then Ambassador until 1946
Gusev, F. T.	Envoy to Canada 1942–3. Ambassador to Britain 1943–46
Kollontai, Alexandra	Envoy to Sweden 1930–45
Lebedev, V. Z.	Ambassador to Allied governments in London 1943–4
Litvinov, M. M.	People's Commissar for Foreign Affairs July 1930 – May 1939. Ambassador to United States 1941–3
Maisky, I. M.	Ambassador to Britain 1932–43
Molotov, V. M.	People's Commissar for Foreign Affairs May 1939 – March 1949
Oumansky, K. A.	Ambassador to United States 1939–41. Ambassador to Mexico 1943–5
Sobelev, A. A.	Counsellor at the London Embassy 1942–5
Vinogradov, S. A.	Ambassador to Turkey 1940–8
Vyshinsky, A. Y.	First Deputy Commissar for Foreign Affairs 1940–6

The People's Commissariat for Foreign Affairs was renamed the Ministry of Foreign Affairs in 1946

Notes

1 Prelude: Anglo-Soviet relations to the beginning of 1941

1 For a general survey of Anglo-Soviet relations since 1917 see F. S. Northedge and A. Wells, *Britain and Soviet Communism: the Impact of a Revolution* (1982). On the beginnings of these relations there is S. White, *Britain and the Bolshevik Revolution: A Study in the Politics of Diplomacy 1920-24* (1979).

2 *Documents on British Foreign Policy* (*DBFP*), Second Series (1972), vol. 12, pp. 438-42.

3 Lord Avon, *Facing the Dictators* (1962), pp. 144-63; *DBFP*, Second Series, vol. 12, pp. 771-91; R. Manne, 'The Foreign Office and the Failure of Anglo-Soviet Rapprochement', *Journal of Contemporary History*, vol. 16 (1981), pp. 725-56.

4 Memorandum by Orme Sargent, 13 August 1936, FO 371/20534. Cited in J. Edwards, *The British Government and the Spanish Civil War* (1979), pp. 32-3. See also pp. 145-6 for further evidence of Sargent's suspicion of Russia.

5 I. K. Koblyakov, *USSR: For Peace against Aggression 1933-41* (Moscow, 1976), p. 11.

6 S. Aster, *The Making of the Second World War* (1973), especially pp. 260-319; N. Gibbs, *Grand Strategy: Rearmament Policy* (1974), vol. 1, pp. 719-60; Lord Strang, 'The Moscow Negotiations, 1939' in D. N. Dilks (ed.), *Retreat from Power: Studies in Britain's Foreign Policy of the Twentieth Century* (1981), vol. 1, pp. 170-86; R. Manne, 'The British Decision for Alliance with Russia', *Journal of Contemporary History*, vol. 9 (1974), pp. 3-26, and the same author's 'Some British Light on the Nazi-Soviet Pact', *European Studies Review*, vol. 11 (1981), pp. 83-102; *DBFP*, Third Series (1952-4), vols. 5, 6, 7.

7 D. N. Dilks (ed.), *The Diaries of Sir Alexander Cadogan 1938-1945* (1971), pp. 180-2. J. Harvey (ed.), *The Diplomatic Diaries of Oliver Harvey 1937-40* (1970). On the failure to anticipate the Nazi-Soviet Pact, see F. H. Hinsley *et al. British Intelligence in the Second World War* (1979), vol. 1, p. 46.

8 *Soviet Peace Efforts on the Eve of World War Two* (Moscow, 1976), p. 426. This is an abbreviated version of a two-volume collection of documents which appeared in 1973. For a commentary see J. Herman, 'Soviet Peace Efforts on the Eve of World War Two: a Review of the Soviet Documents', *Journal of*

Contemporary History, vol. 15 (1980), pp. 577–602. For German overtures see *Documents on German Foreign Policy* (*DGFP*), Series D (1956), vol. 7 *passim*.

9 Dilks, *Cadogan*, pp. 217, 219. Harvey, *Diplomatic Diaries*, p. 323.

10 A. Polonsky (ed.), *The Great Powers and the Polish Question, 1941–45* (1976), pp. 16–17.

11 R. A. C. Parker, 'Britain, France and Scandinavia, 1939–40', *History*, vol. 61 (1976), pp. 369–87; D. N. Dilks, 'Great Britain and Scandinavia in the Phoney War', *Scandinavian Journal of History*, vol. 2 (1977), pp. 29–51; J. A. Bayer, 'British Policy towards the Russo-Finnish Winter War 1939–40', *Canadian Journal of History*, vol. 16 (1981), pp. 27–65; E. L. Woodward, *British Foreign Policy in the Second World War* (1970), vol. 1, chaps. 2, 3, 4, *passim*. On British reluctance to get involved in war with Russia see Dilks, *Cadogan*, pp. 235, 253, 259, 263; Harvey, *Diplomatic Diaries*, pp. 337, 345.

12 *DGFP*, Series D (1954), vol. 8, pp. 588–94, 718–22, 752–4. The text of the agreement is at pp. 762–9.

13 For Anglo-Soviet relations from May to December 1940 see Woodward, vol. 1, chap. 15. On Cripps see H. Hanak, 'Sir Stafford Cripps as British Ambassador in Moscow, May 1940 – June 1941', *English Historical Review*, vol. 94 (1979), pp. 48–70; FO 371/32997 is the annual review of 1940 by the Moscow Embassy. Because it was not written until after the evacuation of the diplomatic corps from Moscow to Kuibyshev in October 1941 it lacked adequate documentation and was not included in the Foreign Office confidential print. The same was true of its successor for 1941, FO 371/33026.

14 For Soviet–Japanese relations in 1940 and 1941 see Hosaya Chihiro in J. W. Morley (ed.), *The Fateful Choice: Japan's Advance into South-East Asia 1939–41* (New York, 1980), pp. 13–114; G. A. Lensen, *The Strange Neutrality: Soviet-Japanese Relations during the Second World War* (Tallahassee, Florida, 1972), pp. 1–20.

15 *DGFP*, Series D, (1961), vol. 11, pp. 550–70, 714–15.

16 For Russian dislike of Cripps see FO 371/29475, report from Mallet in Stockholm, 24 January 1941.

2 Developments in 1941 to Eden's Moscow visit

1 FO 371/24849 and 29463; Woodward, vol. 1, pp. 497–8; Dilks, *Cadogan*, p. 347.

2 FO 371/29463. On 29 January Maisky was asked to report to the Soviet government on the lack of consideration shown to Cripps. Hanak, *EHR*, vol. 94 (1979), p. 68.

3 FO 371/29463 and 33026; Woodward, vol. 1, p. 601.

4 FO 371/39500. On 9 March Cripps recapitulated his views as put to Eden in Ankara; Collier minute of 27 March arguing against Cripps, FO 371/29464; Sargent minutes of 28 March and 9 April; Collier minute of 7 April; Cadogan minute of 10 April; Eden minute of 15 April. Dilks, *Cadogan*, p. 372. Lord Avon, *The Reckoning* (1965), p. 263.

5 Hanak, *EHR*, vol. 94 (1979), p. 68. Woodward vol. 1, pp. 611 and 607–9. FO 371/29465.

6 FO 371/29465. On the other hand, in Avon, *The Reckoning*, p. 265, Eden appears
   to attach no great importance to the Soviet–Japanese pact.
7 Hinsley *et al.*, vol. 1, pp. 437–80 on British intelligence about German plans
   against Russia from January to June 1941; Woodward, vol. 1, p. 612; FO
   371/29501; *Foreign Relations of the United States* (*FRUS*), 1941 (Washington,
   1958), vol. 1, pp. 144, 147.
8 Dilks, *Cadogan*, pp. 381–2; FO 371/29465 for the discussion of 28 May; Dilks,
   Cadogan, p. 385 on the meeting of 2 June. FO 371/29466 for Coote minute of
   8 June; Woodward, vol. 1, p. 595 and 621–2 for Eden's conversation with
   Maisky on 13 June. See also, Avon, *The Reckoning*, pp. 268–9.
9 Hinsley *et al.*, vol. 1, pp. 481–2; Dilks, *Cadogan*, p. 390; FO 371/29561 for
   Cavendish-Bentinck's comments.
10 FO 371/29471, Warner minute of 2 November, minutes by Warner, Sargent and
   Cadogan of 12 November, Eden minute of 30 November.
11 FO 371/33026 for background on the economic agreement. This is the review
   of the Soviet Union for 1941. Like its predecessor it was not included in the
   confidential print series; FO 371/29579 for papers on the Beaverbrook–Harriman
   mission. CAB 92/1 for the origins of ASE; J. D. Langer, 'The Harriman-
   Beaverbrook Mission and the Debate over Unconditional Aid for the Soviet
   Union, 1941' in W. Laqueur (ed.), *The Second World War: Essays in Military
   and Political History* (1982), pp. 300–19; J. Beaumont, *Comrades in Arms:
   British Aid to Russia 1941–45* (1980), pp. 23–60; W. A. Harriman and E. Abel,
   Special Envoy to Churchill and Stalin 1941–46 (1976), pp. 82–101.
12 Polonsky, pp. 18–19; Woodward, vol. 2, pp. 23–7; J. Beaumont, 'Great Britain
   and the Rights of Neutral Countries: the Case of Iran, 1941', *Journal of Contemporary History*, vol. 16 (1981), pp. 213–26.
13 H. Hanak, 'Sir Stafford Cripps as British Ambassador in Moscow June 1941 –
   January 1942', *English Historical Review*, vol. 97 (1982), pp. 332–4 and 334 fn.
   Avon, *The Reckoning*, p. 273; Woodward, vol. 2, pp. 11–13; FO 371/29466 for
   Cripps's conversation with Molotov on 28 June; FO 371/29467 for the agreement of 12 July, and see Sargent minute of 9 July.
14 J. Harvey (ed.), *The War Diaries of Oliver Harvey 1941–45* (1978), pp. 29, 34–5.
   CAB 127/64 for Eden to Cripps 25 August and Cripps to Eden 14 September.
   For Cripps's initial praise of Beaverbrook and Harriman see his telegram to
   Eden of 2 October, FO 954/24B.
15 FO 371/33026 on possible destruction of the oilfields. Had the 1941 survey been
   printed this section would have been deleted; Dilks, *Cadogan*, p. 408 on Russian
   military situation. For the views of Ismay and Sargent see K. Young (ed.),
   The Diaries of Sir Robert Bruce Lockhart 1939–45 (1980), pp. 127–28.
16 FO 371/29470, Eden conversation with Maisky 12 November. Minutes by Dew
   of 15 November and Warner of 17 November; FO 371/29471, Warner minute of
   12 November; FO 371/29472, Warner minute of 23 November; Dilks, *Cadogan*,
   p. 412.
17 For the possibility of Eden visiting Moscow see Dilks, *Cadogan*, p. 405; Harvey,
   War Diaries, pp. 27, 34, 37, 61; Avon, *The Reckoning*, p. 282.

3 Eden's visit to Moscow and the Anglo-Soviet treaty

1 FO 371/29472, Eden memorandum for Winant of 4 December; *FRUS*, 1941, vol. 1, pp. 194–5, Hull to Winant 6 December; Cordell Hull, *Memoirs* (1948), vol. 2, pp. 1165–6.

2 P. Lowe, 'The Soviet Union in Britain's Far Eastern Policy, 1941' in I. Nish (ed.), *The Russian Problem in East Asia* (1981), pp. 27–43; Lensen, pp. 78–92.

3 Dilks, *Cadogan*, p. 422; Harvey, *War Diaries*, pp. 75–7; Prem 3, 394/4; Churchill to Eden, 21 December; compare Churchill to Attlee 20 December; Woodward, vol. 2, p. 235.

4 FO 181/963, Cripps interview with Molotov, 19 December; Avon, *The Reckoning*, p. 299; *FRUS*, 1942, vol. 3, pp. 490–1; CAB 65/29, WM(42)1. For extracts from Eden's first meeting with Stalin see Avon, *The Reckoning*, pp. 290–4. For extracts from the second meeting see Woodward, vol. 2, pp. 226–34.

5 FO 371/33133, Dixon minute of 8 January 1942; Howard minute of 11 January; Sargent minute of 11 January; Eden minute of 12 January. FO 371/32740, Sargent minute of 20 January attacking *The Times* for advocating recognition of a Soviet sphere of influence in Eastern Europe; V. Rothwell, *Britain and the Cold War 1941–47* (1982), p. 180 *et seq.* on British attitudes to the Czech government; pp. 193–5 on the Yugoslav–Greek pact; E. Barker, *British Policy in South-East Europe in the Second World War* (1976), pp. 130–2; Young, *Bruce Lockhart*, p. 134.

6 Harvey, *War Diaries*, pp. 85–91; Dilks, *Cadogan*, p. 432; FO 954/25A, Beaverbrook to Eden, 3 March.

7 FO 954/25A, Eden to Baggallay, 12 and 26 February; CAB 127/75, unsigned Foreign Office memorandum dated only February, 1942; *FRUS*, 1942, vol. 3, pp. 504–12, Hull to Roosevelt 4 February, pp. 527–8, 530–1, reports by Matthews on conversations with Cadogan and Law; Dilks, *Cadogan*, p. 437; Harvey, *War Diaries*, pp. 93, 102, 109, 111, 112; Young, *Bruce Lockhart*, p. 150.

8 FO 954/25A, Eden to Clark Kerr, 17, 23 and 27 March; 8, 13 and 16 April; *FRUS*, 1942, vol. 3, pp. 545 and 552; Dilks, *Cadogan*, pp. 443 and 446; Harvey, *War Diaries*, pp. 112–16; Sir Winston Churchill, *The Second World War* (1951), vol. 4, p. 293; *Stalin's Correspondence with Roosevelt and Truman* (New York, 1965), pp. 22–3; *Stalin's Correspondence with Churchill and Attlee* (New York, 1965), p. 44.

9 FO 371/32740, Sargent to Eden, 17 April; Malkin minute of 18 April; Dew minute of 25 April; Sargent minute of 28 April; Cadogan minute of 28 April; Eden minute of 30 April. Prem 3, 399/8, Harvey Watt to Churchill 24 April; Eden minute 28 April; Dilks, *Cadogan*, p. 449; Harvey, *War Diaries*, pp. 118, 120; E. Barker, *Churchill and Eden at War* (1978), p. 240.

10 CAB 66/24, WP(42) 193, 198, 198 (revise), 218; CAB 127/75, Eden to Cripps, 18 May; Woodward, vol. 2, pp. 248–9; *FRUS*, 1942, vol. 3, p. 559; Dilks, *Cadogan*, pp. 450–5; Harvey, *War Diaries*, pp. 121–130; FO 954/25A, unsigned memo of 25 May (use of the first person indicates it is by Eden); CAB 65/30, WP(42) 220, Eden's review of the negotiations; Prem 3, 399/8, Simon to Churchill, 8 May; Desmond Morton's account of interview with Cardinal

Hinsley, 21 May; James Stuart to Churchill, 22 May; Young, *Bruce Lockhart*, p. 161 on Eden's surprise at opposition to the treaty and p. 179 on hostility inside the Foreign Office; Avon, *The Reckoning*, pp. 327–9 does not mention the draft of 6 May.

11 V. M. Mastny, *Russia's Road to the Cold War* (New York, 1979), pp. 58–9; Young, *Bruce Lockhart*, p. 173; Rothwell, p. 186.

12 Prem 3, 399/4, record of 7th meeting between Eden and Molotov at 3.30 p.m. on 9 June.

4 From the Anglo-Soviet treaty to the Russian break with Poland

1 Prem 3, 399/6; Eden to Churchill, 25 January 1944.

2 *FRUS*, 1942, vol. 3, pp. 566–83 for Molotov's talks with Roosevelt, pp. 593–4 for the communiqué. For Foreign Office dismay see FO 371/32909, Cadogan minute of 30 June; FO 371/31513, Warner minute of 17 August.

3 Churchill, vol. 4, p. 305; Woodward, vol. 2, pp. 260–2; FO 371/32909, Clark Kerr's telegram of 28 June; Prem 3, 76/1, telegram of 5 July.

4 R. E. Sherwood, *The White House Papers of Harry L. Hopkins* (1949), vol. 2, pp. 581–2; CAB 79/22 JP(42) 670, 14 July; CAB 65/31 WM(42) 95, 24 July; M. Howard, *Grand Strategy: August 1942 – September 1943* (1972), vol. 4, pp. xv–xxv, Prologue, 'The Decision for Torch'.

5 For a more detailed account of Churchill's first visit to Moscow see G. Ross, 'Operation Bracelet: Churchill in Moscow, 1942' in Dilks, *Retreat from Power*, vol. 2, pp. 101–19.

6 On the exchange of technical information see for example FO 371/43412, Pott minute of 18 May 1944; FO 371/47847, minutes by Galsworthy of 31 December 1944, 8, 10 and 14 January 1945; FO 371/47849, Warner to Ministry of Production, 29 April 1945; FO 371/47850, Lyttleton to Churchill, 2 June 1945, Churchill to Lyttleton, 18 June 1945; FO 371/47911, Report by Brigadier Firebrace on work of the Russian Liaison Group, October 1945, Appendix E.

7 Beaumont, *Comrades in Arms*, pp. 125–6; Prem 3, 392/3, *passim;* Woodward, vol. 2, p. 566; FO 371/43449, Review of the Soviet Union for 1943; *FRUS* 1942, vol. 3, p. 681, Hurley to Roosevelt, 29 December.

8 CAB 79/21 COS(42) 178, 13 June; Hinsley *et al.*, vol. 2, pp. 98–105; CAB 79/22 COS(42) 226, 3 August. FO 181/969 Clark Kerr to Eden, 27 September on Oumansky's conversation with Cowles; Young, *Bruce Lockhart*, pp. 212, 214, 217; DO 121/12, Clark Kerr's talk.

9 *Stalin's Correspondence with Churchill and Attlee*, pp. 70 and 72; *FRUS*, 1942, vol. 3, p. 464, Henderson to Hull, 15 October; Woodward, vol. 2, pp. 278–80; Young, *Bruce Lockhart*, p. 208; FO 371/26954, Cadogan minute of 29 December; *FRUS*, 1942, vol. 3, p. 475; Mastny, *Russia's Road to the Cold War*, p. 74; Hinsley *et al.*, vol. 2, p. 615 fn.

10 Young, *Bruce Lockhart*, p. 210; Harvey, *War Diaries*, pp. 186, 190; FO 181/969, Baggallay to Eden, 27 December; *Stalin's Correspondence with Churchill and Attlee*, p. 80; FO 181/969, Baggallay to Warner, 14 December.

11 Avon, *The Reckoning*, p. 341; Harvey, *War Diaries*, pp. 162–3; FO 371/31513, Warner minute of 9 July.

12 FO 371/31525, *passim;* Prem 4, 100/7, *passim;* Woodward, vol. 5, pp. 10–18, including text of the January 1943 memorandum.

13 FO 371/31535, minutes by Jebb (24 October), Roberts (27 October), Dixon (28 October), Dew (28 October), Warner (28 October), Ronald (29 October), Roberts (1 November), Wilson (2 November), Warner (4 November), Sargent (5 December).

14 FO 371/32740, memo from Barrington Ward to Eden, 16 January 1942, Sargent minute of 20 January.

15 For Churchill's reaction see FO 800/301, Warner to Clark Kerr, 16 March 1943; Young, *Bruce Lockhart*, p. 251. On the improved atmosphere in Moscow see FO 371/36954, Clark Kerr to Foreign Office, 12 and 17 April.

16 Polonsky, pp. 123–7; FO 181/978, Clark Kerr to Foreign Office, 30 April, minute by Reed 8 May; Dilks, *Cadogan*, p. 523; Harvey, *War Diaries*, pp. 249–50.

5 From Katyn to Tehran

1 *Stalin's Correspondence with Churchill and Attlee*, pp. 86–112 *passim;* Dilks, *Cadogan*, p. 515.

2 Dilks, *Cadogan*, p. 517; FO 371/36954 for Clark Kerr's interview with Stalin on 12 April and optimistic report of 17 April; Woodward, vol. 2, p. 560 fn. on peace rumours; FO 371/34186, Halifax to Foreign Office on Litvinov's recall and letter from Russell to Dew, 1 May.

3 FO 371/37010 for Foreign Office reactions to dissolution of the Comintern; FO 371/36983 for Butler's account of conversation with Maisky on 2 June and Eden's minute of 16 June.

4 *Stalin's Correspondence with Roosevelt and Truman*, pp. 67–71; *Stalin's Correspondence with Churchill and Attlee*, pp. 136–41; Woodward, vol. 2, pp. 561–2; FO 181/980, Clark Kerr to Foreign Office 1 July and Cadogan to Clark Kerr 3 July; FO 371/36955, Clark Kerr to Warner 21 June; FO 371/36971 and 43449 on revival of Soviet propaganda about second front; Woodward, vol. 2, p. 560 fn.; Mastny, *Russia's Road to the Cold War*, pp. 79–80.

5 Prem 3, 172/1, Eden to Churchill 28 July; Clark Kerr to Eden, 30 July; Eden to Churchill 31 July; Churchill to Eden, 31 July; Young, *Bruce Lockhart*, pp. 251 and 248–50.

6 FO 181/980, Clark Kerr to Foreign Office, 24 August; Harvey, *War Diaries*, pp. 286–7, 291, 302; *Stalin's Correspondence with Churchill and Attlee*, pp. 148–9; FO 371/37025 for aide-mémoire of 14 September; *Stalin's Correspondence with Churchill and Attlee*, pp. 171–3; Dilks, *Cadogan*, p. 568.

7 CAB 92/2, ASE meetings of 14 and 30 December; FO 341/36928 and Prem 3, 396/1A for cancellation of Tizard mission; Prem 3, 395/18, Eden to Churchill, 1 April 1942; FO 371/36970, Clark Kerr to Warner, 22 July 1943; Warner minute to Cadogan, 4 August; FO 800/301, Clark Kerr to Warner, 20 June; Clark Kerr to Warner, 29 July.

8 FO 371/34339, report of conversation between Bogomolov and Benes; Soviet *aide-mémoire* of 26 July; Prem 3, 355/6, Eden's paper for Cabinet; Woodward, vol. 2, pp. 595-7.
9 The British records are to be found in FO 371/37031. These can be compared with the American records in *FRUS*, 1943, vol. 1, pp. 513-781. These include some material on military matters which was excluded from the Foreign Office records. For accounts by participants see Avon, *The Reckoning*, pp. 410-18; Hull, *Memoirs*, vol. 2, pp. 1274-91; Harriman and Abel, *Special Envoy*, pp. 234-44; Lord Ismay, *Memoirs* (1960), pp. 321-31. For comment on the significance of the conference see Rothwell, pp. 108-11 and Mastny, *Russia's Road to the Cold War*, pp. 111-22.
10 FO 800/409, Eden to Cadogan, 1 November on significance of EAC; Prem 3, 136/3, Eden to Churchill, 27 November, on importance of making EAC effective; Woodward, vol. 2, p. 574 on British personnel in North Russia; FO 371/36936, minutes of ASE meeting of 17 November for Eden's promise; FO 371/34340, Eden to Foreign Office, 24 October, on Soviet-Czech treaty; Cadogan's reply on 26 October; Eden to Foreign Office, 29 October; Harvey, *War Diaries*, p. 313; FO 800/301, notes by Eden and Clark Kerr on 24 October; FO 371/37031, p. 42 of the British records has a footnote giving the text of the exchange of letters between Eden and Molotov; FO 371/30340, Sargent minute of 29 November with undated comment by Eden. The Soviet-Czech treaty was signed on 12 December; see FO 371/43449, review of the Soviet Union for 1943; FO 371/38920, Eden to Macmillan, 30 December 1943, on his attitude to the treaty.
11 For British records of Tehran see CAB 66/45 and Prem 3, 136, *passim*. The American records are in *FRUS, Conferences at Cairo and Teheran 1943* (Washington, 1963). The Soviet records published in *The Teheran, Yalta and Potsdam Conferences* (Moscow, 1969), are restricted to the plenary sessions. Churchill's account is in *The Second World War*, vol. 5, pp. 302-60. See also Avon, *The Reckoning*, pp. 426-8; Dilks, *Cadogan*, pp. 579-81; Ismay, pp. 337-41; Harriman and Abel, *Special Envoy*, pp. 262-83; C. E. Bohlen *Witness to History* (1973), pp. 136-51; on the Italian fleet see the selection of correspondence in Prem 3, 240/3. There is a summary of the episode in Woodward, vol. 2, pp. 604-11. For later developments see FO 371/43276, A. V. Alexander to Eden, 16 June 1944; FO 371/43277, Alexander to Eden, 5 July 1944; Warner to Clark Kerr, 21 July.

6 **From Tehran to Yalta**

1 Prem 3, 172/5, Eden to Churchill, 2 November 1943; FO 181/979, Clark Kerr to the Foreign Office, 6 November; Prem 3, 399/6, Churchill to Eden 16 January 1944; CAB 65/41, WM(44)8, 18 January. On Benes see FO 371/38920, Killearn to Foreign Office, 1 January; Balfour to Foreign Office, 12 January; FO 371/38931, Macmillan to Foreign Office, 4 January; Nichols to Roberts 27 January; Young, *Bruce Lockhart*, p. 288.
2 FO 371/43359, Balfour to Foreign Office, 17 January, minutes by Warner and

Wilson, 26 January; FO 371/43304, Clark Kerr to Foreign Office, 13 February; Dilks, *Cadogan*, p. 597.

3 Young, *Bruce Lockhart*, p. 285; Harvey, *War Diaries*, pp. 330, 334-5; *Stalin's Correspondence with Churchill and Attlee*, pp. 207, 212-13; Polonsky, pp. 23-33, 175-92; FO 371/43289, Churchill to Eden, 1 April. For background on Allied discussion of Polish frontiers see T. Sharpe, 'The Origins of the Teheran Formula on Polish Frontiers', *Journal of Contemporary History*, vol. 12 (1977), pp. 381-91.

4 FO 371/43304, Eden minutes of 31 March and 3 April; Prem 3, 485/8, Churchill to Eden, 31 March; CAB 65/46, WM(44)32, 3 April; FO 371/41823, Clark Kerr to Foreign Office on the Sakhalin agreements, 16 March and 3 April; Churchill to Eden, 3 April; summary of minutes by Northern and Far Eastern Departments; Churchill to Cadogan, 23 April, Eden to Churchill 27 April.

5 Prem 3, 66/7, Churchill to Eden, 4 May, Eden to Churchill, 9 May; Young, *Bruce Lockhart*, pp. 304-5, 309.

6 FO 371/40171, Pink to Young, 5 April 1944, Young minute of 20 April.

7 Barker, *British Policy in South-East Europe*, pp. 229-39, 234-35; Barker, *Churchill and Eden at War*, p. 278; FO 371/40729, Eden minute of 12 May.

8 Prem 3, 66/7, Eden to Clark Kerr, 18 May; Eden to Churchill, 30 May; CAB 65/42, WM(44)65, 18 May; *FRUS*, 1944, vol. 5, pp. 112-31; Hull, *Memoirs*, vol. 2, pp. 1451-8; Prem 3, 66/7, Eden interviews with Gusev, 19 June and 8 July; Churchill to Eden, 1 August, Eden to Churchill, 8 August.

9 Polonsky, p. 34; Rothwell, pp. 169-70; *Stalin's Correspondence with Churchill and Attlee*, p. 241; Churchill, vol. 6, pp. 113-28; for general background on the Warsaw rising see J. M. Ciechanowski, *The Warsaw Rising of 1944* (1974); Mastny, *Russia's Road to the Cold War*, pp. 186-95 on the Slovak rising.

10 Barker, *British Policy in South-East Europe*, pp. 220-1; FO 371/56883, review of the Soviet Union for 1944; FO 181/987, Clark Kerr to Foreign Office, 9 September; CAB 66/51, WP(44)304; FO 371/43335, Sargent minute of 22 June; CAB 66/53, WP(44)436, and see Woodward, vol. 3, pp. 123-31 for a lengthy summary of this paper.

11 CAB 87/68, Soviet proposals for an International Security Organisation, 12 August, covering memorandum by Eden, 5 September. On the development of Foreign Office attitudes to the German problem see Rothwell, pp. 21-73.

12 F. L. Loewenheim, H. D. Langley and M. Jonas (eds.), *Roosevelt and Churchill: Their Secret Wartime Correspondence* (1975), p. 580; *Stalin's Correspondence with Roosevelt and Truman*, pp. 162-3; Harriman and Abel, *Special Envoy*, pp. 354-8; Churchill, vol. 6, pp. 201-3; B. R. Kuniholm, *The Origins of the Cold War in the Near East: Great Power Conflict and Diplomacy in Iran, Turkey and Greece* (Guildford, 1980), pp. 107-8; *FRUS*, 1944, vol. 4, pp. 1009-26; see especially memorandum from Matthews to Roosevelt, 16 October, p. 1018.

13 Prem 3, 66/7, memorandum by Churchill, 12 October; Prem 3, 512/9, Sargent to Eden, 11 October; Eden to Sargent 12 October; Prem 3, 434/2, record of meeting at 3 p.m. on 11 October; Kuniholm, p. 225 for summary table of negotiating positions; Young, *Bruce Lockhart*, p. 358.

14 Woodward, vol. 3, pp. 351, 146-53; Harriman and Abel, *Special Envoy*, pp. 363-4; Mastny, *Russia's Road to the Cold War*, pp. 207-12; Polonsky, pp.

36–7; Avon, *The Reckoning*, pp. 482–88; Rothwell, pp. 128–36 and 171–3; Barker, *British Policy in South-East Europe*, pp. 144–7; J. R. Deane, *The Strange Alliance* (1947), pp. 243–50; D. Carlton, *Anthony Eden: Biography* (1981), pp. 242–6; A. Resis, 'The Churchill–Stalin Secret Percentages Agreement on the Balkans, Moscow, October 1944', *American Historical Review*, vol. 83 (1978), pp. 368–87; FO 371/43306, Dixon (Cairo) to Ridsdale, 22 October.

15 Loewenheim *et al.*, pp. 602, 607; FO 371/40424, Ward minute of 17 March; Young, *Bruce Lockhart*, p. 331.

16 Loewenheim *et al.*, pp. 619, 624, 628 (Roosevelt to Churchill on 13 December warning that he could not give public support); T. M. Campbell and G. C. Herring (eds.), *The Diaries of Edward R. Stettinius 1943–46* (New York, 1975), pp. 191–2, 196; Woodward, vol. 3, pp. 410–24, 457–66; Churchill, vol. 6, pp. 251–66; Carlton, pp. 248–50; T. H. Anderson, *The United States, Great Britain and the Cold War 1944–47* (Columbia, Missouri, 1981), pp. 19–27.

17 Prem 3, 136/3, Eden to Churchill 27 November 1943; FO 800/411, Cadogan, Redman and Kirby to Bridges, 28 November, on McCloy's suspicions of the EAC. There is a summary of the EAC's activities in Prem 3, 137/1. For American records see *FRUS*, 1944, vol. 1, pp. 1–433. See also Lord Strang, *At Home and Abroad* (1956), pp. 201–25, and T. Sharpe, *The Wartime Alliance and the Zonal Division of Germany* (Oxford, 1975), pp. 56–101.

18 FO 371/43351, Clark Kerr to Foreign Office, 10 May; minutes by Wilson and Warner on 19 May, by Coulson and Ronald on 31 May; FO 371/43352, Clark Kerr to Foreign Office 28 June on conversation between Gifford and Krutikov; FO 371/43353, Clark Kerr to Foreign Office, 14 September; Beaumont, *Comrades in Arms*, pp. 177–82; G. C. Herring, *Aid to Russia 1941–46* (1973), pp. 152–9; D. Acheson, *Present at the Creation* (1970), pp. 85–6.

19 FO 371/36970 for Foreign Office criticism of service attitudes to Russia as of December 1943; minutes by Warner (16 December), Cavendish-Bentinck (16 December), Cadogan (22 December) and Eden (24 December); FO 371/43288, Wilson minutes of 18 and 19 January 1944 criticising Martel; FO 371/43361, more criticism of Martel by Cavendish-Bentinck, 4 February and Cadogan 10 February; FO 371/43284 for initial optimism about Burrows, Warner 17 and 22 February, Cavendish-Bentinck (24 February), Eden to Cadogan 24 February; FO 371/43289, Burrows to War Office 15 and 24 April; Burrows to War Office 3 May with minutes by Pott (6 May), Wilson (12 May), Eden (17 May); FO 371/43290, Clark Kerr to Foreign Office 13 July; Young, *Bruce Lockhart*, p. 335; Prem 3, 396/5, Clark Kerr to Eden, 25 September; Harriman and Abel *Special Envoy*, p. 352.

20 Lord Gladwyn, *Memoirs* (1972), pp. 131–2, 137, 143–4; FO 371/40740, minute by Jebb of 19 February; CAB 81/45, 'Basic Assumptions for Staff Studies of Post-War Strategical Problems', 7 June 1944.

21 FO 371/40740, minutes by Sargent and Cadogan of 9 June; FO 371/43336, informal meeting of 4 October between Eden and Chiefs of Staff; G. Ross, 'Foreign Office Attitudes to the Soviet Union 1941–45' in W. Laqueur (ed.), *The Second World War*, pp. 528–32; Rothwell, pp. 114–23.

7 From Yalta to Potsdam

1 Prem 3, 397/3, Ismay minute, 5 January; Eden to Churchill, 27 January and the latter's reply on 28 January. FO 800/414, Eden to Churchill, 28 January on Russian objectives at Yalta. Avon, *The Reckoning*, pp. 507-9; Churchill, vol. 6, pp. 341-2; Rothwell, pp. 480-1, on British enthusiasm for securing Soviet entry; C. Thorne, *Allies of a Kind* (1978), pp. 408-16 on plans for British participation on the attack on Japan.

2 FO 800/414, Cadogan to Eden, 1 January; Eden to Churchill, 4 January; Avon, *The Reckoning*, pp. 404-5; Dilks, *Cadogan*, pp. 692-3; Young, *Bruce Lockhart*, pp. 386, 390; Harvey, *War Diaries*, p. 374; Churchill, vol. 6, pp. 296-8; Loewenheim *et al.*, pp. 647-8; Campbell and Herring, *Stettinius Diaries*, pp. 184-5.

3 FO 371/47881, unsigned memorandum dated 7 January on the desiderata for Yalta. Prem 4, 78/1, part two, Law and Sargent to Eden, 9 February, on the importance of bringing France into the control machinery for Germany. The publication of the *FRUS* volume on Yalta in 1955 stimulated the collection of essays edited by J. L. Snell, *The Meaning of Yalta* (Baton Rouge, Louisiana, 1956). A revisionist account will be found in D. Clemens, *Yalta* (1970). For more recent comments see Mastny, *Russia's Road to the Cold War*, pp. 239-53, and R. Dallek, *Franklin D. Roosevelt and American Foreign Policy 1932-45* (New York, 1979), pp. 506-25. On the repatriation agreement see N. Bethell, *The Last Secret* (1974), and N. Tolstoy, *Victims of Yalta* (revised edn, 1979). For some accounts by participants see Churchill, vol. 6, pp. 302-52; Avon, *The Reckoning*, pp. 512-8; Campbell and Herring, *Stettinius Diaries*, pp. 224-58; Harriman and Abel, *Special Envoy*, pp. 388-417; Ismay, pp. 383-90. British records are in FO 371/50838 and 50839.

4 CAB 78/34 for records of the reparations commission. CAB 87/66-8 on the Armistice and Post-War Committee. On dismemberment see also T. Burridge, *British Labour and Hitler's War* (1976), pp. 125-38; F. King, 'Allied Negotiations and the Dismemberment of Germany' in W. Laqueur (ed.), *The Second World War*, pp. 362-70; Rothwell, pp. 43-4; Woodward, vol. 5, pp. 242-4 and 272-81. FO 371/47860, Roberts to Foreign Office 12 May on Stalin's victory broadcast. FO 181/997, Clark Kerr to Molotov 19 August proposing the winding up of the dismemberment commission and Molotov's reply on 21 August. Mastny, *Russia's Road to the Cold War*, pp. 233-4 on communist planning for post-war Germany.

5 CAB 118/14, Churchill to Attlee, 14 February; Mastny, *Russia's Road to the Cold War*, pp. 253-7; Loewenheim *et al.*, p. 608; Kuniholm, p. 257; Polonsky, pp. 249-63 and Woodward, vol. 3, 490-518 on the Polish question; Loewenheim *et al.*, pp. 689-90, Roosevelt to Churchill, 29 March; FO 181/997, Molotov to Clark Kerr 22 March; Dilks, *Cadogan*, p. 726 and Harvey, *War Diaries*, p. 377 on doubts about San Francisco; *Stalin's Correspondence with Roosevelt and Truman*, pp. 205-6 and 208-10; on the Berne negotiations generally, B. F. Smith and E. Agarossi, *Operation Sunrise* (1979); FO 371/47881, Eden to Clark Kerr, 8 April; FO 181/1004, Clark Kerr to Eden 9 April.

6 Young, *Bruce Lockhart*, pp. 411 and 416; Loewenheim *et al.*, pp. 705 and 709;

Harriman and Abel, *Special Envoy*, p. 440; Lord Moran, *Churchill - The Struggle for Survival, 1940–65* (1968), p. 226 on Roosevelt's appearance at Yalta and see Dilks, *Cadogan*, pp. 705, 709. Dallek, pp. 527–8.

7 Prem 4, 27/9, Halifax to Foreign Office, 11 April; FO 371/47862, Clark Kerr to Foreign Office, 14 April. On the Truman–Byrnes relationship generally see R. L. Messer, *The End of an Alliance; James F. Byrnes, Roosevelt, Truman and the Origins of the Cold War* (Chapel Hill, North Carolina, 1982). On Davies see Anderson, p. 55 and R. M. Hathaway, *Ambiguous Partnership: Britain and America 1944–47* (Guildford, 1981), p. 137.

8 Prem 3, 473 for the Churchill–Truman correspondence. See also the extracts in *Churchill*, vol. 6, pp. 497–9 and 525–6. On Renner, see Mastny, *Russia's Road to the Cold War*, pp. 267–8.

9 Woodward, vol. 3, pp. 357–63; Prem 3, 495/5, Churchill to Eden, 11 March, Eden to Churchill, 15 and 26 March; Prem 3, 473, Truman to Churchill, 30 April, 12, 16 and 21 May, Churchill to Truman 12 and 19 May; Churchill, vol. 6, pp. 484–7; Woodward, vol. 3, pp. 379–80. Prem 3, 495/3, Churchill to Smuts, 26 May; FO 371/48928, minute by Addis, 4 May.

10 FO 371/47882, Halifax to Foreign Office, 23 May; Prem 4, 27/9, Halifax to Churchill 30 June; FO 371/47860, Wilson minute, 25 May; FO 371/47882, Wilson minute 27 May, Clark Kerr to Foreign Office 29 May, Sargent minute, 2 June; Prem 3, 473, Churchill to Truman, 2, 4 and 9 June; Young, *Bruce Lockhart*, p. 443; Churchill, vol. 6, pp. 501–5; Anderson, pp. 69–70; Hathaway, pp 160–2.

11 FO 371/47881, Clark Kerr to Foreign Office 12 April, on UNRRA; FO 371/47882, Roberts to Warner 25 April also strikes a note of cautious disappointment; FO 371/47860, Sargent minute in May, date illegible, on minute by Bruce Lockhart, written on 11 April. Eden saw it at some point after his return from San Francisco on 17 May but made no comment.

12 Prem 3, 396/12, note by Clark Kerr of Churchill's conversation with Gusev; Prem 4, 411, on the standstill in demobilisation of the RAF, which was revoked on 6 July; Prem 3, 396/14, note by Clark Kerr on Eden's conversation with Gusev; FO 371/47854, Warner note of 19 May, minutes by Sargent (21 May) and Eden (24 May).

13 Prem 3, 447/4A, Peterson to Foreign Office, 13 June; Woodward, vol. 4, pp. 206–10; Kuniholm, pp. 257–9. FO 371/47077, Clark Kerr to Foreign Office 26 and 30 June, on sub-Carpathian Ruthenia; FO 371/47078, Nichols to Foreign Office, 2 July, Foreign Office to Clark Kerr 8 July; Clark Kerr to Foreign Office, 4 September with Molotov's reply. Prem 3, 137/1; FO 371/47964, brief on 'Russian shortcomings at the EAC', 10 July; Sharpe, pp. 187–203.

14 FO 371/47860, Sargent on Bruce Lockhart's paper in May, minute, date illegible; Young, *Bruce Lockhart*, p. 467; FO 371/47883, Warner minute of 25 July, Eden, undated minute.

8 From Potsdam to Moscow

1 Prem 4, 80/1, Clark Kerr's telegrams to Foreign Office of 16 July; Prem 3, 430/3, Cadogan to Churchill, 2 July; Prem 3, 430/14, Halifax to Churchill, 7

July; Prem 3, 396/14, Eden to Churchill, 17 July, quoted in part in Avon, *The Reckoning*, pp. 546–7; see pp. 540–1 on Eden's ulcer; on Churchill's health, Moran, pp. 255, 279; Dilks, *Cadogan*, p. 621; Young, *Bruce Lockhart*, p. 307; Harvey, *War Diaries*, p. 385. For the pressure of work on Eden, Dilks, *Cadogan*, pp. 497, 605, 612, 671; Young, *Bruce Lockhart*, pp. 226, 357, 378; Harvey, *War Diaries*, pp. 201, 210, 255, 282, 365.

2 Prem 3, 79/2, private letter from Rowan to Anthony Bevir, 17 July; Dilks, *Cadogan*, p. 777; Prem 4, 79/1, meetings of the British delegation with Attlee and Bevin, 29, 30 and 31 July; Prem 3, 430/14, Attlee to Eden, 1 August; Prem 3, 430/13, Attlee to Smuts, 31 August.

3 British records of Potsdam are in FO 371/50863 – 50866; American documents are in *FRUS, Conference of Berlin* (*Potsdam*) (2 vols., 1960). There is a summary in Woodward, vol. 5, pp. 401–99. See also Churchill, vol. 6, pp. 545–77; Bohlen, pp. 225–42; Harriman and Abel, *Special Envoy*, pp. 484–92; Mastny, *Russia's Road to the Cold War*, pp. 292–304; on the Council of Ministers, P. D. Ward, *The Threat of Peace: James F. Byrnes and the Council of Foreign Ministers* (Kent, Ohio, 1979), pp. 9–17; On Bevin, Rothwell, pp. 222–32; on the loan negotiations, Hathaway, pp. 182–201.

4 American records of the London Conference are in *FRUS*, 1945, vol. 2, pp. 99–559. See also Ward, pp. 18–49; Messer, pp. 125–36; Rothwell, pp. 236–9; *Stalin's Correspondence with Churchill and Attlee*, pp. 375–8; *Stalin's Correspondence with Roosevelt and Truman*, pp. 271–3; J. Knight, 'Russia's Search for Peace: the London Council of Foreign Ministers, 1945', *Journal of Contemporary History*, vol. 13 (1978), pp. 137–57; FO 371/50917, Campbell to Cadogan, 20 September, Warner and Cadogan minutes of 26 September; FO 371/50918, note by Norman Brook, 29 September, on difficulties over records of the conference.

5 FO 371/50826, Roberts to Foreign Office, 14 and 22 September, minutes by Ward (19 September), Hoyer Millar (21 September), Sargent (22 September) and Clark Kerr (2 October); Roberts to Foreign Office, 4 October, Ward minute, 8 October; FO 371/50917, Roberts to Foreign Office, 27 September; FO 371/50919, Bevin to Halifax, 6 October.

6 FO 371/50917, Halifax to Foreign Office, 25 September, says Truman is thinking of a special mission; FO 371/50919, Halifax to Foreign Office, 9 October, on conversation with Byrnes, Ward minute, 15 October, undated minute by Bevin, Foreign Office to Halifax, 16 October. On Dulles and Byrnes, D. Yergin, *Shattered Peace* (1980), pp. 129–130, Ward, pp. 40–1. FO 371/47883, Roberts to Sargent, 23 October; Harriman and Abel, *Special Envoy*, pp. 511–16; FO 371/47857, Warner and Dixon minutes 29 October, Brimelow minute, 12 November; FO 371/50921, Roberts to Foreign Office, 31 October, Hood and Warner minutes, 1 November, Foreign Office to Washington, 6 November.

7 FO 371/47861, Clark Kerr to Foreign Office, 7 and 9 November; FO 371/50921, Halifax to Foreign Office, 14 November; FO 181/1009, Clark Kerr to Foreign Office, 24 November, Halifax to Foreign Office, 5 December, Foreign Office to Washington, 6 December, Clark Kerr to Bevin, 3 December, minutes by Crosthwaite, 4 December, Roberts, 5 December, Clark Kerr, 5 December, Clark Kerr to Foreign Office, 9 December on Turkish situation; FO 371/47856,

Sargent and Cadogan minutes of 3 December; minutes on Rumania by Stewart, 4 December and Williams, 5 December. For Sargent's view, Young, *Bruce Lockhart*, p. 512.

8 On the Moscow Conference and its antecedents see Yergin, pp. 147–151; Messer, pp. 134–6 and 149–55; Ward, pp. 52–77; Harriman and Abel, *Special Envoy*, pp. 523–7; Bohlen, pp. 247–50; Kuniholm, pp. 282–90; Rothwell, pp. 245–6; G. Kennan, *Memoirs 1925–50* (1968), pp. 283–90. American records are in *FRUS*, 1945, vol. 2, pp. 560–826. J. Byrnes, *Speaking Frankly* (1947), should be used with caution. FO 371/50938, Hood minutes of 20 and 24 December; FO 371/50939, Ward minute of 2 January, 1946; FO 371/47858, Ward minute of 5 January, 1946.

9 FO 371/43291, Burrows to Warner, 31 December, 1944 with a copy of his final report, minutes by Warner (24 December) and Wilson (27 December); FO 371/47849, Foreign Office to Moscow, 5 May, with news of Gammell's appointment; record of discussion held in the Foreign Office about the mission's future, 24 May; FO 371/47850, Gammell to Ismay and Nye, 27 June; extract from minutes of Chiefs of Staff meeting at Potsdam, 19 July; FO 371/47851, Gammell to Chiefs of Staff, 4 September.

10 FO 371/47838, Galsworthy minute of 26 April; FO 371/47841, Clark Kerr to War Cabinet, 2 June; FO 371/47842, Anderson to Lyttelton, 26 June, Cadogan minute, 10 July, War Cabinet offices to Moscow, 5 July; FO 371/47843, Brimelow minute of 20 August on interview between Cripps and Borisenko on 7 August; FO 371/47845, Cripps to Kotchourov, 31 December, 1945; CAB 92/9, ASE(45)32 of 22 August and ASE(45)34 of 14 September; Beaumont, *Comrades in Arms*, pp. 199–201.

Bibliography

All books published in London unless otherwise stated

A Public Record Office files quoted or cited

FO 181   Moscow Embassy files
FO 371   General diplomatic correspondence
FO 800   See in particular the Sargent papers (272–9) and the Inverchapel papers (298–303)
FO 954   Avon papers
Prem 3   Operational papers, Prime Minister's Office
Prem 4   Confidential Papers, Prime Minister's Office
CAB 65   War Cabinet minutes
CAB 66   War Cabinet papers
CAB 78   Moscow Reparations Conference
CAB 79   Chiefs of Staff minutes
CAB 81   Post-Hostilities Planning Staff
CAB 87   Armistice and Post-War Committee
CAB 92   Allied Supplies Executive
CAB 111   Allied Supplies Executive and aid to Russia
CAB 118   Collection of Attlee papers
CAB 127   Miscellaneous correspondence of Cripps
CAB 130   Moscow Reparations Conference
CAB 133   Various conference records, including Moscow Foreign Ministers' meeting of December 1945

B Published collections of documents

Documents on British Foreign Policy
  Second Series, vol. 12 (1972)
  Third Series, vol. 5–7 (1952–4)
Documents on German Foreign Policy
  Series D, vols. 7, 8, 11 (1954–61)
Foreign Office Research Department: Review of the Foreign Press 1939–45, 27 Vols. (Munich, 1980)

Foreign Relations of the United States
  Annual volumes 1941-5 (Washington, DC, 1958-69)
  Special series on wartime conferences (Washington, DC, 1955-72)
Kot, S. *Conversations with the Kremlin and Despatches from Russia* (1963)
Loewenheim, F. L., Langley, H. D. and Jonas, M. (eds.) *Roosevelt and Churchill: Their Secret Wartime Correspondence* (1975)
Polonsky, A. (ed.) *The Great Powers and the Polish Question 1941-45* (1976)
Polonsky, A. and Drukier, B. (eds.) *The Beginnings of Communist Rule in Poland* (1979)
Generak Sikorski Historical Institute, *Documents on Polish-Soviet Relations 1939-45*, 2 vols. (1961 and 1967)
Soviet Peace Efforts on the Eve of World War Two (Moscow, 1976)
Stalin's Correspondence with Churchill, Attlee, Roosevelt and Truman, 2 vols. (New York, 1965)
Teheran, Yalta and Potsdam Conferences (Moscow 1969)
War Cabinet 1939-45: Principal War Telegrams and Memoranda, 1940-43, 7 vols. (Nendeln, Liechtenstein, 1976)

C Diaries, memoirs and autobiographies

Acheson, D. *Present at the Creation* (1970)
Avon, Lord *Facing the Dictators* (1962)
Avon, Lord *The Reckoning* (1965)
Barclay, Sir Roderick *Ernest Bevin and the Foreign Office 1932-69* (1975)
Bohlen, C. E. *Witness to History* (1973)
Byrnes, J. *Speaking Frankly* (1947)
Campbell, T. M. and Herring, G. C. (eds.) *The Diaries of Edward R. Stettinius 1943-46* (New York, 1975)
Churchill, Sir Winston *The Second World War*, vols. 4-6 (1951-4)
Deane, J. R. *The Strange Alliance* (1947)
Dilks, D. N. (ed.) *The Diaries of Sir Alexander Cadogan 1938-45* (1971)
Gladwyn, Lord *Memoirs* (1972)
Harriman, W. A. and Abel, E. *Special Envoy to Churchill and Stalin 1941-46* (1976)
Harvey, J. (ed.) *The Diplomatic Diaries of Oliver Harvey 1937-40* (1970)
Harvey, J. (ed.) *The War Diaries of Oliver Harvey 1941-45* (1978)
Hull, Cordell *Memoirs*, 2 vols. (1948)
Ismay, Lord *Memoirs* (1960)
Kennan, G. *Memoirs 1925-50* (1968)
Macmillan, H. *The Blast of War* (1967)
Maisky, I. *Memoirs of a Soviet Ambassador: The War 1939-43* (1967)
Raczynski, Count *In Allied London* (1962)
Reynolds, P. A. and Hughes, J. (eds.) *The Historian as Diplomat: Charles Webster and the United Nations* (1976)
Strang, Lord *At Home and Abroad* (1956)
Truman, H. S. *Year of Decisions* (1955)

Winant, J. G. *A Letter from Grosvenor Square* (1947)
Young, K. (ed.) *The Diaries of Sir Robert Bruce Lockhart 1939–45* (1980)

D Secondary works

Alexander, G. M. *The Prelude to the Truman Doctrine: British Policy in Greece 1944–47* (Oxford, 1982)
Anderson, T. H. *The United States, Great Britain and the Cold War 1944–47* (Columbia, Missouri, 1981)
Aster, S. *The Making of the Second World War* (1973)
Balfour, M. and Muir, J. *Four-Power Control in Germany and Austria 1945–46* (1956)
Barker, E. *British Policy in South-East Europe in the Second World War* (1976)
Barker, E. *Churchill and Eden at War* (1978)
Beaumont, J. *Comrades in Arms: British Aid to Russia 1941–45* (1980)
Beitzell, R. *The Uneasy Alliance* (New York 1972)
Bethell, N. *The Last Secret* (1974)
Burridge, T. *British Labour and Hitler's War* (1976)
Carlton, D. *Anthony Eden: A Biography* (1981)
Ciechanowski, J. M. *The Warsaw Rising of 1944* (1974)
Clemens, D. *Yalta* (1970)
Crowley, E. L. (ed.) *The Soviet Diplomatic Corps 1917–67* (Metuchen, New Jersey, 1970)
Dallek, R. *Franklin D. Roosevelt and American Foreign Policy 1932–45* (New York, 1979)
Dilks, D. N. (ed.) *Retreat from Power: Studies in Britain's Foreign Policy of the Twentieth Century*, 2 vols. (1981)
Dixon, Piers *Double Diploma: the Life of Sir Pierson Dixon* (1968)
Douglas, R. *The Advent of War 1939–40* (1978)
Douglas, R. *New Alliances 1940–41* (1982)
Edwards, J. *The British Government and the Spanish Civil War* (1979)
Gardner, R. N. *Sterling–Dollar Diplomacy in Current Perspective* (New York, 1980)
Gibbs, N. *Grand Strategy: Rearmament Policy*, vol. 1 (1974)
Hathaway, R. M. *Ambiguous Partnership: Britain and America 1944–47* (Guildford, 1981)
Herring, G. C. *Aid to Russia, 1941–46* (1973)
Hinsley, F. H. *et al.* (eds.) *British Intelligence in the Second World War*, 2 vols. (1979 and 1980)
Howard, M. *Grand Strategy: August 1942 – September 1943*, vol. 4 (1972)
Issraeljan, V. *The Anti-Hitler Coalition* (Moscow, 1971)
Jakobson, M. *The Diplomacy of the Winter War* (Cambridge, Mass., 1961)
Koblyakov, I. K. *USSR: for Peace against Aggression 1933–41* (Moscow, 1976)
Kuniholm, B. R. *The Origins of the Cold War in the Near East: Great Power Conflict and Diplomacy in Iran, Turkey and Greece* (Guildford, 1980)

Laqueur, W. (ed.) *The Second World War: Essays in Military and Political History* (1982)

Lensen, G. A. *The Strange Neutrality: Soviet-Japanese Relations during the Second World War* (Tallahassee, Florida, 1972)

Lewin, R. *Churchill as Warlord* (1973)

Mastny, V. M. *Russia's Road to the Cold War* (New York, 1979)

Messer, R. L. *The End of an Alliance; James F. Byrnes, Roosevelt, Truman and the Origins of the Cold War* (Chapel Hill, North Carolina, 1982)

Moran, Lord *Churchill – The Struggle for Survival, 1940-65* (1968)

Morley, J. W. (ed.) *The Fateful Choice: Japan's Advance into South-East Asia 1939-41* (New York, 1980)

Munch-Peterson, T. *The Strategy of Phoney War: Britain, Sweden and the Iron-Ore Question 1939-40* (Stockholm, 1981)

Northedge, F. S. and Wells, A. *Britain and Soviet Communism: The Impact of a Revolution* (1982)

Roberts, W. R. *Tito, Mihailovich and the Allies 1941-45* (New Brunswick, 1973)

Rothwell, V. *Britain and the Cold War 1941-47* (1982)

Sharpe, T. *The Wartime Alliance and the Zonal Division of Germany* (Oxford, 1975)

Sherwood, R. E. *The White House Papers of Harry L. Hopkins*, 2 vols. (1949)

Slusser, R. M. and Triska, J. F. *A Calendar of Soviet Treaties 1917-57* (Stanford, California, 1959)

Smith, B. F. and Agarossi, E. *Operation Sunrise* (1979)

Snell, J. L. *The Meaning of Yalta* (Baton Rouge, Louisiana, 1956)

Thorne, C., *Allies of a Kind* (1978)

Tolstoy, N. *Victims of Yalta*, revised edn (1979)

Ward, P. D. *The Threat of Peace: James F. Byrnes and the Council of Foreign Ministers* (Kent, Ohio, 1979)

Wheeler-Bennett, J. W. and Nicholls, A. *The Semblance of Peace* (1972)

White S. *Britain and the Bolshevik Revolution: A Study in the Politics of Diplomacy 1920-24* (1979)

Woodhouse, C. M. *The Struggle for Greece* (1976)

Woodward, E. L. *British Foreign Policy in the Second World War*, 5 vols. (1970-6)

Xydis, S. G. *Greece and the Great Powers 1944-47* (Thessaloniki, 1963)

Yergin, D. *Shattered Peace* (1980)

E Articles

Bayer, J. A. 'British Policy towards the Russo-Finnish Winter War 1939-40', *Canadian Journal of History*, vol. 16 (1981), pp. 27-65

Beaumont, J. 'Great Britain and the Rights of Neutral Countries: the Case of Iran, 1941', *Journal of Contemporary History*, vol. 16 (1981), pp. 213-26

Bernstein, B. J. 'The Uneasy Alliance: Roosevelt, Churchill and the Atomic Bomb', *Western Political Quarterly*, vol. 29 (1976), pp. 202-3

Burridge, T. D. 'Great Britain and the Dismemberment of Germany at the end of the Second World War', *International History Review*, vol. 3 (1981), pp. 565-79

302   *Bibliography*

Cecil, R. 'Potsdam and its Legends', *International Affairs*, vol. 46 (1970), pp. 455–65

Dilks, D. N. 'Great Britain and Scandinavia in the Phoney War', *Scandinavian Journal of History*, vol. 2 (1977), pp. 29–51

Hanak, H. 'Sir Stafford Cripps as British Ambassador in Moscow, May 1940 – June 1941', *English Historical Review*, vol. 94 (1979), pp. 48–70

Hanak, H. 'Sir Stafford Cripps as British Ambassador in Moscow, June 1941 – January 1942', *English Historical Review*, vol. 97 (1982), pp. 332–44

Herman, J. 'Soviet Peace Efforts on the Eve of World War Two: a Review of the Soviet Documents', *Journal of Contemporary History*, vol. 15 (1980), pp. 577–602

Herring, G. C. 'The United States and British Bankruptcy, 1944–45: Responsibilities Deferred', *Political Science Quarterly*, vol. 86 (1971), pp. 232–59

Kettenacker, L. 'The Anglo-Soviet Alliance and the Problem of Germany', *Journal of Contemporary History*, vol. 17 (1982), pp. 435–55

King, F. 'Allied Negotiations and the Dismemberment of Germany' in W. Laqueur (ed.), *The Second World War* (1982), pp. 362–70

Knight, J. 'Russia's Search for Peace: the London Council of Foreign Ministers, 1945', *Journal of Contemporary History*, vol. 13 (1978), pp. 137–57

Koch, A. W. 'The Spectre of a Separate Peace in the East: Russo-German Peace Feelers, 1942–44', *Journal of Contemporary History*, vol. 10 (1975), pp. 531–47

Kuklick, B. 'The Genesis of the European Advisory Commission', *Journal of Contemporary History*, vol. 4 (1969), pp. 189–201

Langer, J. D. 'The Harriman–Beaverbrook Mission and the Debate over Unconditional Aid for the Soviet Union, 1941' in W. Laqueur (ed.), *The Second World War* (1982), pp. 300–19

Lowe, P. 'The Soviet Union in Britain's Far Eastern Policy, 1941' in I. Nish (ed.), *The Russian Problem in East Asia* (1981), pp. 27–46

Ludlow, P. 'Britain and Northern Europe, 1940–45', *Scandinavian Journal of History*, vol. 5 (1979), pp. 123–62

Manne, R. 'The British Decision for Alliance with Russia', *Journal of Contemporary History*, vol. 9 (1974), pp. 3–26

Manne, R. 'Some British Light on the Nazi-Soviet Pact', *European Studies Review*, vol. 11 (1981), pp. 83–102

Manne, R. 'The Foreign Office and the Failure of Anglo-Soviet Rapprochement', *Journal of Contemporary History*, vol. 16 (1981), pp. 725–56

Mastny, V. M. 'Stalin and the Prospects of a Separate Peace in World War Two', *American Historical Review*, vol. 77 (1972), pp. 1365–88

Mastny, V. M. 'Soviet War Aims at the Moscow and Teheran Conference of 1943', *Journal of Modern History*, vol. 53 (1981), pp. 417–39

Ovendale, R. 'Britain, the USA and the European Cold War 1945–58', *History*, vol. 67 (1982), pp. 217–36

Parker, R. A. C. 'Britain, France and Scandinavia, 1939–40', *History*, vol. 61 (1976), pp. 369–87

Resis, A. 'The Churchill–Stalin Secret Percentages Agreement on the Balkans, Moscow, October 1944', *American Historical Review*, vol. 83 (1978), pp. 368–87

Resis, A. 'Spheres of Influence in Soviet Wartime Diplomacy', *Journal of Modern History*, vol. 53 (1981), pp. 417-39

Ross, G. 'Operation Bracelet: Churchill in Moscow, 1942', in D. N. Dilks (ed.), *Retreat from Power: Studies in Britain's Foreign Policy of the Twentieth Century* (1981), vol. 1, pp. 101-19

Ross, G. 'Foreign Office Attitudes to the Soviet Union 1941-45', in W. Laqueur (ed.), *The Second World War* (1982), pp. 256-74

Sainsbury, K. 'British Policy and Germany Unity at the end of the Second World War', *English Historical Review*, vol. 94 (1979), pp. 786-804

Sharpe, T. 'The Origins of the Teheran Formula on Polish frontiers', *Journal of Contemporary History*, vol. 12 (1977), pp. 381-91

Strang, Lord 'Prelude to Potsdam', *International Affairs*, vol. 46 (1970), pp. 441-54

Strang, Lord 'The Moscow Negotiations, 1939', in D. N. Dilks (ed.), *Retreat from Power: Studies in Britain's Foreign Policy of the Twentieth Century* (1981), vol. 1, pp. 170-86

Strang, Lord 'War and Foreign Policy, 1939-45' in D. N. Dilks (ed.), *Retreat from Power: Studies in Britain's Foreign Policy of the Twentieth Century* (1981), vol. 2, pp. 66-100

For EU product safety concerns, contact us at Calle de José Abascal, 56–1°,
28003 Madrid, Spain or eugpsr@cambridge.org.

www.ingramcontent.com/pod-product-compliance
Ingram Content Group UK Ltd.
Pitfield, Milton Keynes, MK11 3LW, UK
UKHW042153130625

459647UK00011B/1306